This study describes for the first time the most neglected site of political, religious, and literary culture in early modern England: the court pulpits of Elizabeth I and James I. It provides a timely contribution which unites the most fertile strains in early modern British history – the court and religion – and combines archival and bibliographic research from 1558 to 1625, showing how the pulpit stood at the centre of the court's cultural life and gave voice to a surprisingly diverse body of conformist thought.

Dr McCullough shows how previous work has underestimated the place of religion in courtly culture, and presents new evidence of the competing religious patronage not only of Elizabeth and James but also of Queen Anne, Prince Henry, and Prince Charles. The book recontextualizes the political, religious, and literary careers of court preachers such as Lancelot Andrewes, John Donne, and William Laud, and presents new evidence of the tensions between sermon- and sacrament-centred piety in the established church.

The book is published with a diskette containing a definitive calendar of court sermons for the period.

Cambridge Studies in Early Modern British History

SERMONS AT COURT

Cambridge Studies in Early Modern British History

Series editors

ANTHONY FLETCHER
Professor of History, University of Essex

JOHN GUY
Professor of Modern History, University of St Andrews

and JOHN MORRILL
Reader in Early Modern History, University of Cambridge, and Vice-Master of Selwyn College

This is a series of monographs and studies covering many aspects of the history of the British Isles between the late fifteenth and the early eighteenth century. It includes the work of established scholars and pioneering work by a new generation of scholars. It includes both reviews and revisions of major topics and books, which open up new historical terrain or which reveal startling new perspectives on familiar subjects. All the volumes set detailed research into our broader perspectives and the books are intended for the use of students as well as of their teachers.

For a list of titles in the series, see end of book.

SERMONS AT COURT

Politics and religion in
Elizabethan and Jacobean preaching

PETER E. McCULLOUGH
Lincoln College, Oxford

CAMBRIDGE
UNIVERSITY PRESS

PUBLISHED BY THE PRESS SYNDICATE OF THE UNIVERSITY OF CAMBRIDGE
The Pitt Building, Trumpington Street, Cambridge CB2 1RP, United Kingdom

CAMBRIDGE UNIVERSITY PRESS

The Edinburgh Building, Cambridge, CB2 2RU, United Kingdom
40 West 20th Street, New York, NY 10011–4211, USA
10 Stamford Road, Oakleigh, Melbourne 3166, Australia

First published 1998

Printed in the United Kingdom at the University Press, Cambridge

Typeset in 10 on 12 point Sabon [CE]

A catalogue record for this book is available from the British Library

Library of Congress Cataloguing in Publication data
McCullough, Peter E.
Sermons at court: politics and religion in Elizabethan and Jacobean preaching / Peter E. McCullough.
p. cm. – (Cambridge studies in early modern British history)
Includes bibliographical references and index.
ISBN 0 521 590946 9 (hardback)
1. Preaching – England – History – 16th century.   2. Great Britain – Court and courtiers – History – 16th century. 3. Christianity and politics – Church of England – History – 16th century.   4. Preaching – England – History – 17th century. 5. Great Britain – Court and courtiers – History – 17th century. 6. Christianity and politics – Church of England – History – 17th century. 7. Sermons – Church of England – History and criticism. 8. Sermons, English – History and criticism.   I. Title.   II. Series.
BV4208.G7M33   1998
251'.00942'09031–dc21   97–8761
CIP

ISBN 0 521 59046 9 hardback

For TPR, Jr

Of deuotion and promotion

I Met a Lawyer at the Court this Lent,
And asking what great cause him thither sent,
He said, that mou'd with Doctor *Androes* fame,
To heare him preach, he only thither came:
But straight I wisht him softly in his eare,
To find some other scuse, else some will sweare,
Who to the Court come onely for deuotion,
They in the Church pray only for promotion.

Sir John Harington (1615)

CONTENTS

FIGURES

ACKNOWLEDGMENTS

Thanking people publicly – whether from the pulpit or in print – is a dangerous business. But the fear of omissions cannot mitigate the obligation to give thanks and praise to those who have inspired and enabled my work.

The Elizabethan portion of this book first saw light as a doctoral dissertation written at Princeton University. A. Walton Litz's sage counsel transformed seminar ideas into a coherent literary-historical research project. A Donald and Mary Hyde Research Fellowship from Princeton funded a crucial summer's worth of archival work in England, and the Graduate School and English Department gave four years of generous support. But the presiding genius was that of Tom Roche. My debt to his scholarly and personal *caritas* beggars words; a dedication is only a paltry attempt to acknowledge it.

The final shape of the book, in particular its historiographical focus, is the result of the enthusiastic encouragement and acceptance I and my work have received from historians. David Armitage has been a critical inter-disciplinary link from the beginning; and Peter Lake's serendipitous arrival at Princeton gave me for the first time a senior colleague who shared my excitement for this body of neglected material. In addition to his own inimitable guidance, I have him to thank for introducing me to a remarkably kind and generous circle of scholars who have shared references, criticisms, and opinions, and read drafts of the work in progress: Simon Adams, Alastair Bellany, Nicholas Cranfield, Lori Anne Ferrell, Ken Fincham, Andrew Foster, Arnold Hunt, Anthony Milton, and Alexandra Walsham. The transformation from Elizabethan dissertation to Eliza-bethan-Jacobean book was largely accomplished after-hours during successive teaching and administrative appointments at Princeton. The English Department, the Graduate School Office, and the University Committee on Research in the Humanities and Social Sciences all supported my continued research with time and resources.

With thanks to the President and Fellows of Trinity College, Oxford for my election to a Junior Research Fellowship, final revisions were carried out in one of Oxford's most gracious collegiate societies. My students and their senior English tutor, Dinah Birch, offered constant inspiration and encouragement. And the staff of Duke Humfrey's Library in the Bodleian deserve special commendation for bearing with my checking references and transcriptions from the literally hundreds of early printed books that were until then only so many microfilm reels to me.

I gratefully acknowledge permission from the Marquess of Salisbury to quote from the Cecil papers at Hatfield House, and the Jervoise family to quote from manuscripts on deposit at the Hampshire Record Office. The section in chapter 4 entitled 'Preaching to a court papist?' appeared in only slightly different form in *The John Donne Journal* 14 (McCullough, 1997), and is used here by permission of the editors.

Finally, the debts of an academic to his or her family defy description, or, for that matter, a dedication. Jennifer, Hugh, and Eleanor all helped this project along in their own (some more and some less practical) ways; but my debts to them, and to Jenny in particular, are of a magnitude too great to bear yolking to such trivia as this.

NOTE ON SOURCES AND TEXTS

The primary sources used for this study are of two sorts: documents used to establish the institutional and architectural settings of court preaching, and surviving texts or accounts of court sermons themselves. The accounts of the household departments of the King's Works, the Lord Chamberlain, the Wardrobe, and the Treasurer of the Chamber have provided the basis for reconstructing the physical and ceremonial settings of court preaching, as well as important lists of royal chaplains and Lent preachers. A second crucial source for establishing identities of chaplains and preachers was the remarkable run of court Lent sermon lists from 1584–1625 (with the odd year missing) and lists of chaplains (1600–3) found in Westminster Abbey Muniment Book 15 by Dr Anthony Milton. I am deeply indebted to Dr Milton for sharing his transcripts with me at an early stage of this project; I have since been able to consult the documents myself. Further detail about the institutional mechanics of appointing chaplains has been drawn from contemporary biographies of divines who held royal chaplaincies, and the dedicatory epistles to their printed court sermons.

I have adopted a very conservative policy for quoting early modern texts: spelling and orthography is not modernized; any contractions expanded are placed in square brackets. I quote from the earliest possible sixteenth- and seventeenth-century editions of sermons, except those by John Donne, which alone have been canonized in a high-standard scholarly edition. For those sermons that received Victorian editions that, though textually modernized, are still used as standard (John Jewel, Edwin Sandys, Lancelot Andrewes, Joseph Hall), I quote from the first early modern editions but also include references to their nineteenth-century successors. Place of publication is always London unless otherwise noted.

ABBREVIATIONS

Alum. Cantab.	*Alumni Cantabrigiensis*
Alum. Oxon.	*Alumni Oxoniensis*
BL	British Library
Bodl.	Bodleian Library, Oxford
CCCC	Corpus Christi College, Cambridge
CPR	*Calendar of Patent Rolls*
CSPD	*Calendar of State Papers, Domestic*
CSPI	*Calendar of State Papers, Ireland*
CSPS	*Calendar of State Papers, Spanish*
CSPV	*Calendar of State Papers, Venetian*
CUL	Cambridge University Library
DNB	*Dictionary of National Biography*
HKW	*History of the King's Works*
HMC	Historical Manuscripts Commission Reports
HRO	Hampshire Record Office (Winchester)
LP	*Letters and Papers . . . of the Reign of King Henry VIII*
McK	McKerrow, *Printers' and Publishers' Devices, 1485–1640*
McK&F	McKerrow and Ferguson, *Title-Page Borders Used in England & Scotland 1485–1640*
PRO	Public Record Office
SJCC	St John's College, Cambridge
STC	Pollard and Redgrave, *A Short-Title Catalogue of Books Printed in England, Scotland, and Ireland . . . 1475–1640*, 2nd edition
WAMB	Westminster Abbey Muniment Book
Wing	Donald V. Wing, *Short Title Catalogue of Books Printed in England . . . 1641–1700*
YML	York Minster Library

Introduction

Preaching before Prince Henry in 1609, his chaplain Daniel Price descanted on the proverb 'that Godlinesse is no good Courtier'.[1] That same conventional wisdom from anti-court satire has left its mark on the historiography of early modern England. For despite recent revolutions in the study of both religion and the royal courts under the Tudors and Stuarts, there has been a stubborn resistance to acknowledging any significant intersection between the two. Popular perceptions of Elizabeth I and her successor James VI and I have no doubt reinforced the assumption that 'court religion' in their reigns is a contradiction in terms: Elizabeth had little time or patience for clergy and 'her court was probably more secular in spirit and culture than any which had preceded it'; James was a religious pedant with no morals and a knack for appointing indolent bishops.[2] In institutional terms, religion at court has been consistently presumed to be synonymous with the musical establishment of the Chapel Royal, which itself has been relegated to the status of a decorative 'outer layer' of the royal household.[3] The institutional apparatus and personnel responsible for the ministry of the word at court have been completely neglected – a bizarre gap in the historiography of the greatest preaching age in England. Paul's Cross has received due analysis as a national pulpit and barometer of doctrinal change,[4] but the pulpit at the very heart of political power in the period, the court pulpit, has been virtually ignored. Similarly, literary and artistic studies of the court have turned a blind eye to court religion – its music, service, and sermons – in favour of secular art forms like Shake-

[1] Daniel Price, *The Spring* (1609), sig. E2^r.
[2] David Loades, *The Tudor Court* (1992), 183; D. H. Wilson, *King James VI and I* (New York, 1956); G. P. V. Akrigg, *Jacobean Pageant* (Cambridge, Mass., 1962), 303–20; H. R. Trevor-Roper, 'James I and His Bishops,' *History Today* 5 (1955), 571–81.
[3] Loades, *Tudor Court*, 176–7; Neil Cuddy, 'The Revival of Entourage: the Bedchamber of James I, 1603–1625', in David Starkey, ed., *The English Court from the War of the Roses to the Civil War* (1987), 182.
[4] Millar MacLure, *The Paul's Cross Sermons 1534–1642* (Toronto, 1958); Nicholas Tyacke, *Anti-Calvinists: the Rise of English Arminianism c. 1590–1640* (Oxford, 1987), 248–65.

spearean drama, the masque, and portraiture. Both literary scholars and historians, for example, have effectively shown how court masques could blend political criticism with courtly compliment.[5] But the most frequent and influential literary enterprise that could be used both to trumpet and to shout down royal policy at court, the sermon, has gone unexamined. It has been twenty years since Professor Elton called for court studies to transcend 'reveries on accession tilts and symbolism' and 'pretty pictures of gallants and galliards'.[6] In terms of taking the court seriously as a power centre in secular politics, Elton's call has been heeded. Moreover, studies of court culture have offered increasingly sophisticated assessments of the political valence of courtly art forms.[7] Absent from both, however, is the necessary acknowledgment that religion at court, particularly its presentation and consumption from the court pulpit, was a crucial cultural and political 'point of contact' in Elizabethan and Jacobean England.

In the past two decades ecclesiastical historians have completely redrawn the map of religion in early modern England. According to the best recent work, Protestantism had not won the day with the Elizabethan Settlement of 1559. In fact, that settlement was won legislatively only after a cliff-hanging ordeal in Parliament and then in practical terms through the gruelling evangelical efforts of an understaffed clergy and overworked bishops who had to preach to parishioners not necessarily running to embrace the new faith. The consensus that was established by the century's end among the clergy and in the universities was, however, a resolutely Calvinist one. The reign of James I, moreover, was not a period of ecclesiastical mismanagement, but rather the halcyon days of a sermon-centred Protestantism threatened only by the gathering clouds of ceremonial and sacramental churchmanship that would destabilize church and state under William Laud. Recurrent in all of these revisionary interpretations are the religious tastes and convictions of Elizabeth and James themselves, and the importance of their chapels and pulpits as indicators of religious change. Godliness and courtliness, or rather religion and the royal court, were not the oil and water they have been assumed to be. Thus, the

---

[5] See, for example, Kevin Sharpe, *Criticism and Compliment: the Politics of Literature in the England of Charles I* (Cambridge, 1987); and Martin Butler, 'Ben Jonson and the Limits of Courtly Panegyric', in Kevin Sharpe and Peter Lake, eds, *Culture and Politics in Early Stuart England* (Basingstoke, 1993), 91–115.

[6] G. R. Elton, 'Tudor Government: the Points of Contact. III: the Court', *Transactions of the Royal Historical Society*, 5th ser. 26 (1976), 225.

[7] Starkey, *English Court*; Simon Adams, 'Eliza Enthroned? The Court and its Politics', in Christopher Haigh, ed., *The Reign of Elizabeth I* (Athens, Georgia, 1987), 55–77; Linda Levy Peck, *Northampton: Patronage and Policy at the Court of James I* (1982); Peck, *Court Patronage and Corruption in Early Stuart England* (Boston, Mass., 1990); Malcolm Smuts, *Court Culture and the Origins of a Royalist Tradition in Early Stuart England* (Philadelphia, Pa., 1987).

Elizabethan Reform Bill was helped through the Lords by its carefully choreographed endorsement during the court Lent sermons of 1559. But Elizabeth's own personal distaste for sermon-centred piety and preference for a conservative scenic apparatus for worship, however, sent confusing, if not distressing, signals about her church's ecclesiology to domestic and foreign observers alike. James I, far from being an ignorant governor of his church, has emerged not only as more than an amateur theologian, but also an astute judge of clerical talent who chose his bishops exclusively from an élite corps of preaching royal chaplains. It was from his court pulpit that men such as Lancelot Andrewes and John Buckeridge preached the avant-garde sacramental and ceremonial churchmanship that has been described as the missing link between Hooker and Laud.[8]

None the less, while the most ground-breaking recent scholarship takes us repeatedly to court pulpits and chapels, we have lacked a proper understanding of how they were staffed and what influence they bore on court culture and national politics. It is this gap in the institutional and cultural history of the Elizabethan and Jacobean courts that this study tries to fill. The court pulpit set in its fully reconstructed context demands the revisionary attention of the several academic disciplines reassessing early modern British culture. As the most visible, frequent, and carefully noted literary genre at court, sermons should adjust the ahistorical scholarly obsession with the royal patronage of public players and the courtly masque. Examination of royal tastes in preaching also reveals unopened windows into the souls and minds of princes whose religious convictions have notoriously evaded biographers. The political and doctrinal heterogeneity of the sermons preached in the royal pulpit reveal it as a crucial arena of conflict in sixteenth- and seventeenth-century debates over the ecclesiology of the Church of England.

Court sermons can be readily defined as sermons preached under the auspices of a royal household. These would not necessarily be before a prince, since separate service and sermon were routinely offered for

---

[8] Norman Jones, *Faith By Statute: Parliament and the Settlement of Religion, 1559* (1982); Patrick Collinson, *The Religion of Protestants: the Church in English Society 1559–1625* (Oxford, 1982); Collinson, 'Windows in a Woman's Soul: Questions About the Religion of Queen Elizabeth I', in *Elizabethan Essays* (1992), 87–118; Kenneth Fincham and Peter Lake, 'The Ecclesiastical Policy of King James I', *Journal of British Studies* 24 (April 1985): 169–207; Kenneth Fincham, *Prelate as Pastor: The Episcopate of James I* (Oxford, 1990); Peter Lake, 'Lancelot Andrewes, John Buckeridge, and Avant-Garde Conformity at the Court of James I', in Linda Levy Peck, ed., *The Mental World of the Jacobean Court* (Cambridge, 1990), 113–33; Tyacke, *Anti-Calvinists*. These views, particularly those touching the Jacobean and Caroline church, have not gone uncontested. See Kevin Sharpe, *The Personal Rule of Charles the First* (New Haven, Conn., 1992); and Julian Davies, *The Caroline Captivity of the Church: Charles I and the Remoulding of Anglicanism* (Oxford, 1992).

members above and below stairs, and preaching for both proceeded whether the monarch attended or not. In addition, court sermons cannot be restricted to those preached in a royal palace or manor since sermons were duly provided for the court in country houses, episcopal palaces and cathedrals during royal progresses. But who were the 'court preachers'? Attention to the institutional structures that provided ministers to preach at court calls the very concept of such a category into question. After the Reformation, preaching was the primary responsibility of the prince's Chaplains in Ordinary, a group of ministers who came to court at most two months during the year on a *rota* ordered by the Lord Chamberlain. Court service was never the primary responsibility of the royal chaplains, who were always beneficed elsewhere. Even the two court officers who oversaw court religious practice, the Lord High Almoner and the Dean of the Chapel Royal, were bishops with full episcopal duties. Perhaps only the almoner, who from the 1580s routinely preached the sermons *coram principe* on major feast days, could be considered a 'court preacher' in the strictest sense. Members of the royal chaplaincy were an élite group who benefited from access to the court, but were not permanently attached to it. Because they were not waged members of the royal household and are therefore absent from surviving subsidy rolls, they have slipped through the cracks of all institutional studies of the court.[9] But a royal chaplaincy, and therefore court preaching, was a necessary step to any higher preferment in the church. As recent work has shown, a court chaplaincy was a prerequisite for promotion to the episcopal bench under James I and Charles I;[10] this study adds that an audition in the court pulpit was the last hurdle in securing a chaplaincy from both Elizabeth and James. Moreover, the case of the royal chaplains lends supportive detail to the two most compelling, and competing, models of the court's institutional structure that have emerged since Elton's *crie de cœur*. David Starkey has insisted that 'the history of the court is the history of those who enjoyed . . . access' to the monarch in the privy chamber. As a result, he has emphasized the strict institutional and geographical structures that defined the court as a physical place, and thereby limited political influence to an élite group of royal attendants. A wealth of supportive physical detail has been added to this argument by Simon Thurley's pioneering study of early Tudor court architecture.[11] Malcolm Smuts, however, has chafed at this restricted model and called attention to the court's 'polycentric' nature, where focal points of influence included not only the royal apartments, but the London

---

[9] Notably, Starkey, *English Court*; and Loades, *Tudor Court.*
[10] Fincham, *Prelate as Pastor*, 24, 26, 305–6; Davies, *Caroline Captivity*, 39–42.
[11] Starkey, *English Court*, 5. Simon Thurley, *The Royal Palaces of Tudor England, Architecture and Court Life 1460–1547* (New Haven, Conn., 1993).

houses of magnates and ambassadors, the Inns of Court, lesser courtiers, and visiting landowners.[12]

Delivering one's mind in a sermon while standing in a pulpit *vis-à-vis* the prince certainly qualifies as 'enjoying access' to the monarch. Therefore, an understanding of the geography of the court, the architecture of the royal chapels and outdoor pulpits, and the steps taken to restrict preachers' access to them is absolutely crucial to appreciating how politically important court sermons were. Yet the preachers and chaplains who did gain pulpit access under both Elizabeth and James were not members of a tiny corps of privy chamber servants. Since they held university fellowships, parochial benefices and ecclesiastical dignities elsewhere, with service at court taking up only a few months in a year, they provide yet another example of the 'periphery' which Smuts has reminded us was so influential in defining court culture. Moreover, royal chaplains, like most others who sought patronage at court, were rarely creatures of the court, but rather depended on sponsorship from other great patrons to receive an introduction there. The court chaplains in both reigns were a markedly diverse group – a cross-section of the political and religious interests being pressed upon the centre by the realm's great lay and clerical patrons. The sermons preached by these men displayed a similar ecclesiological and doctrinal heterogeneity. At court in the early years of Elizabeth's reign, one might have heard both the shrill anti-Catholicism of the controversialist William Fulke and the irenic sacramentalism of the Queen's Almoner, Edmund Guest. On successive days in a Jacobean Lent the court would have seen and heard the two poles of early Stuart ecclesiology in sermons by the inveterate enemies William Laud and George Abbot. Within the boundaries of a broadly defined conformity, the court pulpit was a site of conflict not consensus, as attention to the surviving texts of these sermons, both in print and manuscript, will show. Court sermons, with the important exception of those very few printed by royal command, were not 'official' or 'court' position-papers.[13] Court preachers were just as likely to come to court trying to influence royal opinions as they were to parrot them. Close examination of court sermons such as Richard Fletcher's post-mortem justification of the execution of Mary Queen of Scots, or John Burgess's 1604 critique of James's clerical subscription policy[14] – two equally daring

---

[12] Smuts, *Court Culture*; Smuts, 'Cultural Diversity and Cultural Change at the Court of James I', in Peck, ed., *Mental World of the Jacobean Court*, 102–6.

[13] An objection raised by Sharpe (*Personal Rule*, xxii) to relying on court sermons as evidence during the Caroline regime. But for the theological and ecclesiological diversity even of Caroline court preaching, see Kenneth Fincham and Peter Lake, 'The Ecclesiastical Policies of James I and Charles I', in Fincham, ed., *The Early Stuart Church, 1603–1642* (Basingstoke, 1993), 38. For court sermons printed by royal authority, see Appendix.

[14] See below, pp. 84–90, 141–7.

sermons that met with quite different royal responses – teaches us much about the rules governing veiled speech and the finer points of how to school a prince successfully.

Patrick Collinson has reminded us that the years 1559–1625 saw the confirmation and consolidation of Protestantism in English society. However, if the year 1603 can be called 'that almost irrelevant date' in a study of the national church, it cannot be called such in a study of the court.[15] The history of the court is necessarily the history of the individual personalities who presided over it.[16] Elizabeth's and James's churchmanship differed as much as their styles of kingship: the English queen inclined to private prayer and the corporate liturgy, whereas the Scottish king was devoted to the academic and disputative stimulation of sermon-hearing. So, against the backdrop of ecclesiastical continuity between these reigns, two very different royal postures towards preaching not only influenced religious regimens at court, but made the court itself a locus of contention over the proper place of preaching within the service of the visible church. Indeed, the lines drawn in pulpit debate at the courts of Elizabeth, James, and, even more importantly and less known, the household of Charles when Prince of Wales, were in fact the battle-lines for religious war in the 1630s.

Elizabeth clearly recognized the importance of showing herself at sermons in her court, and she nurtured a very select number of preachers as personal favourites; but just as she was not a zealous preaching patron in her church at large, so she never made her court a particularly amenable place for preachers. Still, Elizabeth studiously preserved pre-Reformation court sermon customs, most importantly the series of three sermons preached *coram regina* in each of Lent's six weeks, and she patronized a court preaching style noted for its stylistic sophistication. Thus, a distinguished tradition of preaching already thrived at court upon the arrival of James VI and I in the spring of 1603. But with that arrival began the heyday of preaching at Whitehall. James's passion for sermon-hearing – which surpassed his oft-noted pastimes of hunting and play-going – and the routines for attendance at service and sermon that he brought with him from Scotland radically altered the practice of religion at the English court. The accession of the new king not only saw at least a doubling of the number of sermons preached weekly at court, but also reoriented public worship in the chapels royal from prayerbook service to attendance at sermons.

James did not come from Scotland alone, however, for he was the head

---

[15] Collinson, *Religion of Protestants*. Collinson, 'The Elizabethan Church and the New Religion', in Haigh, ed., *Reign of Elizabeth* (Athens, Ga., 1987), 194.

[16] Starkey, *English Court*, 4–6.

of the first royal family in England since Henry VIII. Soon after his accession, both his queen consort and eldest son, Prince Henry, were given their own household establishments, complete with Chaplains in Ordinary with their own sermon rotas. These three Jacobean courts, the third inherited by Prince Charles after Henry's premature death in 1612, tripled the number of royal centres of ecclesiastical patronage. The chapels at Whitehall, Denmark House, and St James's developed their own distinct pulpit characteristics that dramatized the ecclesiological varieties – and divisions – that marked the Jacobean church. Attention to the chaplains that served Queen Anne at Denmark House and the surviving sermons they preached before her sheds some light on the perennial mystery of her rumoured Roman Catholicism. At Whitehall, James's preachers, fittingly, displayed the wide range of Jacobean conformity. The king's taste for good preaching transcended ecclesiastical faction, and he could praise and reward with equal enthusiasm the anti-Catholic Calvinism of John King and Joseph Hall, the numinous sacramentalism of Lancelot Andrewes and John Buckeridge, or the eloquence of John Donne (who, ecclesiologically, inhabited a muddled space somewhere in between). Across the park at St James's, however, a strikingly homogeneous college of preacher-chaplains dedicated to evangelical reform at home and Protestant militarism abroad flourished under Prince Henry and, much less known today, also under his brother and successor Prince Charles.

THE *CALENDAR OF SERMONS PREACHED AT COURT, 1558–1625*

The supplement on disk, a calendar of all the known sermons preached at court during the two reigns, compiles all known contemporary records of individual Elizabethan and Jacobean court sermons. Since it is the foundation upon which this study was built, and is in itself a substantial resource for further advanced research, the reader should be aware of its contents and arrangement here.

First, this 'Calendar' differs from the related list of Paul's Cross sermons compiled by Millar MacLure in its attempt to record not only printed sermon texts, but also those texts that survive only in manuscript, as well as notice of sermons surviving in contemporary letters, diaries, domestic and foreign state papers, and royal household accounts.[17] The bibliography of printed sermons is in many ways not representative of court preaching during the period, and the inclusion of unprinted sources does much to correct the picture of who preached at court, the doctrinal and formal

---

[17] Millar MacLure, *Register of Sermons Preached at Paul's Cross 1534–1642*, revised and expanded by Peter Pauls and Jackson Campbell Boswell (Ottawa, 1989).

changes over the course of the reigns, and how printing was related (or not) to royal policy and patronage. The 'Calendar' begins with Elizabeth's accession on 17 November 1558 and ends with James's funeral at Westminster Abbey on 7 May 1625, and lists 1,257 sermons known to have been appointed or preached at these courts. No catalogue of this sort could ever pretend to be complete. I have attempted, however, to assemble a definitive list of those Elizabethan and Jacobean court sermons printed before 1640. The primary bibliographical source has of course been the invaluable second edition of the *STC*.[18] Every effort has been made to include sermons published in collections as well as those printed at a later date. This core group of texts includes 42 Elizabethan and 236 Jacobean court sermons: a total of 278 printed court sermons.[19]

A brief description of the 'Calendar' format should help students and researchers determine its suitability for their needs and interests and facilitate its use. Public or political events that had a direct influence on court preaching, such as Elizabeth's prohibition of preaching on 27 December 1558, are collated within the 'Calendar' and distinguished from sermon entries by italic type. When available, the following information appears for each sermon entry: both calendar and liturgical date, place preached, name and rank of preacher, Scriptural text, a précis of the sermon, and bibliography. The following should be noted about these categories:

Date

- Years have been adjusted to correspond with a New Year's Day of 1 January. When a sermon's year cannot be definitely determined, it appears in the 'Calendar' at the latest possible date preached, or, when even such a limited dating is not possible, it is placed in the final section, 'Sermons of Uncertain Date'.

- Days of the week, as well as dates, are included to emphasize the inherent difference between weekday, Sunday, and holiday sermons.

- The liturgical date or occasion appears after the calendar date. For those sermons not preached on a sanctioned holiday (i.e. a major feast, fast, or saints' day) the number of the week of the liturgical season – either

[18] A. W. Pollard and G. R. Redgrave, *A Short-Title Catalogue of Books Printed in England, Scotland, and Ireland . . . 1475–1640*, 2nd edn, 3 vols. rev. W. A. Jackson, F. S. Ferguson, and Katharine F. Pantzer (1986–91). Alan Fager Herr, *The Elizabethan Sermon, A Survey and Bibliography* (published PhD thesis, University of Pennsylvania, 1940), is based on the first edition of the *STC*. Also important, though to a lesser extent for the period under consideration, has been Donald Wing, *Short Title Catalogue of Books Printed in England . . . 1641–1700*, 2nd edn, 3 vols. (New York, 1972).

[19] Of this number, 169 (28 Elizabethan, 141 Jacobean) were printed as well as preached in the period under consideration (1558–1625). The increase in the final total is due primarily to posthumously printed collections of sermons by Andrewes (1629) and Donne (1640, 1649, 1661).

Advent, Epiphany, Lent, Easter, or Trinity – is given (e.g. 'Friday, Lent 2', or 'Sunday, Trinity 23'), according to the Calendar approved in the Elizabethan Settlement of 1559.[20] The progress of the liturgical year influenced the frequency, subject matter, and even the location of court sermons.

Place
- If known, the presence of members of the royal family is noted here.
- The locations given are as specific as possible, with speculations marked by a query (?).

Rank
- After the preacher's name appears his academic degree and the most significant benefices held previously, at the time of the sermon, and successively. Of course, space would not allow potted biographies; I have attempted outlines only to show the trajectory of a career and the probable role of court preaching in it.
- All biographical information, unless otherwise cited, is taken from the *Dictionary of National Biography.*

Scriptural Text
- When known, the chapter and verse taken as the preacher's text appears using the chapter names assigned in the Authorized ('King James'') Version of 1611. If the text is a proper or lesson appointed for the day, that is noted. Because the texts chosen tell much about the occasion of the sermon and the preacher's treatment of that occasion, I print the text as well as the citation. For exceptionally long texts, I give a summary. In cases where no sermon text survives, quoting the Scripture expounded by the preacher at least captures a hint of the subject matter of the lost text. Since so many sermons of the period – most notably, but not only, those of Lancelot Andrewes – are essays in the most minute textual exegesis, I quote the translation used by the preacher, when known. In printed sermons, the preacher's text always heads the sermon itself. Therefore, page references after a text indicate the page of the printed sermon where the text is given. When I supply a text, I quote from the Geneva Bible for sermons before 1611, and the Authorized Version for those after.

---

[20] See *The Book of Common Prayer, 1559,* ed. John Booty (Washington, DC, 1976), 36–47, 77–246. I retain some liturgical nomenclature that, although not recognized by the Prayer Book, did not pass out of common usage (e. g. 'Ash Wednesday', 'Passion Sunday', 'Palm Sunday').

Summary

- Where texts or extended accounts of the sermon survive, I provide brief summaries or outline. More extended accounts are provided for texts not available in modern editions or on microfilm.
- Dedicatees are cited where known.

Bibliography

- The final portion of each entry attempts to gather both bibliography and all known contemporary reference to the sermon. The first bibliographic reference after the summary of the sermon represents the primary source used. In the case of sermons printed during the period covered by the 'Calendar', this will always be the *Short-Title Catalogue* (*STC*) number followed by a transcription of the title page.[21] Modern bibliography will also appear if available. Finally, reference is given to any known contemporary commentary upon or notice of the sermon.

The diskette format should facilitate a flexible, wide-ranging number of searches by any of the above categories (e.g. Scriptural text, place of publication, *STC* number, author name, etc.). The 'Calendar', then, functions not only as an exhaustive bibliography and tool for further research, but also as an independent narrative of primary sources that testifies to the significance of preaching at the courts of Elizabeth I and James I.

[21] I follow the guidelines for this kind of transcript set down by Fredson Bowers in his *Principles of Bibliographic Description* (Princeton, N.J., 1949), pp. 138–9, except that I *do* indicate line-endings.

The architectural settings of Elizabethan and Jacobean court preaching

A preacher at court stepped into a pulpit unlike most others in England. This was due not only to the fact that he spoke before the most august assembly in the realm, but because a court preacher *in situ* had to negotiate a spatial relationship with his auditory that was markedly different from the normal parochial setting. In addition, he found himself in the midst of an elaborate iconographic scene of architectural, artistic, liturgical, and even living human components that made assertive claims about church, commonwealth, and monarchy. Court sermons were preached in surprisingly varied venues, ranging from the formal ceremonial setting of the chapels royal to the grand civic scale of Whitehall's outdoor Preaching Place. Since these varied sites influenced the content as well as the delivery of court sermons, a reconstruction of the physical settings, including the seating arrangement of the prince and the court, must be considered in order to understand what made a sermon at court different from one preached anywhere else in the realm.

'COPIES, AND REPRESENTATIONS OF HEAVEN': THE CHAPELS ROYAL

The court's religious life centred around the chapels royal. It was here that the Prayer Book offices of matins and evensong were sung daily by the Gentlemen and Children of the Chapel Royal, here that the monarch and court received communion on principal feast days, and here that courtiers in special favour might solemnize their matrimony or see their children baptized.[1] With the very significant exception of the outdoor pulpit at Whitehall, discussed later, these domestic chapels were also the primary settings for the sermons preached before the English court. Most of the principal manors and palaces that Elizabeth inherited upon her accession

---

[1] See *The Old-Cheque Book . . . of the Chapel Royal, from 1561–1744,* ed. Edward F. Rimbault, Camden Society, n.s. 3 (1872).

had chapels as some of their most substantial buildings, a feature common not only to royal, but also to most noble houses; the chapel, with the great hall and the presence chamber, formed the ceremonial and social heart of the principal Tudor-Stuart royal manors.

The most important regular residences of Elizabeth and James – their 'standing houses' – were Whitehall, the primary London seat in Westminster, formerly Wolsey's York House; St James's, a smaller, less-frequented palace across St James's Park from Whitehall built by Henry VIII probably as a satellite court for his illegitimate son, Henry, Duke of Richmond; Greenwich, Elizabeth's birthplace, built by her grandfather, Henry VII; and, up the Thames from London, Henry VII's showpiece palace of Richmond, Henry VIII's expansion of Wolsey's Hampton Court, and the ancient castle of Windsor. Only Windsor, Hampton Court, and St James's still stand, and only the latter two retain their Tudor chapels, although even these have been drastically altered in the intervening centuries.[2] Perhaps because of this lack of surviving structures and the almost total absence of detailed plans or descriptions of the Tudor chapels royal, there has been little attempt to describe or reconstruct the appearance and liturgical life of these very influential centres of early modern court culture until very recently.[3] Recent pioneering work on life in the Henrician palaces, however, provides an invaluable frame of reference from the early Tudor period. To this can be added accounts of the King's Works, visitors' descriptions, and household rules and regulations for chapel attendance surviving from the reigns of Elizabeth, James I, and Charles I, to reveal the plans, iconography and liturgical routine that composed the court sermon setting.

With the exception of Richmond, considered separately, the royal chapels in the 'standing houses' – Whitehall, Hampton Court, St James's, Greenwich, and Windsor – shared the same plan, and, for the purposes of understanding the sermon's setting in them, can be described collectively. It should be noted here, to avoid confusion, that the chapel royal at Windsor was distinct from the castle's collegiate chapel of St George. When residing at Windsor, the sovereign's religious duties were performed in a smaller chapel in the Upper Ward's complex of private and state apartments. Thomas Platter's account of his tour of Windsor Castle during Elizabeth's

---

[2] Windsor's domestic Chapel Royal was razed in the early nineteenth century. At Hampton Court, only Henry VIII's ceiling remains; at St James's, the 1540 ceiling is the only surviving Tudor work. See Simon Thurley, *The Royal Palaces of Tudor England, Architecture and Court Life 1460–1547* (New Haven, Conn., 1993), 198, 202–3. I am grateful to Dr Thurley for sharing proofs of his work with me before its publication. See also G. D. Heath, *The Chapel Royal at Hampton Court*, Borough of Twickenham Local History Society Paper Number 42, 2nd impression (1983).

[3] Thurley, *Royal Palaces*, ch. 12.

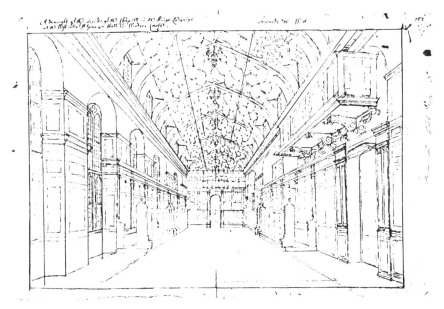

Fig. 1. Wenceslaus Hollar, 'A Draught of the inside of the Chapell in the King's Lodgings . . . in Windsor Castle, towards the West'. The only reliable contemporary interior view of a chapel royal. Though unfinished, the sketch records the chapel as renovated by Elizabeth I in 1570–1, with the oriel windows of the royal closet over the west end (Bodleian Library, University of Oxford, MS Ashmole 1131, fols. 168v–169r).

reign makes the distinction clear. Platter's first stop was the 'mighty church' or chapel of St George. From there, he ascended to the royal apartments in the Upper Ward, where he passed from the Presence Chamber into the domestic chapel where 'the queen listens to the sermon when she is at Windsor'.[4] Rebuilt by Edward III at the west end of the Great Hall, this chapel was completely renovated under Elizabeth in 1570–1.[5] As the only extensive ecclesiastical building project carried out by the queen, the Windsor domestic chapel is significant as evidence of the requirements for worship in the post-Reformation royal household, and Hollar's sketches of it preserve the only complete views of any Tudor chapel interior (Figure 1). Two components of the structure and seating arrangement in these chapels are crucial to a proper understanding of the spatial dynamics between monarch, minister, and court. Briefly put, the sovereign sat in an enclosed

[4] Clare Williams, ed. and trans., *Thomas Platter's Travels in England 1599* (1937), 205, 209–11.
[5] *HKW*, vol. III, 322.

gallery over the west end, while principal household officers and courtiers sat below in two facing sets of stalls against the north and south walls that formed an axis between the pulpit and communion table at the east end and the royal gallery at the west. The element of the chapel plan that made these chapels 'royal' was of course the gallery, referred to in the period as the royal 'closet' or 'pew'.

At Whitehall, Hampton Court, and St James's, the closets were especially large owing to their placement over ante-chapels that crossed perpendicular to the bodies of the chapels proper. Dr Thurley has shown how this plan, introduced at New College, Oxford in the fourteenth century, influenced Wolsey, the builder of what became both the Whitehall and Hampton Court chapels royal. The significant amount of extra space in the ante-chapel's ground floor accommodated the lay members of the cardinal's household, the chapel proper being occupied by the clerical and choral members.[6] These ante-chapels similarly provided standing-room in Elizabethan and Jacobean times for members of the household and visitors who were not allowed by precedence and rank to sit in the stalls. Finally, the royal closet was connected by a passage or lobby to the first-floor royal apartments and presence chamber, and spiral turret staircases called 'vices' descended from the closet to the main chapel level below (Figure 2).

The elevated position of honour for the monarch in church or chapel rearticulated a continuous and vigorous theme in Western royal or palatine chapel architecture begun by Charlemain at his influential chapel at Aachen, or Aix-la-Chapelle (805).[7] Although it served routinely as a parish and collegiate church, Charlemain's Church of Our Lady was also built as the court chapel of his winter palace.[8] Here, possibly for the first time, the sovereign sat in a throne in an upper story ('gallery', 'logia', or 'tribune') over the chapel's west end.[9] A long enclosed gallery, also at the first-floor level, connected the *kaiserloge* with the palace's great hall and private apartments, and a pair of spiral staircases provided access from the first to the ground-floor level of the chapel – precisely the plan of the palace

---

[6] Thurley, *Royal Palaces*, 197.

[7] For the continuity of the tradition through the Middle Ages, see A. Verbeek, 'Die architektonische Nachfolge der Aachener Pfalzkapelle', in W. Braunfels and P. E. Schram, eds., *Karl der Grosse. Lebenswerk und Nachleben*, vol. IV, *Das Nachleben*, (Dusseldorf, 1967), 113–56.

[8] Ludwig Falkenstein, 'Charlemagne et Aix-La-Chapelle', *Byzantion* 61 (1991), 235–6, 255–9.

[9] E. Baldwin Smith, among others, has argued that Byzantine court precedents inform Charlemain's elevated position of honour in *Architectural Symbolism of Imperial Rome and the Middle Ages* (Princeton, N.J., 1956), ch. VII. But this has been qualified by Adolf Reine, *Zeichensprache der Architektur: Symbol, Darstellung und Brauch in der Baukunst des Mittlealters und der Neuzeit* (Zurich, 1976), 314, and Falkenstein, 'Charlemagne', 282–4. I am grateful to Professors John Pinto and Daniel Curcic for these references.

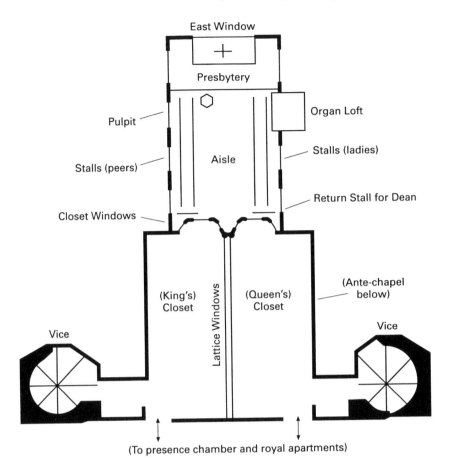

Fig. 2. Conjectural floor plan of the chapel royal, Hampton Court, under the Tudors and Stuarts (based on the plan in Heath, *Chapel Royal at Hampton Court* with seating based on James I's rules for chapel attendance, British Library Add. MS 34324, fol. 215).

chapels at Tudor and Stuart Whitehall, Hampton Court, Greenwich, St James's, Richmond, and Windsor. This arrangement became common in royal abbeys and chapels throughout Europe at least through the Baroque age, with Mansart's Chapelle Royale de Versailles with its colonnaded royal *tribune* (1710) as the apotheosis of the form.[10]

---

[10] For the quotation of the Aachen arrangement in seventeenth- and eighteenth-century Protestant and Catholic palace chapels see Reinl, *Zeichensprache der Architektur*, 319. For Mansart's quotation of Aachen at Versailles, see Guy Walton, *Louis XIV's Versailles* (Harmondsworth, 1986), 195–6.

Even in Tudor England, the gallery or 'closet' had become a much more elaborate affair than Charlemain's marble throne perched between stolid arches above the body of the church. In fact, the closets as we know them from contemporary descriptions and account books were elaborately furnished chambers that doubled as both chapels in miniature and as elevated pews for watching service or sermon below in the main chapel. Caution must be used, however, when discussing palace closets. The early Tudor monarchs heard mass in small closets attached to their privy chambers, and came to the larger chapel closets only on ceremonial occasions (hence also 'holyday closets'). Elizabeth and James continued to use the smaller privy closets, or oratories, for their daily devotions, and processions to the chapel closet to hear sung morning or evening prayer, to hear a sermon, or to attend communion occurred only on Sundays and feast days. The privy closet, actually a two-celled chamber, was located off the important gallery that led from the semi-public presence chamber to the closely guarded privy chamber. Nearest the presence chamber stood an entry to a room furnished with a communion table. Separated from this by a screen or lattice window was a smaller room, entered from the privy chamber, wherein the prince could kneel for private devotions, or hear the service said in the room adjoining (see Figure 3).[11] Thus the orders for Prince Henry's household at St James's (1610) required that when the Prince heard morning and evening prayer 'in his Oratory' (the privy closet) the ushers of both the presence and the privy chambers were to require attendants there 'to repayre unto ye said Oratorye, where they shall give their attendance in such devout and reverent manner as appertaineth'.[12] Sometimes, but not consistently, contemporary accounts refer to the chapel closet as 'the greate Closett', clearly distinguishing it from the smaller closet in the privy apartments, but often when the great closet is meant, only 'Closett' is used.[13] Only the chapel royal at Richmond diverged from the plan, with an elevated closet at the west end. Henry VII built Richmond as the architectural centrepiece of his newly founded dynasty, and unveiled it during festivities that followed the marriage of Prince Arthur to Katherine of Aragon in 1501.[14] The chapel, at 96 feet long and 30 feet wide, was the largest of the Tudor chapels royal. The chapel had passageways at the ground and first floor levels that connected it to the royal lodgings, and, rather than closets at the west end, the king's and queen's closets stood

[11] Thurley, *English Royal Palaces*, 125–6, 198–9. Elizabethan and Jacobean wardrobe warrants for chapel and closet furnishings invariably refer to the 'communion table'; 'altar' is never used.

[12] BL MS Add 39853, fols. 16–18.   [13] *Old Cheque-Book*, 169, 171.

[14] For the significance of Richmond Palace to the new Tudor dynasty see Gordon Kipling, *The Triumph of Honour: the Burgundian Origins of the Elizabethan Renaissance* (The Hague, 1977), 3–10.

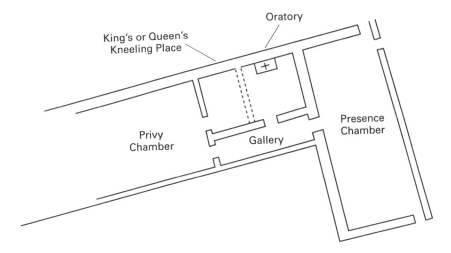

Fig. 3. Plan showing the privy closet or oratory between the presence and privy chambers at Whitehall (based on Simon Thurley, *Royal Palaces of Tudor England*, plan 13).

above opposite sides of the choir in the east end, thereby placing the preacher directly below the sovereign (see Figure 4).[15]

We know very little about the piece of chapel furniture that was specifically the preacher's domain, the pulpit, except that in the chapels royal it was probably wooden and removable. Since all the chapels predated the Reformation, they were not conceived as preaching halls, but rather as buildings where mass could be sung daily, with a wide central aisle for liturgical processions, special ceremonies, such as installations to the Order of the Garter, and the solemnization of diplomatic treaties. Since before the 1530s sermons were usually only preached during Lent and on a few high feast days of the church year, a stationary pulpit would have been an obtrusive encumbrance. Thus, in a pre-Reformation description of a gentleman usher's duties for Ash Wednesday, we find special mention that 'warning ought to be gevin to the Sᵣiant of the vestry . . . to make ready the chapell . . . and to p[re]pair a pulpett for a Sermon'.[16] The accounts of the Comptroller of the Queen's Works for 1590–1 show that 'a newe pulpit' made of 'wainscotting' was built for the queen's chapel at Richmond at a

[15] *HKW*, vol. IV, 226–7. A similar arrangement was adopted at St George's Chapel, Windsor, where the massive oriel window of Henry VIII's closet looks directly over the high altar. See Sir William St John Hope, *Windsor Castle: an Architectural History*, 2 vols. (1913), vol. II, 428 and plate LXIV.
[16] BL MS Sloane 1494, fol. 20ʳ.

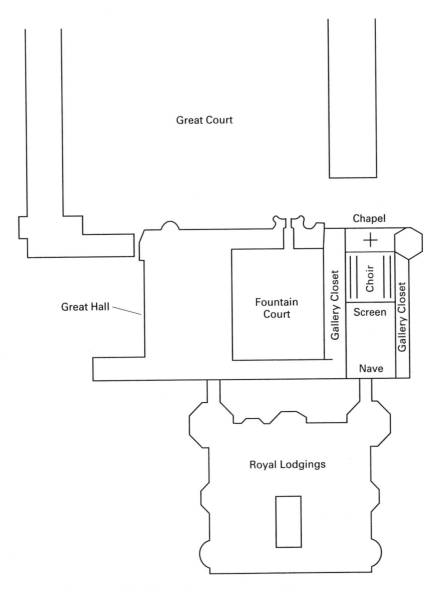

Fig. 4. The principal buildings of Richmond Palace, showing chapel and chapel closet seating. (Based on the plan in *HKW*, vol. IV, 226.)

cost of 22s, and the parliamentary survey of that palace taken in 1649 listed among other 'things useful for a chapel' a 'removable pulpit'.[17] The description of the 1613 marriage of Princess Elizabeth in the Whitehall chapel suggests that the pulpit there was also portable, since the author specified that the preacher 'went into the pulpit, which stood at the foot of the step before the Communion table'. The front of the pulpits were normally draped with an embroidered pulpit cloth, as that observed by von Wedel when he visited Greenwich during Christmastide, in 1584: the chapel itself was 'hung with golden cloth' and the pulpit 'covered with red velvet embroidered with gold'.[18] With the pulpit placed against the step that separated choir from presbytery, court preachers addressed a sovereign seated at a distance of between 35 and 50 feet, depending on the chapel.[19] At Richmond, however, with its royal closets at the east, the preacher stood literally under the monarch's nose, or, considering that the pulpit was raised by several steps, he was, as Sir John Harington put it, 'vis a vis, to the Closet'.[20]

Both before and after the Reformation the closets were elaborately furnished and fitted with eucharistic furniture. Henry VII's closet at Richmond was 'richly hangid with silke and travasse carpet and cusshons' and the altar therin 'also hangid and platid with riche relikes of gold and precious stone.' Henry VIII had his closet altars decked with statues of his favourite saints.[21] Elizabethan and Jacobean warrants for closet stuffs never differentiate between the privy and the chapel closets, but both had to be able to accommodate sovereign and attendants, and were richly appointed with hangings, linens, and service books. In April 1595, Elizabeth ordered to be delivered to her Clerk of the Closet 'for our seruice there', fine linen and cloth of gold 'for two communion Tables'; for the attending chaplains cloth 'for two Communion Towells', 'foure surplises gathered', and 'two Bibles in Englishe'; and, for those worshipping with her in the closet, 'two dosen of seruice bookes'.[22] James's warrants similarly

---

[17] PRO E 351/3225, fol. 7ᵛ; John Nichols, *The Progresses and Public Processions of Queen Elizabeth*, 3 vols. (1823), vol. II, 413.

[18] Lupold von Wedel, 'Journey Through England and Scotland . . . in the Years 1584 and 1585', ed. and trans. Gottfried von Bulow, in *Transactions of the Royal Historical Society*, N.S. vol. IX (1895), 262.

[19] The smallest chapel royal, Greenwich, had a probable length from closet window to east end of 52 feet (Baldwin, *Chapel Royal*, 98), while the largest, Whitehall, had a length of some 70 feet (*HKW*, fold-out Plan VII). I have allowed 15 and 20 feet respectively for the depth of each presbytery.

[20] Sir John Harington, *A Supplie or Addicion to the Catalogue of Bishops to the Yeare 1608*, ed. R. H. Miller (Potomac, Md., 1979), 152.

[21] *The Receyt of the Ladie Kateryne*, ed. Gordon Kipling, Early English Text Society no. 296 (Oxford, 1990), 73. John Bickersteth and Robert Dunning, *Clerks of the Closet in the Royal Household* (Stroud, 1991), 6.

[22] BL MS Add 5750, fol. 40. The orders for items in pairs might suggest furnishings for the

ordered bibles and service books 'for o[ur] owne vse bound accordingly', cloth of gold 'findged with gold and silke' for the communion tables, a traverse hung with 'Crimson Taffata', and Turkey carpets for the royal chair.[23]

As a pew the chapel closet functioned in much the same way that any modern royal box does, but with the addition of the windows that separated the closet from the chapel below. But more exactly, there were closets above the west ends of the chapels royal, since, as at Hampton Court, Henry VIII provided one each for himself and his consort by dividing the chamber in half with a partition of carved woodwork and lattice windows.[24] It is not known which side Elizabeth occupied – the queen's or the king's – during her maiden reign. The two closets were duly kept by James and Anne, as is seen in the routine payments in the Treasurer's Accounts for readying both, as in October 1607, when a gentleman usher and yeomen were paid for 'making ready the Chappell and Clozett at Whitehall on both the kinge and Queenes side against Allhallowtide'.[25] No doubt attending the prince in the closet was a coveted sign of favour, and, even in his or her absence, the closet was still a desirable vantage point. When Lady Anne Clifford and her husband, the Earl of Dorset, went to court on a January Sunday morning in 1617 and were disappointed in their hopes of seeing the queen go to chapel, Clifford and other court ladies seized the opportunity to listen to the sermon standing in the royal closet.[26] The closets in James's reign were also routinely used as a vantage point for foreign ambassadors to view the Garter ceremonies when they were held at Whitehall. In 1622, for example, James invited the States Commissioners to watch from the 'Chappell Closet on the Queens side', and the Spanish Ambassador 'to possess that of the Kings side'. The Spaniard, however, 'would never indure' the Netherlandish ambassadors so near himself, 'where there was but a thin Wainscot Board between them, and a Window to be opened at either of their pleasures, which might be an occasion of scandall, and distemper'.[27]

Elizabeth and James, like their predecessors and successors, always heard the services and sermons conducted in their chapels seated at their closet

two sides – 'King's' and 'Queen's' – of the great closet, or one each for the great and privy closets. Warrants for 'stuffs' for the closets were routine, and varied little during the reigns of Elizabeth, James, and Charles. Other surviving warrants are found in *ibid.*, fols. 41 (1601), 42 and 43 (for Queen Anne, 1603, 1604) and the wardrobe warrants for the three reigns, PRO LC 5/35, 5/36, 5/37 and 5/38.

[23] PRO LC 5/38, fol. 4.   [24] Heath, *Chapel Royal at Hampton Court*, 8–9.

[25] PRO E351/543, fol. 188ᵛ.

[26] *The Diary of Lady Anne Clifford*, intro. Vita Sackville-West (1924), 49.

[27] Sir John Finett, *Finetti Philoxenis: Som Choice Observations of Sᵣ John Finett . . . Master of the Ceremonies* (1656), 106–7.

windows. At Hampton Court the closet pews projected into the chapel as bay windows, and Hollar's sketch of the west end of Elizabeth's Windsor chapel shows similar oriel windows in her closet there (Figure 1). Both Elizabeth and James routinely opened the windows into the chapel to thank, or even to criticize, their preachers for their pains at the end of their sermons. When Matthew Hutton, Bishop of Durham dared to advise Elizabeth in a 1593 sermon to settle the succession on her Scottish cousin, the auditory expected a retort from the queen, but instead, 'when she opend the window', wrote Sir John Harington, 'we founde our selues all deceaved, for verie kyndlie and calmly . . . she gaue him thanks for his verie learned Sermon'. Elizabeth's Bishop of St David's, Anthony Rudd, was not so fortunate after he advised the ageing queen in a 1596 sermon at Richmond to prepare her soul for death. Elizabeth, '(as the manner was) opened the window but she was . . . far from giving him thanks', and observed instead that 'the greatest Clerks are not the wisest men'. [28] James, too, was known to voice his opinions from the closet, as at Christmas 1622, when something in the Bishop of London's sermon 'gave the King so litle content that he grew lowde, and the bishop was driven to end abruptly'.[29] Conversely, after Lancelot Andrewes's sermon for Christmas 1616, the king reportedly stood up in the closet window and proclaimed, '"Before God, never man spake like him from the days of the Apostles."'[30] During a court sermon, a preacher not only had to face the presence of the sovereign, but also stand alone in an elevated pulpit more on a level with the prince than anyone else in the chapel, knowing all the while that before stepping down, the sovereign would pass judgment on his performance from above.

From inside the chapel looking up to the closet, preacher or courtiers would see the sovereign centred over the west end, not only framed in the window, but surrounded by the heraldic devices of the monarchy, as at Hampton Court where Henry had the facades of the closets 'suitably garnished with the royal arms, painted and gilded with fine gold and bice [light blue], set out with fine colours'.[31] From their vantage points above the body of the chapel the monarchs could both watch and hear the service below and still remain in privacy. The closet window simultaneously advertised the princely presence while it guarded it – the sovereign was a kind of present absence, a hovering, presiding genius, removed but more keenly felt because of that removal. Since the courtly congregation faced each other, and not the closet, the monarch was not the direct focus of

[28] Harington, *Supplie or Addicion,* 172, 153.
[29] John Chamberlain, *The Letters of John Chamberlain,* ed. N. E. McClure, 2 vols. (Philadelphia, Pa., 1939), vol. II, 470.
[30] Thomas Plume, 'Dr Plume's Notebook', ed. Andrew Clark, *Essex Review* 15 (1906), 20.
[31] PRO E 14/244, quoted in *HKW,* vol. IV, 135.

visual attention unless a preacher chose to take advantage of this most powerful visual aid by directing attention upward, as Lancelot Andrewes did in a sermon preached before James and his visiting brother-in-law, King Christian of Denmark, in 1606. After reading his text from the 144th Psalm – 'It is He that giveth salvation unto Kings: who delivereth David His servant from the perilous, or malignant sword' – Andrewes no doubt gestured to the closet when he continued, 'For behold *Kings* . . . Behold our *King* . . . whil'st at once we heare the words, of the Text, we have as it were, a Commentary thereof before our eyes.'[32]

The iconographic schemes in the chapels royal emphasized dynastic as much as religious claims. At Richmond the walls bore carvings of the English kings 'whoes lif and vertue was so abundaunt that it hath pleasid Almighti God to . . . recount as sayntes', including 'Saint Edward, King Cadwaleder, Seint Edmond, and many moo'.[33] Henry VIII quoted this dynastic imagery in the court chapels that he renovated or built during his reign. Upon taking York Place, later Whitehall, from Wolsey, Henry had new stalls made for the chapel that were embellished with carved 'beists standyng apon them', trails of Tudor roses, and 28 'pannells with the proporsyon of kyngs in them'.[34] In addition, in every available space heraldic badges appeared – on 'the grette organes in the Chappell' at Greenwich, flanking the west door of the chapel at Hampton Court, and sprinkled across the Holbein ceiling of the chapel at St James's.[35] According to Dr Richard Eedes, chaplain to both Elizabeth and James, God had 'trauailed many yeeres as it were in childbed . . . how hee might bring forth vnto himselfe a Church'. After conceiving the Early Church in humility and persecution he 'cast his fauor toward princes' and only then did the church find her glorious maturity as 'she *grew vp into a kingdome*' nursed by princes.[36] Iconographic assertions of precisely this view surrounded Eedes as he preached that sermon at Whitehall, from the royal arms to the panel portraits of saintly kings who had 'travailed many yeeres' to establish the English church. But Elizabeth and James, too, were living parts of that iconography. At Richmond they sat on a level with the statues of Edward, Edmund, Cadwallader, and the 'many moo' that looked down into the chapel, thus asserting the Tudor, and then Stuart, claims to legitimate succession from Britain's ancient kings.

So standard was the arrangement of elevated chapel closet that English

[32] Lancelot Andrewes, *XCVI Sermons* (1629), 1009; Lancelot Andrewes, *Works,* 11 vols, ed. J.P. Wilson and James Bliss (Oxford, 1841–54), vol. V, 235.

[33] Kipling, ed., *Receyt of the Ladie Kateryne*, 73. *HKW*, vol. IV, 227.

[34] Bodl. MS Eng. Hist. b.192/2, fol. 4; quoted in *HKW*, vol. IV, 315.

[35] *HKW*, vol. IV, 105, 135, 242.

[36] Richard Eedes, 'Princes to bee Nurces of the Church', in *Six Learned and Godly Sermons* (1604), fols. 62^{r-v}, 64^r, 62^v.

sovereigns expected similar accommodation wherever they attended service or sermon. When Elizabeth planned a progress visit to Canterbury in 1573, one of Archbishop Parker's biggest headaches, in addition to how to house the queen's entourage, was how appropriately to imitate a royal closet or pew for Elizabeth to hear a sermon. Hoping that 'it might please her Majesty to hear the dean preach', Parker assured Lord Burghley that 'her Highness might go to a very fit place, with some of her lords and ladies, to be there in a convenient closet above the heads of the people to hear the sermon'.[37] When Elizabeth kept Lent 1585 at Somerset House in the Strand, she spent over £600 fitting the adjacent Savoy Hospital chapel as a proper chapel royal for her use.[38]

Similar accommodations at the great country estates visited by Elizabeth and James during their annual summer progresses were quite easy to make, since the architectural theme of a two-story chapel with an elevated gallery had been adopted not only in royal, but also in noble houses.[39] The Elizabethan–Jacobean 'prodigy houses', which included Lord Burghley's Theobalds (1585), and his son the Earl of Salisbury's Hatfield House (1612) – both of which became Jacobean royal mansions – were built for the express purpose of accommodating the monarch and court on their visits, and had chapels with suitable elevated west-end pews.[40] In fact, perhaps the only facade of an Elizabethan or Jacobean royal closet to survive today is that associated with Holdenby House, Sir Christopher Hatton's Northamptonshire mansion built in 1578–83 in homage to his patroness, Queen Elizabeth, and purchased by James in 1608.[41] Mark Girouard has suggested that the immense carved screen that is now separated into two parts and used as a chancel screen and an entrance to the west-end vestry at Holdenby Church were in fact part of a whole that formed the screen at the west end of the chapel in Hatton's house (see Figure 5). Girouard speculates that the lower portion formed the screen through which worshippers entered the lower body of the chapel. About the upper range he suggests that 'it looks as though it was intended to open into or out of something' and ventures that 'it is tempting to see it as the remains of a first-floor gallery'.[42] The upper portion probably is indeed the

---

[37] Matthew Parker, *The Correspondence of Matthew Parker*, ed. John Bruce and Thomas Perowne (Cambridge, 1853), 442–3.

[38] *HKW*, vol. IV, 254.

[39] Mark Girouard, 'Elizabethan Holdenby', *Country Life*, 166 (1979), 1287–8.

[40] John Summerson, 'The Building of Theobalds, 1564–1585', *Archaeologia*, 97 (1959), 107–26; Lawrence Stone, 'The Building of Hatfield House', *Archaeological Journal*, 112 (1955), 100–28.

[41] The surviving Tudor chapels at Hampton Court and St James's do not retain their original closet facades.

[42] Girouard, 'Elizabethan Holdenby', 1401.

Fig. 5. A Victorian reconstruction of the screen from the west end of the chapel in Holdenby House, Northamptonshire (1578–83). Large portions of the screen have been reused in Holdenby parish church. (Photograph: *Country Life*.)

remains of the first floor gallery, but the rounded central arch was meant to frame not a door opening 'into or out of something', but rather the queen herself. Burghley said that Hatton's mansion was 'consecrated to her Majesty', and Hatton himself longed for the day that 'that lady saint may sit in it to whom it is dedicated'. This bold screen with an arch supported by royal lions – and at one time crowned with the royal arms on its pediment – would have been a suitable niche for Hatton's patron saint.[43] Elizabeth never saw Hatton's architectural homage to her, Hatton dying in 1591; but it was here – probably from behind the great carved screen – that James I heard many sermons during his sojourns at Holdenby during summer progresses.

The symbolic significance of the elevation of the closet must be empha-

---

[43] Girouard, 'Elizabethan Holdenby', 1289. The Queen's arms – not Hatton's – were emblazoned over the porch.

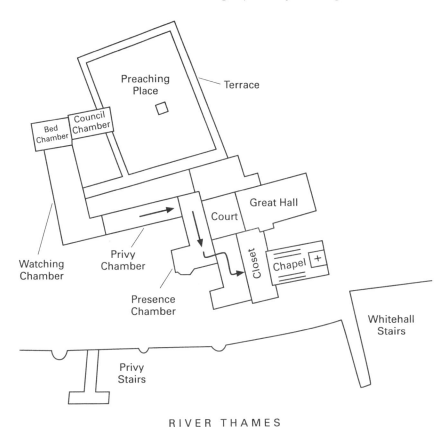

Fig. 6. The principal buildings of Whitehall Palace, showing the route of processions to Chapel. (Based on the plan *HKW*, vol. IV, 309.)

sized and considered in the context of the sovereign's movements to and from chapel services (see Figure 6). Henry VIII's attendance of public service in his palace chapels was primarily motivated not by religous devotion, but by the desire to parade the royal person – increasingly cloistered in the recesses of the privy apartments – before the court and suitors.[44] During Elizabeth's and James's reigns, the Sunday and holy-day processions to and from chapel continued as a major ceremonial event that particularly dazzled foreign visitors. The early modern tourists Paul Hentzner and Lupold von Wedel provide the best descriptions of the ceremony. Sundays at court, more than any other day of the week, were

[44] Thurley, *Royal Palaces*, 198–9.

marked by 'the greatest attendance of nobility' as bishops, counsellors, officers, and gentry pressed into the Presence Chamber where they 'waited the Queen's coming out . . . from her own apartment when it was time to go to prayers'. As the queen emerged from her privy chambers, her guard formed an aisle in the midst of the crowd 'as far as the queen walked through . . . to the chapel'. The procession formed according to strict rules of precedence: 'First went Gentlemen, Barons, Earls, Knights of the Garter, all . . . bareheaded'. Immediately before the queen walked the Lord Chancellor or Keeper of the Great Seal, who was flanked by two earls, one bearing the sceptre, the other the sword of state. As the queen herself moved down the Presence Chamber 'she spoke very graciously' and received petitions and letters from suitors and ambassadors, all of whom 'fell on their knees' as the royal person passed.[45] Chapel processions could also have their lighter moments. A servant wrote to Nathaniel Bacon in 1585 that 'Hir Majestye was verye pleasante upon Asche Wednesdaye'. With the procession about to proceed, the gentlemen ushers called for the Lords 'to go on afore', but then someone called back that the chapel door was shut. Elizabeth quipped 'that was a good skewce for those that refused to com to churche at all'. Such banter not withstanding, in no other routine event was the *majestas* of the Elizabethan, and later the Jacobean, court so dramatically staged.[46]

In fact, the processions to and from chapel provided an opportunity for a weekly version in miniature of Elizabeth's most calculated spectacles, the summer progresses. Here the queen staged on a regular, more intimate basis manifestations of her court's splendour and her own majesty and magnanimity. This was Elizabeth at her best as a public-relations virtuoso. As she moved down the chamber, she spoke very 'graciously' to subjects and foreigners, and deployed her impressive multilingualism to best effect. Hentzner noted that her dignified kindness 'occasioned the acclamation of *God save the Quene Elizabeth*!', to which the sovereign responded with the refrain '*I thancke you myn good peupel.*'[47] The procession to chapel could even imitate the summer progress's brilliant use of close, and closely controlled, contact with commoners. At Richmond the long gallery leading to the royal closet looked down into the central courtyard, where many spectators gathered who could not gain access to the presence chamber or the chapel. Thomas Platter noticed that on the way to the closet, Elizabeth

[45] *England as Seen by Foreigners in the Days of Elizabeth and James the First*, ed. William Brenchley Rye (1865), 104–5; von Wedel, 'Journey Through England', ed. von Bulow, 250–1.

[46] Nathaniel Bacon, *The Papers of Nathaniel Bacon of Stiffkey*, 3 vols., ed. A. Hasell Smith and Gillian M. Baker (Norwich, 1979–88), vol. II, 303.

[47] *CSPV 1558–1580*, 524–5; Rye, ed., *England as Seen by Foreigners*, 105.

took time to look 'down from a window in the gallery on her people in the courtyard'. They 'all knelt' and the litany that Hentzner heard in the presence chamber at Greenwich was rehearsed between gallery and court-yard. After this exchange, the people remained on their knees until Elizabeth 'made them a sign with her hand to rise, which they did with the greatest possible reverence'.[48]

James I of England, when James VI of Scotland, was accustomed to an entirely different architectural arrangement and degree of ceremony when attending the services of the kirk. Lupold von Wedel, who visited James's court immediately after seeing Elizabeth's, was struck by the difference in the two British monarchs' chapel attendance, and his accounts paint a fascinating diptych. Instead of watching a procession to chapel, von Wedel arrived at a church near the court's seat at Perth, took a seat 'not very distant' from the king's chair, and waited with the congregation an hour 'in entire silence' for the royal arrival. When the king entered with his entourage 'he seated himself in a very common chair that showed no ornament whatever' and his attendants remained standing behind him. After singing five psalms, the bishop of St Andrew's preached, five more psalms were sung, and 'the king left the church, mounted his horse, and rode home'. After this encounter, von Wedel's summary judgment was that 'the court does not show much royal splendour'.[49] Small wonder, then, that James, upon his accession to the English throne, continued what Neil Cuddy calls 'the pompous epiphanies of the Tudor procession to the Chapel Royal'.[50] Although James had a reputation in both Scotland and England for laxity in court ceremonial, and never had Elizabeth's flair for inspiring awe and devotion to the royal person, he appreciated the symbolic importance of the routine chapel processions. In 1623, observing 'a gen[er]all breache of the a[u]ncient & lawdable orders of o[ur] Court', he began a general 'reformac[i]on' of court manners with rules for chapel attendance. Those rules began with a frank affirmation of the symbolic importance of 'o[ur] going & cominge from the Chappell', wherein 'all men keepe their ranckes orderly & distinctly, & not break them . . . but p[ro]ceed both for o[ur] honour & y[er] reputac[i]on, that being one of y[e] most eminent & frequent occasions wherby mens ranckes in p[re]cedency are distinguished & discerned'.[51]

Most significantly, the Scottish chapels royal did not have elevated

[48] Williams, ed., *Thomas Platter's Travels*, 228.
[49] Von Wedel, 'Journey Through England and Scotland', 245.
[50] Neil Cuddy, 'The Revival of Entourage: the Bedchamber of James I, 1603–1625', in Starkey, ed., *The English Court from the War of the Roses to the Civil War* (1987), 182.
[51] BL Add MS 34324, fol. 215[r]. The influence of James's Chapel Dean, Lancelot Andrewes, must be assumed here. Charles I repeated this clause verbatim in his own expanded rules for chapel attendance (PRO LC5/180, 16).

galleries for the sovereign, who instead sat in a chair next to the pulpit. The principal chapels of James's Scottish kingdom were those at Holyrood Palace in Edinburgh and Stirling Castle, both of which were of single-storey construction. Rather than being elevated above and screened from the pulpit, James sat at the foot of and was screened with the pulpit. To explain, the Holyrood chapel was first occupied in 1571 and renovated by James in 1583. At the time 'ane honorabill saitt' was made for the king 'togidder withe ane chanchelar [the *cancellus*, or perforated screen] wall of tymmer withe ane trym powpeit and fformes and saittis encirclat rownd abowt' and 'without the chanchelar wall certane formis to be maid'. The main body of the chapel, then, contained the pulpit, royal seat, and 'fformes and saittis' for the royal entourage, while 'formis' for other members of the household were placed without the screen ('chanchelar').[52] The seating arrangement of this plan is best illustrated by a contemporary account of Prince Henry's baptism, held in 1594 in the chapel built by James at Stirling expressly for that event: 'In the middest of the Chappell Royall, within the partition, where the King's Majestie, the Ambassadours, and Prince with his convoy, were placed, there was a new pulpit erected; the same was richly hung with cloth of gold: all the pavement within this partition was prince-like laid with fine tapestrey.'[53]

Just as the English arrangement of elevated closet-over-chapel articulated the royal supremacy by placing the monarch literally above the nobles and clergy, the Scottish custom summed up the kirk's insistence that it was not subject to earthly princes. The English and Scottish chapels provide a neat ecclesiastical correlative for the respective arrangements of the domestic apartments. As Cuddy has summed it up, 'the English court was designed for the preservation and manipulation of distance; the Scots for the management of relatively free and open access'. James, determined to assert the royal supremacy over causes ecclesiastical and plagued by his 'rash-headie' Presbyterian preachers in Scotland, must have revelled in the Tudor chapel arrangements he found in England.[54] The enforced chapel attendance of the Scots Presbyterians Andrew and James Melville at Hampton Court in 1606 – part of James's efforts almost literally to force the royal

---

[52] From a survey by Sir Robert Drummond, Master of the King's Works, printed in Charles Rogers, *History of the Chapel Royal of Scotland* (Edinburgh, 1882), xciv. This chapel was pulled down in 1671 (ibid., xcv).

[53] Nichols, *Progresses of . . . Queen Elizabeth*, vol. III, 358. For the Chapel Royal at Stirling, which still stands, see The Royal Commission on the Ancient and Historical Monuments of Scotland (RCAHMS), *Stirlingshire*, 2 vols. (Edinburgh, 1963), vol. I, 211–13. Another single-cell, one-story Stuart chapel survives at Falkland Castle. See RCAHMS, *Fife, Kinross, and Clackmannan* (Edinburgh, 1933), 139–40.

[54] Cuddy, 'Revival of Entourage', in Starkey, *English Court*, 179. The 'rash-headie' epithet for Puritan preachers is James's own from *Basilikon Doron: The Political Works of James I*, ed. Charles Howard McIlwain (Cambridge, Mass., 1918), 6.

supremacy and episcopacy down their throats – must have given James a special satisfaction. After years of sitting at the foot of their pulpits, the tables were turned and James looked down from the height of the chapel closet upon them as they were preached to by the obedient bishops and doctors of the church of which he was supreme governor.

James's *coup de grace* came in 1617, when, in advance of his progress to Scotland, a major objective of which was to secure conformity to English ecclesiology, he ordered a massive refitting of the Holyrood chapel royal to bring it in line with its English counterparts. As if to make the point of imposition more forcefully, fittings, which included organs, stalls, and statues of the apostles and evangelists, were to be carved in London by English craftsmen and shipped north for installation by the same artisans. By far the most substantial part of the job, however, was a carved 'wall' or screen with a 'faire enterie' below and 'twa bay wondokes abone the same enttrie for the King and Quenes clossit with faire oppening wondokes for ther Majestis to louke downe to the Chapell throw' – nothing less than a full-scale double closet *à la* Whitehall or Hampton Court. James was determined to exercise his prerogative in Scottish ecclesiastical causes, and he saw to it that his royal supremacy received its appropriate structural expression in his northern chapel.[55]

The practical end of the Sunday and holy day processions was to escort the sovereign to the closet above the chapel. Charles I's rules for the chapel processions, which seem in all verifiable points to mimic earlier practice, stated that any 'Lords or others' who were eligible by rank to sit in the body of the chapel for service could not 'go beforehand into the said Chappell but waite upon Vs, till we be sett in Our Chayre in the closet'.[56] Unless the queen or king was to receive communion publicly in chapel, which seems to have taken place only on the great feasts of Christmas, Easter, and Whitsunday, she or he never descended from the closet. The prince's religious life, as well as private life, was largely passed above stairs. Elevation and distance, both symbolic and literal, characterized the royal role in the court's religious services. The screen of the latticed windows separating closet from chapel provided the physical and psychological distance necessary to maintain what Shakespeare's Henry IV termed his 'presence like a robe pontifical,/ Ne'er seen but wondered at'.[57]

[55] *Accounts of the Masters of the Works for Building and Repairing Royal Palaces and Castles*, 2 vols., ed. Henry M. Paton, John Imrie, and John G. Dunbar (Edinburgh, 1957, 1982), vol. II, 441. I am very grateful to Aonghus MacKechnie for this reference. See also David Calderwood, *History of the Kirk of Scotland*, 8 vols., ed. T. Thomson (Edinburgh, 1842–59), vol. VII, 244.

[56] PRO LC5/180, 18. No royal orders or precedent books detailing the protocols of chapel attendance survive from Elizabeth's reign.

[57] *1 Henry IV*, III.ii.57–8.

It should be added here that many lesser royal houses did not have proper chapels. Of the Tudor establishments, Nonsuch is a case in point: built by Henry VIII as a grandiose hunting lodge, it provided no formal space for worship. Thus when Thomas Platter visited in 1599, he joined the queen and court for sermon in the Presence Chamber, where the sovereign sat in her elevated chair of state and the ministers officiated standing on the floor below. Similar arrangements marked service and sermon time at Jacobean Royston and Newmarket.[58]

Chapel symbolism provided a perfect backdrop for the preachers who addressed the monarchical defenders of the faith in England. During chapel sermons, Elizabeth and James reigned from above in the closet, a fact emphasized by the preacher's bows to the closet after he ascended the pulpit steps. Harington captured the scene memorably in his memoir of Matthew Hutton, Archbishop of York: 'I no sooner remember this famous and worthie Prelate but I thinke I see him in the Chappell at Whitehall, Queene Elizabeth at the window in the Closet, all the Lords of the Parliament Spirituall and temporall about them, and then after his three Coursies that I heare him out of the Pulpit thundering [his] text.'[59] Many preachers also confirmed or reiterated in their sermons the implicit symbolism of the monarchs occupying literally the highest seat in the chapel. In the course of his high general praise for Lancelot Andrewes, Harington singled out that preacher's talent for raising in his sermons 'a ioynt reverence to God and the Prince, to the spirituall and civile Magistrate, by vniting and not severing them'.[60] On 24 February 1591, Andrewes took as his text for a sermon before Elizabeth at Greenwich Psalm 127:20: '*Thou diddest leade Thy people like Sheepe, by the hand of* MOSES *and* AARON.' The preacher's ultimate point centred on the last phrase of the text, which revealed the manner of government ordained by God: 'onely with the hands or regiments *Ecclesiasticall* and *Civill*'. These two components, in the types of Aaron the High Priest and Moses the civil leader, '(as the two *Cherubims* did the *Arke*) over-spread and preserve every estate', and 'a maymed and lame estate it is, where either is wanting'. In the queen's chapel, Andrewes stood before, and was part of, a huge *tableau vivant* of the ideal Tudor body politic: the ecclesiastical hand of Aaron served at the Holy Table and preached from the pulpit, while Moses's civil hand, the officers and peers, sat in ordered ranks in the stalls. Elizabeth sat above both; or, as Andrewes made clear, 'over these twaine did He yet set another, even the power and authority *Regall*, in place of the *Head* . . . and to it, as

---

[58] Thurley, *Royal Palaces*, 63–4; Williams, ed. and trans., *Platter's Travels in England*, 192–3; Rye, ed., *England as Seen by Foreigners*, 150–1.

[59] Harington, *Supplie or Addicion*, 170–1.   [60] Harington, *Supplie or Addicion*, 140.

supreme, vnited the regiment of both'.[61] The very architectural arrangement of the chapels royal made exactly this claim.

Preachers' defences of the royal supremacy grew more articulate during the reign of James, when the symbolism of the chapel royal interiors resonated even more strongly in the sermons preached there.[62] For his sermon at Easter 1611, Andrewes chose a text with an architectural metaphor perfectly appropriate to the chapel royal setting to give one of his fullest Jacobean treatments of the concept of the king as absolute and divinely ordained ruler over both church and state. In that year Easter Sunday fell on 24 March, also James's Accession Day. Andrewes took full advantage of the coincidence, and chose as his text Psalm 118.22: '*The Stone, which the Builders refused, the same Stone, is become . . . the Head of the Corner.*' The bishop first applied his text prophetically to Christ, and then, in an historical sense, to King David; but, as Andrewes noted, he chose the text especially because it 'will sort with *Ours*, or with any Prince: in like manner banded against, and sought to bee put by, as *He*: and yet, after brought by God, to the same place, that *Dauid* was'. The place to which Christ, David, and James were all brought was an exalted throne. After being scourged, crucified, and buried, Christ rose from the grave and then ascended to a seat '*ad Caput Anguli*'; after being pursued and persecuted by Saul, David was Crowned King of Israel; and in spite of countless plots and schemes against his life and accession to the English throne, James became the '*head of this Kingdome*' in a manner 'like to *Christs* case'.[63] Whereas Christ had been elevated as a keystone that capped or united the 'corners' of Jew and Gentile, bond and free, quick and dead, the text applied to the prince proved that the king was the keystone of power over 'the two estates, *Ciuill* and *Ecclesiasticall*, which make the maine *Angle*, in euery Gouernement'.[64] In the chapel royal on that Easter Sunday, James sat in the royal closet as a living keystone, literally 'raised up' over the estates of his realm.

As we have seen in the Holyrood chapel, James himself was not unaware of the power of architectural and iconographical statements of royal policy. As Newman has recently argued, James 'had a lively sense of the role which

[61] Lancelot Andrewes, *XCVI Sermons*, 282–3; *Works*, vol. II, 32–3.

[62] For the increasing frequency of expressions of both the divine right of kings and royal absolutism under James, see J. P. Somerville, *Politics and Ideology in England, 1603–1640* (1986), 47, citing a shift in Andrewes's own writings.

[63] Lancelot Andrewes, *A Sermon Preached Before His Maiestie . . . On the 24 of March last* (1611), sig. A3ʳ, 3, 18, 33–34; *Works*, vol. II, 270–89.

[64] *Works*, vol., II, 30. Richard Meredeth applied this metaphor to James in terms of the union of England and Scotland (*Two Sermons Preached before his Maiestie* [1606], 9–10); and Patrick Collinson, in *The Birthpangs of Protestant England* (New York, 1988), 9, calls attention to its application to Elizabeth in 1588.

buildings could play in the projection of a royal aura and the embodiment of royal policy,' but Newman's attention, like others' before him, focuses upon James's secular projects, especially the Banqueting Houses of 1609 and 1621, to the exclusion of the first Stuart king's ecclesiastical commissions.[65] Later in the reign, James commissioned Andrewes to supervise the renovation of the chapel royal at Greenwich, and the result was an architectural reification of the theories of divine right and royal supremacy that he had declaimed from the court pulpits. As Dean of the Chapel, Andrewes received the king's commission in May 1623, 'to cause Greenwich Chapel to be new repaired and gilded, being much decayed, as not having been new furnished since Queen Mary's days'.[66] Not insignificantly, the Surveyor of the King's Works who supervised what was the total renovation of the chapel interior was Inigo Jones.[67] So Andrewes, like Ben Jonson in his masques, must have collaborated with the master architect to create an architectural space, this time ecclesiastical, that provided a physical complement to the verbal expression of the ideals of the Jacobean monarchy and its court. Stephen Orgel has shown how in Jones's designs for court masques the 'one focal point' of the entire hall was the king's seat, and how the audience, seated according to strict rules of precedence, 'at once became a living emblem of the structure of the court'.[68] The banqueting hall so arranged for a masque, then, quoted the interior of the chapels royal: the king presided from an elevated seat in the rear (the west end), the peers were ranged in facing rows of box seats (the stalls), the dramatic action (the sermon or the liturgy) took place in the front (the east end). This suggests not only that court religious ritual, including the delivery of sermons, was a performative dramatic spectacle (this merely states the obvious), but also that the Stuart masque was in its very staging imbued with a distinctly religious ceremonialism.[69]

[65] J. Newman, 'Inigo Jones and the Politics of Architecture,' in Kevin Sharpe and Peter Lake, eds, *Culture and Politics in Early Stuart England* (Basingstoke, 1993), 231.

[66] Thomas Birch, ed., *The Court and Times of James the First*, 2 vols. (1848), vol. II, 400.

[67] *HKW*, vol. IV, 116–18. Colvin calls this not one of Jones's 'more important works', but none the less 'the first example in England of a classical interior conceived partly in terms of painted relief and partly in the round' (118).

[68] Stephen Orgel, *The Illusion of Power: Political Theater in the English Renaissance* (Berkeley, Calif., 1975), 10–11.

[69] The analogues between court religious practice and the masque are significant and the subject of another study in progress. As Orgel points out, the origins of the Stuart masque lie in the pageants staged by the gentlemen and boys of the Henrician Chapel Royal, and college chapels frequently served as royal theatres (*Illusion of Power*, 1975, 9–10, 14–17, 39). The parallel between chapels and banqueting halls (as arranged for a masque production) lends weight to David Harris Sacks's suggestive comment that the masques' 'meanings . . . may have been Platonic, but their functions were what may be called religious' and that 'the masque . . . stood to court life as the taking of communion stood to

Fig. 7. The solemnization of the Spanish Marriage Treaty in the Whitehall Chapel Royal, July 1623. The architectural details – and Catholic ornament – of the chapel interior do not correspond with more reliable contemporary descriptions. Detail from an anonymous Dutch engraving (British Museum, Department of Prints and Drawings).

Howard Colvin has suggested that the 1623–5 renovation of the Greenwich chapel was carried out as compensation to English Protestantism for the sumptuous Roman Catholic chapels being built for the Spanish Infanta. Further evidence to support this theory is the fact that James's commission for the Greenwich renovation coincided almost to the day with the laying of the cornerstone of the Catholic chapel at St James's.[70] The Whitehall chapel royal had, in 1621–2 (also during Andrewes's deanship), already been renovated with an eye towards the Spanish marriage negotiations. That work included repainting the Tudor ceiling and refurbishing a scheme of wall paintings that included human figures.[71] At the same time the king seems to have reintroduced the silver crucifix that had been such a lightning rod for godly wrath in Elizabeth's chapel in the 1560s. Sir Thomas Knyvett

church life': 'Searching for "Culture" in the English Renaissance', *Shakespeare Quarterly* 39 (1988), 471.
[70] *HKW*, vol. IV, 116; Birch, *Court and Times of James*, vol. II, 400.
[71] *HKW* vol. IV, 341.

reported in October 1621 that 'the Kings Chappell at Whithall is curiously painted and all the images newe made and a silver crusifix amaking to hange therin, against the spannish Ladys coming'.[72] All was in place when, after sermon on Sunday 20 July 1623, James and the Spanish Ambassadors processed into the chapel at Whitehall to swear to the articles of the marriage treaty – an event that inspired the only known depiction (probably quite stylized) of the chapel's interior (see Figure 7). James's chapel renovations in the 1620s, with their painted images and silver crosses, certainly must support the recent argument that anti-Calvinists like Dean of the Chapel Andrewes began to enjoy unprecedented influence at court in the 1620s. However, there was a large dose of political expediency at work as well, because James knew that only their ecclesiology, and not mainstream Calvinism, could possibly secure a marriage settlement with Spain.[73] The chapel renovations no doubt were ordered in the same spirit as James's instructions to Matthew Wren and Leonard Maw, the two royal chaplains dispatched to minister to Prince Charles and his servants during his secret excursion to Madrid in 1623. According to James himself, these chaplains were to observe all ceremonies 'as neare the Romane forme as can lawfullie be done for it hath ever bene my waye to goe with the churche of rome *usque ad aras*'.[74]

In the chapels royal, *usque ad aras* meant that, like Elizabeth before him, James would tolerate images and a crucifix for the political expediency of mollifying Catholics. But also like his predecessor, for James the royal supremacy was not negotiable. If the Jones-Andrewes renovation at Greenwich accommodated Catholic tastes for images, it vigorously asserted the supremacy of the British monarch over his church by emphasizing that ancient architectural symbol of imperial power over the church – the elevated royal tribune, or closet, over the west end. In the renovation, the ceiling was repainted, and the two side walls and the east end were, as Colvin interprets the original accounts, painted with 'a scheme of architectural mural painting'.[75] However the west end was glorified not with *trompe-l'œil* architecture but with a massive wooden structure that framed a new closet window with five large columns on pedestals decorated with clusters of hanging fruit, over which were raised both the king's and the prince's arms 'borne by two boyes with two victories on each side of

[72] *The Knyvett Letters (1620–1644)*, ed. Bertram Schofield (1949), 56. The crucifix was *in situ* by May 1623. See Birch, *Court and Times of James*, vol. II, 400. For the Elizabethan crucifix *cause-célèbre*, see Margaret Aston, *England's Iconoclasts* (Oxford, 1988), 306–14.

[73] Kenneth Fincham and Peter Lake, 'The Ecclesiastical Policy of King James I', *Journal of British Studies* 24 (April 1985), 201–2.

[74] BL Harley MS 6987, fols. 29–31, in *Spain and the Jacobean Catholics*, 2 vols., ed. A. J. Loomie, S. J., Catholic Record Society nos. 64, 68 (1973, 1978), vol. II, 185–86.

[75] *HKW*, vol. IV, 117.

them'.[76] Serjeant Painter John de Critz painted the pillared frame white and the window casements gold, the boys' hair gold too, and their draperies and the palm fronds they bore green. While the east end was painted in similarly bold colors, and probably included a series of life-sized prophets and saints, the west end, with its three-dimensional carved work, received the most dramatic, plastic treatment. The façade of the Greenwich chapel closet, then, was not at all unlike the white, sculptured façade of the contemporary Whitehall Banqueting House, the classical and 'strongly sculptural treatment' which Newman has called an innovatory, 'unprecedented presence' in Jacobean London.[77]

However, if preachers such as Andrewes could celebrate the monarch in chapel as the keystone of the arch of government, many others viewed the sovereign shut in the chapel closet as an extremely rare opportunity for a one-sided audience with a captive king or queen. To the preachers who came to court with explicit and direct criticisms for their rulers, the chapel interior also had significance. Pam Wright has very summarily pointed out that under Elizabeth 'the key to political power at court remained – as it always had been – access to the sovereign'. Two factors unique to the Elizabethan court made access to its sovereign more difficult to obtain. First, the queen's Privy Chamber was a *sanctum sanctorum*, or 'a barrier or a cocoon', that kept the queen 'consciously above and beyond the fray' of factional struggle. Secondly, nothing buttressed this restriction of privy access more than the fact that the queen's closest attendants were necessarily women.[78] For the Aarons of Elizabeth's church, the inaccessability of the queen made the occasion of the court sermon one of the most important ways to influence or criticize Elizabeth's ecclesiastical policies. Whenever she sat in chapel, her closet became an extension, both literal and metaphorical, of the privy chamber: never setting foot below stairs, the queen and her attendants moved from the private apartments through the presence chamber, and then to the closet, itself almost as much a cocoon as the bedchamber. If the chapels royal were both geographically and institutionally one of the decorative 'outer layers' of the court, we must remember that the 'inner' layer, most strictly defined as the prince's privy apartments, looked into that outer layer in the form of the closet.[79] The oriel window of that private space protruded into the chapel's very public arena of politico-

---

[76] PRO E351/3257 quoted in *HKW*, vol. IV, 116. Does the erection of the Prince's arms suggest that he occupied the queen's closet after his mother's death?

[77] Newman, 'Politics of Architecture', 235–6.

[78] Pam Wright, 'A Change in Direction: the Ramifications of a Female Household, 1558–1603', in Starkey, *English Court*, 159.

[79] Cuddy, 'Revival of the Entourage', in Starkey, *English Court*, 182.

religious debate, and directly faced a pulpit that could be filled on any given day by a preacher as willing to criticize as to praise.

When a preacher such as Edward Dering took the court pulpit he did not emphasize or celebrate the symbolic distance that separated queen from congregation. On the contrary, he tried to eliminate it. Dering (1540?–76) a Cambridge divine, chaplain to the Duke of Norfolk, and member of Archbishop Parker's household, was poised on the edge of a stellar career when, in 1569, probably under the influence of Thomas Cartwright's radical Protestantism during the Vestiarian Controversy, he turned antagonist of the ecclesiastical *status quo*.[80] In February he preached before the queen in an unknown chapel royal on the text, 'He chose Dauid his servant also, & tooke hym from the shepefoldes' (Psalms 78:70). In his exordium, Dering called on his auditory to remember the mercy God had shown to all present by leading them out of the darkness of popery. From the outset Dering emphasized not the congregation's hierarchy and rank, but the fact that before God all, 'were we neuer so mighty', must be humbly thankful. All must be able to say 'I haue bene bond, but I am free', and also, in an allusion to Elizabeth's incarceration during Mary's reign that included the queen herself in the preacher's call to humility, 'I haue bene a prisoner, I am a Princes'.[81]

To Dering, the glazed facade of the royal closet formed not so much the queen's shield as the preacher's target. After expounding how princes are called as shepherds to protect God's church, Dering lambasted Elizabeth for failing in her pastoral office. In a daring challenge to the distance that separated them, the preacher directly addressed the queen and insisted that she not 'pretende ignorance' of the greatest abuse in the English church, namely 'that hir Ministers bee ignoraunt', indeed 'dum Dogs'.[82] After storming the barrier of deference in this direct address, Dering proceeded to penetrate the closet-fortress and dared to take the royal person by the hand – or perhaps the collar – in a brilliant appropriation of Ezekiel's vision of being snatched up by God and taken on a flying tour of the idolatries committed in Jerusalem. Like Elizabeth in chapel, Ezekiel was sitting 'in mine house, and the Elders of Iudah sate before me' (Ezekiel 8:1). Yet 'the likenes of an hand' that took Elizabeth 'by an heerie locke' was not 'the hand of the Lord God' (Ezeiel. 8:3, 1), but that of her preacher: 'I should leade you along in the spirite as God dyd the Prophet *Ezechiel*'. Suddenly preachers, and not princes, were gods. Dering had prepared the ground for the reversal of the preacher–monarch roles later celebrated by Andrewes

[80] Patrick Collinson, 'A Mirror of Elizabethan Puritanism: the Life and Letters of Edward Dering', in *Godly People: Essays on English Protestantism and Puritanism* (1983), 302–4.
[81] Edward Dering, *A Sermon Preached before the Quenes Maiestie* (1569), sig. Bij^{r-v}.
[82] *Ibid.*, sigs. Ciiij^r, Eiij^v, Eiiij^r.

and Eedes when he looked to the closet and said, 'I beseeche your Maiestie to harken, I wyl speake nothing accordyng to man . . . but that which I wyl speake, shall be out of the mouth of the Lord'. Whereas for Andrewes and Eedes the sovereign had presided over the chapel as God's representative, for Edward Dering the preacher became not only God's mouthpiece, but God's very hand. With Elizabeth by the scruff of the neck, Dering lifted the sovereign out of the cocoon of her private closet, and, like Dickens's ghostly schooling of Scrooge, wafted her to the sites of the various ecclesiastical abuses in her realm – spoiled benefices, corrupt patrons, unfit clergy – and repeated at each venue the refrain that God had spoken to Ezekiel, 'and yet you shall see more abominations then these'.[83]

Cuddy has shown how Elizabeth's jealous guarding of the *entrée* to her royal presence was continued and even further ossified at James's court by that king's restriction of access to his bedchamber. Under James's household orders, even the 'formal officers did not enjoy free access to the king; instead, they had audiences'.[84] Although select preachers, and especially favourite bishops such as Andrewes, benefited from what Kenneth Fincham has described as James's revival of court prelacy, the court sermon still provided one of the few possible opportunities for delivering a petition – or grievance – directly to the king's person. As we shall see in the case of John Burgess, preachers could miscalculate disastrously their petitionary rights in the court pulpit. In 1605, another preacher, Robert Wakeman, fellow of Balliol College, Oxford, in a sermon on the king's duty '*to execute iudgement and iustice*' (2 Chronicles 9:8), commented bravely on the wickedness of those rulers that '*keepe the[m]selues alwaies from the accesse of their subiects*'. Wakeman advised James directly not to concentrate power in a few 'fawning and flattering parasites . . . of Courts', but to listen to the petitions of his 'poorest subiect'. He conceded that 'although by reason of the state of this earthly kingdome, thou canst not so easily graunt accesse vnto thy subiects', and that the king should not be 'faciel of accesse-giving at all times, to al persons', none the less 'in the midst of al the glorie of the Court' he should cast his eyes 'vpon a poore subiect'.[85] There can be little doubt that at least some of the 'poor subjects' Wakeman had in mind were the preachers who, like Dering before them, saw the court chapel as a narrow gateway of access through which they could deliver prescription as well as praise.

Preachers at court, however, did not direct their attention exclusively to the royal closet. Between the preacher and prince sat the courtiers, who

---

[83] *Ibid.*, sigs. Diiij^v, Eiiij^{r–v}.

[84] Cuddy, 'Revival of Entourage', in Starkey, ed., *English Court*, 192.

[85] Robert Wakeman, *Salomons Exaltation: A Sermon Preached Before the Kings Maiestie at None-Such* (Oxford, 1605), 58–9. For Burgess, see 141–7.

were often the primary objects of the preacher's oratorical address. On some occasions the monarch did not attend the sermons preached in chapel, and a vacant royal closet not only shifted the preacher's visual focus, but sometimes influenced the matter of his sermon. When Roger Goad, Provost of King's College, Cambridge, showed up at Greenwich to deliver one of the 1573 Lent sermons and found out that 'hir ma^tie was away' he told the gathered courtiers that 'he was fayne to omit div[er]se thynges wch he most wold haue treated of Lest the speache should haue bene vnconsonant to the auditory'.[86] Other preachers came to court with messages specifically tailored for the members of the royal establishment. However, if we are fully to understand the relationship of preacher to nobility, of pulpit to chapel stalls, some further details of seating must be understood.

When the courtly procession that had formed up in the presence chamber had left the king or queen in the closet, the rest of the entourage would descend the staircases and enter the main chapel through the ante-chapel. As in cathedral choirs and collegiate chapels, the Dean of the Chapel Royal sat in a return stall – one that directly faced the altar – fixed against the west end of the main chapel (the screen or wall dividing chapel from ante-chapel) 'on the right hand of the entraunce'[87] (see Figure 2). The stalls were reserved exclusively for court officers and titled nobility, who were separated on either side of the chapel by sex.[88] In both James's and Charles's rules, and thus presumably also under Elizabeth's, ladies sat on the Dean's side: 'all the stalls beyond [the Dean's] seate . . . be kept only for ladies, & that no man what so ever p[re]sume to come in there, whether there be many or fewe women'. Across the central aisle, 'on the other syde of the chappell', sat the lords where 'none . . . p[re]sume to come into any of the stalls vnder ye degree of a Baron, unlesse he be a privie Councellor, the Captaine of ye Pencioners, and the Captaine of o[ur] garde in regarde of y^er attendance on o[ur] person'.[89]

The upper stalls (closest to the walls) were probably taken by those of the highest rank, with lesser nobility seated in the lower stalls nearer the aisle. Finally, since the surviving regulations are so concerned with limiting access to the stalls, we must assume that there was other seating in the chapel for those who could not 'presume to come' into the lords' and ladies' seats. Charles I's instructions say that staff from 'below=stayres . . .

---

[86] BL Harley MS 6991, fol. 33^r.

[87] BL MS Add 34324, fol. 215^r; see PRO LC5/180, 17–18.

[88] See the Communion rubric in Church of England (liturgies), *The First Prayer-Book as Issued by . . . Edward VI* (Oxford, 1883), 75, that instructs communicants to gather in the chancel, '*the men on the one side, and the women on the other syde*'. The segregation of the sexes also mirrors the separate closets provided for the king and queen.

[89] BL MS Add 34324, fol. 215^r.

in regard they haue Prayers & Sermon for themselues before, though they may come to the second . . . yet they shall . . . but be contented with such other places as they can gett'.[90] The same rules applied to 'any knight or gentleman coming to the Court if they come to the chappell'. Movable benches or seats could have been placed in the centre of the chapel, or those not meriting stalls could simply have stood. This was certainly Sir John Harington's position when he heard a sermon at the Whitehall chapel royal that was filled to overflowing because of the presence of all the Lords, spiritual and temporal, in Parliament-time 1593. He complained that while bishop Matthew Hutton preached, 'my selfe had stood so incommodiously by meanes of the great preasse', and as a result 'heard it not well, but was faine to take much of it on trust on other mens report'.[91]

The peers and courtiers in the stalls were, like the sovereign in the closet, just as likely to be targets for advice and criticism as for praise. Preachers frequently took the court to task for its failure to set a godly moral example for the rest of the realm. Eedes, in a sermon preached to the queen and court in Lent 1596 on the text '*Woe bee vnto them that call good euill, and euill good*' (Isaiah 5:20), blamed a nationwide confusion of good and evil on 'mightie men' who 'will presume to doe those things by their places which for their places they should lesse doe then others'. The privy counsellors in the stalls that day also had their ears pricked when Eedes lamented slander and flattery committed by those who 'haue the honour to be the eares of princes' and thereby cause 'Maiestie' to be 'imprisoned within the blind eyes and the partiall eares of other mens affections'.[92]

Other uniquely courtly vices came in for their share of sermon wrath. In 1569–70 Thomas Drant (*d.* 1578?), chaplain to Bishop of London Edmund Grindal and noted in his day as a preacher and poet, coyly conceded that because he spoke 'in the Court, of apparell, the Court will looke that I should handle the matter somwhat solemnely'. However, the auditory, which on this occasion did not include the queen, had another thing coming, as Drant then quipped that not hanging 'on the courtes doome in diuinitie, I will go forwardes'. Therewith he rebuked 'those that be in kinges houses' who 'do accompt of themselues as exempt persons from controlement of preachers'.[93] Often preachers took advantage of the segregation of the sexes in the chapel stalls and divided their criticisms accordingly. In a sermon before James at Whitehall, royal chaplain Robert

[90] PRO LC5/180, 19.
[91] Harington, *Supplie or Addicion,* 173.
[92] Richard Eedes, 'A Sermon of the Difference of Good and Euill', in *Six Learned and Godly Sermons* (1604), sig. 84^r, 97^r, 101^r.
[93] Thomas Drant, *Two Sermons Preached: the One at S. Maries Spittle . . . the Other at the Court at Windsor* (1570?), sig. K[iiij]^v–Kv^r.

Wilkinson drew moral allegories fit for both the lords and the ladies on the unlikely subject of Joseph's many-coloured coat. First, turning to his left with 'Therefore Gentle-women, Good-women, and Sisters in CHRIST, heere is no warrant for Wantonnesse and Superfluitie . . . Yee may by *Iosephs* example paint out your Coates, but take heed of painting your Faces.' Then, to his right, 'Againe, heere is a lesson for men, especially for Courtiers.' The lesson Wilkinson delivered to the men defended Joseph's father's, that is Jacob's, favouritism shown in giving the coat to his youngest son – 'O but giue *Iacob* leaue to giue the partie coloured Coate, binde not the hands of a Prince, for when Subiects assume to limit the Prince, then they presume to bee aboue the Prince' – a witty apology for James's ('*Jacobus*'s) attention to his favourites.[94]

The place of these men and women of noble birth in the chapel provided an accurate metaphor for their place in the realm; just as royal closet and chapel presbytery declared the union of ecclesiastical and civil under the Crown, so the sight of the lords temporal attending service or sermon in the chapel royal recapitulated the Reformation ideal of the Christian common-wealth. Peter Wentworth, chaplain to the Lord Darcy, claimed before the court in 1587 that in former times the 'enuiousnesse . . . of the Papists' had deliberately discouraged princes and magistrates from 'the studie of the word' and had wrongly insisted that matters ecclesiastical were not the province of the monarch and nobles. However, the subsequent Reformation union of church and state under the governance of the prince had bred in the royal household itself a 'loue of christianitie, and . . . knowledge of the scriptures . . . where before the commo[n] sort especially haue passed their time in ribaldrie, and vnseemely talke'. For Wentworth, the assembly in the chapel royal not only represented, as it did for Andrewes, the body politic of queen as head, magistrates and priests as arms, but, 'this courte is become the church of Christ'.[95]

The chapels royal distilled perfectly the theory that religious and political, ecclesiastical and civil were not only joined, but inseparable. This theory depended upon the acceptance of precisely the hierarchy that the chapel interior structurally and iconographically declared. The whole of each chapel was spanned by a ceiling decorated to evoke what Lancelot Andrewes described, perhaps with a gesture to the Whitehall chapel ceiling, as 'this great vaulted worke, of heauen ouer our heades'.[96] Henry VIII Crowned his Hampton Court chapel with an especially elaborate vault

---

[94] Robert Wilkinson, *The Stripping of Ioseph* (1625), 45–6.
[95] Peter Wentworth, *A Sermon Faithfullie and Trulie Published: According as it was preached at the Courte* (1587), 18.
[96] Lancelot Andrewes, *A Sermon Preached Before His Maiestie . . . On the 24 of March Last* (1611), 16; *Works*, vol. II, 278.

with a series of pendants hanging from its segments, on which sported cherubs and 'angells holdying schochens wyth the Kynges armes'. The segments of the vault were 'gylt with ffyne golde' as was the motto, or 'Kynges wordde' – *Dieu et mon droit* – on each of the sprung arches. The spaces between the ribbed work of the vault finished the entire canopy with a sky of blue ('ffyne byse') spangled 'wyth other ffyne coloers'.[97] If this chapel ceiling, with its cherubs, angels, and blue sky, was designed to inspire thoughts of the high vault of heaven, it was an English or a British heaven. The stars were the royal arms, the constellations spelled the royal motto, and the cherubs and angels sung the praises not only of God, but of God's vicegerent in England, who reigned 'by God and by right'.

In one sense the chapel ceiling was designed as a window through which one could catch a glimpse of heaven above. Yet it was also a mirror meant to reflect the courtly heaven below. For as John Donne put it in one of his first court sermons, 'as Princes are Gods, so their well-govern'd Courts, are Copies, and representations of Heaven'.[98] The sovereign in the upper reaches of this house of God, literally suspended next to the blue ceiling painted to suggest the heavens, constituted a living picture of divinely ordered hierarchy and the harmonious union of civil and ecclesiastical government under the royal supremacy. Here God's power and blessings were sent down upon a godly monarch, and through her or him given to the magistrates, while they in return learned from the Word preached and from prayers offered how to use that God-given power of government to establish and confirm a religious commonwealth. William Laud captured the symbolic essence of the chapel setting in 1622 when he characterized James as 'a mediate fountaine of Gods goodnesse and bounty streaming to the people'. Similarly, Anthony Rudd, Bishop of St David's, invoked the mediatory role of the king in visual terms not unlike those that surrounded him in the Whitehall chapel when he called upon the court to 'now imagin with me, that *Dauid* sitting aloft in his Chaire of estate looketh downe to his subiects saying, Saluation belongeth vnto the Lord: And then casting vppe his eyes to Heaven, by an Apostrophe to God saith thus. And thy blessing is vppon thy people.'[99] Donne himself acknowledged that 'the Copy cannot be better than the Original', and for

[97] PRO E36/244, quoted in Heath, 'Chapel Royal at Hampton Court', 7. Accounts for renovations during James's reign make it clear that ceilings with similar iconographic programmes covered the Jacobean, and probably the Elizabethan, chapels at Whitehall and Greenwich. See PRO E351/3257, Greenwich, taskwork; and *HKW*, vol. IV, 341.

[98] *The Sermons of John Donne*, 10 vols., ed. George R. Potter and Evelyn M. Simpson (Berkeley, Calif., 1953–62), vol. I, 223.

[99] William Laud, *A Sermon Preached at White-hall, on the 24. of March, 1621* (1622), 6; Anthony Rudd, *A Sermon Preached before the Kings Maiestie at White-hall vpon the Ninth of Februarie. 1605.* (1606), sig. A1ᵛ.

that matter, that even God's heaven had its fallen angels.[100] As we shall see, the preacher's duty of recalling prince and court to the ideals that the chapel setting involved made the royal chapels one of the most important – and hitherto most neglected – political theatres in early modern England.

THE PREACHING PLACE AT WHITEHALL

Not all Elizabethan and Jacobean court sermons were preached in the relatively intimate surroundings of the chapels royal. One of the great testaments to the early sixteenth-century flourishing of pulpit oratory, and to the use of the pulpit as government mouthpiece, was the construction of a substantial outdoor pulpit in what had been the Henrician Privy Garden, and was known variously as the Sermon Court, the Preaching Place, or the Chapel Court. The continuator of Stowe's *Annales*, Edmund Howes, dated the construction of the courtyard pulpit during the reign of Elizabeth's half-brother, Edward VI. In his account of the year 1547–8, Howes wrote that there 'was a Pulpit set vp in the Kings priuie Garden at Westminster, and therin Doctor *Latimer* preached before the King, where he might be heard of more then foure times so many people as could haue stoode in the Kings Chappell'.[101] Documentary evidence, however, has proven that the Preaching Place is Henrician, not Edwardine. In an undated petition to Queen Elizabeth, Robert Trunckey, 'an Artificer and straunger borne', requested a Crown pension on the grounds of 'good s^rvice' done 'in the tyme of the raigne of your right noble Father', and cited, among other work, his construction of 'the nowe preaching place w^tin your highnes Pallace at Westm'.[102] Howe, like the many commentators that have reproduced his statement, probably made the not illogical assumption that the construction of this monument to court preaching dated from Latimer's Edwardine heyday.[103] Although he gave no source, Howe did provide a convincingly specific date for the pulpit's inauguration, 'the 17. of March, being Wednesday'.[104] Latimer indeed preached in the Lent of 1548; but 17 March 1547–8 was a Saturday – not a Wednesday as the chronicler records, and the faulty date weakens his assertion. Moreover, a letter written by the Venetian Ambassador in February 1559, corroborates the Henrician existence of the outdoor pulpit. The ambassador was 'much

---

[100] Donne, *Sermons*, vol. I, 223.
[101] John Stowe, cont. Edmund Howes, *Annales of England . . . Continued unto 1631* (1631), 595.
[102] London County Council, *Survey of London*, 41 vols. (1900–), vol. XIV, 169.
[103] See Peter Heylyn, *Ecclesia Restavrata* (1661), 57, and Allan G. Chester, *Hugh Latimer, Apostle to the English* (Philadelphia, Pa., 1954), 165.
[104] Stowe, cont. Howes, *Annales*, 595.

scandalized' by the 'outrageous' things preached against the Pope and all things Catholic in the presence of the new Queen Elizabeth by Dr John Scory 'at the Court in the place where, during the reigns of Kings Henry and Edward, [he] used to preach'.[105]

Howe's explanation of the Privy Garden pulpit as a platform custom-made for Latimer can perhaps be explained as yet another testament to the influence of Foxe's *Actes and Monumentes*, or 'Book of Martyrs'. In the biography of Latimer that precedes the famous account of his martyrdom, Foxe lauded Latimer's evangelical preaching during the reign of Edward VI. After Latimer's cautious silence during the latter years of Henry VIII, the accession of the more devoutly Protestant Edward meant that 'the golden mouthe of thys Preacher, long shut vp before, was now opened agayne'. Latimer preached 'al the tyme of the said king' in the counties, in London churches, and at Paul's Cross, but most 'especially before the king at the court'. Foxe went on to specify that the court sermons were preached 'in the same place of the inwarde garden, which was before applyed to lasciuious and courtlye pastimes' where Latimer now 'dispensed the fruitful woorde of the glorious gospell of Iesus Christ . . . before the kyng and hys whole Courte, to the edification of many'.[106] Immediately beneath this character sketch is the only illustration in the entire *Actes and Monumentes* that does not depict a martyrdom or persecution: the famous woodcut of Latimer preaching from the outdoor pulpit to a throng of courtiers in the garden yard, with King Edward listening from the council chamber window above (see Figure 8). Foxe's eagerness to contrast the 'lasciuious' Henrician reign with the reign of the 'glorious gospell' under Edward VI, coupled with the influential illustration that forever fixed Latimer, Edward, and the Privy Garden pulpit in the same frame, probably skewed Howes's, and subsequent generations', chronology of English court preaching.

The *Actes and Monuments* woodcut preserves a fairly accurate picture of the physical arrangement of the Preaching Place.[107] Lupold von Wedel's description of the courtyard in 1584 shows how little it had changed since Edward's days:

Then we were brought to a grass plot surrounded by broad walks below and above, enabling many persons to promenade there. In the middle of the place a pulpit is erected, with a sounding board above. When the queen commands preaching here, the walks are filled with auditors.[108]

The courtyard itself measured some 200 by 275 feet, and thus provided a

---

[105] *CSPV 1558–1580*, 30–1.   [106] John Foxe, *Actes and Monumentes* (1563), 1353.
[107] See Thurley, *Royal Palaces*, 199–200; *HKW.* vol. IV, 313–14; and *Survey of London*, XIII, 60–1, 88–9, 119.
[108] Von Wedel, 'Journey Through England and Scotland', 236.

Fig. 8.   The Preaching Place at Whitehall: Hugh Latimer preaching before Edward
VI, from John Foxe, *Actes amd Monuments*, 1570 (Bodleian Library, University of
Oxford, shelfmark Mason.F.144, p. 1908).

surface area of some 55,000 square feet, certainly more standing room than
was available in the chapel, and large enough to accommodate the 5,000
people that the Venetian Ambassador reported seeing at Dr Scory's sermon
in Lent 1559.[109] On the north and east sides stood an elevated terrace or
walk that allowed access to the Privy Lodgings and the Council Chamber
and in sermon time provided extra standing room. It was from the
windows of the Council Chamber, which protruded into the courtyard,
that the sovereign listened to the sermon. Both the Terrace and Council
Chamber are clearly seen in the Foxe woodcut, and the whole arrangement
with 'the Preachinge Place' (pulpit), 'The Close wake wch goeth to the
loginges', the 'Chapell Courte', and the protruding Council Chamber, is
recorded in architect John Smythson's plan of James's 1609 Banqueting
House (see Figure 9). The Preaching Place seems to have continued to
double as a garden. This is suggested not only by von Wedel's description of
it as a 'grass plot', but also because Elizabethan Works accounts show that
it was decorated with a series of vertical posts bearing carved and brightly

[109] *CSPV 1558–1580*, 30–1.

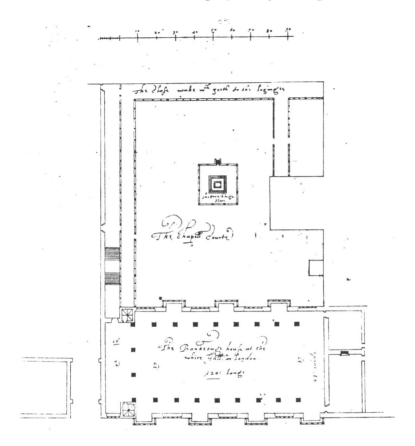

Fig. 9. Robert Smythson, plan of part of Whitehall Palace, 1609 (British Architectural Library, RIBA, London). Smythson's plan for James I's first Banqueting House also captures the physical centrality of the preaching at court: the outdoor pulpit (labelled 'The Preachinge Place') facing the protruding council chamber in the midst of the open courtyard (here anomalously the 'Chapell Courte'). On two sides of the court are the elevated gallery (left) and 'the close wake [walk] wch goeth to the Loginges' (top), the latter with its spur gallery to the council chamber (top right).

painted heraldic beasts like those that stood in the Great Garden on the palace's south side. In 1571–2, for example, repairs 'aboute the preaching place & the Tarrase' included 'newemliking and repayring of the beastes and figures', for which carvers were paid to make 'vij Lyons', 'twoe boyes', and 'the figure of Iustice'. Painters were duly paid for painting these 'diuers figures of beastes and others . . . & also diu[er]se bases & pillasters'.[110]

---

[110] PRO E351/3206, fols. 3ᵛ, 4ᵛ. For the Great Garden, *HKW*, vol. IV, 313.

Just as he did inside the chapel, a preacher in the outdoor Preaching Place stood amidst the colourful emblems of the Tudor monarchy.

The Whitehall Preaching Place had two important architectural antecedents: the medieval outdoor pulpit and the court chapel's royal closet. The picture of a preacher addressing a large audience *en plein aire* should not be viewed as an icon of the Protestant passion for preaching, but rather as proof of the continuity between some medieval Catholic and Reformation Protestant practice in England. One of the results of the sermon's evolution during the Middle Ages as a religious activity severed from the context of the mass was the construction of outdoor stone pulpits built as variations on the familiar market cross, but on the hallowed ground of either churchyard cemetery or convent or monastery yard. The most famous example, of course, and one with a strong post-Reformation legacy, was Paul's Cross, built as early as 1241 in the north-eastern precinct of the London cathedral's cemetery. Also prominent in London were the pulpit crosses at St Mary's Spital, St Mary of Bethlehem, and St Michael's Cornhill, with provincial examples scattered across England.[111] But the great innovation of the Whitehall pulpit lay in the fact that it was erected on secular, not sacred, ground. Henry VIII did not discover preaching as much as the political power of the pulpit. Of course, English monarchs had used the pulpit at Paul's Cross as a state mouthpiece for centuries before him. But the erection of a pulpit on the very secular ground of the king's Privy Garden symbolized a radical turn towards the Tudor subjection of church to state under the 'Supreme Head' of the king.

The Council Chamber above the Privy Garden-turned-Preaching Place provided a perfect surrogate for the chapel's royal closet. The building itself projected several feet into the courtyard, and its windows opened out into it, thus imitating the protrusion of the royal closet's oriel windows into the body of the chapel. As in chapel, the sovereign had the best seat for both seeing and hearing; but, most importantly, the council chamber 'pew' allowed the monarch a seat, as Archbishop Parker knew was crucial, 'above the heads of the people'. John King, in an iconographic study of the woodcuts from Foxe's *Actes and Monuments*, emphasizes that in the portrayal of Latimer preaching before Edward VI 'the king and cleric seem to be on very nearly the same level plane', and thus emphasizes the 'proper ordering of church and state' in the reformed commonwealth.[112] Although this might have been the symbolic intention of the artist or even of Edward VI, Queen Elizabeth at least never suffered herself to be considered on a

---

[111] G. R. Owst, *Preaching in Medieval England* (Cambridge, 1926), 195–201. For Paul's Cross, see Millar MacLure, *The Paul's Cross Sermons 1534–1642* (Toronto, 1958), 3–19.

[112] John N. King, *Tudor Royal Iconography: Literature and Art in an Age of Religious Crisis* (Princeton, N.J., 1989), 164.

plane – literally or symbolically – with her clergy. Although elevated in the pulpit, Elizabeth's preachers were her subjects, and she reminded them of that whenever necessary. When Alexander Nowell, the venerable Dean of St Paul's, made the mistake of speaking too roundly against religious images and the saints in the Preaching Place in 1565, the queen said bluntly from her window, 'Do not talk about that.' At first Nowell did not hear the queen's warning, so she 'raised her voice and pointedly said to him, "Leave that, it has nothing to do with your subject, and the matter is now threadbare."' The Dean could hardly retain his composure long enough to bring his sermon to an abrupt end.[113] Like the royal closet, the Council Chamber was directly connected to the Privy Chambers, and Elizabeth treated it as an extension of her private apartments from which she could come and go as she pleased. When, on the first Sunday in Lent, 1579, Elizabeth tired of hearing a preacher warn of the destruction that awaited herself and her country if she married the Catholic Duc d'Alençon, she rose from her window seat, turned her back to the pulpit, and walked out.[114]

The outdoor pulpit at Whitehall seems to have been used mostly for the important series of court sermons preached during Lent, and James and his family, like his predecessor, attended many of the sermons preached there during that season; by the 1640s the pulpit was even referred to as 'the Lenten pulpit'.[115] Elizabeth even seems to have attempted to preserve the open-air context of the Lent sermons when she and her court were absent from Whitehall. On the second Wednesday in Lent (3 March) 1574, the queen was the guest of Archbishop Parker at Lambeth Palace. The preacher appointed for the day, Dr John Piers, duly came to Lambeth, but did not preach in the household chapel. Instead, in imitation of the Whitehall Preaching Place, a pulpit was set up in the inner fountain court. The queen and some of her nobles and ladies listened from windows in the upper-storey galleries of the buildings that flanked the court, while those of lesser rank stood around the pulpit in the yard.[116] In 1585, when Elizabeth kept Lent at Somerset House in the Strand, she had a new 'preaching place' or 'pulpit howse' built at her own expense for the season's sermons.[117]

The much more public nature of the Preaching Place, where middle-class Londoners could outnumber courtiers, might have demanded different standards of deference from preacher to prince, and even heightened the theatricality of the event. Surely it is significant that the two known

[113] *CSPS 1558–1567*, 405.   [114] *CSPS 1568–1579*, 658–9.

[115] Anon., *A Deep Sigh Breath'd Through the Lodgings At White-hall* (1642), sig. A2ᵛ.

[116] Nichols, *Progresses . . . of Queen Elizabeth*, vol. I, 384. Nichols mistakenly repeats the story under the incorrect date of Lent, 1572–3 (vol. I, 325).

[117] *HMC Bath*, vol. IV, 159; PRO E351/3219, fol. 12ᵛ.

sermons with which the queen publicly expressed dissatisfaction were preached in the Preaching Place. After Lent 1578, the year in which the queen sequestered Archbishop Grindal, an anonymous courtier wrote to a Cambridge head that Elizabeth was displeased with the recent round of sermons, because they had

entered into Dissensions of Matters properly appertaining to Matters of Government: rather by private Advice to be imparted to her self, or to her Council, than in Pulpits, to the hearing of the vulgar People, which are not apt to hear such Things: Especially thereby to catch lightly Occasions, to think either sinisterly or doubtfully of the Head, and of her Government.[118]

What offended Elizabeth more than having government matters treated in a pulpit (not something she liked, to be sure) was having them handled from a pulpit surrounded, as the Preaching Place was, by 'the vulgar people'. Elizabeth could put up with some fierce drubbings, like those from Cole and Dering, when in the privacy of her chapel; but Alexander Nowell and the unknown preacher who criticized the French marriage suffered public humiliation at the queen's hands for engaging some of the same issues in front of the populace.

When Camden remarked that she used to frequent 'the *Lent-Sermons* dress'd in Mourning, as the gravest and most primitive Habit', the external details of Elizabeth's attentiveness and dress were not merely anecdotal, but to the point.[119] Just as on summer progress, or in procession, Elizabeth wanted to be seen at these outdoor sermons. Ironically, it was that same audience made up of so many of the *vulgus* that caused Elizabeth, at least in part, religiously to attend the Lent sermons. The Spanish ambassador reported that they were preached in such a large courtyard 'so that the people on all sides may hear as great crowds go', but added that 'the Queen tells me that more go to see her than to hear the sermon'.[120] A contemporary observer recorded the complete picture of the queen listening to Dr Piers preach in the Lambeth courtyard when he wrote that the 'people from below divided their attention between her Majesty and the preacher (*Populus . . . partim reginam, partim concionatorem, intuitus est*)'.[121] Just as the processions to and from chapel afforded a carefully choreographed display of prince and court for visitors and dignitaries, the Lent sermons allowed a London burgher the rare chance to catch a glimpse of the sovereign. Moreover, since both Elizabeth and James rarely attended any

---

[118] John Strype, *Annals of the Reformation*, 2nd. edn, 3 vols. (1725–28), vol. II, 541. Strype suggests Leicester or Walsingham as the likely author.
[119] William Camden, *The History of Queen Elizabeth*, in *A Complete History of England*, 3 vols (1706), vol. II, 371.
[120] *CSPS 1558–1567*, 405.
[121] Nichols, *Progresses . . . of Queen Elizabeth*, vol. I, 325, 384.

kind of public worship in London, outdoor sermons at Whitehall were one of the few chances these princes had to make a public display of piety, to show their people that they were indeed godly magistrates who esteemed godly preaching. As we shall see, the two did not take equal advantage of the opportunity.[122]

[122] Elizabeth and James both attended Paul's Cross only once; see Millar MacLure, *Register of Sermons Preached at Paul's Cross 1534–1642*, revised and expanded by Peter Pauls and Jackson Campbell Boswell (Ottawa, 1989), 66, 115.

2

Tudor court preaching and Elizabeth I

MEDIEVAL AND EARLY TUDOR PRECEDENTS

Court preaching in England was not the product of the Reformation. Thanks to John Foxe's influential Protestant view of English history, first-generation reformers such as Latimer, Hooper, and Ridley get all the credit in the popular imagination for initiating a tradition of bold pulpit oratory before monarchs and magistrates. However, David had his Nathan, Felix his Paul, and Theodosius his Ambrose. In sixteenth-century England, Latimer and his fellow patriots were only the most recent clerical actors in an established drama of court preaching that stretched back through the Middle Ages to what must have been the first court sermon on the island, St Augustine of Canterbury's convincing exposition of Christianity to King Ethelbert of Kent in the seventh century. To be sure, the reformers placed a previously unheard-of emphasis on preaching – in Latimer's sum, 'take a waye preachyng, and take a way saluacion'.[1] But Latimer was not the first to upbraid 'vnprechinge prelates', for preaching, like any other expression of Christian piety, enjoyed periods of both vogue and neglect. If the age of Shakespeare and its obsession with preaching has an analogue in English history, it is the age of Chaucer. David Knowles has called the last half of the fourteenth century 'the golden age of the popular sermon in medieval England', and that popularity found expression in courtly household chapels as well as in the friary churches and at provincial market crosses. John of Gaunt patronized – in addition to Chaucer – the Carmelite friars William Badby (*fl.* 1380) and Richard Maidstone (*c.* 1475–1530), who established reputations as eloquent court preachers. Badby, like Latimer at the court of Edward VI or Andrewes before James I, drew an audience to his sermons 'as to a show'. A third Whitefriar, John Swaffham, was said to

---

[1] Hugh Latimer, *Seven Sermons before Edward VI, On each Friday in Lent, 1549*, ed. Edward Arber (Birmingham, 1869), 108.

51

have won the bishopric of Bangor in 1376 for his preaching before the court of Edward III.[2]

Historians agree that preaching in medieval England reached its apogee in the last decades of the fourteenth century largely because of social change and instability, 'when social troubles, plagues, war and Lollardy opened a field for evangelists, orthodox or heretical'. Social ills provided much the same grist for preachers' mills as they had for Chaucer's and Langland's.[3] Similarly, the social and religious upheavals of the Tudor Reformation fuelled the next great age of English preaching, with powerful orators on both sides pitting their rhetorical skills against each other in an on-going pulpit debate over the future of the English church. Throughout the pre-Reformation centuries, however, preaching would have been part of the court's religious practice. In addition to the permanent clerical staff of the Chapel Royal, members of the royal family chose personal chaplains and confessors who could be called upon to preach before the household. The weekly Sunday sermon so familiar after the Reformation was rare throughout Christendom, and preaching at the medieval court, like most cathedral preaching, was probably limited to major religious feast days or state occasions. Cathedral practice varied from the Bishop of Sodor and Man's ambitious injunction for preaching on every Sunday and holy day (1350), to Archbishop of York Nevill's lenient one-per-quarter requirement (1466).[4] The holy days typically marked by a sermon would have included, at a minimum, Christmas, Easter, and Whitsunday.

The high season for preaching, however, whether at court, cathedral, monastery, or parish church, was Lent – a medieval tradition that persisted at the English court until the eighteenth century. Church councils repeatedly enjoined sermons in every church on each of Lent's forty days, but this *rota* probably remained more an ideal than a reality. The Quattrocento and Cinquecento papal courts heard sermons only on the Sundays of Lent.[5] The same Lenten Sunday minimum was the pre-Reformation norm at the English court. Evidence for this routine is found in a surviving manuscript handbook of court officers' duties. Although the handbook dates from the early years of Charles I's reign, it contains extracts from what must have been a similar book, dating at least from the Roman Catholic years of

---

[2] David Knowles, *The Religious Orders in England*, 3 vols. (Cambridge, 1955–71), vol. II, 153; G. R. Owst, *Preaching in Medieval England* (Cambridge, 1926), 66, 221.

[3] Knowles, *Religious Orders*, vol. II, 153; W. A. Pantin, *The English Church in the Fourteenth Century* (Cambridge, 1955; Toronto, 1980), 183–4.

[4] Owst, *Preaching*, 146, n. 1. For parochial practice, see H. Leith Spencer, *English Preaching in the Late Middle Ages* (Oxford, 1993), 31–2.

[5] Owst, *Preaching*, 146, n. 4; Spencer, *English Preaching*, 32–3; John O'Malley, *Praise and Blame in Renaissance Rome: Rhetoric, Doctrine and Reform in the Sacred Orators of the Papal Court, c. 1450–1521* (Durham, N.C., 1979), 30.

Henry VIII's reign, and probably from the reign of his father. This manual provides an exhaustive description of gentlemen ushers' duties for state and liturgical ceremonies.[6] The pre-Reformation instructions for Ash Wednesday appoint that 'where euer the kinge shalbe that day' the Serjeant of the Vestry should 'p[re]pare a pulpett for a Sermon . . . and soe eu[er]ie Wedsday & friday in Lent if the king[es] devotion be such. But Sermons must be had on Sondayes of Lent by custome of the king[dom].'[7] Thus, the pre-Reformation English court, like its counterparts throughout Europe, always heard sermons on the five Sundays of Lent, with midweek sermons preached at the discretion of the king.[8]

The early years of the sixteenth century witnessed a revival of preaching at the universities and in London. With generous endowments from his patroness, the Lady Margaret Beaufort, mother of Henry VII and a devoted patroness of preaching, Bishop John Fisher, also Chancellor of Cambridge, established a university preachership in 1504 that required the incumbent to preach in parochial churches and at Paul's Cross. In the same year, Fisher received permission from the Pope to appoint twelve Doctors in Divinity to preach on itinerant circuits. Meanwhile, Dean John Colet (1466–1519), already famous for his Oxford lectures on the Pauline epistles, revived regular preaching from the pulpit of St Paul's Cathedral. Both men owed their ecclesiastical preferments to royal patronage, and their revival of preaching enjoyed royal approval and encouragement.[9] The precedents for an evangelical preaching clergy under the auspices of the Crown were therefore set years before Henry VIII's halting moves towards a Protestant Reformation and Edward VI's later deployment of itinerant preaching chaplains and patronage of preaching prelates such as Latimer, Ridley, and Hooper.

As Henry VIII's divorce proceedings against Katharine of Aragon pro-

[6] BL MS Sloane 1494. Large portions of the book can be dated on internal evidence. There are repeated provisions for seating in the case that 'a Cardinall of this realme be p[rese]nt that day' (fol. 14[r]), suggesting a date before 1529. In addition, the instructions for Ash Wednesday note that 'if the prince be p[rese]nt a stoole is to be p[re]pared for him by the gent[leman] vsher in the closet by the kinge.' (fol. 20[v]). Since this reference to a prince occurs with the provisions for the presence of a cardinal, we may assume that the prince referred to is either Prince Arthur or Prince Henry, attending service with Henry VII. The Chapel Royal ceremonies described juxtapose pre-Reformation practice and the reformed Jacobean and Caroline instructions.

[7] BL MS Sloane 1494, fol. 20[v].

[8] Payments for Lent sermons in the Henrician Treasurer of the Chamber's accounts confirm this pattern; these will be calendared in Fiona Kisby's University of London doctoral thesis, 'The Early-Tudor Royal Household Chapel', 1485–1547 (1996).

[9] Michael K. Jones and Malcolm G. Underwood, *The King's Mother: Lady Margaret Beaufort, Countess of Richmond and Derby* (Cambridge, 1992), 210–11. Edward Surtz, *The Works and Days of John Fisher* (Cambridge, Mass., 1967), 55–6. John B. Gleason, *John Colet* (Berkeley, Calif., 1989), 257–60.

gressed in the early 1530s, court preaching – like preaching throughout England – became politicized in a way that set many precedents for its manipulation by subsequent monarchs, both Tudor and Stuart. This is not to suggest that court sermons were void of secular political content before Henry's infamous divorce. Colet, for example, had openly rebuked the king's military offensive against France in his sermon *coram rege* on Good Friday 1515.[10] After 1529, however, Henry deliberately pressed into service as preachers before the court aggressive reformers who, despite their significant doctrinal differences with king and establishment, were none the less willing to declaim the invalidity of Henry's first marriage and to decry the usurping power of the Pope. Latimer had attracted Henry's attention for his support of the royal supremacy and divorce in sermons preached at Cambridge in 1529. It was for this, and not his Lutheran theology, that Latimer became the first Protestant preacher to address the court when he appeared in the pulpit at Windsor in Lent 1530.

Recent work has called needed attention to Anne Boleyn's patronage of evangelicals such as Latimer and Nicholas Shaxton, which gave the reformers a foothold in the court itself as early as 1530. Preaching was, of course, also the most effective means for Henry's chief reforming ministers, Thomas Cromwell and Archbishop Thomas Cranmer, to promulgate the Acts of Succession and Supremacy passed by Parliament in 1534. Cromwell exerted a tremendous pro-government influence in the dioceses through patronage of reform-minded preachers and a series of injunctions requiring all preachers to denounce papal authority.[11] Similar care was taken to ensure that the court pulpit sounded only government truths in the king's 'great matter'. When days before Easter 1534, news reached England that Pope Clement VII had judged in favour of the divorced Queen Katharine, Henry commanded that the preachers for that great feast attack the Pope. The Imperial ambassador lamented that 'they have acquitted themselves desperately, saying the most outrageous and abominable things in the world'.[12] In June of that year, Cranmer issued orders for preaching and prayers before sermons. These included a special clause for court preachers that instructed them to pray only for the Church, King Henry 'the only and supreme head of this catholic church of England', for Queen Anne, and for 'the lady Elizabeth' – thus summarizing before each court sermon the Acts of Succession and Supremacy.[13]

---

[10] Gleason, *John Colet*, 57–60.

[11] Joseph Block, 'Thomas Cromwell's Patronage of Preaching', *Sixteenth Century Journal* 8 (1977), 37–50.

[12] *LP*, vol. VII, 192–3.

[13] Thomas Cranmer, *Miscellaneous Writings and Letters*, ed. John Edmund Cox (Cambridge, 1846), 460–2.

Bishop Fisher – as did Sir Thomas More – suffered execution in June 1535 rather than accept the royal supremacy. Other conservatively minded prelates chose to moderate their views rather than face a similar fate. Within a month of Fisher's beheading, Henry's Dean of the Chapel Royal, Richard Sampson, also Bishop of Chichester, preached a sermon, presumably in favour of Henry's new title, which Chapuys felt certain was 'against his conscience'.[14] Anti-papal sermon propaganda even followed Katharine of Aragon to her grave. At her funeral early in 1536 at Peterborough Cathedral, Fisher's successor to the see of Rochester, John Hilsey, 'preached the same as all the preachers of England for two years have not ceased to preach, viz, against the power of the Pope . . . and against the marriage of the said good Queen and King'.[15]

If Henrician court preachers spoke unanimously against papal authority – which they seem to have done, albeit with varying degrees of enthusiasm – they none the less vocalized the deep divisions in theology and churchmanship between a conservative and a progressive application of Reformation. In short, the court Lent sermons dramatized the nation's religious divisions. Lent 1538 featured the entire spectrum of debate ranging from conservatives such as Dean of the Chapel Richard Sampson and royal chaplain Nicholas Wilson, moderates such as Thomas Starkey, to the reforming extreme of Latimer's suffragan, Bishop of Bristol Henry Holbeach, and Bishop of Rochester John Hilsey, both then in the midst of violent campaigns of iconoclasm.[16] The conservative reaction that followed the passage of the Six Articles in June 1539 also manifested itself in the Lent rotas. Lent 1540 found Latimer under house arrest – a ward of Sampson's, no less. Other allies of Latimer who had held the court pulpit in the preceding years – men such as Jerome Barlow, Vicar of Stepney, and Hilsey of Rochester – disappeared from the rota.[17] The majority of the Lenten Sundays now went to the conservative voices of John Longland of Lincoln, Cuthbert Tunstall of Durham, and Sampson, with only Holbeach and the moderate William Barlow of St David's representing the committed reformers. Wednesday and Friday sermons were taken by royal chaplain Wilson and the leader of the conservatives, Stephen Gardiner of Winchester.[18]

---

[14] *LP*, vol. VIII, 433.   [15] *LP*, vol. X, 106.   [16] *LP*, vol. XIII.2, 526.

[17] Barlow was burned at Smithfield for heresy on 30 July 1540. He had preached before Henry at Whitehall the previous Lent (Passion Sunday, 9 March 1539) and received the regular honorarium of 20s. (*LP*, vol. XIV.2, 305). Hilsey died late in 1538 and his *cathedra* was filled by the conservative Nicholas Heath.

[18] Charles Wriothsley, *A Chronicle of England During the Reigns of the Tudors from 1485–1559*, 2 vols., ed. William Douglas Hamilton, Camden Society n.s. 18 and 20 (1875, 1877), vol. I, 113. For Gardiner's appointment to preach see *The Letters of Stephen Gardiner*, ed. James Arthur Muller (Cambridge, 1933), 168.

The turbulence of the 1530s inspired a passion for preaching and sermon-going probably not equalled in England since the heyday of the fourteenth-century friars-preachers. There can be no doubt that, especially in London's parish churches, the frequency of preaching increased significantly, although more as a result of divisive political and doctrinal debate than for the homiletic and pastoral reasons envisioned by Fisher and Colet two decades before. There is no proof, however, that the frequency of preaching at court increased; for example, sermons every Sunday, except in Lent, remained unheard of. The pre-existing occasions for court sermons – the major feast days, and especially the five-week Lent series – continued without supplement. However, what were once perfunctory parts of the court routine now became occasions of public and political significance.

Henry died at Greenwich on 28 January 1547, at the close of the Epiphany season, and within one month the court Lent sermons heralded the ecclesiastical changes to be wrought under his son and successor, Edward VI. The Spanish ambassador wrote on 7 March that 'there is preaching every day before the King, and the preachers seem to vie with each other as to who can abuse most strongly the old religion, he who excels the others in this respect being most highly favoured'.[19] Small wonder, then, that civil servants as well as foreign ambassadors treated news of court Lent sermons with the seriousness of any other intelligence that might serve as a barometer of political and religious change.[20] But holy day sermons and an annual Lent series did not pass muster with the ascendant reformers who threatened 'eternal damnation to such as preacheth not'.[21] Acutely aware of the court pulpit's wider influence, several reformers specifically petitioned for more court preaching. In the dedicatory epistle to Archbishop Cranmer prefacing *The Image of God, or Laie ma[n]s booke* (1550), Roger Hutchinson lambasted those of the king's chaplains who 'pretend they be true preachers of God's word' but neglect their duties both at court and at their benefices, and only 'once a year, or twice peradventure, doth preach a sermon before the king, or at the Spittle, or at Paul's cross . . . to uphold their good names'.[22] John Hooper – soon to be Bishop of Gloucester, and later Marian martyr – was even more direct in his sermons preached before King Edward on the seven Wednesdays of Lent 1550. In the sixth sermon he recommended that 'in your case your highness would have before you every Sunday one sermon'. Hooper under-

[19] *CSPS 1547–49*, 50.
[20] See 'The Letters of Richard Scudamore to Sir Philip Hoby, September 1549–March 1555', ed. Susan Brigden, *Camden Miscellany* vol. XXX (1990), 124.
[21] *Early Writings of Bishop Hooper*, ed. Samuel Carr (Cambridge, 1843), 466.
[22] *The Works of Roger Hutchinson*, ed. John Bruce (Cambridge, 1842), 5.

stood that only a soundly Protestant monarch and Council could guarantee a soundly Protestant state, and he seized the opportunity to urge the regular reinforcement of that confession before king and council through godly court preaching. Therefore, he ended his last sermon not with the routine exhortation to 'permit not the mass', but instead reiterated his hope that 'it may please you to command more sundry times to have sermons before your majesty', adding that, since 'there is in the year eight thousand seven hundred and sixty hours, it shall not be much for your highness, no, nor for all your household, to bestow of them fifty-two in the year to hear the sermon of God'. The preacher left his auditory with the promise that a failure to sponsor and be converted by pure preaching would 'condemn both king and council to death'.[23]

Hooper's confidence was not misguided, as he attributed his subsequent elevation to the bishopric of Gloucester to the king's and council's satisfaction with these very sermons.[24] Such admonitions seemed to work, for Edward became a zealous sponsor of court preaching. The young king's personal involvement in the appointment of his preachers, and his whole-hearted engagement with the doctrines they espoused surpassed that of his father, and prefigured the sermon-going enthusiasm of James I. In April 1550, Edward ordered sermons to be preached every Sunday without exception at court, and made a probationary court sermon, 'in or out of Lent', a prerequisite for obtaining a royal benefice.[25] During the same spring a horrified Spanish ambassador saw the young king, 'but too good by nature', become a precocious Protestant under his preachers' tutelage, 'so that in the court there is no bishop . . . so ready to argue in support of the new doctrine as the King, according to what his masters tell him, and he learns from his preachers'. However, if the ambassador can be believed, Edward could even turn the tables and school his preachers, 'whose sermons he often writes with his own hand before everybody; and this seems to be a source of pride to his courtiers that the King should dictate the very words of the sermons and choose for himself those who shall preach'.[26] Hooper's exhortations had not fallen on deaf ears.

Edward also listened to the calls for a reformation of royal chaplaincies. As early as 1547, Lord Protector Somerset had set about the reformation of Edward's household clerical staff. According to surviving lists, conservative chaplains were summarily discharged, including the King's Almoner, Bishop of Worcester Nicholas Heath.[27] Among the 'names of the kynges

---

[23] Hooper, *Early Writings*, 541, 558.
[24] *Original Letters Relative to the English Reformation*, 2 vols., ed. Hastings Robinson (Cambridge, 1846, 1847), vol. I, 87.
[25] Strype, *Ecclesiastical Memorials*, 3 vols (Oxford, 1822), vol. II, 1, 334.
[26] *CSPS 1550–52*, 63.   [27] BL MS Royal 7.C.xvi, art. 15, fol. 92ʳ.

maiesties servauntes as ar nuely placed in ordinary' only Heath's replace-
ment, Dr Richard Cox is named, leaving the selection of 'Chapleyns &
Clerke of the closet' entirely to Somerset: 'So many and such as my lorde
protector shall appoint'.[28] Under Henry VIII court chaplains functioned as
confessors and assisted at the celebration of the divine service in the chapel
royal, preaching only occasionally; but Edward took the radical step of
turning these court chaplains into outriding preachers. Evangelical
preaching received its most significant royal endorsement with the December 1551 appointment of 'six chaplains ordinary, of which two [are] to
be present and four always absent in preaching' in the outer provinces of
the realm.[29] In keeping with the populism urged by radical voices such as
Latimer, Hooper, and Thomas Lever, the court chaplain's cure became not
the court but the shires.

Edward's Catholic half-sister Mary, who succeeded him in July 1553, did
not fail to recognize the importance of preachers and preaching for the re-
establishment of English Catholicism, and took steps to counter the
Protestant evangelism of the previous reign – what she termed 'those errors
and false opinions disseminated and spread abroad by the late preachers' –
with 'good preaching'.[30] Despite the tolerant spirit of her proclamation on
religious matters of 15 August, the letter of the document inhibited all
preaching by unlicensed preachers. The job of licensing an acceptable
preaching clergy fell to Mary's trusted bishop of Winchester and Lord
Chancellor, Stephen Gardiner, who was instructed to approve any such
'grave, learned and discreet persons, as shall seem meet to him, to preach in
any cathedral church, parish church or chapel within the realm'.[31] At her
court, Mary made a point to showcase orthodox Roman Catholic priests
who could preach well – certainly a conscious rejoinder to years of
Latimerian lampoons about the oxymoronic concept of a Roman Catholic
preacher. Mary's first Lent (1553–4) featured the brothers John and
Nicholas Harpsfield, respectively Archdeacons of St Paul's and Canterbury,
and James Brooks, Bishop of Gloucester and Master of Balliol College,
Oxford, all of whom were eloquent preachers trained in the Catholic
humanist tradition of Colet and Fisher. The Venetian ambassador noted in
1556 that 'during all this Lent six or eight priests have preached so well
and learnedly, and with such piety, that I can say with truth that I never

---

[28] BL MS Royal 7.C.xvi, art. 17, fol. 96ʳ. Cox was also tutor to Edward.
[29] *The Chronicle and Political Papers of King Edward VI*, ed. William K. Jordan (Ithaca,
    N.Y., 1966), 101.
[30] *CSPV 1557–1558*, 1647; David M. Loades, 'The Piety of the Catholic Restoration in
    England, 1553–1558,' in James Kirk, ed, *Humanism and Reform: the Church in Europe,
    England and Scotland, 1400–1643* (Oxford, 1991), 295.
[31] *CPR, Philip & Mary*, vol. I, 77.

heard better in all my life'.[32] Finally, Marian court preachers, no doubt with royal approbation, used print to further Catholic doctrine as it was expounded in the chapel royal. Thomas Watson, Bishop of Lincoln, and a preacher favoured by the queen, set out two of his court sermons from Lent 1554 that expounded the doctrine of transubstantiation in the mass and became the classic statement of Marian sacramentalism.[33] Elizabeth Tudor inherited a family tradition of putting the household pulpit to good, or at least expedient, use; but, as we shall see, her personal opinion of sermons may have been lower even than her Catholic sister's, and the heyday of the court pulpit would have to await the accession of a Stuart.

'TUNING PULPITS': THE ARRANGEMENT OF SERMONS FOR THE COURT OF ELIZABETH I

Laud's biographer Peter Heylyn recalled that Queen Elizabeth, 'when she had any business to bring about amongst the people, she used to *tune the Pulpits*, as her saying was; that is to say, to have some Preachers in and about *London*, and other great Auditories in the Kingdom, ready at command to cry up her design'.[34] During the tense months between her accession and the parliamentary settlement of religion there is evidence that the court pulpit was carefully 'tuned' – but to what extent by the queen herself or her ministers we may never know. At the bottom of the first memorandum that Cecil scratched on the day of the queen's accession, 17 November 1558, he reminded himself 'to consider the condition of ye prechar at Pawles Cross that no occasion be gyven to hym to stirr any dispute towchying the governance of ye realme'.[35] On 27 December 1558, a royal injunction inhibited all preaching in England.[36] Meanwhile, writs were issued on 6 December 1558 for the assembly of the reign's first Parliament on 23 January 1559. With all other pulpits in London silenced, Parliament opened after two days' delay on 25 January 1559 with a sermon preached by Richard Cox, former chaplain and tutor to Edward VI, and recently returned from exile in Frankfurt. In this, the first sanctioned

---

[32] W. C. Campbell, 'Sermons and Religious Treatises', in *The Thought and Culture of the English Renaissance: an Anthology of Tudor Prose, 1481–1555*, ed. Elizabeth M. Nugent (Cambridge, 1956), 319; CSPV 1555–1556, 434.

[33] Thomas Watson, *Twoo Notable Sermons, Made ... Before the Quenes Highnes, Concernynge the Reall Presence of Christes Body and Bloude in the Blessed Sacrament* (1554).

[34] Peter Heylyn, *Cyprianus Anglicus* (1671), 153.

[35] PRO SP 12/I/fol. 3, quoted in Norman Jones, *Faith by Statute: Parliament and the Settlement of Religion, 1559* (1982), 31.

[36] Edward Cardwell, ed., *Documentary Annals of the Reformed Church of England*, 2 vols. (Oxford, 1844), vol. I, 208–10.

sermon of the reign, Cox decried popery and begged the queen to free England from its tyranny.[37]

The bill for the supremacy was introduced two weeks later on Thursday, 9 February 1559 – certainly not coincidentally the day after the inauguration of the Lent court sermons. Cecil or the queen, in a brilliant gambit of pulpit policy, took advantage, as Henry and Edward had done, of the coincidence of two great court events: a Lent and a Parliament. On Ash Wednesday, 8 February, 1559 Cox again preached the only legally sanctioned sermon in the realm, this time from the queen's own pulpit in her palace courtyard, from which, according to the Venetian Ambassador, he 'said so much evil of the Pope, of the bishops, of the prelates, of the regulars, of the Church, of the mass, and finally of our entire faith . . . that I was much scandalized'.[38] More significantly, the entire Parliament had been adjourned to hear Cox's sermon. The Lent sermons went forward for the next six weeks in perfect step with the Parliament. The pulpit was filled with returned exiles such as Cox, and loyal Protestants such as Matthew Parker who had passed the Marian years in hiding in England. As the bills for reformation encountered resistance in the House of Lords, the court preachers countered with a sustained barrage of anti-Catholic propaganda.[39] The Venetian ambassador observed that 'the Court preachers in the presence of her Majesty and the people' were 'doing their utmost to convert' the recalcitrant Lords 'by their false arguments that the Pope has no authority'. Prophetically, he remarked that 'for this and other reasons' the reform bills would eventually pass the Upper House.[40]

The preachers at court during the spring of 1559 were a remarkably well-tuned choir indeed. These were heady times for the leaders of the Protestant cause, and differences that had estranged some from others while in exile were buried for the time being in the face of a very real Catholic opposition in the Lords; but within even a year of the Settlement of 1559, factional strife began to mark ecclesiastical as well as civil politics, and the court pulpit rarely sounded univocally. The primary reason for the heterogeneity of preachers and their sermons at court during the reign was the existence of several channels whereby a preacher could receive an invitation to preach there. To appreciate the variety among both the

---

[37] *CSPV 1558–1580*, 23; Jones, *Faith by Statute*, 83.

[38] *CSPV 1558–1580*, 30.

[39] For this Lent, see the 'Calendar' (supplement on disk); also *The Diary of Henry Machyn*, ed. John Gough Nichols, Camden Society no. 42 (1848), 189–90; Jones, *Faith by Statute*, 88, 97.

[40] *CSPV 1558–1580*, 46. These contemporary accounts hardly support the estimate that after the silencing of preachers elsewhere sermons at court 'were preached . . . on general topics not inciting controversy', Alan Fager Herr, *The Elizabethan Sermon: a Survey and a Bibliography* (published PhD thesis, University of Pennsylvania, 1940), 13.

patrons and the preachers of Elizabethan court sermons requires a knowledge of the several departments of the royal household and the quite
separate ecclesiastical hierarchy that had a say in who would preach before
the queen and court. Elizabeth's reign saw the transference of some control
over preachers from the Dean of the Chapel Royal, to two important
secular court officers – the Lord Treasurer and the Lord Chamberlain –
who worked in tandem with the Archbishop of Canterbury to assemble
preaching rotas that would satisfy the factional wishes of prominent
courtiers, ecclesiastics, and of course the final arbiter, the queen herself.
Although, as we shall see, the Lord Chamberlain would retain his influence
over preaching through control of the royal chaplains throughout the early
Stuart period, under James a return to more clerical control over preaching
at court would occur, with a revival and redefinition of the court offices of
Dean of the Chapel Royal and Clerk of the Closet.

Although most court sermons were preached in the chapels royal, under
Elizabeth preaching had no administrative connection with the household
department of the same name. Since at least the fifteenth century, the
Chapel Royal as a department (as opposed to a building) was a body of
priests and singing clerks (the Gentlemen of the Chapel) and boys (the
Children of the Chapel), with a staff (Serjeant, Yeoman, and Grooms of the
Vestry), presided over by a Dean and Sub-Dean. The Chapel was one of the
few court departments that answered directly to the sovereign, rather than
to one of the two principal household officers, the Lord Chamberlain for
staff above stairs, and the Lord Steward for staff below stairs. The Dean
was appointed by the monarch, and, on the model of cathedral chapters or
collegiate foundations, the Dean and adult members of the Chapel formed
its governing body. Meeting in regular chapters, the Gentlemen elected new
members, disciplined those who neglected their duties, and elected the Sub-
Dean.[41] The Chapel Royal was responsible for the liturgical life of the
court. In pre-Reformation times, high mass, vespers, Lady mass, and
diriges for deceased members of the royal house were sung daily at
appointed hours. The Dean and the other ordained members sung and

---

[41] The primary sources for the pre-Reformation Chapel establishment are the 'Establishment
of the Royal Household' (*c.* 1136) in Richard Fitzneale, *Dialogus de Scaccario . . . and
Constitutio Domus Regis: the Estimate of the Royal Household*, ed. and trans. Charles
Johnson (Oxford, 1983), 129; Dean of the Chapel William Say's (*c.* 1448) description,
Liber Regie Capelle, ed. Walter Ullman and D. H. Turner (1961); and Edward IV's
household ordinances, the 'Liber Niger Domus Regis' in *A Collection of Ordinances and
Regulations for the Government of the Royal Household* (1790), 13–86. For Henry VIII's
Chapel, see the 'Eltham Ordinances' in *Ordinances and Regulations*, 135–207. For the
Elizabethan and Jacobean Chapel, *The Olde Cheque-Book . . . of the Chapel Royal*, ed.
Edward F. Rimbault, Camden Society n.s. 3 (1872). The only summary history is David
Baldwin, *The Chapel Royal: Ancient and Modern* (1990). A major reassessment of the early
Tudor Chapel is Fiona Kisby, 'The Early-Tudor Royal Household Chapel'.

assisted at the celebration of the masses, and with the lay or 'singing clerks' and children performed the choral duties at the daily services. After the Reformation, the Gentlemen and Children of the Chapel sung matins and evensong daily, and ante-communion on Sundays and feast days, except during regularly observed vacations in summer and after major feasts, during which service was sung only on Sundays or holy days.[42] The Chapel Royal always attended when the court lay at one of the prince's standing houses, but did not follow on summer progresses. Preaching was not one of the responsibilities of the ordained Gentlemen of the Chapel; rather, these men served as members of the choir, sung the Gospel and Epistle and otherwise assisted at divine service. Though they sometimes did style themselves 'chaplains', they should not be confused with the household chaplains who filled the preaching rota.[43] The Chapel Royal must therefore be understood as an exclusively liturgical and musical foundation. As Heylyn described it, the duty of the Chapel and its Dean was 'to look unto the diligent and due performance of Gods Publick Service, and order matters of the Quire'.[44]

The Chapel Dean, however, in previous reigns, had exercised considerable control over who preached at court. An official description of the Dean's duties during Edward IV's reign stated unequivocally that 'the Deane assigneth all the sermons, and the persons'.[45] This control of the court pulpit seems to have survived until the later years of Henry VIII's reign, when a significant shift in responsibility occurred. Archbishop Cranmer's successful efforts to put Hugh Latimer on the court Lent rota in 1534 reveal that the Dean had responsibility for the list. After receiving the king's permission, Cranmer sent a letter to Dean of the Chapel Sampson 'to desire and require you . . . for to discharge the assignment already appointed, or hereafter to be', in favour of Latimer, and to require the original appointee '(if any such be) to be contented with the same'. Cranmer even went on to request 'that my old acquainted friend, master Shaxton . . . may be assigned likewise to preach the third Sunday in Lent before the king's grace'.[46] Sampson, a conservative, bowed to the king's pleasure, but let Cranmer know that he had completed the Lent list more

---

[42] For Chapel vacations, see *Old Cheque-Book*, 73.

[43] Compare the 1592 decree regarding Gentlemen Extraordinary of the Chapel and signed by the 'sayd companye, Chaplens and Gentlemen of her Majestes sayd Chappell' – the names subscribed being those only of choral members (*Old Cheque-Book*, 63). Similarly, Robert Greene and John Hottofte, styled 'chaplains in the chapel royal' in the patent rolls, were priests choral, not Chaplains in Ordinary (*CPR, Elizabeth*, vol. VII, nos. 201, 204; *Old Cheque-Book*, 2).

[44] Heylyn, *Cyprianus Anglicus* (1671), 158.

[45] *Liber Niger*, in *A Collection of Ordinances*, 49.

[46] Cranmer, *Miscellaneous Writings*, 309.

than 'two months ago', and registered his apprehensiveness about bringing such a radical to court.[47] Cranmer's interference in what Sampson as Chapel Dean clearly considered his responsibility is emblematic of the increase in royal control over preaching in both court and commonwealth under the Tudors.

Elizabeth was even content to let the post of Dean of the Chapel Royal fade into non-existence, but only after the Crown was securely placed on her head in Westminster Abbey on 15 January 1559. One of the greatest obstacles that Elizabeth and her advisors faced at her accession was the bench of Catholic bishops who almost blocked the religious reform bill in the Lords.[48] Even more urgently, however, the queen needed a bishop who was willing to Crown a heretical princess and to celebrate the coronation mass according to her Protestant taste. Elizabeth could not deprive sitting bishops single-handedly in order to appoint more amenable replacements. One of the few ecclesiastical appointments of any public significance the queen could legally make was the Dean of her Chapel Royal. Previous English kings had jealously guarded the Chapel Royal's statutory exemption from the authority of both the Pope and the Archbishop of Canterbury, and the royal deanery's independence suddenly became an even greater privilege. Within one week of her accession, Elizabeth dismissed the Marian incumbent, Bishop Thirlby of Ely, and appointed as her own Chapel Dean George Carew, a Marian conformist and Archdeacon of Exeter.[49] Elizabeth and her Council managed to convince only one bishop, Owen Oglethorp of Carlisle, to perform the actual coronation, thus securing the episcopal participation necessary to make it valid. However, even Oglethorp had recently defied Elizabeth's demands not to elevate the host at the consecration, and it was Dean Carew, using the slightly reformed ceremonies of the Chapel Royal, who celebrated the coronation mass.[50] The coronation, however, was the zenith of the Elizabethan office of Dean of the Chapel Royal. Carew subsequently received other benefices to hold *in commendam*, including the Deaneries of Windsor and Exeter. He did not have, as has been claimed, an Elizabethan successor in the household Chapel Royal; after his death in 1583 Elizabeth never appointed another Chapel Dean.[51] The daily duties of the Chapel's musical and operational functions had always been carried out by the Sub-Dean, who

---

[47] *LP*, vol. VII, 15–16.   [48] Jones, *Faith by Statute*, 72–81.

[49] *CSPS 1558–1567*, 6. For Carew, see also Joseph Welch, *The List of the Queen's Scholars of St Peters College, Westminster* (1852), 7.

[50] William P. Haugaard, 'The Coronation of Elizabeth I', *Journal of Ecclesiastical History* 19 (1968), 161–70.

[51] *DNB* retails the error that William Day (1529–96) succeeded Carey in the domestic chapel deanery in 1572; in fact he was appointed dean of the royal free chapel of St George, Windsor. See Thomas Rymer, *Foedera*, 17 vols. (1704–17), vol. XV, 708–9.

continued to run the Chapel with the Lord Chamberlain, instead of a Dean, as titular head and liaison with the queen.[52] Since the absence of a Dean did not interrupt the musical and liturgical functions of the Chapel, Elizabeth no doubt saw the vacancy as a simple way to cut household costs.

Significantly, Carew seems not to have been a keen preacher. His only known appearance in the court pulpit – on Ash Wednesday 1566 – came as a result of Parker's need to counter accusations that the Queen's own household Dean was 'altogether unlearned'. Arranging court sermons seems never to have been part of Carew's duties as Dean either. Rather, until the accession of James I, the Archbishop of Canterbury compiled the annual Lent list, while the Lord Chamberlain oversaw the appointment of royal chaplains and their routine Sunday and holy day rota. To begin with the Lent series, the earliest surviving evidence also suggests that the queen's principal secretary, Sir William Cecil, acted as overseer. In January 1566 Archbishop Parker wrote to Cecil that 'I am about to devise for preachers in Lent before the Queen's Majesty'. He asked the Secretary to determine whether Elizabeth would allow the inclusion of Alexander Nowell, Dean of St Paul's, who the previous Lent had offended the queen by preaching too roundly against crucifixes and the saints. On Shrove Tuesday, Parker was still relaying last-minute changes to Cecil. In 1570–1, when Lent began on 28 February, Parker reminded Cecil on 21 January to return an initial draft of the preachers' names, presumably with the Secretary's approval. A week later, Parker wrote again with changes, but complained that 'what will fall out . . . I know not, because they may alter their days', and so concluded that he would not send another copy until Cecil's 'pleasure shall be so to use it', perhaps after the list had been finished.[53] Perhaps not coincidentally, these two records of Cecil's direct involvement with court preaching coincide with moments of ecclesiastical crisis: the Vestiarian Controversy (1563–6) and moves to silence the Cambridge Puritan Thomas Cartwright (1570–1). No doubt Cecil was anxious to screen from the list any preachers who might voice Puritan sympathies *coram regina*.[54] After 1571, and during subsequent crises, Parker and his successors worked not with Cecil but with the Lord Chamberlain. This may suggest that Cecil's oversight was needed as a supplement to that of Elizabeth's first Lord Chamberlain, William Lord Howard of Effingham.

Thomas Radcliffe, Earl of Sussex, was appointed Lord Chamberlain in 1572. Radcliffe had served both Mary and Elizabeth as Lord Deputy of Ireland, and as Lord Lieutenant of the North he had secured high favour

---

[52] Baldwin, *Chapel Royal*, 248–9; *Old Cheque-Book*, 33–9.
[53] Matthew Parker, *The Correspondence of Matthew Parker*, ed. John Bruce and Thomas Thomason Perowne (Cambridge, 1853), 254, 260–1, 377–8.
[54] I owe these points to Simon Adams.

with Elizabeth for his efficient suppression of the Northern Rebellion in 1569–70. Parker wrote to Sussex on 9 January 1573 with the 'names of such preachers as may serve the Queen's Majesty this Lent' and the body of his letter makes it clear that Radcliffe was new to the job of Lent sermon coordinator. The first list was to be shown to the queen 'to know her pleasure, whom she will accept, and whom she will reject'. Parker kindly included 'in another paper' a list of alternates 'for that your lordship may have store of persons named to supply such rooms as her Highness shall mislike'. He also added a bit of wisdom no doubt gained from experience: 'Your lordship may think that I do this somewhat too soon, but I pray you consider that some of these may alter their rooms according to their business and health'.[55] Lenten appointments, then, were in the gift of the Archbishop, with the Lord Chamberlain acting as intermediary with the queen. The conclusion of Parker's letter – 'And when her Highness is resolved, if it please your lordship to signify her pleasure unto me, I shall do further accordingly' – makes clear that royal assent was the final step in appointing Lent preachers.

Having secured the sovereign's approval, the Lord Chamberlain sent the Lent list back across the Thames to Lambeth, where the Archbishop proceeded to 'do further accordingly', or commence the trying process of securing the appointees' attendance at the proper time. Some, especially younger men eager to make an appearance at court, gladly accepted. In the winter of 1564–5, Matthew Hutton (1529–1606), then Master of Pembroke Hall, and Regius Professor of Divinity at Cambridge, and later Bishop of Durham and Archbishop of York, acknowledged Parker's letter and promised 'that god willinge, I will not ffaile to make repaire to the court agai[n]st that day there'.[56] However, since many of the appointed preachers were elderly bishops who resided in their sees, the inconvenience of travel, poor health, and the bitter weather of an English Lent could wreak havoc with the best-laid plans of Archbishops and Chamberlains. So Richard Cox of Ely, although he fully intended 'to give myne attendance', warned that he might be late as he was 'not yet clere of these wyntrye & fennish morres'.[57] Finally, there were purely bureaucratic headaches. This March 1565 missive from Bishop Robert Horne of Winchester was probably enough to try even the mild Parker's patience:

i suppose your grace in your last letters doo mistake my daye of preaching: for in your former leters you appointed to me passion sonday & i wolde gladlye have had palme sondaye or rather good fridaye: wherevpon i have so apointed weightie & necessarie busines . . . in Hampshire on palme sondaye & all that weeke folowinge

55 Parker, *Correspondence*, 416.
56 CCCC MS 114, vol. II, 915.   57 CCCC MS 114, vol. I, 441.

. . . wherefor i praye your grace, i maye ether be all together dispensed w[ith]all, or else kepe passion sonday.[58]

Lord Chamberlain Sussex's trials in arranging the Lenten series also included negotiating two great *causes-célèbres* of the late 1570s: the sequestration of Elizabeth's second Archbishop of Canterbury, Edmund Grindal, and the furore over the queen's proposed marriage to the Catholic Duc d'Alençon. Grindal succeeded Parker at Canterbury early in 1576, and must have continued the seasonal archiepiscopal duty of arranging the Lent sermons, since he submitted to Sussex the expected preliminary list for the queen's approval in January 1577.[59] But by May of that same year, after his confrontation with Elizabeth over the Puritan 'prophesyings', the Archbishop was sequestered at Lambeth Palace by royal command. Grindal was initially allowed to appoint his own 'vicars general' to exercise his now defunct signatory authority, but on 20 January 1578 the queen and Council named their own appointees.[60] Grindal was allowed to continue to execute spiritual duties, such as the consecration of new bishops; however, he was not allowed to coordinate the Lent court sermons with Sussex. That duty, with several other administrative tasks, devolved instead upon Bishop of London, John Aylmer (1521–94), ally of the new royal favourite Sir Christopher Hatton, and a man who during his two-decade tenure in London earned a reputation as a scourge of Puritans and Catholics alike.[61] On 27 January 1578, with Lent only two weeks off, Aylmer wrote a letter to Sussex, despairing that two bishops 'signified vnto me that theie cannot come vppon the daies appointed for them to Preache by reason of Sicknes', and that he could not hope to complete the rota 'yf wee shuld put out Readman and Blage being twoe of the Archb. Chaplaines'.[62] William Redman and Thomas Blague were both chaplains to the disgraced Archbishop, and Redman, if not Blague, owed his preferment in the church to his archiepiscopal patron.[63] Aylmer and Sussex knew that Elizabeth probably would not want so much as to see two of Grindal's creations in her pulpit – she was known to carry pulpit grudges[64] – and might very well have anticipated untoward criticisms of the queen and pleas on Grindal's

[58] CCCC MS 114, vol. I, 435.   [59] BL MS Harley 6992, no. 34, fol. 69.

[60] Patrick Collinson, *Archbishop Grindal, 1519–1583: the Struggle for a Reformed Church* (Berkeley, Calif. 1979), 249–50.

[61] Collinson, *Archbishop Grindal*, 263, 268. For Aylmer, see Sir John Harington, *A Supplie or Addicion to the Catalogue of Bishops to the Yeare 1608*, ed. R. H. Miller (Potomac, Md., 1979), 46–50; and John Strype, *Historical Collections of the Life and Acts of . . . John Aylmer* (1701).

[62] BL MS Harley 6992, no. 46, fol. 92ͬ.

[63] Grindal lobbied both Burleigh and the queen for Redman's preferment to the Archdeaconry of Canterbury in 1576: *The Remains of Archbishop Grindal*, ed. William Nicholson (Cambridge, 1843), 360.

[64] See below, 76–99.

behalf from the pulpit should the two be allowed to preach. Whether a shortage of preachers in Lent 1578 forced Aylmer and Sussex to gamble with Redman and Blague, we do not know.[65]

The following Lent (1579) Sussex must have thought an even greater challenge. Elizabeth was on the brink of marriage with the French Catholic Duc d'Alençon. At court, Robert Dudley, Earl of Leicester, led the opposition to the proposed match, and certainly no pulpit could have sounded Leicester's opposition more directly to the queen than her own. But Sussex was in charge of the Lent series, and he was one of Leicester's inveterate political enemies and the leading proponent of the Alençon match. No doubt Sussex made every effort, as he and Aylmer had done the year before, to prevent open criticism of the queen's prerogative. But popular sentiment, and possibly Leicester's influence, overwhelmed any barriers that Sussex might have put in place. The Spanish ambassador wrote that 'in the sermons preached before the Queen they speak very violently about this marriage'. An unnamed preacher on the first Sunday in Lent 'said that marriages with foreigners would only result in ruin to the country' and proceeded to invoke the memory of how Queen Mary had 'married a foreigner, and caused the martyrdom of so many persons, who were burnt all over the country'. Before the sermon ended, Elizabeth stormed out. The ambassador, however, concluded his account of the sermon not with the queen's dramatic exit, but with this analysis: 'They are also attaching much importance to the fact that preachers are constantly saying this to the Queen and that she takes no steps, from which it may be inferred that they are inspired from high quarters.'[66] Although there was no shortage of anger at the proposed marriage, 'high quarters' might very well have been Leicester House.[67] In such circumstances not even the careful screening of preachers by the Lord Chamberlain could completely censor the court pulpit. Even Elizabeth's respected Whitgift could have trouble placing his chosen preachers at court. In 1592, he could only tentatively appoint royal chaplain William Tooker because 'some such as have interest in this matter' – presumably the queen – wished him out; and in 1593, Lord Chamberlain Hunsdon insisted on the deletion of two preachers' names, observing that the queen 'm[ar]veleth yo[ur] grace would putt them in'.[68]

---

[65] The Lent list for this year does not survive. Any displeasure on the queen's part, however, soon dissipated. Blague became the queen's chaplain as early as 1582, and Elizabeth elevated Redman to the bishopric of Norwich in 1594.

[66] *CSPS 1568–1579*, 658–9.

[67] For Leicester as a patron of moderate Puritanism, see Simon Adams, 'A Godly Peer? Leicester and the Puritans', *History Today* 40 (1990), 14–19.

[68] WAMB 15, fols. 8ʳ, 10ʳ (the two preachers' names in Hunsdon's letter are now heavily crossed out).

Sussex's inability to weed out the Lent rota preachers unsympathetic to the French marriage was due not only to the great unpopularity among the clergy of such a marriage, but to the fact that finding suitable preachers of any persuasion to fill the pulpit every Sunday, Wednesday, and Friday during Lent – twenty-one sermons in all – was a difficult task. As we shall see in the following chapter, the chapel royal or the Preaching Place could be hostile arenas and some preachers were willing to forgo chances for preferment to avoid it. But, even more generally, the surviving Lent lists, especially those from early in the reign, lend some supportive detail to the picture of the Elizabethan episcopate as rather tired, if not demoralized, and the number of well-educated clergy under them somewhat thin on the ground.[69] The preachers put on display during Lent at Elizabeth's court were significantly junior in both years and rank to those we will find at the court of her successor. The earliest surviving Elizabethan list is that for Lent, 1566.[70] Seven years after the Lent of the Elizabethan settlement when leading lights of the English Reformation had taken the court pulpit, Parker and Cecil could rally only four bishops – Grindal of London, Horne of Winchester, Guest of Rochester, and Scambler of Peterborough – four Deans, and four doctors of divinity without ecclesiastical dignities, leaving the fourteen remaining slots (including five supernumeraries) to young MAs (Masters of Arts). To be sure, those MAs included four archdeacons and some of the luminaries of the late Elizabethan church, among them Edmund Freke (successively Bishop of Rochester, Norwich, and Worcester), John Aylmer, and the future primate, John Whitgift, and most of them were soon to proceed to DD (Doctors of Divinity). By contrast, the rota for the last full Lent of King James's life (1624) contained seven bishops, seven deans, five doctors of divinity without dignities, and only one MA.[71] The 1566 list, with its paucity of church dignitaries and slight episcopal presence, captures the personnel crisis of the fledgling Elizabethan church, and suggests a reason other than the queen's distaste for clergy for their low profile at her court.[72]

The survival of a near-continuous run of Lent lists for the years 1584–1603 also reveals important patterns of how places were assigned to

---

[69] Patrick Collinson, *The Religion of Protestants: the Church in English Society 1559–1625* (Oxford, 1982), 35–7, 39–42, 94.

[70] Printed in John Strype, *Life and Acts of Matthew Parker* (1711), appendix, 75.

[71] WAMB 15, fol. 45ᵛ. The lone MA was the king's chaplain George Warburton (1580–1641), later DD (1636), and Dean of Gloucester and of Wells (1631).

[72] For the different status of clerics at the courts of Elizabeth and James, see Kenneth Fincham, *Prelate as Pastor: The Episcopate of James I* (Oxford, 1990), 35–6. For the socio-economic status of the Elizabethan bench, see Felicity Heal, *Of Prelates and Princes: a Study of the Economic and Social Position of the Tudor Episcopate* (Cambridge, 1980), chs. 9 – 11.

preachers.[73] Basically, in keeping with Henrician practice, Sunday sermons in Lent were taken by bishops. Although no complete lists survive, Henry Machyn's careful monitoring of the Lent court sermons 1559–62 shows that, almost without fail, a lord bishop marked the solemnity of the Lord's day, while weekdays were taken by preachers of lesser rank.[74] In addition, certain days in Lent became associated with particular preachers and ecclesiastical offices. From 1561–92, a full thirty-one years, the Lent series was begun on Ash Wednesday by the sage reformer and Dean of St Paul's, Alexander Nowell (1507?–1602).[75] Favourite preachers, some of them men who, because they never committed their sermons to print, have now faded into near-obscurity, regularly appeared several times in a single Lent. In 1586, for example, two preachers highly favoured by the queen, Thomas Neville (*ob.* 1615) and Thomas Dove (1555–1630), both then Cambridge MAs, preached three times a piece.[76] More importantly, during the course of Elizabeth's reign, sermons for the most solemn days on the rota – Palm Sunday, Good Friday, and Easter – became associated with the office of Lord High Almoner. The withering away of the Chapel Royal Deanery under Elizabeth completed a process that had begun with the Reformation of divorcing prelacy from court and secular offices. With the notable exception of Whitgift's appointment to the Privy Council in 1586, bishops no longer sat on the Council board, did not carry the privy seal, or serve as Lord Chancellors, and did not represent the Crown on embassies; even episcopal palaces in the capital were alienated to lay peers. The last vestige of a court dignity – other than appearing in its pulpits – that remained the prerogative of bishops was the royal almonership.[77] Supported by a Sub-Almoner and a small staff, the Almoner was responsible for distributing royal charity, both left-overs from the court tables, and gifts of money. Most prominently, the Almoner assisted the queen at the Royal Maundy, the ritual distribution of gifts to selected poor men or women on Thursday in Holy Week.[78] Given the absence of a Chapel Dean at Elizabeth's court,

[73] WAMB 15, fols. 13–31; only 1596 is missing.
[74] *Diary of Henry Machyn*, ed. Nichols, 189–90, 227–30, 251–3, 276–9. For his court sermon entries, see the 'Calendar' on the disk supplement. Only the 1566 Lent list reprinted by Strype departs from the bishop-on-Sunday rule.
[75] Machyn, *Diary*, ed. Nichols, 251, 276; Parker, *Correspondence*, 235, 254; WAMB 15, fols. 13ʳ–13ᵛ, 14–20.
[76] WAMB 15, fol. 14. Neville, a client of Whitgift, was successively Dean of Peterborough (1590) and Canterbury (1597), and Master of Trinity College, Cambridge (1593). Dove was successively Dean of Norwich (1589) and Bishop of Peterborough (1601).
[77] Heal, *Of Prelates and Princes*, 278.
[78] David Loades, *The Tudor Court* (1986), 43–4; payments to the Almoner are annual entries in the Elizabethan and Jacobean accounts of the Treasurer of the Chamber (PRO E351/541–543). For the Royal Maundy, see John Nichols, *The Progresses and Public Processions of Queen Elizabeth*, 3 vols. (1823), vol. I, 325–7; and Baldwin, *Chapel Royal*, 322, 378.

the Almoner was the highest-ranking cleric in the royal household and therefore appropriate as the household's preacher on holy days. So, beginning with the earliest of the Lent lists in the surviving series, that for 1584, and thereafter through the reign almost without exception, we find the queen's Almoners preaching on Palm Sunday and Easter.[79] In terms of rank on the bench, Elizabeth's Almoners do not compose a 'particularly prepossessing list', and indeed they held minor sees such as Rochester, Bristol, and Chichester.[80] If these men were appointed for their ability to serve the court as red-letter day preachers and trustees for the queen's charities – duties requiring frequent attendance at Whitehall – the virtual attachment of the post to the nearby see of Rochester early in the reign and its presentation to the favoured court preachers Fletcher and Watson at its end not only make perfect sense, but make clear that this was one clerical appointment that Elizabeth took seriously. The importance of preaching for the post is further suggested by the prominence of future incumbents in the Lent lists prior to their appointment. Near the end of Almoner John Piers's life, his successor in the almonership, Richard Fletcher, obviously stood out with two and sometimes three slots of his own; and three years before Anthony Watson succeeded Fletcher in 1595, he had assumed Alexander Nowell's prominent Ash Wednesday position as well as others during mid-Lent.[81] Several preachers not Almoners, such as Nowell, retained the same day for many years, presumably out of either routine, or as recognition of a special facility with the theme or tone demanded by the day; Thomas Dove, for example, was given every Good Friday from 1590–1601.[82] The oft-noted series of sermons that Lancelot Andrewes preached to James's court on holy days, then, were not the remarkable phenomena they have been taken to be. By virtue of his sermons' survival, we do have his great Jacobean series for Christmas and Easter, but, had the threads of bibliographical fate been cut another way, we might have instead Alexander Nowell's Elizabethan series for Ash Wednesday or Thomas Dove's for Good Friday.

The discussion of the appointment of preachers at Elizabeth's court has

[79] The Elizabethan Almoners and the dates they held the office, based on payments to them in the Chamber Accounts (PRO E351/541–3), were William Bill, as Dean of Westminster (1558–61); Edmund Guest, as Bishop of Rochester (1562–72); Edmund Freke, as Bishop of Rochester (1572–6); John Piers, as Bishop of Rochester and Salisbury (1576–89); Richard Fletcher, as Bishop of Bristol and Worcester (1590–5); and Anthony Watson as Bishop of Chichester (1595–1606).

[80] Heal, *Of Prelates and Princes*, 278. Heal includes George Underhill, Bishop of Oxford from 1589–92, among her list of Elizabethan almoners; however, he does not appear as such in the Chamber accounts.

[81] WAMB 15, fols. 13–17, 21–3.

[82] WAMB 15, fols. 19–29. In 1602, having been elevated to the bishopric of Peterborough, Dove moved to a bishop's Sunday slot (fol. 30).

so far focused on the annual Lent series. To address the other regular occasions for sermons and the supply of preachers for them we must consider first the place of the sermon in the reformed liturgy, and then address the role of the Lord Chamberlain. Elizabeth's 1559 *Book of Common Prayer* provided collects and lessons for holy communion to be celebrated every Sunday and holy day of the year, and the rubrics for that service specify that after the Creed there should follow a 'sermon, homily, or exhortation'.[83] But it is an anonymous preacher who gives us the most accurate summary of the Elizabethan court's religious routine in his condemnation of its '*negligence*' in attending 'the monthly *sacrament[es]*, & the *weekly sermons*, & the *dayly prayers*'.[84] In lieu of weekly communion, Elizabeth's (and James's) court heard the abbreviated service of 'ante-communion' on all but one Sunday of each month. This followed the order of holy communion through the Psalms, lessons, Gospel, prayers, and Creed, and concluded with the prayer for 'Christ's Church militant here in earth' that immediately preceded the Eucharistic portion of the service. When preceded by matins and the litany, this was the usual Sunday order of service in most parish churches in Elizabethan and Stuart England.[85] The queen and her court attended chapel in the late morning immediately before dinner. The German traveller Paul Hentzner noted that the 1598 Sunday service he heard at Greenwich 'scarcely exceeded half-an-hour'.[86] And a more detailed account by a Venetian ambassador in 1575 makes clear that the ferial Sunday order was ante-communion without sermon. The queen processed to the household chapel at Windsor,

> where she remained about twenty minutes until the service there ended. This service consisted, first of all, of certain Psalms chanted in English by a double chorus of some thirty singers. A single voice next chanted the Epistle; after this another voice chanted the Gospel, and then all voices together chanted the Belief [Creed]. This concluded the service, and we with the rest then returned into the presence chamber to see the Queen once more.[87]

It needs to be remembered that sermons in the context of the medieval mass – *inter missarum solemnia* – were probably rare. Scholarship on this point varies, but the general consensus favours the view that late medieval sermons, especially those preached in more privileged social settings, evolved into free-standing events in their own right, preceded by a lengthy

---

83 *The Book of Common Prayer 1559: the Elizabethan Prayer Book*, ed. John Booty (Washington, D.C., 1976), 251.

84 BL MS Add 41499a, fol. 21ᵛ.

85 John Harper, *The Forms and Orders of Western Liturgy from the Tenth to the Eighteenth Century* (Oxford, 1991), 180–1. *Book of Common Prayer*, ed. Booty, 247–54.

86 William Brenchley Rye, ed., *England as Seen by Foreigners in the Days of Elizabeth and James the First* (1865), 105.

87 *CSPV 1558–1580*, 525.

prayer, and usually delivered in the afternoon.[88] Here lies another link between pre- and post-Reformation liturgical practice in England, for the Elizabethan (and Stuart) court Lent series followed precisely this model.[89] The sermon as an exercise severed from service explains the existence of early modern preachers' extensive 'prayers before sermon,' prayers that would be inappropriate in the context of a prayerbook service because of their length and repetition of petitions already contained in the liturgies.[90] In addition, the removal of the sermon from the context of the service also suggests an explanation for why the majority of court sermons do not take as their texts the lessons or Gospel appointed for the day.[91]

Even Sunday and communion-day sermons seem to have been severed somewhat from the context of divine service, despite the prayerbook rubric calling for their place in the midst of the communion rite. Tobie Matthew noted in his sermon diary that on Sunday, 3 November 1594, he preached to the Court at Richmond 'in Coena Domini', which suggests that his sermon might have been preached at the time appointed for communion or that he simply preached on a day when the Lord's Supper was kept.[92] Lancelot Andrewes, however, insisted that sermons should not intrude upon the service of communion and preferred them, at least in theory, to be preached immediately after the Litany (said every Sunday after morning prayer) and before the communion.[93] This was certainly the form observed on Easter 1593, when, according to Sub-Dean Anthony Anderson's narrative account, the queen came down from the royal closet into her traverse near the altar 'after the Holy Gospell was redd', to receive the communion celebrated by her Almoner, Bishop Fletcher. However, the account makes clear that no sermon was preached between the time when the queen entered her traverse and her departure from the chapel at the end of the service. But we also know from the Lent lists that Fletcher preached the Easter sermon that year before the queen – either before the communion

---

[88] Owst, *Preaching in Medieval England* (Cambridge, 1926), 145, and Harper, *Forms and Orders*, 111–12, cite the routine separation of sermon from service. More recently, Spencer, *English Preaching*, 71, has argued the contrary.

[89] For the time of the sermons, compare Machyn's diary entry for 24 March 1559, when he heard a sermon at court, 'and at v of the cloke yt ended; and contenentt her chapell whent to evy[ning song] . . . and after done a goodly anteme song' (*Diary*, 1848, 229). Peter Heylyn, writing a century later, noted that the Lent sermons were preached 'in the afternoon' 'according to the ancient custom' (*Cyprianus Anglicus*, 1671, 126).

[90] See P. J. Klemp, ed., 'Lancelot Andrewes' "Prayer Before Sermon": a Parallel Text Edition', *Bodleian Library Record* vol. XI, no. 5 (1984), 300–19.

[91] For the Biblical texts of the court sermons, see supplement on disk.

[92] YML Add MS 17, 43.

[93] Andrewes, 'Notes on the Book of Common Prayer', in *The Works of Lancelot Andrewes*, 11 vols., ed. J. P. Wilson and James Bliss (Oxford, 1841–54), vol. XI, 150–1.

service or, like Lent sermons, in the afternoon.[94] More evidence from the Jacobean period, such as Hampshire MP Sir Robert Paulet's diary note that on Palm Sunday morning 1610 he heard a sermon in the chapel and 'after this was a comunion', confirms the supposition that the sermon fell outside – if only slightly outside – the reformed ideal more familiar today of incorporation within a single liturgical service.[95]

Who, then, appointed preachers for routine Sunday sermons? The Lord Chamberlain's involvement with the arrangement of the Lent rota did not represent his only, or indeed his chief, dealings with the court pulpit. As the supervisor of all staff that served above stairs, he had always had authority over the sovereign's chaplains, and it was this group of clerics who were responsible for filling the pulpit on a regular basis. The chaplains were a clerical group at court wholly distinct from the priests and clerks of the Chapel Royal. They were not in fact a static body, but a select group beneficed elsewhere, and appointed to attend on a monthly rota. In the broadest sense a court chaplain was to serve the daily spiritual needs of the sovereign and to be available as a counsellor and example to members of the household. Edward IV provided bouge of court, or court-rations, for four chaplains monthly and required two to take their meals in the king's chamber, and the other two in the hall, thus distributing their presence evenly through the major divisions of the household.[96] At Elizabeth's court, however, the chaplain's most prominent duty was to preach to the household or the queen during his month in attendance.

Whereas sermons for the Lent series and major feast days were arranged by special invitation, routine sermons were supplied by this fixed staff of chaplains. Like most other court departments, the chaplaincy had regular full appointees, the Chaplains in Ordinary, and supernumerary Chaplains Extraordinary. The number of ordinary chaplains attending monthly in Elizabeth's time remains unclear. One complete list of Elizabethan chaplains survives, dated 19 February 1602, and shows twenty-five 'Chaplens in Ordinarie' and nineteen 'Chaplens Extraordinarie'.[97] James I, like Edward IV, was served by at least four each month. But did Elizabeth make do with two? John Manningham recorded that at her death two ordinary chaplains attended. And Henry Isaacson, Lancelot Andrewes's amanuensis and biographer, claimed that when Andrewes was appointed Chaplain in Ordinary in 1589, 'there were then but twelve', a surprisingly small

[94] Rimbault, ed., *Cheque-Book*, 150–1; WAMB 15, fol. 22. Anderson's account mentions Fletcher as the celebrant at the communion.

[95] Hampshire Record Office 44MGA/F6 (Jervoise MSS), fol. 6ʳ. I am grateful to Dr Eric Lindquist for sharing a portion of his transcript. For the Jacobean service-sermon relationship, see below, 155–67.

[96] *Liber Niger*, in *A Collection of Ordinances and Regulations*, 35.

[97] WAMB 15, fol. 2.

number, which, unless supplied by extraordinary chaplains, would have required two months' annual service per pair.[98] Whatever their number, the ordinary chaplains were an élite group of men distinguished as university divines, able preachers, and members of the ecclesiastical hierarchy. Of the twenty-five in the 1602 list, eighteen were doctors of divinity, and eight of those were deans. The nineteen extraordinary chaplains were, by contrast, a much more junior assemblage of seven doctors and twelve masters or bachelors, with only one holding any ecclesiastical dignity greater than a prebend. The conspicuous absence of bishops from both lists suggests that upon elevation to the episcopal bench, divines ceased to serve as chaplains, an inference supported by Lord Chamberlain Hunsdon's complaint in 1598 that because *'diverse of Her Majesties Chaplaines have bin advanced to sundrie . . . Preferments'*, they *'have and do discontinue their Attendance at the Court'*.[99] Episcopal presence in the court pulpit, then, was by special, rather than routine, appointment, and reserved for public or solemn occasions, namely Sundays in Lent and feast days.

The Lord Chamberlain's authority in the selection of the queen's Chaplains in Ordinary, and the importance of preaching as a criterion for the appointment, is well illustrated by the career of Dr Richard Field (1561–1616), a divine valued by both Elizabeth and James, and a noted ecclesiastical historian. Early in September 1598, Lord Chamberlain Hunsdon wrote to Field that, based on the recommendation of *'such as seem to know you'*, Field was *'to make your Repair to Court by the 23. Day of this Instant Month . . . at what time, I wish that you will be readie to Preach in that Place'*. From this sermon *cum* audition, or in the Lord Chamberlain's terms, *'better Knowledge of your Sufficiencie'*, Field would later *'understand Her Majesties farther Pleasure for your Approbation and Preferment to Her Service'*. Field duly preached before Elizabeth, and *'being approved of'*, was sworn Chaplain in Ordinary by the Lord Chamberlain before he left the court.[100] A court chaplaincy was an honour coveted by any who had serious designs on higher preferment in the church. First, the appointment carried with it the lucrative statutory right to hold up to three livings *in commendam*.[101] This right, however, put a royal stamp of approval not only on pluralism but also on non-residency, making royal chaplains a target of more progressive reformers.

Certainly, resentment of pampered non-preaching chaplains inspired

---

[98] *The Diary of John Manningham of the Middle Temple, 1602–1603*, ed. Robert Parker Sorlein (Hanover, N.H., 1976), 211; Andrewes, *Works*, XI, viii.

[99] Nathaniel Field, *Some Short Memorials Concerning the Life of that Reverend Divine Doctor Richard Field* (1716–17), 7–8.

[100] Field, *Short Memorials*, 7–8.

[101] Stat. 21 Hen. VIII, c.13, cited in R. C. Bald, *John Donne: a Life* (Oxford, 1970), 307.

Bishop Hooper's exhortations for Edward VI to hear weekly sermons at court, as well as Edward's own decision to make four royal chaplains into rural evangelists. In the Elizabethan Convocation of 1563, Bishop Alley's proposed rules for clerical discipline allowed the queen's chaplains to be non-resident only during the time of their attendance at court, but this stipulation was quietly dropped.[102] As late as 1586, Puritan petitions to Parliament complained that royal chaplaincies bred complacency; the consciences of chaplains and other 'double or treble beneficed men' had been 'seared up from tender remorse' for the spiritual needs of those in their parochial cures 'by reason of attendance in princes courts, or in other noble men and prelats services'. In the same year, another petitioner complained that, although he did not question that 'her most excellent Matie, her highnes court and household should be served of the best of that calling', too many ministers held royal chaplaincies and used the 'pretence of her Maties service to the depriving of us of such meanes as are needfull for the salvation of our soules'. If the queen would only pay her chaplains for services rendered, what this petitioner termed 'competent pentions for their convenient maintenance out of her Maties cofers and treasurie', rather than calling them away from the cures which they were already paid to serve, the queen and her church would be better served.[103]

Though a chaplaincy at court may have removed a minister from his parish, it nevertheless gave him unprecedented access to, or at least exposure in front of, a queen who was not otherwise generous of her time and attention to churchmen. Recent historians have established the virtual necessity of first holding a royal chaplaincy before elevation to the Jacobean and Caroline bench of bishops, and evidence suggests that a royal chaplaincy, or even a good sermon at court, was at least considered a help up on to the Elizabethan bench.[104] When Griffith Lewis wrote to Sir Robert Cecil in 1601 to beg the see of Llandaff, he complained that he had dutifully served the queen as ordinary chaplain 'these 17 years . . . in all which time I never received any promotion but only the poor deanery of Gloucester'.[105] And in June of the same year Whitgift wrote to Cecil to further the suit of Robert Humstone for the Irish see of Down and Connor. Among his qualifications, Whitgift noted not only Humstone's recommendations from other patrons, but that 'I my selfe allso heard him preach yesterday at the *Cowrte* . . . and do iudge him thereby to be worthie of the

---

[102] William P. Haugaard, *Elizabeth and the English Reformation* (Cambridge, 1968), 177–8, 351.

[103] *The Second Parte of a Register . . . Intended for Publication by the Puritans about 1593*, 2 vols., ed. Albert Peel (Cambridge, 1915), vol. II, 11, 78–9.

[104] Fincham, *Prelate as Pastor*, 24, 305–6; Julian Davies, *The Caroline Captivity of the Church: Charles I and the Remoulding of Anglicanism* (Oxford, 1992), 39–42.

[105] *HMC Salisbury* XI, 20–1.

Commendac[i]on given vnto him'. Humstone was duly nominated to the see.[106] Accordingly, patrons sought chaplaincies for their clients with some determination. A full month before Elizabeth was crowned, the Earl of Westmoreland petitioned Cecil for his kinsman, George Neville (1509–67), Marian Archdeacon of Carlisle, 'to be one of the Quenes Ma^tes chaplins ordenarye', and vouched not only for the candidate's 'honeste co[n]versa-c[i]on' but also his willingness 'to set fourthe in his Cures and elles wheare, all suche good & vertuous doctrine, as by the quene her highnes Authoritie, shalbe frome time to time set forthe'.[107] At the reign's end, when Whitgift wrote on behalf of his own chaplain, William Barlow, he reminded Cecil that he had 'divers tymes moved that Dr barloe might be admitted her Maties Chaplaine' but saw that 'some that have lesse deserved, and are not so worthye, have bene admitted w^t lesse suet'.[108] But, whether recruited by the Lord Chamberlain or recommended by the Archbishop, a preacher at Elizabeth's court had to please his royal mistress, and the rigours of that demand will concern us next.

CORAM REGINA: PREACHING BEFORE ELIZABETH I

Perhaps the greatest obstacle confronting a preacher in one of Elizabeth's pulpits was the queen's own attitude to sermons and sermon-going. Unlike her half-brother and her successor, Elizabeth did not consider frequent attendance at preaching necessary either for herself or for her subjects. The fact that she showed no great commitment to a preaching ministry at court after the returned exiles had served their political purpose during the Lenten Parliament of 1559 was distressing to those who had hoped for the consummation of Reformation under Elizabeth. In January 1560, Thomas Sampson, a celebrated Edwardine preacher and Marian exile, wrote to Peter Martyr asking how he could possibly serve in the English church not only while a crucifix and candles adorned the queen's chapel, but when – *horribile dictu* – the Lord's supper was celebrated there 'without any sermon'. Given this state of affairs, he cried, 'Oh! my father, what can I hope for, when the ministry of the word is banished from court?'[109] As we have seen in the previous chapter, the queen often heard service with no sermon on ferial Sundays, a practice that regressed from Edward's re-

---

[106] Cecil MSS, Hatfield House, vol. LXXXVI, art. 86 (calendared in *HMC Salisbury*, vol. XI, 220); *CSPI 1600–01*, 300, 360.

[107] PRO SP 12/1/36.

[108] Cecil MSS, Hatfield House, vol. LXXXVI, no. 95 (calendared in *HMC Salisbury*, vol. XI, 232). Barlow (*obit.* 1613) appears on the 1602 list of royal chaplains.

[109] *The Zurich Letters* 2 vols., ed. Hastings Robinson (Cambridge, 1842, 1845) vol. I, 63.

forming zeal and that reflected the queen's own liturgical and prayer-centred piety.

William Camden provides the best contemporary description of Elizabeth's churchmanship. In addition to private prayers in her privy closet, 'the first thing after she rose', the queen 'attended the publick Service at her own Chappel, at the appointed Times, and always on *Sundays* and *Holy-days*'. Of her attendance at sermons Camden says only that she 'used to frequent the *Lent-Sermons* dress'd in Mourning, as the gravest and most primitive Habit'. But even more tellingly, he adds that 'she would often mention what she had read of her Predecessor *Henry* III. "That he had much rather put up an humble devout Petition to God himself, than hear the finest Harangues about him, from the Lips of others."'[110] And preaching? Perhaps the most infamous measure of the queen's attitude to pulpit evangelism was her suppression of the 'prophesyings', those training sessions for lesser-educated ministers that, in some settings, bred a Puritanism perceived to threaten both episcopacy and the royal supremacy. After Archbishop Grindal's refusal to restrain the exercises in 1576 – stunned that his sovereign could consider three or four preachers per county sufficient – Elizabeth suppressed both the prophesyings and Grindal.[111] Furthermore, the queen who was willing to restrain preaching in the shires was willing to do so in her own court too. If on some Sundays she heard no sermon at all, she also had no qualms about cutting short sermons that were already underway. In 1599 a Swiss traveller watched at Nonesuch while Elizabeth listened to a preacher, but 'not for long however'; the day being 'warm and late', she instructed an attendant to 'sign to the preacher to draw to a close, as the time was going on, which straightway happened'.[112] Elizabeth gave no visible signs in her own household of heeding the impassioned pleas from the leaders of her church for an increase in preaching. The court sermon rotas remained largely unchanged from Mary's days, with sermons on some Sundays and holy days and thrice weekly during Lent. On many occasions what the godly scorned as the 'bare reading of Scripture' and, still worse, choral settings of the prayerbook service and anthems, constituted the whole of God's worship in the chapels royal. So for men like the anonymous preacher who

---

[110] William Camden, *The History of Queen Elizabeth* in *A Complete History of England*, 3 vols. (1706), vol. II, 371. Some significance has been attached to the queen's collection of 'private prayers'. See William P. Haugaard, 'Elizabeth Tudor's Book of Devotions: a Neglected Clue to the Queen's Life and Character', *Sixteenth Century Studies Journal* 12(2) (1981), 103; but see Patrick Collinson, 'Windows in a Woman's Soul: Questions about the Religion of Queen Elizabeth I', in *Elizabethan Essays* (1992), 87–118.

[111] Patrick Collinson, 'The Elizabethan Church and the New Religion', in Christopher Haigh, ed., *Reign of Elizabeth* (Athens, Ga., 1987), 181; and *Archbishop Grindal*, 233–76.

[112] Clare Williams, ed., *Thomas Platter's Travels in England 1599* (1937), 192–3.

told the queen and court that the power of the keys was neither priestly absolution nor 'the bare publishing and hearing of the words', but 'the worde of God preached', preaching to Elizabeth was by no means preaching to the converted.[113]

Given Elizabeth's natural disinclination towards sermon-hearing, she and her court earned a reputation as a demanding auditory that required sermons of a distinct style and nature. First and foremost, court sermons had to be short. As Thomas Drant epigrammatically put it at Windsor in 1570, 'our scantling to preach in the Court is a most short scantling'.[114] Archbishop of York Edwin Sandys began one of his sermons before the queen with the acknowledgment, 'But I minde breuitie, because I knowe before whom I speake. Fewe woords will be sufficient for the wise.'[115] Most surviving sermons could have been delivered easily within the space of an hour. More important even than length was the preacher's demeanour in the pulpit. A 1571 letter from Archbishop Parker to Cecil makes clear how vigilant the keepers of the queen's sermon rotas had to be to provide suitable preachers. Parker, then in the process of compiling that year's Lent list, wrote that John Bullingham had that day preached before him in his chapel at Lambeth. Although Parker was sure Bullingham was 'an honest true-meaning man', after hearing him preach he was convinced that he had unwisely acted upon others' recommendations by having once preferred Bullingham to preach before the queen: 'I intend hereafter not to do so again', Parker concluded. Why? 'I would her Highness had the best', the Archbishop explained, and in Bullingham 'I perceive neither *pronunciationem aulicam* nor *ingenium aulicum*; not meet for the court'. The unfortunate preacher was therewith pulled from the Lent list, and replaced by another.

'Courtly delivery' and a 'courtly wit' – degrees of sophistication in both elocution and invention – were therefore minimum expectations that another early Elizabethan preacher, James Calfhill, failed to meet. In July 1564, scholar–lawyer Dr Walter Haddon informed Parker of a sermon by Calfhill (1530?–70), Lady Margaret Professor of Divinity at Oxford, that was so shrill that it gave offence in every part and pained Haddon even to recall it. We have no indication of the matter of Calfhill's sermon, for it was the manner of its delivery, evidently a brazen challenge directed at the queen herself, that offended. 'More moderation is required in the Queen's presence', Haddon lamented, 'more reverence, more shamefacedness.' Calf-

[113] Anon., *A Godlye Sermon: Preached before the Queenes most Excellent Maiestie* (1585), 88.

[114] Thomas Drant, *Two Sermons Preached. the One at S. Maries Spittle . . . the other at the Court at Windsor* (1570), sig. Ii^v.

[115] Edwin Sandys, *Sermons Made by the most reuerend Father in God, Edwin, Archbishop of Yorke* (1585), 124; *The Sermons of Edwin Sandys*, ed. John Ayre (Cambridge, 1841), 144.

hill had failed to observe the decorum demanded by the dignity of the Court – '*quas illius theatri celebritas postulat*'. Jeremiads like Calfhill's would not only insult the queen and court; as Haddon put it, unless preachers brought a more calming spirit with them into the court pulpit their rashness would only make the 'damned religion' of Rome more attractive.[116]

Although Elizabeth was no obsessive sermon-goer, indeed perhaps because of that, she seems to have nurtured a few select preachers as personal favourites. We have already seen this reflected in the appointment of preachers such as Thomas Dove and Alexander Nowell to multiple appearances in the Lent lists and the preferment of men such as Richard Fletcher and Anthony Watson to the office of Lord High Almoner. The question of what pleased the queen about these men and their sermons is worth pursuing, and can be reconstructed in some further detail through contemporary testimonies of who her favourite preachers were and, in some cases, their extant court sermons.

Sir John Harington attested to the queen's high esteem for Thomas Dove's preaching. Although no sermons by him survive, Harington's estimate of Dove's court preaching tells us something about the rhetorical style preferred by the queen. Harington refuted the Puritan proposition that denied that 'Rhetoricall figures and tropes, and other artificiall ornaments of speach taken from prophane authors, as sentences, Adages, and such like, might be vsed in Sermons' by citing Elizabeth's love for Dove's sermons, which were, he said, 'as well attended and adorned' with the 'tropes and figures' as 'anie of his predecessors'. When Elizabeth first heard him, Harington says, 'she thought the holy ghost was discended againe in this Doue'.[117] Even among the more godly preachers who came to court, the flowers of rhetoric appear. Thomas Drant, although he gave 'these tender courtlinges' a severe drubbing at Windsor in 1570, did so with style. His choice and application of text was itself a bit of courtly *sprezzatura*: Genesis 2:25 – 'They were bothe naked, *Adam* and *Eue*, and blushed not' – afforded disquisitions on mortality, the necessity for military preparedness (a nation not being caught with its pants down, as it were), and the abuse of apparel. Rhetorical devices like anaphora and alliteration ('For some one stroke, at some one time, to some one person, from the princes hand, doth let many thousandes of buffets, and bloes'), a poet's facility with metaphor ('*Xerxes* that made the sea land with ships'), and even chiming puns ('I would haue thee wholy holy') animated the sermon and sweetened an

---

[116] Parker, *Correspondence*, 378, 218–19 (author's translation). Haddon's concluding words were, 'Nisi mansuetiores spiritus posthac concionatores ad aulum attulerint, metuo ne multum ex eorum temeritate damni religio sit acceptura'.

[117] Harington, *A Supplie or Addicion*, 147–8.

otherwise bitter pill.[118] The most extreme form of stylish prose, John Lyly's painfully ornamented and balanced 'Euphuism', which enjoyed a vogue among courtiers in the middle of the reign, also sounded from the court pulpit, although briefly.[119] One HB's (Hugh Broughton's) *Moriemini*, a sermon preached *c.* 1580, turned Lyly's passion for rhetorical schemes and tropes to the use of godly admonition:

For, that euerie prentise should prate of Princes, and euerie Cobler seeme a Counsellor, and euerie Iack Straw deuise a new law, and euerie medling mate mislike the whole state, is neither commendable by the word of God, nor tollerable in a Christian common-wealth.[120]

Not every flourish, however, was for pleasure. In the hands of some preachers, rhetorical ornament could produce powerful, dramatic oratory that advanced the preacher's argument. William James (1542–1617), chaplain to Leicester and successively Dean and Bishop of Durham, preached and printed the reign's most memorable court sermon against church papistry by animating Edwardine admonition with rhetorical elaboration and a clever manipulation of the relationship between orator and auditory. The cadences and tropes of ornamented prose, as well as the clever aphorisms, played their part throughout: conforming Catholics 'mingle Christ and Belial, the Church of God and Idols, the Gospell and popery, religio[n] and mockery'; these 'playne Herodians' alliteratively 'grunt and grone at the preaching of the Gospell'; and, as the preacher concluded, these 'Bladders puffed vppe with winde, are good for nothing but to make footballes'.[121] Having established the nefariousness of these hidden adversaries, James seized the opportunity to challenge them directly as they sat in the chapel stalls. In an indignant direct address, the preacher thundered out repeated challenges to court papists, demanding, 'Answer me O ye Samaritanes.' Then, employing the rhetorical device of *rogatio*, he transformed his sermon into a dramatic dialogue between himself and a courtier sympathetic to his Catholic-minded fellows. Literally interrupting his own invective, James, taking the first person, anticipated and gave voice to the objections many must have wanted to make: 'But O Sir, it is for their conscience, be good to them, shew mercy', 'But he is my friend', 'O but he hath done me good.' Having appropriated the possible objections to his

---

[118] Drant, *Two sermons*, sig. Kv^v, Ij^r, Ivij^v, Iij^v, Lij^r.

[119] For Lyly's prose romances, see *Euphues. The Anatomy of Wit* (1578) and *Euphues and His England* (1580), and their vogue, see C. S. Lewis, *English Literature in the Sixteenth Century* (Oxford, 1954), 312–17. For Euphuism in sermon prose, see J. W. Blench, *Preaching in England in the Late Fifteenth and Sixteenth Centuries* (Oxford, 1964), 192–202.

[120] H. B. [Hugh Broughton?], *Moriemini: A Verie Profitable Sermon Preached before her Maiestie at the Court* (1593), 7.

[121] William James, *A Sermon Preached before the Queenes Maiestie* (1578), sigs. Biiij^v, Bv^v.

thesis, the preacher was of course able to rebut these objections with his own refrain, 'But answere me O ye English Samaritanes, O ye recusantes that dishonour God ... shal a strange proud Italian Priest withdrawe you?', 'O ye Samaritanes, seeke the Lord while he may be founde.'[122] Sermons, even those of admonition, were performance pieces, and the court expected virtuosity from its preachers – *pronuntiationem aulicam, ingenium aulicum*. Understanding this, we can appreciate the warmth and degree of approbation in John Chamberlain's brief remark that Richard Eedes 'was very well liked in court for his sermon this Lent which they say was all needle-worke'.[123] One year later, James I would be similarly impressed with the verbal finery of the preachers who met him in the English court.

If Archbishop Parker knew which preachers would not satisfy the queen, he also knew which ones would. When Richard Curteys (1532?–82), Bishop of Chichester, was suggested as a likely candidate for the archbishopric of York in 1569, Parker did not approve, citing his desire to have Curteys 'nigher to serve the court' and his fear of having too many 'mean chaplains to be toward the prince'.[124] Curteys was noted for his sermons, having been appointed preacher to both the University of Cambridge and his own St John's College, as well as chaplain to Archbishop Parker and the queen.[125] In the epistle to the reader prefixed to the first of Curteys's sermons to appear in print, one Thomas Browne said that he set out the sermon after hearing that it was especially liked by the queen among the many 'notable Sermons preached this Lent'. In fact, she 'commended most graciously that sermon ... so much that some noble Peeres, and many other desired a copie of the same'. Curteys's sermons displayed the qualities that Parker summed up as '*ingenium aulicam*'. Most significantly, Curteys avoided harsh declamations against abuses and leavened his admonitions with praise. Quite apart from the familiar chorus of chastisement for the insufficiency of English clergy, for example, Curteys praised England as a sacred walled garden served by a wise and effective clergy, and over which God had set their queen, '*Miriah*, to set foorth his glory'. Far from replacing criticism with empty praise, though, Curteys's strategy of first emphasizing the positive allowed him to chastise England's sins not as wilful rebellion against God but as an almost understandable complacency that could be easily corrected. 'Wee of the Churche of Englande, are

[122] *Ibid.*, sig. Ciij^r–Cv^v, Cviij^v.
[123] *The Letters of John Chamberlain*, 2 vols., ed. Norman McClure (Philadelphia, Pa., 1939), vol. I, 147.
[124] Parker, *Correspondence*, 350.
[125] For Curteys's preaching as the likely source of his high regard by Parker and Elizabeth, see Roger B. Manning, *Religion and Society in Elizabethan Sussex* (Leicester, 1969), 70.

vnthankfull to God for our Treasures, and Iewels', he said, 'we grow secure and carelesse.'[126] Carelessness in Curteys's eyes did include the oft-lamented abuse of the clergy by lay patrons, but in his sermon, the point is made not by means of a frontal attack on the queen's and court's wilful negligence, as Edward Dering had done four years before, but in the context of praise for the gluttony of riches showered on England.

The following Lent (1575), Curteys again showed his skill at easing the tensions between the estates that were often heightened by other preachers who came to court. Just as the body of Christ had many members, Curteys said, not all equal, but all equally necessary to the whole, so too the Christian commonwealth stood most soundly when the different estates said to one another in charitable interdependence, 'help you vs in our lot, and we will helpe you in your lot'. Metaphorically mending fences broken by the estrangement of the laity and the clergy, Curteys explained that,

Noble men be the posts of the Christian Church and common welth, Ministers the rayle, & the people the pales which as long as they be tied and fastned togither with the feare of God, obedie[n]ce to their Prince, & mutuall loue one to an other, they must needes stand & prosper: for a threefold line is hardly broken.

Then he concluded with a triumphant Protestant review of English history that was bound to please. God had led his people out of 'the Egipt of error, blindnesse, and superstition' by his 'noble Moses', King Henry VIII, who had seen the true church 'but did not goe ouer Jordayne to it, but dyed in the Land of Moab'. Edward VI had been the Joshua who had led the way into the Promised Land, but under Mary the people 'forgat the Lorde their God, & serued Baal and Asteroth'. Then from prison and exile the children of God 'cryed to the Lord whyche raysed vp a gratious Debora, by whome God . . . caused his Churche of Englande to prosper in healthe, wealthe, peace, pollicie, learninge, religion, and many good giftes and graces'.[127] With the ability to serve up such godly nationalistic optimism, it is no surprise that Parker wanted Curteys close to Whitehall.

Preachers, of course, could change their colours to suit the royal audience, as one last sermon by Curteys shows. In both 1574 and 1575 Elizabeth issued commands for the suppression of those 'vain exercises', the prophesyings. Her injunctions were on the whole quietly ignored by bishops and preachers alike, and by the spring of 1576, with Grindal enthroned at Canterbury, the queen's exasperation with her bishops' complacency in the matter mounted until the first of her confrontations

---

[126] Richard Curteys, *A Sermon preached before the Queenes Maiestie . . . at Grenewiche,* (1574), sig. Aij^r, Bvj^r–Bvij^r, Ciiij^r, Cv^r.

[127] Richard Curteys, *A Sermon Preached before the Queenes Maiestie at Richmond* (1575), sig. Ciij^r, Ciiij^r, Cviij^v–Dj^v.

with the ill-fated primate in July.[128] With the queen incensed by reports of unruly prophesyings breeding Presbyterianism in the shires, Curteys preached before her on the third Sunday in Lent (25 March) 1576 and maintained that foremost among the dangers facing the faithful were those ministers who were 'puffed vp with vain glory to get them selues a name, and that the chaungeable people may flock to their sermons, and their Lectures, and their Churches, and their Discipline, drawn and fed with their fond Nouelties, whereof the simple be to to desirous'. Although the bishop asserted the right of all believers to read the Scriptures, he warned against interpretation by the unlearned, which was 'to be curiouse and to busy abooue your capacities'. Each estate should read Scripture as it pertained to its own station and calling; mere householders, for example, needed only 'to feare God, obey their Prince, looue their neighboure', only to be 'sure Gods worde is true, although you doo not see how'. If certain Scriptures were 'darck', he said, let the ignorant 'with the blessed Uirgine *Mary*, lay the same vp in their harts, and suspend their Iudgement'.[129] This could have been Queen Elizabeth herself summarizing her objections to the prophesyings, exercises which, as she put it in a 1577 royal letter, tempted 'assemblies of a great number of people, out of their ordinary parishes . . . to be hearers of their disputations and new devised opinions upon points of divinity, far unmeet for vulgar people'.[130] But one of the staunchest episcopal patrons of the prophesyings was none other than Richard Curteys.[131]

Although Curteys might not have thought that the exercises he sponsored in his diocese encouraged the kind of lay proselytizing that he criticized in his sermon, events swirling around him at the time suggest that he had every reason not to risk the loss of the queen's favour. The prophesyings that Curteys sponsored in Chichester diocese were indeed planting the seeds of Presbyterianism in Sussex. At the same time, Curteys was battling charges brought to the Privy Council and Star Chamber by the gentry of his diocese in reaction against his programme of rural evangelism – disputes that would, as in Grindal's case, lead to Curteys's suspension in 1577. Curteys would write 'eloquently' to Grindal in support of the prophesyings in July, so it might be an exaggeration to suggest that he tried to distance himself from them in March.[132] But, perhaps as a well-known supporter of

---

[128] Collinson, *Archbishop Grindal*, 235–7.
[129] Richard Curteys, *Two Sermons . . . the First at Paules Croße . . . and the Second at Westminster before ye Queenes Maiestie* (1576), sig. F7^r, F8^v, G1^r.
[130] BL MS Lansdowne 25, no. 44, quoted in Collinson, *Archbishop Grindal*, 248.
[131] Manning, *Elizabethan Sussex*, 188, 190–2; Collinson, *Archbishop Grindal*, 237; Collinson, *The Elizabethan Puritan Movement* (1967; Oxford, 1990), 173.
[132] Manning, *Elizabethan Sussex*, 104, 110–11, 118–19, 188.

this type of evangelism, he took the opportunity of a court sermon to try to show the queen that her fears of it were unnecessary and unfounded.

Were preachers that pleased the queen little more than flatterers? There can be no denying that Elizabeth loved courtly compliment and praise, and her preachers as well as her poets could serve it up in large portions. But it is perhaps too easy to dismiss, or even vilify, both the queen and her preachers for vanity and flattery, respectively, when praise and compliment not only often cloaked otherwise offensive advice, but also articulated truths that the flatterer, as well as the flattered, believed, or at least thought it necessary to believe. Alexander Nowell put the first case quite succinctly: when charged with flattering Elizabeth in a sermon, he responded that 'he had no other way to instruct the queen what she should be, but by commending her'.[133] Such a strategy was no innovation of Nowell's, but a time-honoured way to instruct one's betters through praise of an ideal. The second case, more difficult to define, might be approached through Sir John Harington's remembrance of Bishop of London John Aylmer (1521–94). 'When there was talke of daungers, and rumors of war, and invasions', Harington says, 'then he was commonly chosen to preach in the Court, and he would doe yt in so chearfull a fashion, as not only showd he had courage, but would put courage into other.'[134] Just as in times of crisis, the right preacher could inspire the court with his optimism, so too a complimentary sermon deployed at the right time could confirm the queen herself in a course of which she was otherwise unsure.

Such seems to have been the job of another of Elizabeth's favourite preachers, Richard Fletcher, in the days of the queen's guilty fury after the execution of Mary, Queen of Scots. Fletcher (*ob.* 1596), father of the dramatist John Fletcher, is perhaps best remembered for the two great indiscretions of his life: his self-righteous hounding of Mary Stuart at her trial and execution, and his injudicious second marriage to a rich widow in 1595, the latter of which indiscretions earned him the queen's disgust and banishment from court.[135] But before his disgrace, his was one of the most successful careers of any preacher at Elizabeth's court, and perhaps the closest any Elizabethan bishop came to the Jacobean model of a court preacher-prelate. Educated at Cambridge through the gift of Archbishop Parker, Fletcher was one of the vanguard of Cambridge clergy imported to Sussex to evangelize Chichester diocese under Richard Curteys. Parker, or perhaps even Curteys, introduced Fletcher to the queen, and she was taken with his preaching. According to Harington, he possessed those two virtues requisite for the queen's pulpit, a 'comly' person and 'courtly' speech, and

---

[133] Ralph Churton, *The Life of Alexander Nowell* (Oxford, 1809), 92.
[134] Harington, *Supplie or Addicion*, 48.
[135] For Fletcher's marriage, see Harington, *Supplie or Addicion*, 54.

Elizabeth rewarded him first with a Crown living in 1575, and then made him her ordinary chaplain in 1581; thereafter, he was successively Dean of Peterborough (1583), Bishop of Bristol and Lord High Almoner (1589), Bishop of Worcester (1593), and of London (1594).[136]

Mary Stuart's final prison, the castle at Fotheringay, Northamptonshire, lay within the diocese of Peterborough. Fletcher, then Dean of Peterborough, served as chaplain during Mary's trial and execution. He greeted the queen's Commissioners and preached before them on 12 October 1586, and at the hour of Mary's execution on 8 February 1587, Fletcher began to deliver a series of admonitions to the condemned queen that taunted her for her traitorous Catholicism. Mary, however, refused to be badgered and cut him off. Fletcher instead led the Protestant Commissioners in their own prayer while the condemned queen prayed her rosary. After the executioner's axe had fallen for the third and fatal time, it was Fletcher alone who broke the stunned silence in the hall with, 'So perish all the Queen's enemies!'[137]

A contemporary narrative of these events circulated widely in manuscript and has formed the basis for most subsequent retellings.[138] But included in one manuscript volume of the 'proceadynge[s] against the Quene of Scotte[s]' now at St John's College, Cambridge, is a document not usually considered in the sequence of events. This volume contains not only the familiar accounts of the scaffold scene and the 'manner of hir funerall[s]', but also the complete text of the sermon preached before Elizabeth 'immediatly after the execuc[i]on of the Queene of Scotte[s] by the Deane of Peterburghe'.[139] When word reached Elizabeth that her rival, but sister, queen had met her end, she flew into a legendary rage. She then denounced her Council, imprisoned Secretary Davison, and even refused to admit Burghley to her presence until March. When Parliament reassembled exactly one week after the execution, a motion in Commons to tender thanks to the queen for executing justice was quashed, probably, Sir John Neale assumes, by those 'near to the Queen [who] must have shuddered at the thought of her probable reaction'. And it was before this angry

[136] Manning, *Elizabethan Sussex*, 76–8; Harington, *Supplie or Addicion*, 50. For further background, see Patrick Collinson, 'Cranbrook and the Fletchers', in *Godly People: Essays on English Protestantism and Puritanism* (1983), 399–428.

[137] Nichols, *Progresses . . . of Queen Elizabeth*, vol. II, 495–507.

[138] Copies include BL Harley MS 1300; CUL MS Gg.III.34, arts. 26, 29; CUL Add MS 335, art. 9; Folger MS E.a.1, fols. 6ᵛ–22ᵛ.

[139] SJCC MS I.30, fols. 49ᵛ–67ᵛ; foliation is my own and subsequent references appear in the text. A much fuller treatment of this sermon is Peter McCullough, 'Out of Egypt: Richard Fletcher's Sermon to Elizabeth after the Execution of Mary Queen of Scots', in Julia Walker, ed., *Dissing Elizabeth: Negative Representations of Gloriana* (Durham, N.C., 1998).

mistress, and at this very time, that Dean Fletcher had to preach.[140] Many years later, Harington said that Fletcher 'could preach well, and would speake boldly, and yet keepe *Decorum*, he knew what would please the Queene, and would adventure on that, though it offended others'. The Council presumably counted on Fletcher's good looks and smooth tongue to calm the livid Elizabeth. But, much more daringly, Fletcher used his pleasing 'parts', as both his physical appearance and oratorical skills were called, not merely to mollify the queen with platitudes, but to seize the moment of Mary's very popular execution to call for yet more action against Catholics.[141] Fletcher used praise of Elizabeth as the divinely appointed protectress of the church not only to confirm the justice and wisdom of Mary's execution, but to insist that she use her new-found advantage over her enemies to further the work of Reformation.

The text Fletcher declaimed after ascending the pulpit was Matthew 2:19–20: 'The Angell of the Lorde appeared to Ioseph in Egipt in a dreame, sayeng arrise, and take vpp the childe and his mother and returne into the Lande of Israell for they are deade that sought the chylde[s] Lyfe' (49^v). The last phrase must have made the court hold its breath – the connection between Herod and Mary was clear enough, but how would Fletcher apply the whole text? How could he broach the topic of the execution while Elizabeth was in an 'irrational fury'?[142] After an exordium that safely summarized the verse's context in the Nativity narrative, the preacher dwelt on the holy family's flight into Egypt, and deftly moved his discourse away from possible application to Mary Stuart, the persecuted queen who had fled to England, by aligning Elizabeth with Mary and Joseph in exile. To do so, Fletcher first drew the moral lesson that God never abandoned the just to prison or exile, but ministered to them by his angels. 'In wch dignitie, and ministerie of holy Angelle[s]', he asked the queen, 'howe hathe youre kyngdome, yor self, and yor people bene magnyfyed manye yeares'. That magnification had begun with her accession, when God 'made the fetters of yor feare and captiuitie to fall from yor feete' to the eternal shame of those who clamored 'against youre most iuste and naturall succession'. Further, Fletcher continued, God delivered his servants not only in times of distress, but in times of seeming safety, as when the angel came to Joseph who was 'layed into his bedd and place of forgetfulnes' (54^v–55^r). With this the preacher stepped much closer to the present moment. Elizabeth, for

[140] J. E. Neale, *Elizabeth and her Parliaments*, 2 vols. (1953, 1957), vol. II, 137, 141–3, 166; Wallace MacCaffrey, *Elizabeth I* (1993), 352. Mary was executed on Wednesday, 8 February, making Sunday, 12 February the most likely date of the sermon's preaching; the House reconvened on Wednesday 15 February.

[141] Harington, *Supplie or Addicion*, 53. Harington's *Supplie*, written for Mary's grandson, Prince Henry, omits any reference to the famous role that Fletcher played at her end.

[142] MacCaffrey, *Elizabeth I*, 352.

the nearly twenty years of Mary's exile in England, had not allowed her knowledge of the Scottish queen's plots for her deposition to force her to give in to demands for Mary's execution. Elizabeth had been, in the terms of Fletcher's text, asleep on a bed of dangerous forgetfulness. But God had sent the same 'blessed servyce to you', he told the queen, 'as even it was to Iosephe. to be warned and infourmed of yor enemyes secret maliciousnes by ye Angell of god, by divine and miraculous intelligence' (55^v).

The 'intelligence' that had roused the queen was no angel's, but Sir Francis Walsingham's. The spymaster had managed to route Mary's correspondence across his own desk, which had provided him with the proof of her complicity in the Babington Plot and had finally prompted Elizabeth to order her trial.[143] So miraculous was this intelligence to Fletcher, 'that even in the tente[s] of the kinge of Aram, yt ys sayde as sometyme in the dayes of Elizens the prophete who ys yt y^t betrayethe oure councell vnto the kinge of Israell'. Indeed, the plotters' counsel had been betrayed, but Fletcher did not give Walsingham direct credit, for it was 'the Angell of the Lorde, the divine instincte of ye wisedome of the holy ghoste' that had saved the queen. Therefore, the preacher told her, 'it is marvelous and memorable and shalbe shewed to all posteritie when yor soule shalbe translated, what god . . . hathe don for yo^u in Egipte' (55^v, 56^v). This first part of Fletcher's sermon fitted the troubling events of the winter of 1586–7 into the familiar frame of a providentialist Tudor history. Elizabeth was God's chosen queen, delivered against all human odds repeatedly since her birth. 'God hath never forgotten you', Fletcher declared, 'hee forgate you not in yor cradle, but was yor hope when you hanged vppon yor mothers brest', and so too 'hee forgetteth you nott yesterdaye and to daye to open vnto you the conspiracies of yor enemyes' (56^v–57^r). So Elizabeth's very real fears that she had in fact traduced God's laws by killing a divinely appointed prince were, Fletcher insinuated, groundless. The execution of Mary was not a sinful action by the queen, but an act of deliverance by God. With one of the arch-enemies removed, 'there be more on o^r syde then be against vs', Fletcher proclaimed, and to grieve over such a God-given victory was to deny God's providential watch-care over his chosen prince and people (55^r).

So the angel's 'oracle' to Joseph – '*Surge*: Aryse and take the Chylde, and his mother and returne into the lande of Israell' – became Fletcher's own for his queen. Although Marian imagery was applied to Elizabeth in the later years of her reign, and has become one of the *données* of studies of her iconography, Fletcher applied to her a more politically insightful Biblical type, that of Joseph. Mary had borne and nursed Christ, making her a type

---

[143] MacCaffrey, *Elizabeth I*, 347–50.

of the church, the mother of Christ's body in the world. From this medieval iconography it was not an illogical step for preachers such as Richard Eedes to praise Elizabeth, defender of the faith, as one whom 'God hath honoured . . . so far beyond other princes, as to make a *virgin Queen the best nurce* of the religio[n] of him, who had a *virgin to his Mother*'.[144] Though Elizabeth had demurred at the title 'head of the church', the royal supremacy ensured that she was in fact precisely that. She not only nursed the Church of England, but was its governor, just as Joseph had been the governer of his charges, Mary and the infant Jesus. Hence the angel's call to Joseph was also Fletcher's to Elizabeth: 'Arise Iosephe, whye sleepest thou, and looke vnto thy charge . . . w[ch] have taken vppon yo[u] the tuition of Christe, the care of his churche, and conducte of his people' (60[r]). Elizabeth was to be not only a nursing mother, but also a governing father who would lead her charge, the church, out of the land of bondage – the fear and threat of Mary Stuart and the Catholic Egypt she represented – and back into the Israel of true religion.

Yet Elizabeth not only lay upon a bed of security, she wept there without cause. At the opening of the heated parliamentary session in the autumn of 1587, Sir Christopher Hatton had urged Mary's execution by applying the exemplum of David and his traitorous son, Absalom: '*Ne pereat Israel, pereat Absalom* (Absalom must perish, lest Israel perish).'[145] Now, three months later, Fletcher, playing the angel to Elizabeth's Joseph, called the queen out of her stupor of guilt and rage by retelling this same chastisement of David for mourning Absalom. His daring reapplication of the exemplum captured the pathos of a prince mourning for a fellow (or sister) prince, but insisted that sage counsellors could recall their sovereigns from indulgent filial sympathy to a concern for God's and the nation's good. As Fletcher recounted, 'howe sate David that good kynge soroweing and lamentynge after the most righteous and honourable execution of Iustice that ever was in Israell, tyll Ioab his faythfull counselor came vnto him', the Biblical context was gradually overtaken by its contemporary application until Joab's advice to David became indistinguishable from Fletcher's own to the queen:

aryse and speake comfortablye to thy serv[a]unte[s] that have done thys thinge, w[ch] if thou doe not, I sweare vnto thee by god, there will not one man abyde w[th] thee this night. Thou wilte loose the harte[s] and love of all thy faythefull subiecte[s], and that wilbe worse vnto thee then all the evill that ever befell thee from thy youthe hitherto (60[v]–61[r]).

---

[144] Richard Eedes, 'The Principall Care of Princes to Bee Nurces of the Church', in *Six Learned and Godly Sermons* (1604), 82[v].
[145] Neale, *Parliaments*, vol. II, 107.

Here, Fletcher spoke as much for the Council – the queen's servants 'that have done thys thinge' – as for himself. For the Lord Treasurer and the Council to suffer under the queen's wrath was a dangerous public show of a feeble commitment to advancing the true church and securing the nation. For the sake of the state, the queen had to reconcile herself to her trusted councillors: '*Surge* Debora, *surge* Baracke: Arise Debora arise Baracke: Arise prynce, aryse counsell, and aryse people' (61ᵛ). Here, then, is fruitful evidence to support Neale's thesis that 'the Court, united in wanting Mary's death, was in a subdued mood of revolt against their Queen's reaction to it'. But if her counsellors were 'cowed' and 'cringed before the wrath of the Prince', there was still a preacher whose high favour with the queen could allow an articulation of the court and Council's 'subdued revolt' and implore the queen for reconciliation.[146]

Still, Fletcher's peroration was motivated by a desire not only to pacify the queen, but to seize the opportunity of Mary's death to exhort his sovereign to the further 'perfectinge and fynyshinge of the tabernacle' (61ᵛ). Ignorance of Christ within the queen's own realm had made Mary's treasonous plottings possible, and, with Mary dead, attention had to be turned to the planting of the true church in the unreformed, and therefore rebellious corners of Elizabeth's dominions. Ireland, where Spanish troops had mounted an invasion aimed at deposing Elizabeth and freeing the Queen of Scots in 1579–80, was to Fletcher 'as that poore woman in the gospell' that 'bleedethe and can not touche the hemme of Christes vesture'; and in England, the 'coulde partes towardes the pole' were 'frozen in theire dregges' (62ᵛ) by the absence of the gospel's warm light.[147] This work could now be accomplished, Joseph could arise and return to Israel, for 'the whore of babilon wᵗʰ all her detestable enormities . . . are dead'. Now was the time for Elizabeth to move against popery, for Mary's death had thrown the forces of Catholicism into disarray. 'I beseeche yoᵘ', he cried, 'all the hoste of those Insolente & cruell Assirians doe . . . but flye and be confounded: when holophernes their chyefe captayne lyethe headles by the hande of Iudithe: ffollowe therefore vppon them.' And so, with the she-Holofernes's head in her hand, England's Deborah was to find her true comfort, her true rest, her true reward by propagating the Gospel and riding on in 'the charyott, the tryumphant chariott of Iustice' against God's enemies (65ᵛ, 67ʳ). Fletcher, in keeping with Harington's later estimate of his preaching, had indeed spoken 'boldly' and yet kept '*Decorum*'. By

---

146 Neale, *Parliaments*, vol. II, 142–4.
147 For the Spanish invasion of Ireland, see MacCaffrey, *Elizabeth I*, 340–1; for the glacial pace of reform in the North, see Sandys, *Sermons*, ed. Ayre, 154; Christopher Haigh, 'Puritan Evangelism in the Reign of Elizabeth I', *English Historical Review* 92 (1977) 30–58; and Collinson, *Archbishop Grindal*, 189–90.

recalling Elizabeth to her established iconographic role as both England's Deborah and its Judith – a governing judge and a righteous avenger[148] – Fletcher avoided direct criticism of his angry queen, and instead urged her through an oblique form of praise to continue to fulfil her office of governor and protectress of God's church.

Not every sermon of admonition preached before Elizabeth was so decorous. As we have seen in Edward Dering's infamous 1570 attack on the queen's negligent shepherding of her flock, Elizabeth as well as her court came in for some round criticisms from their preachers. But it would be inaccurate to take a sermon such as Dering's as representative of sermons preached *coram regina*. The very popularity of Dering's sermon in printed editions should itself alert us to the fact that it was probably not run-of-the-mill fare at Whitehall or Windsor. Dering delivered a rebuke to his queen that was sensational enough to sustain eleven new editions, more than any other Elizabethan sermon, court or otherwise.[149] Significantly, the last edition was printed in 1603: the titillation of Dering's jeremiad died with its subject.

It also seems dubious to assume, based on the assertiveness of a sermon such as Dering's, that Elizabethan preachers – especially those who came to court – saw the queen 'as by nature subordinate to themselves' and used their sermons 'as a species of self-advertisement' of their authority over her.[150] As Professor Collinson has remarked, 'few English Protestants have held such a "high" doctrine of the ministry as Edward Dering', and his performance at court was more an expression of Dering's own peculiar 'sense of his own office as the very mouth of God' than a paradigm for pulpit addresses to the queen.[151] Clergy in the early Elizabethan establishment committed to the construction of a viable reformed church were indeed an embattled group. Their heart-felt need to evangelize the shires ran up against not only a queen unconvinced of the need to plant preachers in every parish, but also against lay peers who grubbed for alienated church property and lay patrons who appropriated church livings.

Small wonder then that a recurrent refrain in the court sermons of first-generation Elizabethan bishops such as John Jewel (1522–71) was the call for support of a preaching clergy. Faith, Jewel saw, could not be imposed by statute. The people, he lamented at court, 'are commaunded to change

---

[148] For the Elizabethan currency of these two Biblical types, see Elkin C. Wilson, *England's Eliza* (Cambridge, Mass, 1939), chs. 1, 2; and John N. King, *Tudor Royal Iconography: Literature and Art in an Age of Religious Crisis* (Princeton, N.J., 1989), 225–8.

[149] Patrick Collinson, 'A Mirror of Elizabethan Puritanism: the Life and Letters of "Godly Master Dering"', in *Godly People*, 305.

[150] Margaret Christian, 'Elizabeth's Preachers and the Government of Women: Defining and Correcting a Queen', *Sixteenth Century Journal* 24 (1993), 561, 565.

[151] Collinson, 'Mirror of Elizabethan Puritanism', 299–300.

their religion, and for lacke of instruction, they know not whither to turne them: they knowe not, neither what they leaue nor what they should receiue'.[152] Another court sermon afforded him the chance to look directly in the eye many of the magnates who hoarded church property and to say, 'you, whosoeuer you are, that by such meanes haue decayed the Lordes House, and abridged the prouision and maintenaunce thereof, and see the miserable wracke of Gods Churche . . . oh remember you haue the patrimonie due vnto them that shoulde attend in the Lordes house'.[153] But Jewel, for all his insistence that without the guidance of preachers the nation was but a 'shippe which is tossed by the tempestes amiddes the surges and rockes of the Sea', understood – unlike Dering – that agitation for more royal patronage of a preaching ministry without showing due reverence for the queen and her supremacy was folly.[154] Whereas Dering scolded Elizabeth for her failure to use her royal prerogative for the propagation of the Gospel – 'And yet you in meane while that al these whordomes are committed . . . you sit still and are carelesse, let men do as they list' – Jewel only praised the royal supremacy in high, though general, terms, omitting any direct comments on whether the sovereign present used her power rightly. After insisting on the nation's need for preachers, Jewel added this vital coda: 'Notwithstanding we ought to praye to God, that hee will stirre vp and set foorth men to instruct his people: yet that nothing embarreth the authority of princes.' The queen was at the helm, and evangelism could only proceed as commanded by her. Only in this context of praise for the royal prerogative did the bishop then offer the same conclusion, albeit differently broached, as Dering. 'It pertaineth therefore', Jewel said, 'also to kings and Princes to send out labourers into the haruest.'[155] Elizabeth could be schooled, but she was much more likely to listen to those like Jewel who acknowledged their role as counsellors subordinate to the prince's authority. This was a lesson that Dering ultimately learned when the queen herself, not having forgotten his previous appearance before her and incensed at his sympathy for Thomas Cartwright in the Admonition Controversy, silenced Dering's preaching.[156] The whole clerical establishment, indeed the nation, saw Elizabeth's unwillingness to be challenged by her clergy in church matters when Grindal

---

[152] John Jewel, *Certaine Sermons* (1583), sig. L8^{r-v}; also *The Works of John Jewel*, 4 vols., ed. John Ayre (Cambridge, 1845–50), vol. II, 1024.

[153] *Certaine Sermons*, sig. K3^v; *Works*, vol. II, 1015.

[154] Jewel, *Certaine Sermons*, sig. L5^v; *Works*, vol. II, 1022. *Pace* Christian, 'Elizabeth's Preachers', 562–3, Jewel does not apply the ship metaphor, a familiar type of the church, to the queen, thereby making her 'merely . . . an object'.

[155] Jewel, *Certaine Sermons*, L6^r; *Works*, vol. II, 1022.

[156] Collinson, 'Mirror of Elizabethan Puritanism', 312.

learned the bitter lesson that Elizabeth was not willing to play Theodosius to any churchman's Ambrose.[157]

Was there any degree of distrust of government by a woman in the sermons that offered advice to Elizabeth? At her death there was some relief that the nation was finally to be governed by a man, a sentiment expressed by many, including royal chaplain Henry Hooke in a 1604 sermon before James. At the succession of the new king, according to Hooke, Elizabeth had 'died not, but was reuiued in one of her owne bloud; her age renewed in his younger yeeres . . . who stood vp a man as it were out of the ashes of a woman'. The 'elect might hope', he said, 'that what was not possible for a woman to effect, man should be both able and industrious to performe'.[158] But such sentiments were largely suppressed in the court pulpit during the queen's life. Thomas Drant's 1570 chastisement of Elizabeth's reluctance to punish the Northern rebels more severely can be read as a rebuke of fond womanish clemency, and Anthony Rudd's injudicious 1596 sermon on 'the most reuerend age of my most deare and dread Soueraign' undoubtedly hinted at the queen's famous vanity, but it is easy to mistake for 'traditional misogyny' the very traditional preacher's pose of offering advice to the magistrate.[159] On the whole, most royal sins decried from the court pulpit were not gender specific – failure to maintain a preaching clergy, leniency toward Catholics, avoidance of military intervention abroad – and were later directed at King James as often as they had been at Queen Elizabeth. Only one significant dispute among Elizabeth's preachers at court can be wholly attributed to her sex, and that was her refusal to marry and produce an heir to secure the succession. Thomas Cole, echoing the petitions of Elizabeth's second Parliament, complained before the queen at Windsor in 1564 that he found it very hard to expound Isaiah 49:23, where 'it appeareth that the . . . Church of god is here taken for the nurceling, & the kings & their Queenes . . . are here noted for nouriers and nourices', because 'the proper qualities of Godly tender nourices' were 'wanting in those that are lawfully placed for nourices'. 'These qualities', Cole grumbled, 'would haue bene easelier co[n]ceaued in this place, if it had pleased God, to haue shewed his mercye vpon vs, in giuing your Grace a nurceling of your own wombe'.[160] No doubt it was in

---

[157] For Grindal's appropriation of Ambrosian advice to the emperor see Collinson, *Archbishop Grindal*, 242–5; and *Religion of Protestants*, 24–7, 29–30.

[158] Henry Hooke, *A Sermon Preached before the King* (1604), sig. Ciij^r, Ciiij^r.

[159] Drant, *Two sermons*, sigs. Ivij^v–Kij^r; Anthony Rudd, *A Sermon Preached at Richmond before Queene Elizabeth* (1603), 49–50. Christian, 'Elizabeth's Preachers', 566–7, 569–71, 576.

[160] Thomas Cole, *A Godly and Learned Sermon, Made this Laste Lent at Windesor before the Queenes Maiestie* (1564), sig. Avj^v–Aij^r. Formal parliamentary appeals for the Queen to marry were delivered in 1559, 1563, 1566, and 1576. See Dean of St Paul's Alexander

response to criticisms like Cole's that Elizabeth and her preachers later fostered the iconography of the queen as Virgin Mother of Christ's body in England. Thus the queen's spinsterhood could be transformed from a liability – as Cole put it, 'that chaste estate of Matrimonie' was 'more profitable in my co[n]scie[n]ce to your realme & people than Uirginitie' – into a blessing.[161]

No matter how admonitory her preachers became, Queen Elizabeth refused to play the part of the female victim. If anything, she played the man with her preachers, if by that can be meant not only refusing to be bullied by them but also dogging them herself. As we have seen, she used the public forum of the outdoor Preaching Place at Whitehall to 'utterly dismay' Dean Nowell for his attack on the cross and saints on Ash Wednesday 1565, a smart he still felt a full year later. When Tobie Matthew hinted broadly that the queen was not forthcoming with deserved preferments, she opened her window and said, 'Well, whosoever have missed their rewards, you . . . have not lost your labour.' With this remark Matthew 'was hit home for his sauciness'. Anthony Rudd, after touching on that greatest of *arcana imperii*, the queen's age, was rewarded with one of the queen's trademark ripostes from the closet window and temporarily banished from the court. The Preaching Place at Whitehall did in fact double as an arena for bloodsports, including bull- and bear-baiting and wrestling. With such rough-handling of preachers possible, the Preaching Place must have seemed a latter-day Coliseum to nervous preachers such as Richard Vaughan, who accepted his appointment in Lent 1593, 'verie desirous to haue been spared . . . knowinge myne owne infirmities, & the terro[r] of the place'. Even William Barlow, the preacher who had done the ruling Cecil élite no little service during the Essex crisis by preaching the official Paul's Cross justification of the Earl's execution, was not exempt from the queen's government of her preachers. Diarist John Manningham noted that Barlow 'received a checke at hir Majesties, because he presumed to come in hir presence when shee had given speciall charge to the contrary, because shee would not have the memory of the late Earl of Essex renewed by him'.[162] For preachers who came to Elizabeth's court, the royal supremacy had a very special meaning.

Finally, some account must be made of the noticeable changes in the

Nowell's complaint in the queen's presence at the opening of Parliament 1563 that her virginity was 'a plague': Nowell, *A Catechism*, ed., G. E. Corrie (Cambridge, 1853), 228.

[161] Cole, *A Godly and Learned Sermon*, sig. Aij[v].

[162] Parker, *Correspondence*, 235, 254; *Memoirs of the Reign of Queen Elizabeth*, 2 vols., ed. Thomas Birch (1754), vol. I, 47; Harington, *Supplie or Addicion*, ed. Miller, 151–4; WAMB 15, fol. 12[r]; Manningham, *Diary*, 87. For bloodsports in the Preaching Place, see PRO E351/543, fol. 173[v], and *Dudley Carleton to John Chamberlain 1603–1624: Jacobean Letters*, ed. Maurice Lee, Jr (New Brunswick, N.J., 1972), 110.

sermons preached at court over the near half-century of Elizabeth's reign. Patrick Collinson has pointed out that Elizabeth's Injunctions of 1559 prescribed papal usurpation as the topic for the minimum quarterly sermons to be held in all parishes, and he wonders, 'but surely not for ever and ever?'[163] To read the sermons and descriptions of sermons, preached at court during the first twenty to twenty-five years of the reign inspires exactly the same question, for anti-Catholic disputation dominates that body of material to a striking degree. The first Lent series, with its calculated assault on Roman Catholicism aimed at winning support for the reform bills in Parliament, set the tone for much of what followed in the succeeding decades. Significantly, the first court sermon printed during the reign was John Jewel's so-called 'Challenge Sermon', a refutation of seven points of Roman Catholic doctrine and practice that Jewel challenged any papist to defend out of Scripture and the early Fathers. It was preached first at Paul's Cross in November 1559, but repeated at the court and again at Paul's Cross during Lent 1560, and sparked a voluminous print debate between Jewel and the deprived Dean of Westminster, Dr Henry Cole. In early printed editions of the sermon, the controversy between Jewel and Cole received top billing, with the sermon itself added as a kind of appendix.[164] Subsequent court sermons, or at least those that survive, concerned themselves largely with the business at hand of settling the newly reformed church.

Throughout the 1560s and 1570s preachers such as Dering, Thomas Cole, and Drant, as well as Jewel and Sandys, urged the establishment of a preaching clergy as the only way to fend off popish wolves. The hotter Protestants among them agitated for the further cleansing of the English church of the dangerous remaining 'Popish dregges' such as ceremonies, images, and vestments.[165] And Rome was vilified with a passion: in 1566 Thomas Godwin, Dean of Christ Church, accused Roman churchmen of deliberately 'forginge and counterfeytinge' the works of the Fathers to suit the papacy's own perversions of the truth; in 1570 William Fulke (1538–89) proved Rome to be the latter-day Babylon and seat of the anti-Christ; and in 1578 William James, as we have seen, decried the insidious persistence of church papistry and recusancy.[166] But, of course, threats to religious uniformity came from within the reforming camp as well, and the controversial character of much court preaching before the 1580s owed

[163] Collinson, 'Elizabethan Church', in Haigh, ed., *Reign of Elizabeth*, 184.

[164] Jewel, *The Trve Copies of the Letters betwene . . . Iohn Bisshop of Sarum and D. Cole, vpon Occasion of a Sermon that the Said Bishop Preached before the Quenes Maiestie* (1560); *Works*, vol. I, 1–80.

[165] Cole, *A Godly and Learned Sermon*, sig. Eviij^v.

[166] CCCC MS 340, 169; William Fulke, *A Sermon Preached at Hampton Court* (1570); James, *A Sermon Preached before the Queenes Maiestie* (1578).

something to the struggle against Protestant nonconformity. The most notable surviving sermon in this vein was Whitgift's Lent 1574 sermon before the queen at Greenwich.[167] Preached less than two months after he had delivered to Burghley the manuscript of his last salvo in the Admonition Controversy, Whitgift's only surviving court sermon, and one of only two of his sermons ever printed, provided a précis of the establishment's response to the Presbyterian challenge.[168] In this concise sermon Whitgift deployed much of the rhetoric that would distinguish conformity as he defined it during his archiepiscopate and that of his successor. Here too were seeds of many of the views on church polity nurtured in the Jacobean court pulpit by his chaplain, Lancelot Andrewes, including the stigmatizing of Puritanism as populist anarchy, the yoking of Puritanism and popery as twin adversaries, and confidence in the church hierarchy as the guardian of order and stability.

There are, however, what might seem to be exceptions to the controversial character of court preaching early in the reign, but these exceptions tend only to prove the rule. Edmund Guest (1518–77), successively Bishop of Rochester and Salisbury, preached a Lent sermon at court in 1560 on the elementary text, 'Repent and believe the Gospel' (Mark 1:15), that replaced overt sectarian controversy with homiletic moral instruction appropriate to the liturgical season at hand. First using Seneca, Socrates, and Plato, as well as Augustine, to call the court to self-examination and self-denial, Guest then elaborated upon the Ten Commandments as the ways in which believers could fulfil the Gospel command to keep God's law and to love their neighbours as themselves. His call for Roman Catholics to repent – 'Wherfore youe that have defended and followed poperie & sup[er]stition repent youe of it. youe that have persecuted or hated the truthe repent you of it' – while strong, did not approach the scorn of, for example, William James's taunt to 'ye English Samaritanes'. Guest seemed to hold out a hand of conciliation not extended by other preachers, a gesture underscored by the catholicity of his exempla. In addition to ancient philosophers, Guest even enlisted Sir Thomas More and his 'boke of comforte agenst tribulation' in the service of urging those present to 'beware of delaies in leving synn in turninge to god'. Far from repeating the reformers' litany about England as an elect nation, predestined and privileged to receive the truth, Guest went on to conclude his sermon with the decidedly un-Genevan

[167] John Whitgift, *A Godlie Sermon Preached before the Queenes Maiestie at Grenewiche* (1574); also *The Works of John Whitgift*, 3 vols., ed. John Ayre (Cambridge, 1851–53), vol. III, 566–85.

[168] Whitgift, *Works*, vol. III, 601–2. For Whitgift and the Admonition Controversy, see Peter Lake, *Anglicans and Puritans? Presbyterianism and English Conformist Thought from Whitgift to Hooker* (1988), 13–66.

assertion that 'this sayeng of Christ repent and beleve . . . doth unfaynedlie belong to all men and shall turne to all mens salvation that kepe it. And that all men be not saved it is not because god wold not but because we will not.'[169]

Such an emphasis on free will and universal grace would not be heard again until the 1620s. In Lent 1565, Guest gave the Spanish ambassador some comfort by preaching a Good Friday sermon that, rather than entering 'into other questions or disputes on religious points as they usually do', instead insisted on the real presence of Christ in the Eucharist.[170] At a time when the pulpit was dominated by preachers whose anti-Catholicism and sacramental theology had been cast in Germany and Geneva, these seemingly conciliatory words of Guest's must have been in themselves inflammatory – small wonder indeed that Guest was the subject of table-talk that labelled him a Lutheran and a free-will man.[171] Yet this was the man that Elizabeth had appointed as her second Lord High Almoner. Why? Guest's more moderate approach to the conversion of Roman Catholics and his less-than-Zwinglian view of the sacrament might have been amenable to the queen, who may herself have had an affinity for the Augsburg Confession. Guest also shared Elizabeth's conservative sympathy for the scenic apparatus or worship, and was one of the only bishops who acted on the queen's 1560 order to protect church monuments from iconoclasm.[172] But as we have seen in a previous chapter, the office of Almoner was associated at least by the end of the reign with a favoured preacher, and Guest's moderation (or conservatism) in the pulpit no doubt suited the queen's personal taste for decency and order, as well as her eagerness to prove to conservative subjects and Catholic dignitaries alike that hers was not a reactionary, heretical church. As the Spanish ambassador's report after Guest's Good Friday sermon shows, the strategy was not without some success.

Guest provides an important link between the first generation of Elizabeth's preachers, those with first-hand experience of the Edwardine reformation and Marian persecution, and their successors, men raised and educated in an established Protestant church who rose to positions of leadership in the 1580s. Although shifts of this sort are never sudden,

---

[169] CCCC MS 104, printed in Henry Geast Dugdale, *The Life and Character of Edmund Geste* (1840), 193, 197–8, 200.

[170] *CSPS 1558–1567*, 419.   [171] Collinson, *Elizabethan Puritan Movement*, 206.

[172] Collinson, *Elizabethan Puritan Movement*, 32–3; Collinson, 'Windows into a Woman's Soul' in *Elizabethan Essays*, 108–18; Margaret Aston, *England's Iconoclasts* (Oxford, 1988), 318. Although Guest argued against transubstantiation in the 1540s, in 1563 he was a leading advocate of revising the Thirty-nine Articles away from a Zwinglian position toward an affirmation of the Real Presence. See Haugaard, *Elizabeth and the English Reformation*, 250–3.

Grindal's death and the translation of Whitgift to Canterbury in 1583 seems as much a pivotal year in the history of preaching at court as it was for the religious and political nation at large. Preachers of Dering's or Coles's nonconformist stripe were deprived from their livings during Whitgift's subscription campaign of 1583–4, and at the same time the court pulpit ceased to provide a platform for strict Puritan criticisms of the established church. Not until the nonconformist John Burgess took the pulpit at Greenwich in 1604, carrying the banner of those ministers who had pinned their reforming hopes on the new king and his Hampton Court Conference, would a preacher attack the *status quo* to the sovereign's face in the manner of Edward Dering.[173]

Rather, court sermons in the 1580s and 1590s asserted the settled, disciplined church polity constructed by Whitgift and Hooker. As at Elizabeth's accession, so upon Whitgift's translation to Canterbury the Lent sermons played an important role. During his first Lent as archbishop (1584), Whitgift used the court sermons to assert and defend his subscription campaign against Puritans, with some hearers nonplussed at hearing his appointees try 'to persuade her Majesty and the world that there was and is a great schism in the Church' caused by factious nonconformists.[174] Institutionally, Whitgift's influence can be seen in the appearance of the primate's own clients in the Lent lists after 1584. Whitgift's understudy, Richard Bancroft, made his debut in Holy Week of 1585. In Lent 1598, following the publication of Hooker's seventh book of the *Laws of Ecclesiastical Polity* – dedicated to Whitgift – Hooker was appointed by the archbishop to preach before the queen on mid-Lent Wednesday, 29 March.[175] Of more influence in the court pulpit, especially in the next reign, were two other Whitgift chaplains, John Buckeridge and Lancelot Andrewes. Andrewes preached his first Lent sermon at court on 11 March 1590, and Buckeridge (1562?–1631) in 1597, the Lent following his appointment to Whitgift's household. Fittingly, Andrewes's sermon articulated a Whitgiftian insistence on the inseparability of sacred from civil government under the head of the Christian prince.[176]

The conformist case for the royal supremacy had been hammered out in detail by Whitgift during the Admonition Controversy of 1572–4, and would be elaborated upon in florid detail by Andrewes from the 1590s onwards. Taking full advantage of the optimism bred by the triumph over

173 For Burgess and his sermon, see below, 141–7.
174 BL MS Add 48039, fol. 26, quoted in Collinson, *Elizabethan Puritan Movement*, 247.
175 WAMB 15, fol. 26. This is Hooker's only known appearance in the court pulpit.
176 WAMB 15, fols. 19, 25; Lancelot Andrewes, *XCVI Sermons* (1629), 263–72; also Andrewes, *Works*, 11 vols., ed. James Wilson and J.P. Bliss (Oxford 1841–54), vol. II, 3–15.

Presbyterianism and the scattering of the Spanish Armada – the twin threats of parity and popery – Andrewes preached in Lent 1590 on King David's 'arch of governement'. He identified the two pillars thereof as the worship of God and the execution of justice, each of which strengthened the other: '*Religion* rooting *Iustice within*; *Iustice* fensing *Religion without*, and they both making an arch of governement irremovable.'[177] Just as Whitgift insisted that 'I make no difference betwixt a Christian common-wealth and the church of Christ', Andrewes called 'Divinitie the Back-bone of the Prince's Law; and consequently Religion, of the Common-wealth'. But without a beam uniting the two pillars, he said, 'they both sinke'. The missing beam or keystone was, before he even named it, punningly inscribed by Andrewes in his summary of the two pillars: 'GOD, and *Right*, the *Pillers*', quoting the royal motto *Dieu et mon droit* that glittered on the ceilings and royal closets of the queen's chapels. Not subject to either clergy or council, priests or Parliament, the prince was 'the *first* and the chiefe *Person* in any governement . . . upon whom both these leane'.[178]

To this classic conformist view of the royal supremacy, Andrewes added a novel concern sympathetic to one that would soon be set down in Hooker's *Laws*. In Professor Lake's summary, Hooker's defence of church ceremonies as things more than indifferent 'was little short of the reclama-tion of the whole realm of symbolic action and ritual practice from the status of popish superstition to that of a necessary, indeed essential, means of communication and edification'. For Hooker, churches were one of the few places where the divine attributes of majesty and splendour could be glimpsed.[179] So, we find Andrewes preaching at Elizabeth's court, and perhaps in her chapel, where, along with her infamous silver crucifix, more outward ceremony and splendour was lavished on divine service than anywhere else in her realm. Here Andrewes described the godly prince's care for the pillar of religion not in terms of planting preachers, but in terms of King David's care for the ark. 'And, when it was brought backe', Andrewes said, David 'sett such an order for the Service of it, by the *Levites*; for maintenance so bountifule; so reverend for regard; so decent for order; so every way sufficient, as the care of the Temple might seeme to reigne in his heart'.[180] Whereas Jewel had pleaded with the queen for prophets, Andrewes lauded a Levitical priesthood that served God pri-marily not in the pulpit, but in the ordered and reverent ministry of the church's liturgical service. Had Elizabeth been succeeded by a prince whose

---

[177] Lancelot Andrewes, *XCVI Sermons*, 267; *Works*, vol. II, 10.

[178] Whitgift, *Works*, vol. III, 313, quoted in Lake, *Anglicans and Puritans?*, 50. Andrewes, *XCVI Sermons*, 265–8; *Works*, vol. II, 7–10.

[179] Lake, *Anglicans and Puritans?*, 165, 167.

[180] Andrewes, *XCVI Sermons*, 269; *Works*, vol. II, 13.

churchmanship was similar to her own, Andrewes's vision of service performed throughout the realm as it was in the chapel royal, with preaching by no means the primary public service of God, might have been realized. But the Scottish King would bring to Whitehall a love for sermons that would radically alter the place of the sermon not only in the service in the chapel royal, but in the court's social and cultural life as well.

⟨ 3 ⟩

James I and the apotheosis of court preaching

Next to Anthony Weldon's 'wisest fool in Christendome', 'amateur theologian' and 'theologian-king' rank as two of the most widely retailed sobriquets for James VI and I. But James's penchant for engaging in pamphlet wars with Roman Catholic controversialists abroad, and the persistent portrait of him as a religious pedant has overshadowed his remarkable patronage of preaching at court.[1] While more recent studies of Stuart court culture have briefly acknowledged the royal taste for sermons by Lancelot Andrewes and John Donne, the predominance of sermons over other literary forms (most notably drama) at the Jacobean court, and their tremendous impact on the court's cultural life and the polity of the Jacobean Church requires further attention.[2]

ACCESSION AND SUCCESSION: 'THIS CHANGE . . . WITHOUT CHANGE'?

When Elizabeth died on Thursday, 24 March 1603, much was made of the coincidence of both her birth and death with the church's Marian feasts.[3] But perhaps more liturgically significant at the time, at least for her

---

[1] The traditional picture is summed up in David H. Willson, *King James VI and I* (New York, 1956). For James as bumbling 'amateur theologian', see G. P. V. Akrigg, *Jacobean Pageant* (Cambridge, Mass, 1962), 303–20, and H. R. Trevor-Roper, 'James I and his Bishops', *History Today* 5 (1955), 571–81. These portraits have been fundamentally revised in Jenny Wormald, 'James VI and I: Two Kings or One?', *History* 68 (1983), 190–1; Kenneth Fincham, *Prelate as Pastor: the Episcopate of James I* (Oxford, 1990); and Kenneth Fincham and Peter Lake, 'The Ecclesiastical Policy of King James I', *Journal of British Studies* 24 (April 1985), 169–207.

[2] The importance of religion at James's court has been most sympathetically acknowledged in Graham Parry, *The Golden Age Restor'd: the Culture of the Stuart Court, 1603–42* (New York, 1981), ch. 10. Strangely Parry's discussion of James and preaching draws only on sermons preached about the king, but not at his court.

[3] John Chamberlain, *The Letters of John Chamberlain*, 2 vols., ed. Norman E. McClure (Philadelphia, Pa., 1939), vol. I, 189; Daniel Price, *A Heartie Prayer* (1625), 32; William Camden, *The History of Queen Elizabeth*, in *A Complete History of England*, 3 vols. (1706), vol. II, 653.

101

chaplains, counsellors, and her successor, was the fact that Elizabeth died on Thursday in the second week of Lent, with the court Lent sermons in full swing. The young Queen Elizabeth, as we have seen, had used the court sermons during the first Lent of her reign to brilliant political effect by turning the Whitehall Preaching Place into a court annex of Parliament for the purpose of pushing a reformed religious settlement. Now, in this, her last Lent as queen, and James's first as English king, the court pulpit, with its thrice-weekly sermons by some of the establishment's best preachers, became a mouthpiece for stability that heralded the new king. But the now-Jacobean court preachers did not hesitate to warn the king as well as subjects against innovations in civil and ecclesiastical government – in effect, to ensure that the succession was indeed a 'change . . . without change'.[4]

Not unlike the continuance of preaching at the new Elizabethan court while it was suppressed elsewhere, Cecil and Whitgift seem to have made special efforts to keep the court sermon routine going as a means of allaying public fears about the succession. John Manningham, who heard the last sermon preached at court before the queen's death, followed the court pulpit with special attention during the months between Elizabeth's passing and James's arrival, and his diary gives an important glimpse of what was said there during that heady time. According to Manningham, on the Sunday immediately following the queen's death, Giles Thomson, Dean of Windsor, 'whoe at thys tyme attendes still with Dr Parry as chaplein', could not keep his appointment to preach at Whitehall. He should have taken his turn 'by course' as one of the two chaplains in ordinary attending for the month. Thomson, however, was relieved of that duty, perhaps because of the strain of attendance during the queen's final illness and the conveyance of the body to Whitehall late the previous night. There must also remain open the possibility that Thomson was not deemed the appropriate preacher for the first court sermon preached after the queen's death. Appointed to take his place was John King, Vicar of St Andrew's, Holborn, a noted evangelical preacher and later Bishop of London. Although James had been publicly proclaimed the day before at both court and City, worries over possible Catholic opposition to the succession still beset the public. King therefore warned against 'intestine discord' and offered thanks for what few could have been completely sure of, the successful and peaceable transfer of power.[5] Similarly on 6 April, Wednesday in the fourth week of Lent, John Overall, Dean of St Paul's, took as his text Christ's

---

[4] Richard Eedes, *Six Learned and Godly Sermons: Preached some of Them before the Kings Maiestie, some before Queen Elizabeth* (1604), 1ʳ.

[5] John Manningham, *The Diary of John Manningham of the Middle Temple, 1602–1603*, ed. Robert Parker Sorlein (Hanover, N.H., 1976), 211, 213. Thomson was among those of

warning to '*watch and pray that yee enter not into temptation*' (Matthew 26:41), something 'fit for those tymes, in this change, least wee be tempted to desyre innovacion' – probably a glance not only at Catholics, but also at Puritans, both of whom hoped James would be the champion of the one and the scourge of the other.[6]

On the same day that Overall preached that message from the Whitehall pulpit, James VI and I entered his new kingdom at Berwick. After a ceremonial reception at the city gates, the king, in his first public act in England, processed to Berwick church, where he heard 'a most learned and worthy Sermon' by the Bishop of Durham, Tobie Matthew.[7] With this began a concatenation of court sermons – those preached at Whitehall at the waning court of the deceased Elizabeth (not officially disbanded until her interment on 28 April), alternating all the while with those preached before the ascendant court of King James on its progress south to London. On Sunday, 10 April, for example, we know that three court sermons were preached – one at Newcastle, and two at Whitehall. At Newcastle, James again heard the diocesan, Tobie Matthew. We know nothing of Matthew's sermon itself, but the text he chose, 2 Chronicles 15:1,2 is suggestive: 'The Lord is with you, while ye be with him: and if ye seke him, he wil be founde of you, but if ye forsake him, he wil forsake you.' James was welcomed by most, or at least by those who knew best. Matthew himself had been an outspoken opponent of a Scottish succession to the English throne but now preached before the king, prayed at his table, and played host to him at the episcopal palace in Durham.[8] But sermons of welcome were from the start hedged with advice. Bishop Matthew's Old Testament text could be a summary of the many sermons James heard in the first year of his reign, all of which praised him as God's anointed and the chosen king of Britain, but also hinted that God's favour would be withdrawn quickly if he deviated from the civil and ecclesiastical policies inherited from his predecessor. Indeed, while Matthew preached in Northumberland, Giles Thomson preached a similarly advisory sermon at Whitehall on Psalm 2:10, 11: 'Be wise nowe O ye Kings, be learned O ye judges; serve the Lord with feare, and rejoyce unto him with reverence.' According to Manningham, Thomson stressed kings' subjection to God. Taking a wry look at courtiers' frantic jockeying for position at the new court, the dean called attention to the 'strang doctrine, that those whom al desyre to be servants unto should

Elizabeth's former chaplains designated by Whitgift as 'fitt to preach' before James (WAMB 15, fol. 2).

[6] Manningham, *Diary*, 223–4.
[7] John Nichols, *The Progresses, Processions, and Magnificent Festivities of King James the First*, 4 vols. (1828), vol. I, 62–7.
[8] Manningham, *Diary*, 245; YML Add. MS 18, 70.

be taught that themselves must serve an other: yet this is the highest point of honour, to serve God'.[9] And in Thomson's mind, 'to serve God' probably meant to maintain the *status quo* in the English Church.

The preachers who addressed James in the first months of his English reign also conveyed in their sermons a keen awareness, if not a nervousness, about the Stuart king's absolutism – known predominantly from *The Trew Law of Free Monarchies* (1598) as well as *Basilikon Doron*[10] – and they insisted on their right to offer warnings and advice. Not surprisingly, finding the *aurea mediocritas* between kingly justice and mercy was a common refrain. Thomas Blague, preaching before James on the day of his entry into London, pressed the king to temper mercy with judgment, memorably noting that 'he that blowes his nose too hard, wrings out blood'.[11] More explicitly, Anthony Rudd took as his text for a June 14 sermon Psalm 101:1, '*I will sing mercie and iudgement, to thee O Lord will I sing*', and identified it as a text written by a king to show 'how he will behaue himselfe in his kingdome . . . both in the Court, and in the countrie'. Rudd expounded this proper kingly behaviour as 'touching the gouerment of the kingdome by way of practise of mercie toward the good, and of iudgement against the bad'.[12] And Bishop of Winchester Thomas Bilson, in the king's coronation sermon on July 25, after affirming the divine right of kings in no uncertain terms ('Yea the very Robes, which they weare, are sanctified'), entered a significant caveat to the subjection of peoples to kings:

Howbeit when Princes cease to command for god, or bend their swords against God, whose Ministers they are: we must reuerence their Power, but refuse their willes. It is no resistaunce to obey the greater before the lesser, neither hath any man cause to be offended, when god is preferred.[13]

This was resistance theory not unlike that retailed by Bilson in his 1585 tome defending resistance by French and Dutch Calvinists, a theory that was, in Dr Sommerville's estimate, 'going out of vogue among the higher clergy' even by the 1590s. If reservations about absolutism 'were rapidly disappearing from the armoury of apologists for the established church' in

[9] Manningham, *Diary*, 232.

[10] See Maurice Lee, Jr, *Great Britain's Solomon* (Urbana, Ill., 1990), 82–5; Jenny Wormald, 'James VI and I, *Basilikon Doron* and *The Trew Law of Free Monarchies*: the Scottish Context and the English Translation', in Linda Levy Peck, ed., *The Mental World of the Jacobean Court* (Cambridge, 1991), 36–54.

[11] Thomas Blague, *A Sermon Preached at the Charterhouse, before the Kings Maiestie* (1603), sig. B4ᵛ.

[12] Anthony Rudd, *A Sermon Preached at Greenwich before the Kings Maiestie* (1603), sig. A4ʳ, A6ʳ. See also Rudd's *Sermon Preached to the Court at White Hall* (1604).

[13] Thomas Bilson, *A Sermon Preached at Westminster before the King and Queenes Maiesties, at their Coronations* (1603), sig. B1ᵛ, B6ʳ.

the years after James's accession, in the first few months after that accession, they enjoyed a brief Indian summer in the court pulpit.[14]

The guarded approach taken by court preachers to their new king is best seen in the first sermon preached before James by Richard Eedes, Dean of Worcester, formerly Chaplain in Ordinary to Elizabeth, and newly entered into the same service to James. In August, 1603, Eedes, like Bilson, Rudd, and Blague, wanted to ensure that court preachers could safely offer James and his court prescription as well as praise. He reflected graciously on 'this office . . . to the which for some yeares I haue ben employed in this Court, vnder the religious reigne of the peerelesse Queene of the world, my many waies most gratious ladie and mistris'. Even more graciously, he spoke of his chaplaincy as that office 'to the which I am now againe called in this change (as I may well say) without change; a change of the person, but not of the bloud royall; a change of the Gouernour, but not of the Religion and gouernment of the land'. He defined his royal chaplaincy as an office through which God 'doth wholly intend the good of those princes to whom we are sent, and hath an end to make them not only *good Christians . . .* but *good kings* also'. But making good kings good Christians required the freedom to teach kings 'so to guide the helme of their civile gouernement, as they are guided and directed by the rule of heauen'. Eedes went on to lament that, 'especially in the courts of princes', the preacher suffered from a lack of credibility with his hearers, having 'become rather an instructer than a correcter, a disputer than a commaunder'. To effect God's work in the court, preachers needed to ascend the pulpit not as 'suiters, and by way of entreatie', but 'in the stile of *a commander . . .* or *with a rod* for the advauncement of that kingdome, *which is not in word but in power'*. Eedes then warned that if the court did not have 'eares patient of reproofe, or hearts that will yeeld to haue their stonie hardnesse broken' by preachers, God would 'proceed against disobedience with the *yron Scepter* of his wrath, and *crush them in pieces euen like potters vessels,* though they be neuer so mightie'.[15]

The court sermons, then, do not reflect what has been described as a nationwide sigh of relief, or burst of optimism, at the death of an aged queen whose reign would have been remembered more kindly if it had ended ten years sooner.[16] Instead, the preachers James inherited from Elizabeth held her up as an exemplum to the new king and asked for

[14] Thomas Bilson, *The True Difference between Christian Subiection and Unchristian Rebellion* (Oxford, 1585); J. P. Somerville, *Politics and Ideology in England 1603–1640* (1986), 11, 47.

[15] Richard Eedes, in *Six Learned and Godly Sermons,* 1r–2ʳ, 16ʳ⁻ᵛ, 17ʳ.

[16] For the twilight of Elizabeth's popularity, see Christopher Haigh, *Elizabeth I* (1988), 160–2, 164–6.

continuity, not change. For John Hopkins, preaching to James before February 1604, Elizabeth's memory was one that 'of all other cannot be forgotten, but will euer be as sweete perfume in the house of God'. For it was she who found 'the Church defaced' and 'against the liking of all her neighbour Princes . . . and also contrary to the will of most of her counsell . . . clensed the Temples . . . and established the Church in that state & condition, that the florishing thereof hath bin famous through the world'. For this service, Hopkins argued, Elizabeth was blessed with a long life and a peaceful reign. By implication, James needed to perform similarly to guarantee the same results; the new king needed not to depart from Elizabethan practice, but to fulfil and continue it.[17]

DEAN OF THE CHAPEL, CLERK OF THE CLOSET, AND THE 'MULTITUDE OF *SCOTS*'

Even before Elizabeth's death, the increasingly certain prospect of a Scottish succession, with the attendant threat of an influx of Scottish Presbyterianism, was enough to cause Archbishop Whitgift and his lieutenant, Richard Bancroft, Bishop of London, to blench. Neither prelate waited idly for the inevitable to happen, but rather tried to build as many bulwarks as possible to protect the English church from the Scottish invasion.[18] One such defence was to maintain a firm grip on court religion, including the chaplains who would serve and preach there before the king. Shortly after the accession, a list was drawn up headed 'The Names of such as were her late Ma[tes] Chaplens and other persons likewise Fitt to preache beefore his Ma[tie] if occasion bee offered'. This list, with emendations and additions in Whitgift's own hand, included thirteen Elizabethan Chaplains in Ordinary, all seasoned court preachers, eight of whom were deans. Appended were nineteen others that were 'no Chapleins', but either no strangers to the court pulpit (like John Buckeridge and John King) or prominent university men (such as brothers George and Robert Abbot and James Montagu).[19] Whitgift clearly wanted to have chaplains and preachers in place when James arrived from the north, no doubt to counter and, it was hoped, to supplant, the influence of any Scots preachers that might have accompanied him. Whitgift seems to have succeeded in large part, since Elizabeth's Chaplains in Ordinary evidently became James's *en bloc*, something suggested not only by Eedes's personal testimony, but also by other

[17] John Hopkins, *A Sermon preached before the Kings Maiestie* (1604), sigs. A4[v], A5[r].
[18] See Jenny Wormald, 'Ecclesiastical Vitriol: the Kirk, the Puritans and the Future King of England,' in John Guy, ed., *The Reign of Elizabeth I: Court and Culture in the Last Decade* (Cambridge, 1995).
[19] WAMB 15, fol. 6.

surviving lists dating from before July 1603. First, among a rash of household servants sworn in at Greenwich in May were eleven Chaplains in Ordinary. All were English, and all veterans of Elizabeth's pulpit: seven of her Ordinary chaplains (Griffith Lewis, John Bridges, William Tooker, Thomas Blague, Paul Thomson, Francis Burgoyne, and Robert Wright), three of her Extraordinary chaplains (Richard Alison, William Hilliard, and John Fox), and John Aglionby, an Elizabethan court Lent preacher.[20] Another Whitgift list of approximately the same date recorded the names of 'Chaplaines in Ordinary' and included all but two of the Elizabethan chaplains labelled 'fitt to preach' in his earlier list, and recorded as promoted to Ordinary rank several of those formerly designated 'fitt to preache' but not then chaplains.[21] Here lies the institutional manifestation of the conservatism expressed thematically in the reign's first court sermons. With respect to the chaplains' rota at least, James's accession was, thanks to Whitgift, a 'change without a change'.

However, this same impulse on the part of the English ecclesiastical élite to close ranks against Scottish influence also led to one of the most significant changes from Elizabethan to Jacobean court religious practice. Peter Heylyn provided the best summary of how at the beginning of James's reign,

Bancroft, then Bishop of *London*, conceiving into what dangers the Church was like to run, by the multitude of *Scots* about him, thought it expedient that some Clergy-men of Note and Eminence should be attendant always in and about the Court. And thereupon it was advised, that to the Bishop *Almoner* and the Clerk of the Closet a Dean of the Chappel should be added, to look unto the diligent and due performance of Gods Publick Service, and order matters of the Quire.[22]

Accordingly, Dr James Montagu was put forward and accepted by James as his first incumbent of the revived Deanery of the Chapel Royal. As a candidate probably hand-picked to please both the Scots and the English, Montagu was a brilliant choice. First, he was not an Elizabethan court insider. Montagu's name does not appear in Whitgift's Elizabethan Lent preacher lists, and the first notice of him in the court pulpit comes from Manningham, who heard him at Whitehall on 8 April 1603, two weeks after Elizabeth's death.[23] In addition, as first Master of Cambridge's newest

---

[20] PRO LS 13/168, fol. 70. Aglionby did receive mourning blacks as a chaplain for Elizabeth's funeral (PRO LC 2/4/4 fol. 70ᵛ).

[21] WAMB 15, fol. 4ʳ. I date the list on fol. 4ʳ after that on fol. 6, based on the promotion of John King, John Aglionby, 'Dr Hayward', Thomas Mountfort, and James Montagu from 'no Chaplein' status on fol. 6 to Ordinary on fol. 4ʳ. The identification of the second hand as Whitgift's was made by Anthony Milton and confirmed by Patrick Collinson.

[22] Peter Heylyn, *Cyprianus Anglicus* (1671), 158.

[23] Manningham, *Diary*, 225–31. Montagu was added by Whitgift to the list of those fit to preach before the new king, and he also appears in the list of the royal chaplains who

Puritan seminary, Sidney Sussex College, Montagu came with impeccable Calvinist credentials. But with this he also brought a commitment to episcopacy that could be counted on by the Whitgiftian establishment to resist Presbyterianism. Thus, Bancroft and Whitgift put forward a candidate for the royal deanery that, under the guise of being the king's own creation, could, they hoped, be one of their own.

The plan worked, for Montagu swiftly became James's most trusted clerical confidante: on his own testimony, the new Dean was 'always with his Matie' in his peregrinations between court and country. The Venetian ambassador observed in 1607 that James lived 'in almost absolute retirement in the company of one man, a Dean, very learned'; and that consummate social climber, Francis Bacon, reminded himself in a 1608 memorandum to 'sett on foote and mainteyn acces' with three men, Montagu, Humphrey May, and John Murray.[24] These last two were Scots, May a groom of the Privy Chamber and Murray groom of the Bedchamber. The Scots may have monopolized access in terms of the inner chamber establishment, but the clerical avenue to the king was a decidedly English one.[25] Indeed, the Scots' religious influence at court was never more than minimal. Among the Scottish attendants James appointed to accompany him south in April 1603 were eight clergymen: two bishops, David Lindsay of Ross and Peter Rollock of Dunkeld; and five ministers, Patrick Galloway, Andrew Lamb, John Spottiswood, Gavin Hamilton, and Alexander Forbes.[26] Of this number only Patrick Galloway maintained a visible profile in the early days of James's English court. Galloway, who as king's chaplain had preached at Prince Henry's baptism, acted as a liaison at court between Scots Presbyterians and English Puritans until after the Hampton Court Conference, when he returned north to minister in the Chapel Royal at Holyrood. While in England he earned the contempt of some English courtiers for his shrill calls from the pulpit for the execution of the Bye and Main Plot conspirators.[27] Dudley Carleton referred to the whole Puritan interest at the Hampton Court Conference as 'Patrick Galloway and his

received mourning blacks in Elizabeth's funeral procession. (WAMB 15, fol. 6; PRO LC 2/ 4/4, fol. 54^r).

[24] Folger Shakespeare Library MS X.d.428, art. 59; *CSPV 1607–10*, 74; *The Letters and the Life of Francis Bacon*, ed. James Spedding, 7 vols. (1862–74), vol. IV, 40.

[25] Neil Cuddy, 'The Revival of Entourage: the Bedchamber of James I, 1603–1625', in David Starkey, ed., *The English Court* (1987), 202–3.

[26] John Spottiswood, *History of the Church of Scotland*, 3 vols., ed. M. Russell (Edinburgh, 1847–51), vol. III, 138.

[27] John Nichols, *The Progresses and Public Progressions of Queen Elizabeth*, 3 vols. (1823), vol. III, 360; Patrick Collinson, *The Elizabethan Puritan Movement* (1967; Oxford, 1990), 451; Charles Rogers, *History of the Chapel Royal of Scotland* (Edinburgh, 1882), xcvii; *Dudley Carleton to John Chamberlain 1603–1624: Jacobean Letters*, ed. Maurice Lee, Jr (New Brunswick, N.J., 1972), 49, 57.

crew'. But the others, even if they did attend the king as far south as London, were too important to James's plans for planting episcopacy in Scotland for the king to keep them about him in the southern kingdom. These ministers, all royal chaplains sympathetic to ecclesiastical government by bishops, were the cornerstones of James's Scottish episcopate: Spottiswood was appointed Archbishop of Glasgow in July 1603; Forbes Bishop of Caithness in 1606, and Lamb Bishop of Brechin in 1607, and Hamilton, dean of James's Scottish Chapel Royal, Bishop of Galloway in 1610.[28]

Only one Scot, Dr John Gordon, received preferment in England early in the reign and maintained a presence in the royal pulpit. Educated largely in France, and a chamber servant to Queen Mary as well as Charles IX, Henri III, and Henri IV, Gordon returned to England at James's accession and took English orders only upon the king's grant of the Deanery of Salisbury in October 1603. In October of the following year, he preached a sermon before the king that urged the ratification of union between England and Scotland. Although the ostensible theme was the woe that would befall a nation *'diuided against it selfe'* (Matthew 12:25), the sermon must have only fuelled the burning resentments between the Scottish and English factions at court. Gordon not only warned the English against monopolizing 'preferments, offices, and dignities as well Ecclesiasticall as Temporall, excluding from thence the fellow arme of the North', but told the court that they should be thankful for James's 'laudable modestie' in using the term 'Britains' to describe his subjects, 'seeing that the South part is fallen to his royall person, both by the lawe of God, and nature; the name of the former kingdome might haue beene imposed to this kingdome, which is last fallen in his power'.[29] But Gordon never seems to have attended as an Ordinary Chaplain, nor was he ever listed into the Lent rota. Two Scots who did become Ordinary Chaplains, and thus regular preachers at court, migrated after the succession, and were to some extent anglicized at Oxbridge: John Young, son of James's tutor, Sir Peter Young, migrated to Sidney Sussex College, Cambridge, from St Andrew's in 1606, was ordained in 1610, proceeded BD (Bachelor of Divinity) and appointed dean of Winchester in 1616; Walter Balcanquhall, son of a staunch Edinburgh Presbyterian of the same name, was incorporated at Pembroke College, Oxford, from Edinburgh in 1609, and was later Master of the Savoy and a delegate to the Synod of Dort. The Scottish presence of these men in the English court pulpit was exceptional.

In addition to a Dean of the Chapel, Bancroft's plan to guard the court

[28] Hew Scott, *Fasti Ecclesiæ Scoticanæ*, new edn., 10 vols. (1915–), vol. VII, 322, 329–30, 345, 346.
[29] John Gordon, *Enotikon or a Sermon of the Vnion of Great Britannie* (1604), 1, 10, 29.

and Church from Scots Presbyterians included yet another player. In Heylyn's account, the Chapel dean was put forward to supplement the influence of the court's two other resident clerics, the Almoner, and the Clerk of the Closet. Elizabeth's last Almoner, Anthony Watson, Bishop of Chichester, retained the office upon James's accession. But the Clerkship of the Closet received both a new incumbent and significant new duties after Elizabeth's death. Elizabeth appointed her last Clerk, John Thornborough, probably in the Armada year, and he was still so designated in the list of mourners at the queen's funeral, although his presence there is doubtful.[30] Although Thornborough seems to have been in London briefly in 1602, he had been posted from his Irish bishopric to his York deanery in 1599, where he preached before the new King James in April 1603. In July he was replaced in the Clerkship by a fairly unknown priest – Dr Richard Neile.[31] Like Montagu, Neile was probably appointed to the Clerkship through the machinations of Bancroft, and certainly with the blessing of Neile's patron, Sir Robert Cecil.[32] Also like Montagu, Neile was not a familiar face at court. Although he had been educated through the benefaction of Lady Burghley, served both William and Robert Cecil as domestic chaplain, and probably through the latter's influence was appointed Master of the Savoy in 1602, he did not make his debut in the court Lent lists until 1603, was neither an Ordinary or an Extraordinary Chaplain to Elizabeth, and was only sworn chaplain to James when he accepted the Clerkship.[33]

Was the appointment of such a minor figure to the post unusual? Elizabethan precedent suggests not, for throughout the reign the Clerkship had not gone to major ecclesiastical dignitaries. The Clerk's duties, too, seem to have been limited to the custodial tasks of arranging cushions, service books, and other Closet furniture.[34] None the less, the desire to monitor or control the Scots king's private religious practice seems to have heightened an awareness of the potential power and influence inherent in the Clerkship, and the position metamorphosed from a Tudor sinecure to a crucial Stuart point of political contact. The Clerk's principal domain in the palace apartments was a sensitive one. Positioned in what has been called

---

[30] Nichols, *Progresses . . . of Queen Elizabeth*, vol. III, 10; PRO LC 2/4/4, fol. 54. John Bickersteth and Robert W. Dunning, *Clerks of the Closet in the Royal Household* (Stroud, 1991), 16.

[31] Thornborough had been involved in a scandalous divorce and second marriage: *CSPD Addenda 1580–1625*, 392; *CSPD 1598–1601*, 178; *HMC Salisbury*, vol. XII, 330, 576; Nichols, *Progresses . . . of King James*, vol. I, 80–1.

[32] Andrew Foster, 'A Biography of Archbishop Richard Neile' (unpublished Oxford DPhil thesis, 1978), 16.

[33] Chamberlain, *Letters,* vol. I, 179; WAMB 15, fols. 31, 2, 4^r; *HMC Salisbury*, vol. XV, 199–200. Neale was sworn 'chaplein and clerk of his Ma[jesties] Closet the xxvjth of Iuly 1603' (PRO LS 13/168 fol. 90^v).

[34] Bickersteth and Dunning, *Clerks of the Closet,* 7.

the 'no man's land' between the Presence and Privy Chambers, the Privy Closet was literally as close to the king as a servant who was not sworn of the Privy or Bedchamber could get (see Figure 3). As keeper of the Closet, Neile was geographically placed on the king's doorstep, and could therefore monitor, if not control, access to him. In addition, he would have oversight of the celebration of divine service in the Closet, and therefore would be able to ensure the new king's conformity to English rites. With such access to the sovereign's person and influence over his religious routines, we can understand Bancroft's and Cecil's eagerness to hand-pick a Clerk of the Closet for James. In the ensuing reign, the sensitivity of the Clerkship was not lost on Laud either, who chose William Juxon as Neile's successor in 1632 in order that he 'might have one that I might trust near to his Majesty, if I grow weak or infirm'.[35]

For Neile, the Clerkship brought not only personal influence with the king, but public influence on the king and court through the addition of a significant new duty – a part in arranging the court sermon rotas.[36] It is not clear, however, whether Neile assumed responsibility for the preaching rota immediately upon receiving the Clerkship. But his very close ties to both Bancroft and Cecil, who, after 1604, as Archbishop of Canterbury and Secretary of State, would by tradition have arranged the Lent rota, suggests that, even if only as an apprentice, Neile could have begun his career as custodian of the court pulpit upon his appointment as Clerk. However, clear evidence survives to prove that by 1609 Neile, then Dean of Westminster and Bishop of Rochester as well as Clerk, had a part in managing court preaching. In a sermon on Easter Tuesday, 18 April 1609, William Smith, a Cambridge college head and royal chaplain, 'so well baited the great courtiers, whom he termed *suffragatores aulicos . . .* and so schooled the king himself for being led by other men rather than his own judgment' that Dudley Carleton wondered how he 'escaped baiting himself'.[37] Smith evidently regretted his boldness, for within two weeks Neile wrote to Salisbury that Smith 'has desired to preach before his Majesty tomorrow, purposing to crave some pardon for the error of his last sermon, and with some better discourse somewhat to recover his good opinion'.[38]

Neile engineered the preaching rotas with the king's interests in mind. In 1611, he set about satisfying James's request to hear his canons of Windsor preach '*in their Order*' by instructing the Dean of Windsor, Giles Thomson, to notify the prebends of the royal wish. But, wary that '*some of them may*

---

[35] Simon Thurley, *The Royal Palaces of Tudor England* (New Haven, Conn., 1993), 125–6; William Laud, *The Works of William Laud*, 7 vols., ed. J. Bliss and W. Scott (Oxford, 1847–60), vol. III, 216.

[36] Foster, 'Archbishop Richard Neile', 17.   [37] *Jacobean Letters*, ed. Lee, 110.

[38] *HMC Salisbury*, vol. XXI, 46.

not be well, or not so fit' as the king might wish, Neile instructed Thomson
to ensure the presence of Richard Field, one of the canons who was also a
favourite royal chaplain and '*a sure Card*' to satisfy the king.[39] Evidence of
Neile's responsibility for the Lent lists survives from January 1612, when
Neile wrote to Richard Clayton, Master of St John's College, Cambridge,
asking him to tell royal chaplain Valentine Carey 'that I left him this yeare
owt of the bill of the Lent Preachers', not only because he requested to be
omitted the last year, but also 'because he is to wayte imediatly after Lent
in May'. Neile said he would rather have Carey 'furnish himself against' his
Ordinary service when he would be expected 'to preach at the least Two
sermons to the King, and 2. or 3. to the howshould'. Given these demands,
Neile thought Cary was 'like to haue his hands full of preaching to the
King' and could do without a place on the Lenten rota.[40] Also in 1612,
William Westerman, a Hertfordshire vicar and chaplain to Archbishop
Abbot, credited not his powerful patron, but Neile, with securing him a
preaching spot before King James during a progress-visit to St Alban's.[41]

In view of Bancroft's engineering of court religious institutions in
advance of James's arrival, it is striking to note his singling-out for the two
key ecclesiastical appointments at court of two men of such different
theological and ecclesiological stripes as Montagu and Neile. At the time
both men were establishing clear ideological reputations: Montagu as a
Calvinist Cambridge head, and Neile as a nascent anti-Calvinist.[42] In these
two men, as in the royal chaplaincy they oversaw, we can see the outlines
of what has been described as James's deliberate incorporation of 'a wide
range of theological opinion and churchmanship into the ecclesiastical
establishment'.[43] But according to Heylyn, Montagu and Neile were
singled out for their service at the Jacobean court before there was a
Jacobean court or a Jacobean Church of England. Did Richard Bancroft lay
the foundation of James's broad-based ecclesiastical programme? At least
in terms of the court, he might have, for the competing interests of the
factions represented by Montagu and Neile were both represented with
vigour in the court pulpit throughout the reign. Montagu, as we shall see,
was quietly sympathetic with nonconformist ministers, used his influence

---

[39] Nathaniel Field, *Some Short Memorials Concerning the Life of that Reverend Divine Doctor Richard Field* (1716–17), 14.

[40] SJCC MS D105.337.

[41] William Westerman, *Iacobs Well: Or, a Sermon Preached before the Kings most Excellent Maiestie* (1613), sig. &5ᵛ.

[42] For Montagu, see Fincham, *Prelate as Pastor*, 229, 272; Neile's 1600 doctoral commencement theses aligned him with Cambridge Calvinism, but by that time his 'ideas were already in flux': Nicholas Tyacke, *Anti-Calvinists: the Rise of English Arminianism c. 1590–1640* (Oxford, 1987), 110–13. For Neile's episcopal churchmanship, see Fincham, *Prelate as Pastor*, 279–88.

[43] Fincham and Lake, 'Ecclesiastical Policy', 187.

with the king to place evangelical Calvinists around Prince Henry, and maintained a politico-religious alliance with the anti-Catholic Thomas Egerton. Montagu, given the source, might even have been pleased with the Spanish ambassador's obituary notice of him as 'capellan mayor deste Rey y gran Puritano'.[44] Neile, on the other hand, used his position as Clerk to suppress evangelicalism and to advance the careers of like-minded anti-Calvinists. Arthur Wilson, no sympathizer with prelacy, remembered with contempt Neile's unique way of censoring sermons preached by godly ministers at court. Sitting in his privileged place next to the king in the chapel closet, Neile, 'when any man preached that had the *Renown* of *Piety*' would 'entertain the King with a *merry Tale* . . . which the King would after laugh at, and tel those near him, he could not hear the *Preacher* for the old *Bishop*'.[45] Perhaps with more impact on the course of history, Neile secured William Laud's first turn in the court pulpit in 1609, a royal chaplaincy for him in 1611, and was instrumental in persuading Laud not to retire from court to a university career when preferments were not quick in coming from the king.[46]

Even if Bancroft was the principal engineer of this strategy of inclusion, it was carefully maintained by James, and the court pulpit displayed the broad range of conformity throughout his reign. In the most positive light, court preaching rotas, with their striking juxtaposition of spokesmen for very different interests in the English church, attest to a commendable inclusivity on James's part. But in a list such as that for Lent 1609, which opened the season with successive sermons by the evangelical Calivinist trio of James Montagu, John King, and George Lloyd, and closed with the proto-Arminian triumvirate of John Buckeridge, Richard Neile, and Lancelot Andrewes, we also can see the fault lines that would rend the church during the next reign. Similarly, John King, scourge of Roman Catholics, was followed in the pulpit in Lent 1613 by Benjamin Carier, a royal chaplain who later in the same year fled England and converted to Rome. Even more paradigmatically, Archbishop Abbot's routine Palm Sunday sermon was for several years followed by a sermon on Tuesday in Holy Week by his nemesis, William Laud.[47] Some texts for these contiguous

---

[44] Fincham, *Prelate as Pastor*, 268–9; *Spain and the Jacobean Catholics*, 2 vols., ed., A. J. Loomie, Catholic Record Society nos. 64 and 68 (1973, 1978), vol. II, 112. Montagu secured a royal chaplaincy for at least one of Egerton's chaplains, John Williams, later himself Lord Keeper, in 1617; see John Hacket, *Scrinia Reserata*, 2 parts (1693), vol. I, 31.

[45] Arthur Wilson, *The History of Great Britain, Being the Life and Reign of King Iames the First* (1653), 152.

[46] Heylyn, *Cyprianus Anglicus*, 59–60; Laud, *Works*, vol. III, 134.

[47] WAMB 15, fols. 35ʳ, 39, 40, 42. For Carier, see Chamberlain, *Letters*, vol. I, 483; and Loomie, ed., *Spain and the Jacobean Catholics*, vol. II, 14.

sermons survive and provide evidence of the kind of pulpit debate, or even retaliation, that could occur between court preachers.

On Easter Sunday, 24 April 1614 Lancelot Andrewes, the Moses of English anti-Calvinism, delivered an uncompromising call for worshippers to bow at the name of Jesus and to kneel for communion as obligatory recognitions of Christ's sacrifice and Real Presence in the Eucharist. God, he said, 'will not haue the inward parts onely . . . No: mentall deuotion will not serue: He will haue, both corporall and vocall, to expresse it by.' Of his text – '*at the Name of* Iesus, *euery knee should bow*' (Philippians 2:10) – he said curtly, 'the words be plaine, I see not how we can auoyd them'.[48] But the very next Sunday, James Montagu placed his own domestic chaplain in the court pulpit, evidently for the first time, to deliver a direct rebuke to Andrewes's ritualism. Norwich Spackman took as his text Matthew 9:13: 'But go ye and learne what this is: I will haue mercy, and not sacrifice.' To this Spackman shrewdly appropriated Andrewes's notion of inward and outward worship by suggesting that the former was the 'mercy' of his text, and the latter mere 'sacrifice'. For Spackman, the two were not created equal: he continued, '*mercy is so farre beyond sacrifice, and inward puritie aboue outwarde ceremonie*' that it must '*qualifie our* opinion, *which, yet in many, notwithstanding all demonstration, thinkes* formality *to bee* religion'. Leaving no doubt that he engaged Andrewes on genuflection, he concluded with a sarcasm that matched Andrewes's own by insisting that God '*will not haue a bended knee, but an vpright heart . . . not prostrated bodies but humbled soules, and when these things are within, then hang vp your* signes'.[49] In this debate, the king was on Andrewes's side, and the Easter sermon was quickly released from the royal printing house for the public's edification. But, tit for tat, Spackman's sermon was also rushed to press, the title page advertising not the preacher's name, but his service and attachment to Montagu.[50] The public therefore received two very contradictory messages from the king's pulpit on the controverted issue of liturgical ceremony, one from the Calvinist Dean of the King's Chapel (albeit through a spokesman), and another from the king's favourite Arminian preacher. Here, then, inside James's very household, we find further evidence of his masterly balancing of 'inherently antipathetic religious tendencies' through delicate manipulation of patronage. By subtle endorsements of one side (the royal printing of Andrewes's sermon), and

[48] Lancelot Andrewes, *A Sermon Preached Before His Maiestie, at Whitehall, on Easter day last* (1614), 23; *Works*, vol. II, 333.
[49] Norwich Spackman, *A Sermon before his Maiestie* (1614), A4^v, A7^r, 1, 63, 73.
[50] James made a point to receive communion on his knees. See *The Old Cheque-Book . . . of the Chapel Royal*, ed. Edward F. Rimbault, Camden Society n.s. 3 (1872), 172. Spackman signed the dedicatory epistle to his sermon 6 July 1615 (sig. A7^v).

tacit approval of another (indulging his Chapel Dean's indirect opposition), James kept both sides happy – or at least kept them guessing.[51]

It would be inaccurate to assume that the Clerk of the Closet had exclusive control over the court pulpit; as in Elizabeth's time, an élite group of court officials all had some say in who occupied it, and, as we have already seen, factional interests jockeyed for representation in it. First, it remained the Lord Chamberlain's prerogative to swear chaplains into ordinary service in the household. Moreover, he authorized the lists of Lent preachers, though, in both instances, he only ratified the king's wishes.[52] The principal secretaries to the king also continued to exercise influence and administer court pulpit affairs. When Sir Henry Wotton sent his chaplain Nathaniel Fletcher (son of the bishop and brother of the dramatist) home from Venice in 1606 with hopes for further preferment, he commended him to Salisbury with the request 'that by your honourable means he may be put into the list of the preachers at the Court this next Lent'. It was to Cecil that Neile wrote about William Smith's request to make amends for his injudicious Easter 1606 sermon; but in the same letter he observed that Smith had first gained the approval of a third party, Dean Montagu. In 1617, James's wishes for chaplains to attend him to Scotland were vetted by the joint Secretaries of State Lake and Winwood as well as Archbishop Abbot. Finally, during summer progresses, when James liked to sample local preaching talent as much as local hospitality, Neile allowed diocesans to nominate suitable preachers.[53]

None the less, James himself was the final arbiter of court-sermon matters. In purely institutional terms, he influenced the selection of court preachers more than anyone else because of his enthusiastic interest in his royal chaplaincy. As in Elizabeth's time, preaching at court was a royal chaplain's primary responsibility during his month of attendance. As Neile's message to Valentine Carey makes clear, chaplains – presumably attending in pairs – divided the month's sermons between them. That is, each took half of the Sunday and Tuesday sermons before the king, and half of the Sunday sermons before the household. The household services and sermons were held in the early morning, preceding those for the king, as an anecdote involving Neile himself shows. Bishop Andrewes having

---

[51] See Fincham and Lake, 'Ecclesiastical Policy', 206–7.

[52] *HMC Salisbury*, vol. XIII, 199; Julian Davies, *The Caroline Captivity of the Church: Charles I and the Remoulding of Anglicanism* (Oxford, 1992), 42. For Lent, see the 1622/3 Lent list endorsed by Pembroke (WAMB 15, fol. 45ʳ), and John Donne's fear, quoted in Walton's *Life of Donne*, that if 'my Lord Chamberlain believe me to be dead' he will 'leave me out of the Roll': Geoffrey Keynes, ed., *The Complete Walton* (1929), 260.

[53] *The Life and Letters of Sir Henry Wotton*, 2 vols., ed. Logan Pearsall Smith (Oxford, 1907), vol. I, 363; *HMC Salisbury*, vol. XXI, 46; PRO SP14/91/35; Field, *Short Memorials*, 13–14.

preached to the household one morning, the Clerk of the Closet told James that 'he had lost an excellent sermon . . . which, though prepared for household fare, yet would have served a royal palate'.[54] Although Neile could assign preachers for Lent, and grant special appearances by those not in the chaplaincy, it was James, by appointing chaplains, who appointed regular court preachers.

As we have seen, preaching acceptable to the sovereign was the one prerequisite for appointment as an Elizabethan chaplain in ordinary. But James, acting almost impulsively out of his love for good sermons, seems to have appointed chaplains as quickly as he dubbed knights. While on progress, for example, James delighted in sampling local preaching talent. After a good sermon by the Bedfordshire rector Thomas Archer in July 1605, the king had him sworn a Chaplain in Ordinary on the spot.[55] Coming after Elizabeth's very conservative grants of royal chaplaincies – usually only to doctors of divinity who held prebendal or decanal rank – James's doling them out to country parsons must have irritated the old guard. At James's death, sixty-two chaplains received mourning blacks for the funeral procession – Elizabeth had been attended to her tomb by only seventeen.[56] And sixty-two chaplains must have frustrated any attempts to organize these ministers into anything like the orderly monthly attendance possible with Elizabeth's seventeen chaplains. No wonder, then, that Charles, in the first months after James's death, 'observed the multitudinousness of his Fathers Chaplains, and the disorder of their waitings' and set about 'reducing them to a lesser number, and limiting them to a more certain time of attendance then before they were'.[57] Richard Neile may have had titular control over the court sermon rotas, but the influence of other officers, the king, and an oversized chaplaincy must have made tight personal control of them practically impossible.

GOWRIES, GUNPOWDER, AND HOLY TUESDAYS

James, then, was no passive cipher in matters of court religious practice. Indeed, before he reached London he had personally instituted a radical change to the Elizabethan court sermon rota that would persist until the Interregnum. In a sermon preached before the court at Greenwich in June 1603, Anthony Rudd made this allusion to the new sovereign: 'And blessed

---

[54] Andrew Clark, ed., 'Dr Plume's Notebook', *Essex Review* 15 (1906), 20; see also Charles I's rules for chapel attendance (PRO LC 5/180, 19). No printed court sermon identifies itself as having been preached for the humbler auditory, but it is likely that some, given ambiguous titles like 'preached at the Court', could indeed have been 'household fare'.

[55] Nichols, *Progresses . . . of King James*, vol. I, 520–1.

[56] PRO LC 2/6 fols. 40ᵛ–42ᵛ; LC 2/4/4 fols. 54ʳ, 67ʳ, 70ᵛ.

[57] Heylyn, *Cyprianus Anglicus*, 127.

be God who hath put into his head to celebrate euerie Tuesdaye with publike prayer, and preaching in remembraunce of God's mercie towardes himselfe, and Gods iudgement towards his enemies, by that which was acted at Saint *Ionstone* vpon the fifth of August, in the yeare 1600.'[58] Rudd alluded, of course, to James's notorious escape from the conspiracy of the Earl of Gowry and his brother at Perth. But just what had God 'put into his head'? In July of 1603, the Privy Council ordered Archbishop Whitgift to draw up a form of public thanksgiving to be observed annually in every parish in England on the fifth of August, in keeping with a similar statutory observance in Scotland.[59] Did James originally plan to have thanksgivings for his deliverance offered up every Tuesday in every English parish and cathedral church? We may never know, but even if he did, the Council only approved an annual nationwide observance.

However, in the royal household, Rudd's 'euerie Tuesday' was no exaggeration – every Tuesday of the year after James's accession was marked by a sermon at court. Within the first months of the new reign, the Venetian ambassador called the Tuesday sermons routine, noting in November 1604 that 'yesterday, after the sermon, which the King attends every Tuesday besides feastdays, his Majesty touched a number of sufferers from scrofula'. In July of the same year, he noted that after a Tuesday audience with the king, James 'went to hear the sermon, as is his wont', and the ambassador himself remained at court until after dinner – which fixes the Tuesday sermons, like those on Sundays, as late morning affairs, probably preached after morning prayer.[60] So Anthony Maxey could conclude a sermon preached on Tuesday, 8 January 1605 with allusion to '*that wicked, and most dangerous conspiracie, plotted against the Lords anointed*', and to how '*this daye wee doe acknowledge it, with thankefull remembraunce; this daye, wherein, wee are all mette together, in a most happie, and blessed peace; this day doth plainely witnesse, that hee had the deliuerance*'.[61] In August of the same year, the fifth fell on a Monday, but as Thomas Playfere's sermon on Tuesday the sixth makes clear, the state observance was held on the fifth, and the weekly court solemnization of Tuesday duly followed on the sixth. In the sermon's passionate conclusion, the preacher invoked the memory of the Gowries ('detest them, hate them, loathe them, as a toad, or as a viper, or as some hidious mishapen monster') and characterized them as those 'who were the first cause of the solem-

---

[58] Rudd, *Sermon Preached at Greenwich*, sig. B1ʳ–B2ʳ.

[59] Edward Cardwell, *Documentary Annals of the Reformed Church of England*, 2 vols. (Oxford, 1844), vol. II, 59–61; John Strype, *The Life and Acts of John Whitgift* (1718), 561–2; Church of England (liturgies), *A Fourme of Prayer with Thankesgiuing, to be Vsed . . . Euery Yeere theFfift of August* (1603).

[60] *CSPV 1603–1607*, 193, 265.

[61] Anthony Maxey, *The Sermon Preached before the King* (1605), sig. H1ᵛ–H2ʳ.

nizing, or as I may say of the sanctifying of this present day for the day of the weeke, and of yesterday for the day of the moneth . . . with so holy an exercise'.[62] Thus twenty years later, on the last Tuesday before James's interment, his chaplain Phineas Hodson, preaching in the presence of the body, maintained that the king's observance of that 'Vow, whereby hee had tyed himselfe to those weekely Exercises, for his preseruation from the *Traiterous Conspiracy*' meant that 'in two and twenty years (whiles he raigned ouer vs) he heard more Sermons, than all the Princes before him in two hundred'. For once, Jacobean panegyric was also Jacobean truth.[63]

The Privy Council had rationalized the annual English observance of the Scottish deliverance in terms of England's partaking the fruits of it in the person of their new king: 'forasmuch as by his succession to this Crown we are now made partakers of the same blessings, and of the benefit thereof preceeding equally with his subjects of the Scottish nation'.[64] But if any in the English court felt that they had had a superfluous foreign custom foisted upon them by elevating Tuesdays to quasi-sacred status, their doubts evaporated when the Gunpowder Plot of 1605 was discovered on Tuesday the fifth of November. James and his preachers were beside themselves over this coincidence that was no coincidence, but rather proof of God's providential watch-care over His anointed. In his first speech to Parliament after the Plot's discovery (9 November), James 'observed one principal point, that most of all his best fortunes had happened unto him upon the Tuesday; and particularly he repeated his deliverance from Gowry, and this, in which he noted precisely that both fell upon the 5th day of the month'.[65] Now the Tuesday court sermons honoured not just the deliverance of the Scottish king at Perth, but the entire English nation at Westminster. So the Jacobean court observed not only the state services prescribed for the fifth of August and November, but heard a weekly preaching exercise as well, the two types of commemoration becoming such a part of court custom that on Easter 1618 Lancelot Andrewes could cite these deliverance services and sermons as proofs for the Church's right to legislate religious commemorations like Easter and Sundays. 'Take example by our selues', he said. 'For His Maiesties deliuerance the fift of *August* . . . and ours the fift of *Nouember* (being Tuesday both) for these a kind of remembrance we keepe, on Tuesday euery weeke in the yeere', not unlike Sundays, those 'abstracts' of Easter. 'But', he continued, as with

[62] Thomas Playfere, *A Sermon Preached before the Kings Maiestie at Drayton* (Cambridge, 1609), 18.

[63] Phineas Hodson, *The Last Sermon Preached before his Maiesties Funerals* (1625), 22.

[64] Cardwell, *Documentary Annals*, vol. II, 59.

[65] Godfrey Goodman, *The Court of King James the First*, 2 vols., ed. John S. Brewer (1839), vol. II, 116.

Easter, 'when by course of the yeere in their seuerall monethes, the very originall dayes themselues come about: shal we not? doe we not celebrate them in much more solemne maner?'[66] Whether the annual observances on 5 August and 5 November were in fact celebrated in a 'solemne maner' at court begs further enquiry.

From the beginning there had been doubts about the veracity of the king's account of his Scottish 'deliverance'. Lancelot Andrewes is even said to have fallen on his knees before the king to beg for assurance that the royal version was true.[67] Given this dubious background, to endorse the official account of the deliverance by celebrating it with as much verve as possible was an important way to display one's loyalty to James, whether preacher, noble, or foreign ambassador. Since the holiday fell in the midst of the usual summer progress, this could mean high travel costs just to pay compliments to the delivered prince. The Venetian ambassador noted that the Lords of the Privy Council rode the sixty miles from London to Holdenby, Northamptonshire, in August 1610 to observe the holiday, and in 1611 and 1612 he himself travelled all the way to Salisbury for the event – in the latter year he literally drove two horses to death in the rush to arrive on time.[68] And the observance of Gowry Day could be a bacchanalian affair. It was the Gowry celebration attended by James's visiting brother-in-law, Christian of Denmark, in 1606 that inspired Sir James Harington's gossipy and oft-quoted *pièce de résistance* about the drunken débâcle that featured puking masque-maidens and two inebriated kings.[69] More prosaically, the Venetian ambassador concluded that 'the anniversary of the Scotch conspiracy' was most memorable as an occasion for 'unlimited drinking'.[70]

The Gunpowder Plot Anniversary added another day of revelry to the Jacobean court's calendar. Like 5 August, 5 November became a national religious holiday, observed in every church with a specially appointed service and sermon.[71] The court kept the day 'with great solemnity', going 'in state to the chapel' for service and sermon in the morning followed by

[66] Lancelot Andrewes, *A Sermon Preached before his Maiestie at Whitehall, on Easter Day Last* (1618), 47–8; *Works*, vol. II, 426.

[67] John Hacket, *A Century of Sermons,* ed. Thomas Plume (1675), viii.

[68] *CSPV 1610–1613,* 26, 198, 409–11.

[69] Sir John Harington, *The Letters and Epigrams of Sir John Harington,* ed. Norman E. McClure (Philadelphia, Pa., 1930), 118–26.

[70] *CSPV 1623–25,* 414.

[71] Both the 5 August and the 5 November services are based on *The Book of Common Prayer*'s order for Morning Prayer, with special collects, Psalms, and lessons, as well as collects and lections for any service of Holy Communion celebrated on that day. For the nationwide observance, see David Cressy, *Bonfires and Bells: National Memory and the Protestant Calendar in Elizabethan and Jacobean England* (1989), ch. 9.

the king's dining publicly in the presence chamber.[72] The Gunpowder Anniversary also coincided nicely with the Allhallows-tide revels which began on All Hallow's (31 October) and included the major feast of All Saints' (1 November). The addition of the Gunpowder Anniversary in 1606 expanded the holiday at court to almost a full week (31 October–5 November) and by the middle of the reign it became a season, not unlike Christmastide or Shrovetide, marked by theatrical productions. On 5 November 1611, for example, the King's Men acted before their patron Shakespeare's romance of royal deliverances, *The Winter's Tale*. In 1612, Prince Henry's fatal illness interrupted a full slate of dramatic performances begun on All Hallow's Eve, and four years later the All Hallows–Gunpowder week provided a festival setting full of pageants and plays for the creation of Charles as Prince of Wales on 4 November 1616.[73]

The vast majority of the surviving sermons delivered at court on these holy days were by Lancelot Andrewes.[74] As articulations of what we now call Stuart divine-right absolutism, some have found Andrewes's 'political' sermons mere slavish fawning at the king's feet, while more recent studies have yielded more measured theological and political analyses.[75] But it still remains to place these, some of Andrewes's best sermons, more squarely in their court context. Andrewes could be withering about the less-than-pious turn that court feast days took as soon as king and court processed out of the chapel and into the hall or banqueting house. On 5 November 1617, preaching on a verse from the Benedictus – '*That we being deliuered, from the handes, of our enemies, might serue Him, without feare In holinesse* . . .' (Luke 1:74) – he asked sarcastically, 'Were we *liberati*, to become libertines, to sett vs downe, and eate, and to drinke healths, and rise vp, and see a play?'[76] On these occasions Andrewes offered repeated instruc-

---

[72] *CSPV 1603–1607*, 430; *CSPV 1607–1610*, 64.

[73] Yoshiko Kawachi, *Calendar of English Renaissance Drama, 1558–1642* (New York, 1986), 153, 158, 170–1. The Gowry Anniversary also became an occasion for masquing, including Ben Jonson's *The Gypsies Metamorphosed* with lines specially written for 5 August at Belvoir Castle in 1621: *Ben Jonson*, 11 vols., ed. C. H. Herford and Percy and Evelyn Simpson (Oxford, 1925–52), vol. VII, 608; Kawachi, *Calendar*, 183, 185, 194.

[74] Exceptions to Andrewes preaching at court on these days are Tobias Matthew on 5 August 1603, John King on 5 November 1608, and John Hacket on 5 August 1623 or 1624, and 5 November 1623 and 1624: YML Add MS 18, 71; John King, *A Sermon Preached at Whitehall the 5. Day of November.ann.1608* (Oxford, 1608); Hacket, *Century of Sermons*, 731–61.

[75] Paul Welsby, *Lancelot Andrewes 1555–1626* (1958), 135–43, 198–208; Maurice Reidy, *Bishop Lancelot Andrewes, Jacobean Court Preacher* (Chicago, Ill., 1955), 185–211; Nicholas Lossky, *Lancelot Andrewes the Preacher, 1555–1626* (Oxford, 1991), ch. 7; Deborah Shuger, *Habits of Thought in the English Renaissance: Religion, Politics, & the Dominant Culture* (Berkeley, Calif., 1990), 141–50.

[76] Andrewes, *A Sermon Preached before his Maiestie . . . the Fift of Nouember Last* (1618), 5; *Works*, vol. IV, 363.

tion on how to feast properly, enjoining a reorientation of the celebration from flesh to spirit, a case he put strongly in the very first court observance of the Fifth of November (1606). He called for the court to '*order our ioy*', not like the people of Ephraim, who 'kept their King's day . . . by taking in boule after boule, till they were sick again'. These were but the feasts 'that *Malachi* speaks of, there came nothing of their *feasts,* but *dung* (beare with it, it is the *Holy Ghost* his own terme) that is, all in the *belly,* and *belly-cheere*. So they, that sate *down to eat and drink, and rose up to play,* and there was all; that is the *Calves feast,* a *Calfe* can do as much.' What calves could not do and the court should do was to '*bleße,* and be *bleßed* in the *house of the Lord*'. The 'streame of our ioy, must come from the spring-head of *Religion*', Andrewes insisted. Only after a proper sacrifice of praise and thanksgiving in chapel, 'when we have put this *incense* in our phialls, and bound *this sacrifice with cords, to the altar*', can the priest 'blesse you and dismisse you, to eat your *bread* with *joy,* and to drinke your *wine* with a *cheereful heart*'.[77]

Much more than being indignant over gluttony, drunkenness, and play-going, however, Andrewes became increasingly incensed throughout the reign over the court's assumption that showing up for a sermon was somehow sufficient praise and thanksgiving for the great deliverances God had wrought on 5 August and 5 November. In his Gunpowder Anniversary paraphrase of the Benedictus, Andrewes insisted that God had delivered the court from the hands of their enemies that they then might serve him – 'there growes an obligation out of it'. But Andrewes saw the court's notion of religious service, whether the liturgy itself, behaviour in church, or religious life in general as reduced to mere 'eare-seruice': 'All our holiday *holinesse,* yea, and our working day too, both are come to this, to heare (nay, I dare not say that, I cannot prooue it) but, to be at a Sermon.'[78] Nicholas Lossky has observed in Andrewes's Gowry and Gunpowder sermons both a high concentration of the preacher's own 'liturgical creations', mostly elaborate prayers, and a preoccupation with calling the court to 'join deeds to their words'. Although both of these characteristics support Lossky's general thesis that Andrewes used these occasions as 'a pretext' to enjoin works of charity and participation in ecclesial prayer, they can be more specifically linked to Andrewes's critique of the Jacobean court's sermon-centred piety.[79] James's observance of the Gunpowder and Gowry deliverances – both annual and weekly – resulted in an exponential increase in court sermon-hearing. This, coupled with the fact that the holy

[77] Andrewes, *XCVI Sermons,* 898–9; *Works,* vol. IV, 218–19, 221.
[78] Andrewes, *Sermon Preached before his Maiestie . . . the Fift of Nouember Last,* 5, 35; *Works,* vol. IV, 363, 377.
[79] For the reaction against court preaching, see below, 155–67.

days themselves inspired more revelry than piety at court, made them exemplars for Andrewes of the worst kind of Christian practice – one based wholly on the 'ear-service' of sermon-hearing that consequently devalued prayer and failed to translate precepts in sermons into actual deeds and works once outside the chapel. Lossky helpfully observes that each of the Gowry and Gunpowder sermons 'without exception, contains examples, more or less developed, of prayers composed for the occasion'. But these specially designed prayers-within-sermons provided the perfect emphasis, or rather realization, of his pleas to join prayers to preaching, to observe the festivals *'per modum orationis'* as well as *'per modum concionis'*.[80] So, too, his calls for works were tied directly to a critique of sermon-piety. The king and court could, according to Andrewes, troop into chapel in the morning for a sermon, 'haue certaine pangs of *godlinesse* come vpon them at times: be affected for the present, with a deliuery, grow a little *holy* vpon it';[81] but this kind of piety lasted only as long as the sermon. To it had to be added not only the act of public prayer, but, to make the day more than an occasion for feeling smug at a sermon or a mere *'play* or *feasting'*, godly acts of charity and justice had to be performed.[82] As Andrewes summed it up in one of his last Gunpowder sermons, 'Nay, God is *serued* in *righteous* doing, as well, nay better, then in *holy* hearing.'[83]

Finally, as in the kingdom at large, at court the Gunpowder and Gowry sermons were important annual articulations of providential nationalism – the logical outgrowth of the Foxeian myth of England's divine deliverance from the clutches of popery. Not insignificantly, Whitgift instructed the panel of bishops who were to draw up the Gowry Anniversary service to take as their model the order 'used upon the 17th of *November* in our late Sovereign's Time' – Elizabeth's accession day.[84] Icons of Tudor providentialism were metamorphosed into Stuart ones: the deliverances at Perth and the 1605 Parliament simply corroborated the status of Elizabethan England, now Jacobean Britain, as God's elect nation, the recipient of 'such *mercies* and favours of His, *Super* upon ourselves, as (sure) the nations round about us have not seen: and', as Andrewes ventured in 1615, 'I think I may say, not eny nation on the Earth seene the like.'[85] The deliverance

---

[80] Lossky, *Lancelot Andrewes*, 300–8. Cf. also the conclusion of the sermon for 5 August 1614 (quoted here; Andrewes, *XCVI Sermons*, 828–9; *Works*, vol. IV, 100) or that for 5 November 1609 (*XCVI Sermons*, 921–2; *Works*, vol. IV, 259–60).

[81] Andrewes, *Sermon Preached before his Maiestie . . . the Fift of Nouember Last*, 46; *Works*, vol. IV, 382.

[82] *XCVI Sermons*, 1007; *Works*, vol. IV, 404.

[83] *Sermon Preached before his Maiestie . . . the Fift of Nouember Last*, 40; *Works*, vol. IV, 379.

[84] Strype, *Whitgift*, 562. For 17 November, see Cressy, *Bonfires and Bells*, ch. 4.

[85] Andrewes, *XCVI Sermons*, 966; *Works*, vol. IV, 332.

from the Gunpowder Plot in particular formed a Jacobean pendant to the Elizabethan deliverance from the Spanish Armada. According to Andrewes, they were deliverances 'Two such, as no Age euer saw, nor can bee found, in any Story. That of 88. This of [1]605. (both, within the compasse of seuenteene yeeres) One by strand, the other by land . . . a Summer, and a Winter *deliuerance*.'[86]

Since the Fifth of November commemorated the deliverance from a Catholic plot, the handling of court sermons on that day was carefully monitored as a gauge of anti-Catholic sentiment and policy. In November 1609 a servant of the Earl of Rutland informed his master from London that 'the generall opinion is here that a milder course wilbe held with Catholicks'. He cited as proof Salisbury's commendation of the 'quiet behaviour of recusants' and the moderate tone of Lancelot Andrewes's 'publique sermon before the King the 5th of November, a daie used in time past to exasperate'.[87] An example of the kind of Gunpowder sermon 'used in time past to exasperate' had been preached at court the preceding year by John King, a royal chaplain and later Bishop of London. This was one of the few court sermons for the day not preached by Andrewes, and its shrill anti-Catholic rhetoric, which was so well received that it was commanded into print, might explain not only the comment by the Earl of Rutland's servant about past exasperations, but also the decision to put the Gunpowder Anniversary sermon back in the milder Andrewes's hands for many years thereafter.[88] Andrewes's sermon for 1609 was not void of anti-Catholic sentiment; in fact, it was one of his most sustained pulpit attacks on the Jesuits' mission. So what could the Earl's servant have found so encouraging?

Important recent work has shown that Andrewes was preaching this sermon at a time when 'most writers (and many officials) were keener to incriminate as many Romanists as possible . . . whether they were secular or Jesuit'. Moreover, he was preaching on the anniversary of the Plot that galvanized precisely this kind of unilateral anti-Catholicism. By attacking only the most extreme van of popery, Andrewes tacitly took a more moderate position on other forms of Catholic loyalty and practice, thereby giving support to King James's own political distinction between moderate and radical Catholics, and anticipating much in the later Laudian attitudes towards Romanists.[89] But not only did Andrewes eschew popular English

---

[86] Andrewes, *A Sermon Preached . . . the Fift of Nouember Last*, 1617, 11; *Works*, vol. III, 366.

[87] *HMC Rutland*, vol. I, 420.

[88] King, *A Sermon Preached at White-hall*. The title page advertises the sermon as '*Published by commandement*'; for its reception at court, see Chamberlain, *Letters*, vol. I, 269.

[89] Anthony Milton, *Catholic and Reformed: the Roman and Protestant Churches in English Protestant Thought, 1600–1640* (Cambridge, 1995), 241–2, 258–63. James's distinction

anti-Catholicism, he openly, if cleverly, criticized it; in the course of condemning the Jesuits' use of violence 'upon pretense of religion', he censured English Protestants' calls for equally violent retaliation against Catholics. Andrewes's text, a passage from Luke (9:54–6) in which Christ condemns his Disciples' call for fire to rain down on a Samaritan village, afforded an easy, punning application to Jesuit complicity in the Gunpowder Plot:

And was not this, under the termes of *Iames* and *Iohn* and a Town of *Samaria,* our very case, this day foure yeare. We were then in danger of *destroying,* and destroying by the same element, *fire* . . . There were then, that forwarded these *fire*-works, with their *dicimus,* all they could: and they said, they were *Disciples* of IESVS's *societie.*

Having played this anti-Catholic card, Andrewes turned the tables by reminding the court that Christ's rebuke – '*For the Son of man is not come to destroy men's lives, but to save them*' – 'shewed himself on that side that inclined to humanitie and peace'.[90] By implication, Andrewes urged the Golden Rule: do unto Catholics as you would have them do unto you.

John King, however, had decidedly not urged James to turn the other cheek. Instead, noting that the pens and tongues of the papists would malign James's name anyway, he urged the king to really give them something to write about:

I would they had iuster cause . . . That your Maiesty would do them right, and administer iustice vpon them, in the timely execution of your Lawes, and necessary castigation, coercion of their vnrestrainable audaciousnesse . . . Least if iustice goe on to sleepe as it were hir dead sleepe, the tares of disloialty, treasons, and seditions be so thicke sowen in the field of your kingdomes, by those *envious men,* the seedes-me[n] of Rome, that it wil be difficulty and maistry afterwards to remoue them.[91]

The following year Andrewes's emphasis fell on mercy rather than justice. Christ's spirit was that of a dove, not a hawk, and violence in the name of Christ's religion, whether Roman Catholic or Protestant, was to Andrewes a contradiction in terms. Christ was 'the Master of all meekenesse', and 'if this spirit be in you', Andrewes told king and court, 'let all your motions smell of the olive-branch, not of the thunder-bolt; come from *saving grace,* and not from *consuming zeale*'.[92] The juxtaposition of King and Andrewes on Gunpowder Day 1608 and 1609 anticipated the divisions among clergy and court that would blaze after 1618 over intervention in the Palatinate and the proposed Spanish Match. But just as the pairing of the two is

between moderate and radical Catholics was first sketched by Fincham and Lake, 'Ecclesiastical Policy', 182–6.
[90] Andrewes, *XCVI Sermons,* 911–14; *Works,* vol. IV, 242, 245.
[91] King, *A Sermon Preached at White-hall,* 34–5.
[92] Andrewes, *XCVI Sermons,* 918; *Works,* vol. IV, 253.

emblematic of future struggles, so too is the fact that Andrewes, not King, became the preferred preacher for 5 August and 5 November until 1623, while James, over the objections of preachers such as King and his powerful colleague George Abbot, steered a stubbornly pacifist policy abroad while turning a deaf ear to repeated parliamentary and pulpit calls for enforcement of anti-Catholic legislation at home.

SERMONS AND JACOBEAN COURT CULTURE

By commanding the annual observance of the Gowry and then the Gunpowder Anniversaries, James had increased from three to five the number of great religious feasts marked at court by 'Solemne Sermons'.[93] By commanding a weekly Tuesday sermon-commemoration of his deliverance from the Gowries, James had at a single stroke doubled the number of sermons preached at Elizabeth's court. The sermon – not Shakespearean drama, and not even the Jonsonian masque – was the pre-eminent literary genre at the Jacobean court. No other literary enterprise could captivate, inspire, or even anger the king like a sermon. There is something compelling and emblematic – and not to be ignored – in the fact that James's first act upon entering England was to march to Berwick church to hear a sermon; James's institution of the Tuesday court sermons before he had even arrived in London invalidates the claim that the king's famous May 1603 transformation of Shakespeare's acting company, the Lord Chamberlain's Men, into the King's Men was his 'first act in the literary realm'.[94] It might have been his first act in what scholars like to think of as 'literary', but literary tastes and canons, despite a new wave of 'historicism', remain quite ahistorical.

Leeds Barroll has done much to dispel the notion that King James was infatuated with drama, and he reminds us that 'hunting, not plays was the approved solace' of the new king.[95] But to that must be added the fact that James took his preachers hunting with him, and that the one thing that could certainly get him off his horse was a good sermon. When sermon days coincided with hunting days – Tuesdays, for example – the king ordered the usual mid-morning sermon for eight o'clock, so that he could dine immediately thereafter and then take horse.[96] Moreover, the favourite

---

[93] The other three occasions were Christmas, Easter, and Whitsunday. The phrase is John Buckeridge's, from 'A Sermon Preached at the Fvneral of . . . Lancelot Late Lord Bishop of Winchester', appended to Andrewes, *XCVI Sermons*, 21; *Works*, vol. V, 295.

[94] Jonathan Goldberg, *James I and the Politics of Literature* (Baltimore, Md., 1983), 231–9.

[95] Leeds Barroll, 'A New History for Shakespeare and his Time', *Shakespeare Quarterly* 39 (1988), 461.

[96] Thomas Ball, *The Life of the Renowned Doctor Preston*, ed. E. W. Harcourt (Oxford, 1885), 63.

royal hunting grounds around Newmarket and Royston, because of their proximity to Cambridge University, gave James the chance to catch preachers 'as well as hares'. The king agreed with the University on 'a combination . . . for Preachers' that supplied young MAs and BDs to fill the king's hunting lodge pulpit 'whenever he should lye w^{th}in 12 miles of Cambridge'.[97] James took pride in his hunting-lodge *cum* seminary and once boasted, '*I have many great Wits, and of clear Distillation, that have Preach'd before me at* Royston *and* New-Market *to my great Liking, that are under Thirty.*'[98] Among those who made their court debuts as part of the Cambridge–Royston connection were Prince Charles's chaplain John Preston; John Williams, later Lord Keeper and Bishop of Lincoln, who was 'Listed into the Combination of the choicest Preachers' at 'that hunting Court at *Royston*' in 1610; and Williams's biographer, John Hackett, Restoration bishop of Lichfield.[99] The Cambridge 'Combination' even involved some remuneration from the king to the university. A letter dated 8 March 1624[5?] from the University's Vice-Chancellor authorized Sir John Coke to pay Valentine Carey, Bishop of Exeter and a former Cambridge head and Vice-Chancellor, 'those monies due to the preachers before his Majesty at Roiston & Newmarket'.[100] Not only was the king willing to interrupt his hunting for preaching, he was willing to pay for it too – something not done since Henrician times. And in 1610, John Chamberlain, eager to obtain notes from the sermon that Lancelot Andrewes preached at court on Christmas Day 1609, reported that 'the King with much importunitie had the copie delivered him on Tewsday last before his going toward Roiston, and sayes he will lay yt still under his pillow'.[101] If we contrast how much critical attention has been paid to the sparse evidence of James's interest in Shakespearean drama with the scant attention given to evidence like this of his devotion to sermons we must at least begin to see how dubious are the claims for drama's privileged place at the Stuart court. James VI and I did not sleep with a copy of *Macbeth* – much less *The Golden Age Restor'd* – under his pillow.

James liked sermons more than his predecessor: Elizabeth had tolerated them, James revelled in them. Whereas Elizabeth suppressed the prophesyings, James, as part of his commitment to a preaching ministry, saw the Elizabethan ban on the prophesyings lifted in the canons of 1604.[102] Not

[97] Ball, *Preston*, 62.

[98] Hacket, *Scrinia Reserata*, vol. I, 88. For James's time spent in Cambridgeshire as more than time wasted in the hunt, see Wormald, 'James VI and I: Two Kings or One?', 203; and B. W. Quintrell, 'The Royal Hunt and the Puritans, 1604–1605', *Journal of Ecclesiastical History*, 31 (1980), 41–58.

[99] Hackett, *Scrinia Reserat.*, vol. I, 19.   [100] PRO SP14/185/29.

[101] Chamberlain, *Letters*, vol. I, 292, 295.

[102] Fincham and Lake, 'Ecclesiastical Policy', 179–80.

only did James countenance prophesyings and combination lectures in parish churches, but he also brought them in a somewhat modified albeit still recognizable form to his court. Professor Collinson has described the typical Elizabethan prophesying as a series of sermons after which 'the ministers would retire for formal 'censure' of the doctrine preached, to discuss other matters of common and professional interest, and to dine together'.[103] In addition to the traditional Lent series, James enjoyed sermon series of his own design. In his hunting-lodge combination for Cambridge divines, he in effect auditioned promising younger preachers; and at least once he commanded the twelve canons of Windsor to preach before him 'in their Order that he may see what is in them'.[104] After stepping out of the court pulpit, preachers could also expect the king to engage them in some discussion of major points of their sermons. After John Preston's probationary sermon at Finching-Brook, James kissed the preacher's hand 'as the manner was', and then, not unlike the presiding minister at a prophesying, commanded the younger man to attend at his dinner table where he 'had his eye continually upon Mr Preston, & spake of divers passadges in the sermon with much content'.[105] Similarly, after Thomas Mallory, Dean of Chester, preached before James on progress in 1617, the king 'could at his dinner recount the heads and chief points of his Sermon as punctually as if his Highnesse had been acquainted with the preacher's notes'.[106]

James's interest in his preachers' performances was not just religious dilettantism. In addition to listening passively to sermons, he could actively deploy court preaching, even court sermon series, for political ends. When refractory Scottish Presbyterians challenged the king's ecclesiastical authority in 1606, James responded by hauling the ringleaders to Hampton Court, where they were subjected to a carefully orchestrated two-week sermon series that, under the king's watchful eye, schooled them on the royal supremacy and *jure divino* episcopacy.[107] Similarly, as we have seen, the king's 1617 Scottish homecoming was an ecclesiastical progress, painstakingly choreographed to display the purported beauties of conformity with English hierarchy and ceremony. In addition to shipping an entirely new chapel interior and choir north to Holyrood, James brought an entourage of English chaplains and bishops, men Secretary Lake said the king wanted to hand 'to haue some that might sett his ministers as he

[103] Patrick Collinson, *Archbishop Grindal, 1519–1583: the Struggle for a Reformed Church* (Berkeley, Calif., 1979), 234.
[104] Field, *Short Memorials*, 14.   [105] Ball, *Preston*, 64.
[106] Nichols, *Progresses . . . of King James*, vol. III, 407.
[107] James Melvill, *The Autobiography and Diary of Mr James Melvill*, ed. Robert Pitcairn (Edinburgh, 1842), 653–67. For the sermons, see below, note 150.

termed it to school if need were'.[108] The 'able Ministers' chosen reveal a shrewd preaching strategy on the king's part: they included ceremonialist Arminians such as Lancelot Andrewes, Richard Neile, and William Laud, who could preach ceremonial and sacramental worship, and conformist Calvinists such as John Williams, Robert Wilkinson, James Montagu, and Joseph Hall, who could act as doctrinal bridges to the Scots Calvinists while upholding episcopacy. The Dean of the Scottish Chapel Royal, William Cowper, knew what was coming. In May he wrote that in a recent letter James had already 'boasted us with his English doctours, who (as he sayes) shall instruct us in these and in other points, except we refuse instruction'. Faced with the approach of James and his vanguard of English preachers the Dean could only pray, 'God make us wise and faithfule, and keepe us from their usurpation over us, which now is evidentlie perceived'.[109]

James was also a shrewd auditor and a harsh adjudicator of what was preached before him. When Edward Simpson, Fellow of Trinity College, Cambridge, 'fell upon a point of Arminius doctrine' in an October 1617 sermon at Royston, James ordered the Cambridge heads to examine the suspect preacher. The light censure they returned dissatisfied him so much that he a called a conference of the college heads at Newmarket, where the issue was 'narrowly discussed' and the errant preacher ordered to preach a retraction sermon *coram* 'at the Kings return thether after Christmas'. When Simpson reappeared in February 1618, he preached an excellent sermon but not 'what was lookt for and enjoyned him', which resulted in yet another pulpit appearance by royal command.[110] Moreover, James did not like to share his role as adjudicator of court sermons. In 1613, the Privy Council, led by the Earl of Northampton, took it upon itself to question one of the king's chaplains, Thomas Scott, who had 'glaunct at matters somwhat suspiciously' in a court sermon against flatterers and church papists. Upon hearing of the Council's action, James snapped that 'he heard the sermon himself, and was able to judge and yf he had found cause wold have referred him over to the counsaile himself'.[111] Perhaps in monitoring his preachers James found an outlet for the type of direct involvement in governmental debate that Jenny Wormald reminds us was such an impor-

---

[108] PRO SP14/91/35. The king specified that Lancelot Andrewes was to preach 'all the holydays'; see Heylyn, *Cyprianus Anglicus*, 67.

[109] David Calderwood, *The History of the Kirk of Scotland*, 7 vols., ed. Thomas Thomson (1842–59), vol. VII, 245. According to Heylyn, the English preachers also served as James's ears at Edinburgh city sermons (*Cyprianus Anglicus*, 68). See another contemporary account sympathetic to the Scots, in Bodl. MS Carte 77, fols. 158–9.

[110] Chamberlain, *Letters*, vol. II, 121, 140. Copies of Simpson's sermon are CUL MS Ff.5.25 and BL Add MS 5960.

[111] Chamberlain, *Letters*, vol. I, 453–4.

tant feature of James's Scottish kingship: 'as in the state, so in the church the key to royal success was personal intervention by a king who stepped down from his throne and joined in as one of the protagonists in the hurly-burly of debate'.[112]

It should be noted, however, that as much as James was the zealous patron of sermons, he had no patience for overly long ones. In 1618, Chamberlain wrote that, in spite of Bishop of London John King's having preached well and 'very plaine in many points' before the king on Accession Day, it was still 'nothing pleasing, the rather for that he was a full halfe howre too long'. The only known instance of James's interrupting a preacher in the pulpit was his Christmas 1622 humiliation of his new Almoner, George Montaigne, Bishop of London. The courtiers, who found the sermon 'smooth and plausible enough', could come up with no other explanation for the royal outburst than that the sermon's length was 'too much'.[113] As we have seen, Elizabeth's preachers grumbled about the 'short scantling' afforded court sermons as opposed to those preached in parish pulpits or at Paul's Cross. Likewise, in 1606, the king's chaplain George Meriton prefaced the printing of a court sermon with the explanation that 'it is a short Sermon. *For it was preached, not at the* Crosse, *but at the* Court: *The one place requiring length, the other expecting breuity.*'[114] In fact, court sermons were expected to be exactly half the length of a Cross sermon: at the Cross the hourglass was turned twice, but at court only once. When Thomas Playfere published an expanded version of the sermon he had preached before Prince Henry during Lent, 1605, he explained that in the pulpit he had '*deliuered somuch as filled vp the ordinarie time of an hower*', even though '*that was scarse halfe this sermon*'. He had '*vttered no more*', he observed, because '*tediousnes without regard of due time, especially in so high a presence, soonest offendeth*'.[115] This '*strict compasse of time*', to use Playfere's phrase, resulted in a striking uniformity of length that sets the court sermons off formally as a distinct sub-genre of pulpit oratory. Andrewes's court sermons, almost without exception, run from eighteen to twenty modern quarto pages. Donne's are even slightly more concise, usually running to eighteen pages, in contrast to thirty pages for those preached at St Paul's. In the hands of the best preachers, the brevity required of the court sermon could yield the verbal intensity and artistry more frequently associated with poetry of the period.

James's enthusiasm for sermon-hearing elevated what had been a

---

[112] Wormald, 'James VI and I', 197.   [113] Chamberlain, *Letters*, vol. II, 152, 470.
[114] George Meriton, *A Sermon of Nobilitie* (1607), sig. A4[r].
[115] Thomas Playfere, *The Sick Mans Couch* (Cambridge, 1605), sig. A3[r]. For Paul's Cross sermon length, see Millar MacLure, *The Paul's Cross Sermons 1534–1642* (Toronto, 1958), 8–9.

mundane, and perhaps even optional, Elizabethan observance, to a twice-weekly obligation for those resident at court. Whereas Elizabeth assiduously heard sermons only during Lent and then sporadically on Sundays and feast days, at a minimum James expected any members of his Council present at court to attend him to the weekly Sunday and Tuesday sermons, as well as those on major holy days; according to the Venetian ambassador, the king would even cut an audience short in order not to delay a Tuesday sermon.[116] Not surprisingly, early in the new reign preachers who for years had been handicapped by Elizabeth's feeble commitment to a preaching ministry heralded James's privileging of sermons at court as a portent of glory days to come. On Accession Day 1605, Anthony Maxey praised James for having 'the most religious Court . . . that is in Christendome'. And in August of the same year Thomas Playfere praised the court as the centrepiece of the new king's devotion to a preaching ministry:

Neuer heretofore such diligent hearing in the Court, as now a dayes. I dare be bold to say it; All the preachers in England, in verie many yeares by all their exhortations, could neuer haue done halfe so much good in this kind, as the one onely, holy, and happy example hath done, which we see euery day before our eies.[117]

Even though James grieved advanced Protestants by moving decisively against nonconformist ministers in the deprivations of 1604–5, the example of a sermon-hearing king and court could still be held up as proof of James's personal commitment to an evangelical Church of England. Although, as we shall see, James's sermon patronage did not please everyone, it inspired praise throughout the reign. In 1611, the translators of the Authorized Version of the Bible claimed in their dedicatory epistle that among the joys of the succession 'there was no one that more filled our hearts' than James's 'blessed continuance of the Preaching of GODS sacred word amongst us'. As late as 1621 – when James's credentials with the godly needed a boost – his chaplain Christopher Swale could still sing the praises of that 'Religious Vow, you see weekly payed in this place by our royall *Iacob*, I meane our Tuesdayes Exercise; which was deuoutly vowed . . . and hitherto (God be thanked) it hath beene religiously performed'.[118] James's clear endorsement of a sermon-centred piety aligns him even more strongly than has perhaps been recognized with the phalanx of evangelical Calvinist clergy, helpfully described by Kenneth Fincham as 'preaching pastors'. At court, this group was represented most strongly by Bishop John King and Archbishop Abbot, but also included bishops such as James

---

[116] *CSPV 1607–1610*, 307.
[117] Thomas Playfere, *A Sermon Preached before the Kings Maiesty . . . at Woodstock*, 37.
[118] Christopher Swale, *Iacobs Vow. A Sermon* (1621), 13.

Montagu, Tobie Matthew, and Arthur Lake.[119] Montagu's almost unrivalled early influence with James has already been surveyed, and sympathies in churchmanship between James and Abbot, including a mutual commitment to the pulpit, must surely have influenced the king's decision to elevate Abbot to Canterbury over the expected candidate, Lancelot Andrewes, who, as shall be argued, was a pointed critic of James as a consumer and patron of sermons. The court, then, was an amenable place for ministers who saw preaching as the very heart of the national church. Here, for example, a godly Calvinist such as Francis Rollenson could preach a sermon that interpreted the Canticle's wedding banquet not only as a feast for the elect – a 'selected number, not the whole frie of the world' – but as a feast of preaching. In the hands of Andrewes or Buckeridge a Biblical text inviting the faithful to a feast could have led to nothing other than an invitation to the Eucharist. But to Rollenson and many like him who filled the court pulpit, the invitation 'to His table' was to gather around the pulpit.[120]

King James's patronage of court preaching was, however, problematic. Because of his preference for rural Cambridgeshire over the courtly crowds at Whitehall, James failed to make nearly as much of a public statement out of his sermon-going as his predecessor. James did not hear sermons alone, but expected his courtiers and officeholders to attend with him. According to Bacon, the pressure on court grandees to attend court sermons actually resulted in the diminished presence of the Lords at City sermons, thereby eroding an important political link between the court and City. When James was on progress to Scotland in the spring of 1617, the newly appointed Lord Keeper seized the opportunity to rally the lords left in London,

to meet again on Easter-Monday, and go all to the Spital sermon for that day, and, therein to revive the ancient religious manner when all the Council used to attend those sermons; which some neglect in Queen Elizabeth's time, and his Majesty's great devotion in the due hearing of sermons himself with his Council at the Court, brought into desuetude.[121]

---

[119] Fincham, *Prelate as Pastor*, ch. 8.1. Dr Fincham's cautions about overstating this group as a 'factional bloc' are well taken, but as a description of a common churchmanship, the grouping is very helpful. For Abbot's commitment to evangelism, see Fincham, *Prelate as Pastor*, 87, and his 'Prelacy and Politics: Archbishop Abbot's Defense of Protestant Orthodoxy', *Historical Research* 61 (1988), 36–64.

[120] Francis Rollenson, 'The Bridegroom's Banquet', part one of *Sermons Preached Before his Maiestie* (1611), 17, 19. Rollenson was a royal chaplain and part of Lord Keeper Egerton's extensive patronage network of evangelical clergy. See Louis A. Knafla, 'The "Country" Chancellor: The Patronage of Sir Thomas Egerton, Baron Ellesmere', in French R. Fogle and Louis A. Knafla, *Patronage in Late Renaissance England* (Los Angeles, Calif., 1983), 44–54.

[121] Bacon, *Letters*, vol. VI, 167.

James's patronage of the court sermon could, then, be seen as contributing to the growing estrangement of court and City, and herein lies one of the great ironies of the reign: the monarch who so highly esteemed preaching failed to display himself as a preaching-patron outside the court. Though not one to go gadding to sermons, Elizabeth succeeded better in manipulating public displays of sermon-hearing, and nowhere is the contrast between the two sovereigns more clearly seen than in their patterns of attendance at the court Lent sermons. On Camden's testimony, which can be corroborated, Elizabeth piously attended these thrice-weekly sermons.[122] Machyn, for example, observed the queen at the majority of the court sermons preached in the first four years of her reign. Moreover, of the twenty-two Elizabethan court Lent sermons that have survived in print, Elizabeth was present at every one. As we have seen, the queen also made especially good use of the public spectacle of her attendance at outdoor sermons where throngs of people – not all courtiers – paid as much attention to her as to the preacher.[123]

However, James spent the greater part of Lent at his Essex and Cambridgeshire hunting retreats, and when at Whitehall seems to have commanded use of the outdoor Preaching Place very infrequently. During Lent 1610, for example, the Venetian ambassador observed that James had 'seldom stayed two days running' in London. The following year, the king reportedly planned to leave for Royston on 'the second day of Lent' and to 'remain at the chase till Holy Week'. With Anne at Greenwich, the court at Whitehall was 'quite empty' that year until the royal family returned for Holy Week and Easter.[124] Early in the reign there seems to have been some attempt on the part of the royal family to keep up Elizabeth's Lenten practice of showing royal faces in the Council Chamber window over the Preaching Place during sermons, but, as the reign wore on, James avoided it more and more. The accounts of the Treasurer of the Chamber, which list payments to the gentlemen ushers and their assistants for setting up rooms for various ceremonial occasions, record that in 1605, 1606, and 1607 the Council Chamber was readied an unspecified number of times 'for the king and Queene against the preaching'. Royal attendance at outdoor sermons seems to have peaked in 1609 when the Council Chamber was readied 'six severall times', followed by a decline to four times in 1612, twice in 1615 and 1616, three times in 1618, and only once in 1621 and 1623.[125]

[122] Camden, *History of Queen Elizabeth*, in *A Complete History of England*, vol. II, 371.
[123] See above, 48–9. For Elizabeth's Jacobean legacy as 'the special friend of her non-noble subjects', see Curtis Perry, 'The Citizen Politics of Nostalgia: Elizabeth in Early Jacobean London', *Journal of Medieval and Renaissance Studies* 23 (1993), 89–111.
[124] *CSPV 1607–1610*, 450; *CSPV 1610–1613*, 116, 125, 127.
[125] PRO E351/543, fols. 153ᵛ, 173ᵛ, 189ʳ, 211ʳ, 260ᵛ; E351/544 fols. 44ʳ, 59ᵛ, 91ʳ, 132ʳ, 158ʳ. Having a chamber readied does not necessarily indicate that royalty actually attended a

Chamberlain's reports to Carleton about the king's Lenten attendance in the early 1620s fills in this sketch a bit more, and suggests that James withdrew from public sermon-hearing at Whitehall as resentment over his pro-Spanish foreign policy mounted. At mid-Lent 1622, Chamberlain noted that, although he had frequently come and gone between Whitehall and Hampton Court, the king had avoided the afternoon Lent sermons in his chapel until Tuesday in Holy Week.[126] Prince Charles had attended in his place since Ash Wednesday, and if the sermon he heard on Passion Sunday, 7 April, was typical of that year, we might find a reason for James's absence. Thomas Winniffe, one of the prince's own chaplains, and later Donne's executor and successor at St Paul's, 'tooke occasion out of his text' to compare the Spanish general Spinola to Satan, who 'like a greedie wolfe seeketh to devoure the innocent lambe the Palatinat'. For this tart remark, in what Chamberlain heard was 'otherwise an excellent sermon and much applauded', Winniffe spent that Sunday night in the Tower. Significantly, the young preacher did not secure his release by petition to the king or prince, but by supplication to the offended party, the Spanish ambassador Gondomar.[127] Although the Venetian ambassador probably overstated matters when he said in 1620 that Gondomar 'arrogated to himself a practical omnipotence in this Court', the reaction to Winniffe's sermon certainly shows that James censored his court pulpit with Spain and her ambassador in mind. Fear of an outburst like Winniffe's – and the embarrassment of literally countenancing such an insult to Spain from the royal closet – probably kept James away from the 1622 Lent sermons. But preachers throughout the realm continued their pulpit offensive against Spain and James's Spanish foreign policy, finally prompting the August promulgation of the King's Orders for Preachers that forbade mention of state affairs or controverted points of doctrine in any sermon.[128] As the clamour over the hated match rose, James retreated further and further from public view – and public criticism.[129] One week before Lent began in

sermon. In 1622, the Council Chamber was prepared 'fower tymes for his Matie', but on Chamberlain's witness, the King did not attend any sermons at court until Palm Sunday (*Letters*, vol. II, 426–8).

126 Chamberlain, *Letters*, vol. II, 427, 428, 433.
127 Chamberlain, *Letters*, vol. II, 432; Thomas Birch, ed., *The Court and Times of James the First*, 2 vols. (1848), vol. II, 304.
128 For a survey of preachers' criticisms of James's Spanish policy after 1618, see Fincham and Lake, 'Ecclesiastical Policy', 198–202. The Orders are printed in Edward Cardwell, *Documentary Annals of the Reformed Church of England*, 2 vols. (Oxford, 1844), vol. II, 198–206.
129 Compare James's strictly enforced order for nobles and gentry to depart from London for the country during Christmas 1622 (*CSPV 1621–23*, 530), and Neil Cuddy's evidence that at this time 'an *entrée* list was being used to limit access to the king' (Starkey, *English Court*, 221).

1623, Charles and Buckingham shocked even court insiders by taking ship for Spain to woo the Infanta. In England, the godly feared future enslavement to Rome, and even the most pragmatic observers saw the move as foolhardy at best. Not surprisingly, James ignored his Council's petitions and assiduously avoided London, staying in Cambridgeshire until the day before Palm Sunday. On that day he heard Archbishop Abbot in the Whitehall Preaching Place, 'where there had ben no sermons all this Lent, nor the King present at any' in the Chapel until Good Friday, when James heard his Lord Keeper, John Williams.[130]

In sharp contrast to the surviving Elizabethan Lent sermons, of the twenty-three Jacobean court Lent sermon texts that survive, only thirteen specify that the king was present. Two of these were preached in the middle of James's first English Lent when the king, queen and prince were in London for their postponed ceremonial procession through the City and the opening of James's first Parliament.[131] The eleven remaining sermons preached *coram rege* were delivered either on Ash Wednesday, the first Friday in Lent, on or very near Accession Day, or on or after Palm Sunday; that is, James heard Whitehall Lent sermons only during the first and last week of that season, or when his Accession Day happened to fall therein. The Lent sermons, though, proceeded with or without the royal presence. Bills of preachers were dutifully drawn up each January, and those persons left about Whitehall and Westminster still attended the court-sponsored event with relish, as in 1610, when Carleton reported to Sir Thomas Edmonds that 'the Court Sermons have been well and exactly hitherto discharged', with, he was pleased to report, an especially good showing made in the pulpit by fellow Oxonians.[132] Indeed, the series maintained its stature as an event of great cultural importance in the capital, as much a seasonal event as the Christmas revels at court or the Easter theatre season at Bankside. The bills for Lent preachers circulated not only throughout the court and City, but abroad: Laud sent Sir John Scudamore the 1622 list, and Chamberlain kept Carleton *au courant* at his various diplomatic posts by sending him the Lent lists as well as reports, notes, and copies of especially fine sermons.[133] As Andrewes himself noted sarcastically at the

---

[130] *CSPV 1621–1623*, 584; Chamberlain, *Letters*, vol. II, 489. For the crisis of 1621, see Thomas Cogswell, 'England and the Spanish Match', in Richard Cust and Ann Hughes, eds, *Conflict in Early Stuart England: Studies in Religion and Politics 1603–1642* (1989), 107–33.

[131] The preachers were Richard Field and Richard Eedes. See the "Calendar" disk supplement, 16 and 23 March, 1604. The triumphant procession from the Tower to Whitehall was held on Thursday 15 March, and Parliament began on Monday, 19 March. Nichols, *Progresses . . . of King James*, vol. I, 337–424.

[132] Nichols, *Progresses . . . of King James*, vol. II, 286–7.

[133] PRO C115 M24/7758, quoted in Hugh Trevor-Roper, *Archbishop Laud* (1940), 438; Chamberlain, *Letters*, vol. II, 427.

opening of his 1613 Gunpowder sermon, 'It is the common question, *Who Preaches?* Ever, we must know that.'[134] Notes of court sermons could even be recycled as gifts for a court patron. After Bishop James Montagu preached his Ash Wednesday sermon in 1615, humble Benjamin Agar, 'one of ye Pages of his ma^ties chamber in ordinarie', wrote out 'Principall notes' of it 'As they were taken memorit[er]' and presented them to the Lord Chamberlain, William Herbert, Earl of Pembroke. Just as the bishop had opened 'ye Temple doore of virtue' in his sermon, so Agar hoped that Pembroke would open 'ye Temple' of his 'hon:^bl fauour & protection' in exchange for his humble offering to the Earl and acknowledgment of his known 'deuotion to religious exercises'.[135] Enthusiasm for sermons at court was not limited to a pedantic 'theologian-king'.

Some of the best evidence for the social significance of the series lies in the texts themselves. Lancelot Andrewes, who inherited the Ash Wednesday sermon slot with his appointment as Dean of the Chapel Royal in 1618, twice took two consecutive years (1621 and 1622, 1623 and 1624) to treat a single text, each time taking for granted that his auditory had attentively heard the first installment the previous year. In 1622, preaching for the second year on Matthew 6:16, he began, 'ovr last yeares endeavours were out of the two first words' of the text, and reasoned that 'we may then goe forward to the rest'.[136] The court Lent sermon auditory also knew the rota in advance and looked forward to the appearance of favourite or famous preachers. Such a following must have been necessary to understand the punning allusion that opened John Donne's sermon for the First Friday in Lent, 1623. Preaching on John 11:35 ('IESUS WEPT'), Donne began:

I AM NOW but upon the Compassion of Christ. There is much difference betweene his Compassion and his Passion, as much as between the men that are to handle them here. But *Lacryma passionis Christi est vicaria*: A great personage may speake of his Passion, of his blood; My vicarage is to speake of his Compassion and his teares. Let me chafe the wax, and melt your soules in a bath of his Teares now, Let him set to the great Seale of his effectuall passion, in his blood, then.[137]

Knowing that Donne preached as part of an extended sermon series that stretched from Ash Wednesday to Easter, we can understand his contrast 'between the men' who will treat Christ's 'Compassion' and his 'Passion' – the former being Donne himself, and the latter the preacher for the day of

[134] Andrewes, *XCVI Sermons*, 933; *Works*, vol. IV, 277.
[135] Bodl. MS North e.41, fols. 141^r–42^r. Pembroke was a noted patron of conformist Calvinists. See Margot Heinemann, *Puritanism and Theatre: Thomas Middleton and Opposition Drama under the Early Stuarts* (Cambridge, 1980), 272–9.
[136] Andrewes, *XCVI Sermons*, 227; *Works*, vol. I, 398; see also Andrewes, *Sermons*, 249; *Works*, vol. I, 435.
[137] John Donne, *The Sermons of John Donne*, 10 vols., ed. George R. Potter and Evelyn M. Simpson (Berkeley, Calif., 1953–62), vol. IV, 324.

the Passion, Good Friday. The 'great personage' who would fill the pulpit on that solemn day was John Williams, who, as Dean of Westminster, would preach the Good Friday sermon.[138] But since 1621 Williams had also held both the bishopric of Lincoln and the office of Lord Keeper of the Great Seal. Hence Donne's suave allusion, set in the metaphorical terms of his chosen Biblical text and Williams's secular office, to Williams and his coming Good Friday sermon. Donne proposed to 'chafe the wax' of his hearers' hearts with the tears of Christ's 'Compassion', and then promised that five weeks hence Williams, Keeper of the Great Seal, would stand in the same pulpit to 'set to the great Seale' on their hearts with the blood of Christ's Passion.[139]

James, then, did not attend with any regularity the one court preaching event that traditionally and consistently attracted a large, public auditory. Peter Heylyn remembered that the afternoon Lent sermons, 'according to ancient custom', attracted not only the Lords of the Council and household officers, but also a 'great Concourse of all sorts of People which usually repaired thither'.[140] James, unlike Elizabeth, did not consider the court a place where he was 'perpetually on display', and, ever since his Scottish reign, he had assiduously avoided crowds; evidently, that extended even to the 'great concourses' that flocked to hear outdoor sermons in his Preaching Place.[141] Except for the very few days at the beginning and end of the season, however, Lenten access to the king's sermon-going was restricted to those very few who made up the small hunting court, and we see then yet another ramification of the restricted access to James's person that has been discussed as the hallmark of the Jacobean royal household.[142]

In February 1605, James had deputized his Privy Council to hear and judge matters of civil dispute so that he could avoid London and devote himself to the chase, allegedly to preserve his good health.[143] Shortly thereafter, the Venetian ambassador wrote of the 'indescribable ill-humour among the King's subjects' who chafed at finding themselves 'cut off from their natural sovereign, and forced to go before Council'.[144] One of those ill-humoured subjects found his way into the pulpit at Nonesuch on 30 April of that year. Robert Wakeman concluded what was otherwise a panegyric sermon on James's accession by railing against the 'cursed *Machiavels*' who think '*that to keepe the[m]selues alwaies from the accesse*

[138] WAMB 15, fol. 45ʳ.
[139] To my knowledge, this bow to Williams has eluded modern students of Donne, and sheds some new light on the enigmatic relationship between the two men, both former clients of Lord Chancellor Egerton. See R. C. Bald, *John Donne: a Life* (Oxford, 1970), 378–9.
[140] Heylyn, *Cyprianus Anglicus*, 126. [141] Lee, *Great Britain's Solomon*, 142–3.
[142] For the 'rural intimacy' of the hunting entourage, see Cuddy, 'Revival of Entourage' in Starkey, *English Court*, 193.
[143] Chamberlain, *Letters*, vol. I, 201. [144] *CSPV 1603–1607*, 219.

of their subiects is the next way to make them great'. Wakeman saved himself from a trip to the Tower by claiming that his criticisms had nothing to do with his own sovereign, but proceeded to address the king himself:

Although by reason of the state of this earthly kingdome, thou canst not so easily graunt accesse vnto thy subiects: yet for that thou thy selfe art to hope to haue accesse to the presence of the king of heauen, do that to man in earth as thou wouldest haue God do to thee in heaven. Vouchsafe to admitte thy poore brother into thy presence, that thou maist one day bee admitted into the presence of God, and his holie Angels. Vouchsafe to open thy eares to his supplication, that God may open his eares to thy petition.

The preacher conceded that he did not wish 'Kings and Princes to be facile of accesse-giving at all times, and to al persons', but begged that 'in the midst of al the glorie of the Court, they woulde sometime thinke on the oppression of the poore comminalty'.[145] The 'comminalty' watched the court, and, as in Elizabeth's time, they often used preachers at court as both their eyes and their voice. Recent work on Stuart court scandal has shown that Londoners and country gentry kept a close watch on the court's life, and that their reactions to it constituted an important form of political engagement.[146] Sermons such as Wakeman's show that the court was indeed a political 'point of contact' both as an institution and as a manifestation of the royal personality.[147] But court politics were not high politics, hermetically sealed off from public observation and participation. As much as James wanted both his royal person and court matters shrouded from public view, Robert Wakeman's 'comminalty' felt entitled to some access to the courtly point of political contact. The sermons preached there are, of course, only a small part of a much larger picture, but in them we can see the beginnings of the Stuart estrangement between court and populace: James cut himself off from a valuable venue for contact between court and citizenry by increasing the obligation of his lords and courtiers to attend court instead of City sermons, by removing many of those same sermons from Whitehall to his hunting-lodges and by shunning the Elizabethan tradition of regular, visible attendance at the court Lent sermons.[148]

---

[145] Robert Wakeman, *Salomons Exaltation* (Oxford, 1605), 59, 62–3.

[146] Alastair Bellany, 'A Poem on the Archbishop's Hearse: Puritanism, Libel and Sedition after the Hampton Court Conference', *Journal of British Studies* 34 (1995), 137–64; and '"Rayling Rymes and Vaunting Verse": Libellous Politics in Early Stuart England, 1603–1628', in Sharpe and Lake, eds., *Culture and Politics*, 285–310. I am grateful to Dr Bellany for sharing and discussing his work before publication.

[147] For the classic summaries of these points, see G. R. Elton, 'Tudor Government: the Points of Contact, III: the Court', *Transactions of the Royal Historical Society* 5th ser, 26 (1976), 211–28; and David Starkey, 'Introduction: Court History in Perspective', in Starkey, ed., *English Court*, 1–24.

[148] See R. Malcolm Smuts, 'Public Ceremony and Royal Charisma: the English Royal Entry in

Although James withdrew his person from many court sermons, he – much more than Elizabeth – associated himself with selected preachers and their sermons in print. As we shall see in the case of some of Lancelot Andrewes's sermons, the king not only commanded court sermons into print for their rhetorical and devotional merits, but he also had court sermons 'set out' for reasons of policy.[149] His instruction to publish as virtual position papers on episcopacy, the royal supremacy, and Presbyterianism the four court sermons preached before the Scottish Presbyterians at Hampton Court in 1606 was paradigmatic of this use of print.[150] Similarly, in 1617–18, the king sponsored the publication of four sermons preached in his presence that explicitly enjoined Scottish acceptance of some or all of the five Articles of Perth, James's minimum expectations for liturgical and episcopal conformity in Scotland. Robert Wilkinson's *Barwick Bridge: Or England and Scotland Covpled*, preached at St Andrews on 13 July 1617, and printed by the king's English printer in the same year, tried to calm Scottish tempers; and Lancelot Andrewes's sermons for 5 November 1617 and Easter 1618, as well as John Buckeridge's for Passion Sunday 1618, contained extensive defences of two of the controverted articles, the keeping of major holy days and kneeling at communion.[151] Although the court sermons that appeared from the king's printer included two by the evangelical John King and one apiece by the conformist Calvinists John Williams, William Goodwin, Christopher Swale, and Edmund Mason, it was the group of Arminian preachers – Andrewes, John Buckeridge, William Laud, and Walter Curll – who received the majority of James's commands to print.

Setting aside those sermons already discussed as printed for what today we might call their literary merit, and those preached against Scottish nonconformity, we find in the remaining sermons a consistent articulation of James's own visions of a pacifist foreign policy and of the supremacy and sacrality of kings. In 1610, the year of Henri IV's assassination, James sponsored the printing of two of Andrewes's most vigorous denunciations

London, 1485–1642', in A. L. Beier, David Cannadine, and James M. Rosenheim, eds., *The First Modern Society: Essays in English History in Honour of Lawrence Stone* (Cambridge, 1989), 84–6, but see Judith Richards, '"His Nowe Majestie" and the English Monarchy: the Kingship of Charles I Before 1640', *Past and Present* 113 (1986), 83.

[149] For sermons printed by command, see Appendix.

[150] William Barlow, *One of the Foure Sermons Preached before the Kings Maiestie, at Hampton Court* (1606); John Buckeridge, *A Sermon Preached at Hampton Court before the Kings Maiestie* (1606); Lancelot Andrewes, *A Sermon Preached before the Kings Maiestie, at Hampton Court* (1606); John King, *The Fovrth Sermon Preached at Hampton Covrt* (Oxford, 1606).

[151] Andrewes, *Sermon Preached . . . the Fift of Nouember Last, 1617; A Sermon Preached before his Maiestie at Whitehall, on Easter Day Last* (1618); John Buckeridge, *A Sermon Preached before his Maiestie at Whitehall* (1618).

of regicide: first, the sermon for the Gowry Anniversary of that year on the apt text, 'Touch not mine anointed', which explicitly compared the attempt in Scotland to the recent French crime; and second, the Latin Gowry sermon preached before James and Christian of Denmark four years earlier, but revived in print for its now-timely tirade against Jesuit missions to kill Protestant-sympathizing kings. The following year appeared Andrewes's remarkable conflation of Easter and Accession Day themes in a sermon hailing James – analogous to King David and the risen Christ – as the stone *'which the Builders refused . . . become,* (or made) *the Head of the Corner'.* These sermon publications coincided with Andrewes's royally commissioned role in the supremacy controversy with the Jesuit Cardinal Bellarmine, and should probably be read at least in one sense as domestic variations on that international controversy's theme.[152]

When, in the 1620s, James came increasingly under attack for his obsession with the Spanish Match and repeated refusals to intervene in the Palatinate, William Laud, who had been doggedly serving as a royal chaplain since 1611 but had seen little in the way of preferment, came into his own, preaching sermons before James that aped Andrewes's unique style as well as his pacificism and celebration of kingship by divine right.[153] On the king's birthday, 19 June 1621, with Parliament agitating for military intervention in Europe, Laud took as his text Psalm 122:6,7: *'Pray for the peace of Ierusalem; let them prosper that loue thee. Peace be within thy walles, and prosperity within thy Palaces.'* Not very obliquely praising the king and chastizing the war-party, he asserted that peace 'cannot bee accounted onely the Gowne-mans, or the weake-mans prayer' and that 'it is not cowardize to pray for peace: nor courage to call for troubles', and asked, 'can yee do other then *Rogare pacem,* pray for peace in the day, nay Natiuity, the very birthday of both *Peace,* and the *Peace-maker?'* Moreover, taking advantage of Archbishop Abbot's very recent fall from grace for his efforts on behalf of the Palatine, Laud concluded with an opportunistic swipe at his disgraced enemy: God, he said, 'did not intend to leaue out the Priest, whom it concernes most, to preach peace to the people; neither the High Priest, nor the rest, but they should bee most forward in this duty'. While Abbot never regained his favour at court, Laud was only beginning his. Ten days after preaching this sermon, James granted him the bishopric of St David's, and the birthday present he had

---

152 Lancelot Andrewes, *Tortura Torti* (1609); *Responsio ad Apologiam Cardinalis Bellarmini* (1610); *Works,* vols. VII, VIII; Chamberlain, *Letters,* vol. I, 264; Welsby, *Lancelot Andrewes,* ch. 5.

153 William Laud, *The Works of . . . William Laud,* 6 vols., ed. James Bliss (1843–57), vol. III, 135; Heylyn, *Cyprianus Anglicanus,* 60; Chamberlain, *Letters,* vol. II, 391.

given to the king from the pulpit was printed almost immediately by royal command.[154]

In Lent of the following year, instead of his routine appearance in the pulpit on mid-Lent Sunday, Laud was given the Accession Day sermon, probably on the strength of his royal birthday performance. His application of Psalm 21:6,7 (*'Because the King trusteth in the Lord: and in the mercy of the most High hee shall* not miscarry') to David, Christ, and King James paid tacit homage to Andrewes's application of *'the Stone, which the Builders refused'* (Psalm 118:22) to the same trio of kings in his combined Easter and Accession Day sermon of 1611.[155] Laud delivered a fulsome panegyric on kings as the conduits of blessing between God and the people, and, reacting to popular discontent with royal policy, chastized the 'grosse *ingratitude'* of those subjects who complained that the king's blessings were not perfect. 'Well, suppose that, what then?', he asked. Since blessings fell on subjects only from their king, 'they are strain'd . . . through him, through the *Man*, and therefore must relish a little of the Strainer'. Laud had expected James to be present; but even though he did not attend, word of Laud's reminding the Lenten crowd of their debt to James for his many blessings on them must have reached the king's ears, for under 24 March, Laud entered in his diary, 'I preached at Court: commanded to print'.[156] Meanwhile, fears of papist aggression emboldened orthodox Calvinists at court to speak out against James's peculiar way of 'straining' God's blessings to the nation, and they were reprimanded accordingly. Just two weeks after Laud's sermon, Charles's chaplain Thomas Winniffe spent his night in the Tower.[157] Although notes of Winniffe's sermon would circulate in newsletters, James or his deputies saw to it that the king's printer set out whole texts of sermons such as Laud's or that preached by Walter Curll on Low Sunday. Curll, later Laudian bishop of Winchester, warned those 'wishing for war' that if 'the heat of war beat vpon our heads, as it doeth vpon other nations, wee would make more account of the sweete shade of *Peace*, vnder which wee now sit'.[158] As James's dreams of a Habsburg alliance increasingly alienated those committed to a confessional foreign policy, the king indeed found his most friendly court preachers to be those

[154] William Laud, *A Sermon Preached before his Maiesty* (1621), 1, 19, 22, 41. Chamberlain sent Carleton a copy of the sermon on 21 July (*Letters*, vol. II, 391). For Abbot's fall, see Fincham, 'Prelacy and Politics', 51–3.
[155] William Laud, *A Sermon Preached at White-hall on the 24. of March, 1621* (1622), 1–3; Lancelot Andrewes, *A Sermon Preached before his Maiestie . . . on the 24 of March Last* (1611), 1–3; *Works*, vol. II, 270–3.
[156] Laud, *A Sermon Preached at White-hall*, 20–1; *Works*, vol. III, 138.
[157] Birch, *Court and Times of James*, vol. II, 304.
[158] Walter Curll, *A Sermon Preached at White-hall* (1622), 21.

such as Andrewes, Laud, and Curll, whose more liberal theology 'allowed them to endorse his foreign policy'.[159]

There is no evidence of advance censorship of court-sermon texts by church or court officers. The Renaissance papal court, to take a contemporary example for contrast, took formal steps to censor the sermons preached *coram papa*. By the early sixteenth century, the Pope's official theologians, the Masters of the Sacred Palace, were to read a copy of every sermon before it was preached.[160] No comparable measures were taken at the English court. The king's chaplains, like all royal servants, swore an oath of allegiance upon joining the royal household, and thereafter had to be self-disciplining.[161] Late in the reign, in response to increasingly frank pulpit criticism of James's Hispanophilia, there were some efforts to ensure a greater degree of doctrinal and disciplinary uniformity in the court pulpit. In the years surrounding the Synod of Dort (1619), James took steps to muzzle the Arminians, including Lancelot Andrewes, on the contentious issue of predestination.[162] He then increased the policing power of the Dean of the Chapel in September 1619, when orders were drafted requiring all court preachers who were not Chaplains in Ordinary to 'subscribe before the Deane of our Chappell or before one of our ordinarye chaplaynes attendinge' to the three articles 'subscribed vnto in the late queenes tyme' – the royal supremacy, *The Book of Common Prayer*, and the Thirty-nine Articles – before they could preach in his presence.[163] Finally, the August 1622 Orders for Preachers attempted to limit allusion to matters of state or points of controverted doctrine. But these efforts failed to have a tremendous impact on the content of court sermons. First, the injunction against handling points of predestination and grace technically applied only to those preachers 'under the degree of a bishop, or dean' preaching in 'simple auditories' – hardly a description of preaching in James's chapels. While the injunction against discussing 'the power, pre-

---

[159] Fincham and Lake, 'Ecclesiastical Policy', 201.

[160] See John W. O'Malley, *Praise and Blame in Renaissance Rome: Rhetoric, Doctrine, and Reform in the Sacred Orators of the Papal Court, c. 1450–1521* (Durham, N.C., 1979), ch. 1, esp. 17–24.

[161] Millar MacLure suggests that Laud's 1629 order for Paul's Cross preachers to produce a copy of their intended sermon before its delivery was an innovation: MacLure, *Paul's Cross Sermons*, 13. Compare also John Donne's anxiety over how his first sermon before Charles I, preached on the Sunday after James's death, would be received: Bald, *John Donne*, 467–8. I owe this point to Dr John Considine.

[162] Fincham and Lake, 'Ecclesiastical Policy', 190–1.   [163] PRO SP14/110/89.

rogative, jurisdiction, authority, or duty of sovereign princes' was to apply at all places and to all preachers, court sermons continued to contain thinly veiled allusions to the foreign-policy crisis.[164]

Court sermons could, however, be censored after the fact by penal measures taken against preachers who had overstepped their bounds, and those bounds were clearly defined early in the reign in James's response to a sermon preached before him by John Burgess at Greenwich on 19 June 1604. Burgess was a nonconformist minister who, with the tacit indulgence of his diocesan, William Chaderton of Lincoln, and the support of godly patrons such as Lord and Lady Norrys, had quietly ignored the established church's ceremonies since the 1590s.[165] But, like many other godly clergy, his hand was forced in the months after the Hampton Court Conference as King James and Bishop of London Richard Bancroft enforced ceremonial conformity. At the invitation of Dean of the Chapel Montagu – who himself sympathized with the nonconformists, albeit timidly – Burgess came to the Greenwich chapel royal carrying the banner of those godly ministers who would ultimately prefer deprivation to conformity.[166] His sermon, on the apt text, 'ffor my Bretheren & Neighbours sake: I will nowe speake peace unto the: because of the houre of the Lord our God I will procure thye health' (Psalm 122:8–9), landed him in prison and saw him roughly handled at the Privy Council table by Bancroft. The sermon itself and Burgess's letters of supplication to the king and Council written from prison provide us with unrivalled documentation of precisely what in a court sermon would not be tolerated by the royal ear.[167]

We know precisely what James could not tolerate in this sermon from Burgess's letter to the king, wherein he provided a numbered 'account . . . of such things as your Highnesse desireth to be answered in' (25). These

---

[164] Cardwell, *Documentary Annals*, vol. II, 202. For examples, see the 'Calendar' disk supplement, 9 October 1622, and 14 January, 6 April, and 2 September 1623. See Peter Lake, 'The Moderate and Irenic Case for Religious War: Joseph Hall's *Via Media* in Context', in Susan D. Amussen and Mark Kishlansky, eds., *Political Culture and Cultural Politics in Early Modern England* (Manchester, 1995), 55–83.

[165] *HMC Salisbury*, vol. XVII, 617.

[166] Montagu scheduled Burgess in the court pulpit as an audition for appointment as chaplain to Prince Henry. See below, 185–6.

[167] Many copies survive, including Folger MS V.a.351, fols. 126^r–141^r; CUL Add. MS 336, fols. 69–77; Bodl. MS Rawl.D.353, fols. 189–211; Bodl. MS Eng.the.c.71, fols. 40^r–47^v. These all include the sermon and letters to the king and to the Council, except Bod. Eng.the.c.71, which lacks the letter to the Council, but includes a unique letter from Burgess to Bishop Chaderton explaining his nonconformity (fols. 47^{r-v}). William Covell, under Bancroft's patronage, answered Burgess's later refusal to subscribe, but did not address the court sermon itself, in *A Briefe Answer vnto . . . Mr Iohn Burges* (1606). The sermon, with Burgess's letters to King and Council, first appeared in print as *A Sermon Preached before the Late King James . . . with Two Letters in Way of Apology* (1642). I quote from the printed text, collated against the Folger MS; references appear in the text.

seven points of offence can be summarized under two headings – perceived criticisms of the king's character and of his ecclesiastical policy – and they deserve attention here because they seem to have been the two topics that remained beyond the pale of preacherly correction at a court that otherwise indulged a remarkably broad range of opinion in its pulpit. James felt that the preacher had satirized two specific courtiers when he said that the king 'flyeth the company of the wise, and advanceth fooles' (6), and that he would do best to 'hunt away two beasts, the tame beast and the wilde, the flatterer and the false informer' (9). Burgess vehemently denied this accusation, claiming that he did not criticize individuals, but types, 'of which', he added somewhat malapertly, '(there is noe doubt) but your Majesty hath more then two about you' (26). Burgess, however, stood by the portion of his sermon that he called his 'generall discourse of the graciousnesse of Princes to their Subjects', wherein he interpreted the phrase from his text, 'for my bretheren and my neighbours sake', as a call for princes to treat their subjects with affection and respect (25). Here, Burgess said he was 'bound in conscience' to convey to the king his subjects' dismay that 'you grace not your people, you speake not to them, you looke not at them, you blesse them not' (26). With this, Burgess had crossed two boundaries: he had traduced the king's preferred mode of government, that is, the consolidation of favour and power in a select few; and he had questioned the wisdom of James's domestic retreat and detachment from the populace. There is a sincerity in Burgess's claim that he brought these concerns into James's presence out of love, and not out of spite. Convinced that James was not aware of his people's discontent, and that it could be dispelled if only they had a chance to see how godly a monarch James really was, Burgess thought himself called 'to propone such generall discourse, as your Majesty might make use of, for your owne good' (26). But what Burgess considered to be James's remediable social ineptitude was to James a studied mode of good government, and criticism of it skirted treason.

Whereas Burgess's handling of the first half of his text contained some points of offence, his treatment of the second – 'because of the house of the Lord our God, I will procure thy wealth' – was odious to both James and Bancroft. The 'house of the Lord' was of course the Church of England, and to procure its wealth Burgess advised the further reform of rites and ceremonies. He began in somewhat veiled terms by warning that destruction would attend any prince who 'put off to the Prelates all the care of the house of God' (14) – a glance at James's alignment with the episcopal interest at Hampton Court. He then advised that the witness of a godly king was 'surely . . . as strong as any compulsary meanes' to encourage the people's zeal for the church – a response to James's repeated warnings after the conference that religious conformity would be enforced (16). Finally, explaining how he saw fit to 'establish peace in the Church it selfe' (18), Burgess offered the exemplum of Pollio's glasses – Caesar Augustus's reversal of a death sentence imposed on Pollio's servant for having broken a precious crystal glass, and the Emperor's proceeding to break all the remaining glasses 'that they might not be occasion of like rigorous sentence afterwards'. Of this exemplum the preacher said, 'I will not apply it, but do humbly beseech your Majesty to use your owne most godlie wisdome, now to make peace in the Church, when so small a thing will doe it' (19). The 'so small a thing', not at all lost on the king's 'godlie wisdome', was the destruction of all ordinances requiring the observation of church ceremonies, as Burgess's gloss on his own sermon avowed: 'by *Pollios* glasses, I did intend to notifie the Ceremonies for which this Church of God hath bin in vexation above fifty yeeres' (28). The rigorous sentence now exacted for breaking these 'glasses' was that '60. or 70 of yᵉ hablest Ministers in yᵉ Land are like to be put out'.[168] Ultimately, Burgess was among that number of able ministers 'put out' by the deprivations of 1604–5.[169]

The harsh reaction to his June sermon, which presaged the strict line taken by the ecclesiastical authorities six months later, left a perceptible mark on future court preachers and the contents of their sermons. Burgess's fate – temporary imprisonment – was a very rare one for preachers at James's court; in fact, the scenario was not repeated until the crisis over the Spanish Match.[170] However, this was not because all preachers before the king and court never risked a criticism of their noble auditory; rather, they learned how to present them in a manner befitting 'so high *a* presence, *so great an Audience*'.[171] In Burgess's letter to the Lords of the Privy Council, written after his appearance before them and accompanying the required written copy of his sermon, the preacher apologized for only one offence: his 'to sparinge acknowledgement of his Majesties Princely graces, and the unspeakeable good we have by him' (22). As the text of the sermon shows, the preacher had indeed ignored what must have been the Golden Rule of the court pulpit; that is, even if only in the last moments of one's sermon, compliment the prince. It must be insisted that not every court sermon, nor even a majority of them, drips with unctuous flattery. But if a preacher was to offer some criticism of royal policy or behaviour, he could shield himself from the worst of royal discipline by tempering his critique with a

---

[168] Folger MS V.a.351, fol. 141ʳ. The 1642 printed text has 'six or seven hundred' (27).

[169] The most recent count places the number of deprived ministers at between seventy-three and eighty-three: Fincham, *Prelate as Pastor*, 323–6.

[170] Sampson Price was clapped-up in the Tower for an anti-Spanish sermon preached *coram* on July 8, 1621, as was Thomas Winiffe on 7 April 1622: Birch, *Court and Times of James*, II, 265–6, 304.

[171] The phrase is William Westerman's, *Jacobs Well*, sig. &3ᵛ.

disclaimer that the present audience was, of course, not the intended object of criticism.

We have already seen how only one year later, and evidently without reprimand, Robert Wakeman glanced at precisely the same royal failings by carefully denying the obvious application to the king. To take one other example of many, in January 1623 the royal chaplain William Loe broached the forbidden topic of military assistance for the Palatinate when he told James to make use of his 'good measure of *Shipps, Sailers,* and *Munition*' and almost taunted the king with an exemplum of his prede-cessor as Protestant protectress: 'by kings doth god defend his Church . . . Elizabeth our last Soveraigne of pretious memorie, what a Sheild was she to Churches of *Scotland, Holland, Fraunce, Germanie, Denmarke,* and *Geneva?* Was she not alwaies in readines, even throughout her whole Dominions?'[172] Loe had prefaced those fighting words with the disingen-uous, if not obsequious claim that 'ffoule *Presumption* it were in me, if I should haue anie the least thought, that I were meete in any sort to advize his sacred Maiestie, whom I Conceave hath the most prudent, and most provident Counsell in the World'. An even bolder use of the strategy of disclaimer in a prefatory epistle was chaplain Francis Mason's 1621 protestation that, although he chose to preach on David's adultery because '*carnall Concupiscence*' was a sin '*likely to be found in Princes Courts*', he absolutely did not '*take occasion by King* David *to glanse in any wise at the sacred persons of Princes: God forbid*'.[173] So, although both men probably fooled no one, including the king, they had taken precautionary measures against possible accusations of meddling in the affairs of princes by claiming that they offered no advice at all. But Burgess, as he said himself, was 'not acquainted wth such a presence', and made no such accommoda-tion for his schooling of the king (22). In repeated direct addresses to the royal closet, he failed to mediate his criticisms of royal behaviour and policy with either compliment or caveat. To borrow Annabel Patterson's phrase, William Loe, and not John Burgess, understood the 'hermeneutics of censorship'. Preachers such as Loe knew that to handle the *arcana imperii* safely, they had to maintain the fiction that they did no such thing, and this was best accomplished by an insistence on 'authorial intention in controlling meaning', usually by the 'disavowal of allusion'.[174] To the preacher the whole business of preaching was to 'open' or 'apply' a Scriptural text – or, with Patterson, to 'control' the meanings or possible

[172] BL MS Royal 17.A.xl, fols. 23ᵛ, 29ᵛ.

[173] BL MS Royal 17.A.xl, fol. 22ᵛ. Francis Mason, *Two Sermons Preached at the Kings Court* (1621), sigs. A2ᵛ, A3ᵛ.

[174] Annabel Patterson, *Censorship and Interpretation: the Conditions of Writing and Reading in Early Modern England* (Madison, Wis., 1984), 104.

interpretations of a text. So fundamental was the preacher's right to control meaning that disavowals of a clearly intended meaning seem to have been deemed sufficient to exempt the preacher from the punishment he would otherwise have received. Burgess learned this the hard way. His attempts to deny offending allusions (which is not to say they were not intended) and to control the interpretation of his sermon came too late. Had he laced his sermon with the protestations found in his letters of supplication to king and Council he might have avoided imprisonment.

There were also historical particularities at play in Burgess's sermon, the royal reaction against it, and its influence on what subsequent preachers said from the court pulpit. As Fincham and Lake have shown, James considered church ceremonies in themselves as things indifferent, and therefore interpreted nonconformity not as a theological or doctrinal aberration, but as 'open defiance of his authority as supreme governor of the church'.[175] In his desire to accommodate all but the most radical nonconformists in a broad-based church, James and many of his bishops were willing to accept even slight gestures toward conformity as proof of a minister's loyalty to the king. Endorsement of the king's supremacy through subscription and at least token ceremonial conformity then became the cement that bonded men with otherwise antithetical ecclesiological and doctrinal views into one Jacobean church. Paying lip service at court to ceremonial conformity could, like a strategically deployed compliment to the king, license conscientious objections not unlike Burgess's own. Burgess corroborated accusations that the Dean of the Chapel Royal himself, James Montagu, thought that enforced conformity was a sin.[176] Royal chaplain Anthony Maxey, later Dean of Windsor, made no attempt to hide his sympathies for the deprived ministers in a sermon before the king in March 1605 when he mourned,

by lamentable experience doe I know, what strange and wofull effects, these disordered courses haue brought forth. Diuers, in whose vertuous and louely societie, my heart hath often ioyed, and some, for whom nature would cause a man to cry out (would to god I had dyed for thee my brother;) some of these haue forsaken both friends and country[.]

Maxey faulted these men only for their inability to sacrifice scruples over things indifferent for the cause of 'one publike, perfect, and Christian Peace amongst vs', a peace possible only if 'all preach one and the selfe same doctrine, all vse the same ceremonies, thereby to win the people'. Fittingly, having voiced his sympathy for the deprived ministers, he balanced his sermon by concluding with an encomium to the controverted ceremonies –

---

[175] Fincham and Lake, 'Ecclesiastical Policy', 176.
[176] *HMC Salisbury*, vol. XVII, 270, 288.

'especially the vse of the *Corsse* [*sic*], so much excepted aginst' but by which 'the *Standard of Christshonour,* hath euer beene aduanced, and borne aloft in the eye of the Church' – over which his 'brothers' had forfeited their livings.[177] Court pulpit endorsements of ceremonial conformity, like token parochial conformity, became a sure way to ensure one's favour in James's eyes. So Thomas Scott's probationary court sermon, preached on the day he was sworn as chaplain to the king, contained a careful recitation of the ceremonial conformist's creed: in questions over things indifferent, 'childrens baptisme, and the Crosse vsed in baptisme, and many other points concerning the doctrin, discipline and ceremonies vsed in our Church', the 'prohibition of Princes and Prelates' held sway.[178] The deprivations crisis of 1604–5 marked out boundaries for general clerical conformity in the Jacobean church; John Burgess's sermon of June 1604 defined similar ones for the Jacobean court pulpit.

PREACHER AS FAVOURITE: LANCELOT ANDREWES, *STELLA PRÆDICANTIUM*

If James could punish a preacher such as Burgess, he could also advance and reward other preachers whose sermons pleased rather than offended. No preacher has been more associated with James than Lancelot Andrewes (1555–1626). Although Andrewes was an established preacher at court by 1589, his career as bishop and preacher to the court *extraordinaire* was a Jacobean phenomenon.[179] To contemporaries he was '*Stella prædicantium*' and his virtual monopoly over the court sermons preached on the principal feast days of the Jacobean church year – Christmas, Easter, Whitsunday, and the Gowry and Gunpowder Anniversaries – has often been noted.[180]

---

[177] Anthony Maxey, *The Churches Sleepe Expressed in a Sermon Preached at the Court* (1606), sig. A3ᵛ, A4ʳ, B3ʳ, C4ʳ.

[178] Thomas Scott, *Christs Politician, and Salomons Pvritan* (1616), sig. A2ʳ⁻ᵛ, and part 2, 9 (*vere* 11–12), 14.

[179] Andrewes (1555–1626) was made Ordinary Chaplain to Elizabeth in 1589. She preferred him to St Giles's, Cripplegate (1589) and the deanery of Westminster (1601). James elevated him to the bishopric of Chichester (1605), and successively to Ely (1609) and Winchester (1619) as well as appointing him Lord High Almoner (1605–19), Dean of the Chapel Royal (1619), and privy counsellor (1616). The standard biography remains Paul A. Welsby, *Lancelot Andrewes 1555–1626* (1958), which should be used with further reference to Fincham, *Prelate as Pastor, passim*; Peter Lake, 'Lancelot Andrewes, John Buckeridge, and Avant-Garde Conformity at the Court of James I', in Peck, ed., *Mental World of the Jacobean Court,* 113–33; and Lossky, *Lancelot Andrewes, passim,* but especially 7–27.

[180] Henry Isaacson, *Life and Death of Lancelot Andrewes,* in Andrewes, *Works,* vol. XI, xxvi. During the twenty-two years of James's reign, Andrewes preached or prepared seventeen surviving court sermons for Christmas, eight for Ash Wednesday, six for Lent, three for Good Friday, nineteen for Easter, fifteen for Whitsunday, and nineteen for the Gowry and Gunpowder Anniversaries.

Just as oft noted, however, has been the stark contrast between the pious scholar-bishop and the king who so richly favoured him. Andrewes's biographer puzzled over the contrasts in their temperaments and social behaviour, and more recent work has underscored the two men's differences over major points of doctrine.[181] It is worth asking, therefore, why James preferred Andrewes to such pre-eminence in the court pulpit. My answer to that question – that James was eager both to enjoy and to employ Andrewes's formidable learning, and that he was enthralled by Andrewes's unique preaching style – concurs with Dr Fincham's explanation for Andrewes's episcopal advancement under James.[182] But the recovery of further institutional detail about court offices and court preaching revises our understanding of Andrewes's prominence at court.

As we have seen, during Elizabeth's reign certain Lent sermons became associated with specific ecclesiastical dignities or household posts, most notably the Palm Sunday and Easter sermons with the Almonership. James, or perhaps his Chapel Dean and Clerk of the Closet, oversaw a much more extensive standardization of the Lent rotas. Beginning with James's first English Lent (1604), and thereafter without exception, the Ash Wednesday sermon was preached by the Dean of the Chapel Royal, and the Dean of Westminster, who since 1597 had preached on Ash Wednesday, was given the sermon for Good Friday. Also in 1604, the Almoner, while he retained the Easter sermon, was relieved of the sermon for Palm Sunday, which began to alternate between the Bishops of Durham and London, and the Archbishop of York. As Bishop of London in 1611, George Abbot by course took the Palm Sunday sermon, but then continued to preach it throughout the reign after his elevation to Canterbury.[183] By the middle of the reign a Jacobean Lent rota was established that would return at the Restoration and persist into the next century: Dean of the Chapel on Ash Wednesday, Chaplains in Ordinary on the Wednesdays thereafter, bishops on Sundays, and deans on Fridays, with the exception of the Archbishop of Canterbury on Palm Sunday, the Dean of Westminster on Good Friday, and the Lord High Almoner on Easter. These Jacobean pairings of offices with sermons were internalized by Londoners as givens in the court routine. When Chamberlain wrote to Carleton in April 1623 that 'the King came hither the fifth of this present, and the next day (beeing Palme-Sonday) the Lord Archbishop preached at

---

[181] Welsby, *Lancelot Andrewes*, 188–9; Tyacke, *Anti-Calvinists*, 45; Fincham and Lake, 'Ecclesiastical Policy', 190–1.
[182] Fincham, *Prelate as Pastor*, 25, 37.
[183] Neither Whitgift nor Bancroft preached in the Lent series during their archiepiscopates. (WAMB 15).

court', he was confirming that Abbot had kept his traditional day in the pulpit before the king.[184]

Lancelot Andrewes's first known pulpit appearance before James, then, was in his capacity as Dean of Westminster preaching the Good Friday sermon on 6 April 1604. In literary terms, this sermon is arguably one of Andrewes's best, and it contains many of the characteristics for which Peter Lake dubs Andrewes's court sermons ecclesiologically 'avant-garde'.[185] Daringly, Andrewes took as his text Lamentations 1:12 – 'Haue ye no Regard, ô all ye that passe by the way? Consider, and behold, If euer there were sorrow like my Sorrow' – the refrain from the *Improperia*, or 'Reproaches from the Cross' sung in the Roman Catholic rite for Good Friday. That Andrewes was nervous about his choice of text is clear from his exordium, in which he marshalled a host of Patristic precedents for applying the prophet's words 'to our Sauiour *Christ*, And that this very day, the day of his Paßion'. He concluded, somewhat defensively, that 'the Fathers . . . are to me a warrant, to expound and apply this verse (as they haue done before)'. In a brilliant use of the preacher's position raised up in a pulpit before the court, Andrewes, like the deacon chanting the medieval reproaches, addressed his text to the courtiers as if they were the mob at the foot of the cross:

Be it then to vs . . . The speech of the Son[n]e of God, as this Day hanging on the Crosse, to a sort of carelesse people, that goe vp and downe without any manner of Regard of these his Sorowes and sufferings, so worthy of all Regard. Haue ye no regard? ô all ye that passe by the way.[186]

Only his own Good Friday sermon for 1597 anticipated the emphatic Christocentrism of this sermon, with its repeated calls to 'behold and consider' the sufferings of Christ graphically painted by the preacher, and its insistence on the universal efficacy of the grace purchased on the cross.[187] James was clearly taken with Andrewes's performance, for this was the first Elizabethan or Jacobean court sermon to appear from the

---

[184] Chamberlain, *Letters*, vol. II, 489. For Caroline Lent lists, see PRO LC5/183, fol. 2; WAMB 15, fols. 46, 47 (1626, 1628, 1629, 1630, 1631). For the post-Restoration rota, see Edward Chamberlayne, *Angliae Notitia . . . the Third Edition* (1669), 232–3.

[185] Lake, 'Avant-Garde Conformity', 131.

[186] Andrewes, *The Copie of the Sermon Preached on Good Friday* (1604), sigs. A2^{r-v}, A3^{v}–4^{r}; *Works*, vol. II, 140. Rosemond Tuve charted the persistence of the *Improperia* tradition as a literary influence in England in *A Reading of George Herbert* (Chicago, Ill., 1952), 33–47. This Passion sermon by Andrewes should be added to Tuve's catalogue of very probable post-Reformation influences on Herbert's redaction of the *Improperia*, his poem 'The Affliction'.

[187] Expanding on Isaiah's prophecy that Christ will bear the iniquity of all (53:6), Andrewes added, 'All, all, euen those, *that passe to and fro*, and for all this, *regard* neither him, nor his Passion' (sig. D3^{r}). The 1597 sermon is *XCVI Sermons*, 333–48; *Works*, vol. II, 119–37.

royal printing house.[188] In its verbal artistry, its word-painting, its involvement of the auditory as characters in a drama of salvation, the Passion sermon for 1604 was distinct from anything preached at court by contemporary English preachers, and was no doubt unlike anything James had ever heard in Scotland. On coming to England, James had been dazzled by what he perceived as the southern kingdom's vast wealth – its agrarian plenty, its prodigy houses – and at Whitehall he had been equally taken with the splendour of the Tudor Chapel Royal and its service. In Lancelot Andrewes he found a complement to the Chapel's ceremony and music, a preacher who, like vestments, hangings and choral polyphony, could adorn his chapel on solemn feast days.

So, when the bishopric of Chichester and Royal Almonership fell vacant at the death of Anthony Watson in 1605, Andrewes was clearly established as one of James's most admired preachers. This fact, coupled with the longstanding precedent for the Almoner to be the preferred, or ranking preacher at court, no doubt influenced James to make Andrewes his Lord High Almoner as well as Bishop of Chichester. We do not know if Elizabeth's Almoners routinely preached to the household on holy days other than Palm Sunday and Easter. But events late in James's reign, involving the division of court preaching duties between the Dean of the Chapel and the Almoner, suggest that Andrewes's preaching at court on the major festivals was as much a function of his post as Almoner as it was of James's love for his preaching, and, moreover, that James was willing to see Andrewes give up the Almonership and possibly the pulpit prominence that came with it.

In 1618, James's first Chapel dean, Bishop of Winchester James Montagu, died. Andrewes subsequently received the king's *congé d'élire* for the see of Winchester in June 1618; he was sworn into the Chapel deanery on New Year's Day 1619 in the vestry at Whitehall.[189] Accordingly, Andrewes began to preach the court Ash Wednesday sermon previously delivered by Dean of the Chapel Montagu – this institutional fact explains what until now has been the puzzling existence of a run of late Jacobean Ash Wednesday sermons by Andrewes.[190] As we have already seen, there were two Sunday morning services in the Chapel Royal, one for the

---

[188] *The Copie of the Sermon Preached on Good Friday* was the finest quarto printing yet given to a court sermon; six editions before 1618 made this the most oft-printed court sermon of the reign.

[189] Andrewes, *Works*, vol. XI, xi; Rimbault, ed., *Cheque-Book*, 126; HMC *Downshire*, vol. VI, 458.

[190] See Lossky, *Lancelot Andrewes*, 102. After Andrewes's appointment as dean, Lent lists survive for 1622–5 (inclusive), all of which show Andrewes or (in 1625) a substitute for him appointed for Ash Wednesday (WAMB 15, fols. 44ʳ, 45ʳ⁻ᵛ, PRO LC 5/183 fol. 1). Andrewes's court sermons for Ash Wednesday 1620–4 (inclusive) survive: *XCVI Sermons*, 173–262; *Works*, vol. I, 356–454.

household and one for the king and his entourage. This division also held for the major feast days, and it was the Dean of the Chapel's charge to preach at the earlier service, while the Almoner preached to the king at the later one. Assiduous sermon-goers attended both, as Sir Dudley Carleton did on Easter Sunday 1609. He reported to Chamberlain that 'the dean of the chapel [Montagu] to the household and the bishop of Chichester [Andrewes] before the king befitted the solemnity of the time with as good sermons as ever I heard from either of them'.[191] Similarly, on Whitsunday 1614, Archbishop of York Tobie Matthew 'went to the *Court* at *Greenwich*' where he 'heard Two Sermons and waited on his *Majestie*'.[192] But what happened when Andrewes became Dean of the Chapel Royal? As early rumours suggested, it does seem that Andrewes held on to both posts for some months.[193] Because James lay dangerously ill at Royston on Easter 1619, we do not know how the preaching rota would have been arranged to accommodate a Chapel Dean who was also the Lord High Almoner. The king called for Andrewes to attend him on Good Friday, and he preached before the sick king at his hunting estate on Easter Sunday, while the Whitehall sermon was taken by John Donne.[194] According to Camden, however, during the second week of May 1619, George Mountaigne, Bishop of Lincoln, was 'made the King's Almoner, in the place of the Bishop of *Winchester*, who laid it down against his Will'.[195]

With his appointment as Dean of the Chapel, Andrewes had gained exclusive control over the celebration of the liturgy in the king's chapels, and for the first time in the reign he was in a position to enforce the sacrament-centred ritualism for which he had been calling for years from the court pulpit.[196] Indeed, he was not idle. The Whitehall altar was probably railed in during Andrewes's tenure as Dean, and he undoubtedly had a hand in the king's rules for seating and deportment in chapel. The rules, designed to redress 'a gen[er]al breache of the a[u]ncient & lawdable

[191] Lee, ed., *Jacobean Letters*, 110. Chamberlain reported the same arrangement for Christmas 1617 to Carleton (*Letters*, vol. II, 47).

[192] YML Add MS 17, 108.

[193] A correspondent reported in July 1618 that Andrewes would have the deanery and retain the almonership: *HMC Downshire*, vol. VI, 8.

[194] Chamberlain, *Letters*, vol. II, 225; Donne, *Sermons*, vol. II, 197–212. Donne had been sworn chaplain in the spring of 1615; see Bald, *John Donne*, 306–8. Andrewes's sermon for this Easter does not survive.

[195] Camden, *Annals of King James I*, in *A Complete History of England*, vol. II, 652; and *cf.* Chamberlain, *Letters*, vol. II, 247–8. The reasons for James's preferment of Mountaigne are unclear, and might repay further study. He had successively served Essex, Sir Robert Cecil, and, at the time of his appointment to the Almonry, Buckingham (BL MS Stowe 743, fol. 41; Bodl. Add MS D 111, fol. 186, a reference I owe to Ken Fincham). Ecclesiologically, he was akin to Andrewes, but lacked Andrewes's distinction (Tyacke, *Anti-Calvinists*, 191; Fincham, *Prelate as Pastor*, 292).

[196] Lake, 'Avant-Garde Conformity'; Fincham, *Prelate as Pastor*, 276–82.

orders of o[ur] Court' were promulgated at Christmastide, 1622/3, and Andrewes concluded his Christmas sermon with a gloss on them:

If He breathed into us our *Soule,* but framed not our *body* (but some other did that) Neither *bow* your *knee* nor *uncover* your *head,* but keep on your hats, and sitt even as you do hardly. But, if He have framed that *body* of yours, and every member of it, let Him have the honour both of *head,* and *knee,* and every *member* els.[197]

His new-found liturgical control notwithstanding, Andrewes was clearly unwilling to surrender the Almonership, and that unwillingness probably came from his desire to retain the Almoner's rights as preacher to the king on feast days. But Mountaigne did succeed Andrewes as Almoner and ranking preacher to the king, and Camden thought it noteworthy to record the next act in the drama: on 4 June, Whitsunday, 1620, James 'took the Sacrament, which was administred by the Bishop of *Winchester* [Andrewes], and the Bishop of *Lincoln* [Mountaigne], who preached his first Sermon before the King'. This last remark makes no sense except as a commentary on the passing of the Almonership, for Mountaigne had been a royal chaplain since 1608 and preached repeatedly before the king – Whitsunday 1620 was not his first court sermon but his first feast day sermon before the king as Lord High Almoner. The lag between Mountaigne's taking up the charitable duties of Almoner in May 1619 and actually beginning his festival preaching duties *coram* in May 1620 perhaps bears witness to Andrewes's ability to retain the Almoner's preaching slots in spite of losing the office. None the less, on Whitsunday 1620, the long-standing division of duties between Dean and Almoner had been completely restored, with the Almoner, now Mountaigne of Lincoln, preaching the sermon before the king.[198]

However, here matters become more, not less, complicated. For, beginning with the *editio princeps* of Andrewes's collected sermons, the folio *XCVI Sermons* edited by Laud and Buckeridge (1629), and then persisting in its four subsequent folio editions and the now-standard *Works* in the Library of Anglo-Catholic Theology, every sermon preached by Andrewes on Christmas, Easter, and Whitsunday after 1619 is subtitled, 'Preached before King James'.[199] So, in addition to Camden's explicit testimony that Mountaigne preached at the king's Whitsun communion, we have an

---

197 Andrewes, *XCVI Sermons,* 146; *Works,* vol. I, 262. For the chapel rails see Rimbault, ed., *Old Cheque-Book,* 155; and Davies, *Caroline Captivity of the Church,* 20, 209. The orders for chapel attendance are BL MS Add 34324, fols. 215–16.

198 Compare also Chamberlain's account of Easter 1621, when Andrewes was exhausted after preaching to the Lords and then administering the king's communion – attendance at two distinct services (*Letters,* vol. II, 362).

199 The copy-text for sermons in *Works* was the second edition of *XCVI Sermons* (1632). See G. M. Story, 'The Text of Lancelot Andrewes's Sermons', in D. I .B. Smith, ed., *Editing Seventeenth Century Prose* (Toronto, 1972), 11–23.

Andrewes sermon for that same date allegedly preached before the king.[200] Did Laud and Buckeridge, while editing *XCVI Sermons*, programmatically and without sufficient recourse to actual fact title all of Andrewes's festival sermons as preached before the King? Several pieces of evidence suggest that they did. Andrewes's Gunpowder Plot sermon for 1612 – preached the day before Prince Henry's death – received Laud and Buckeridge's designation 'preached before the King'. But John Chamberlain, present at the sermon, reported that the conspicuous absence of both James and Anne was taken by all present as proof positive that the prince was '*plane deploratus*'.[201] In 1622, James lay ill at Theobalds during the first part of Lent, and Chamberlain reported he heard no Lent sermons until Holy Week, yet the folio claims that Andrewes preached his Ash Wednesday sermon before the king.[202]

Closer to the passing of the Almonership from Andrewes, we find an important discrepancy in the title for the quarto edition of his sermon for Easter 1620 and that for the the folio text. The quarto, printed shortly after the sermon's delivery on 16 April, is titled simply, '*A Sermon Preached At White-hall, on Easter day*', the standard title for sermons preached at court but not in the royal presence, making it very likely that this sermon was preached not at the king's communion, but at the household's. Laud and Buckeridge, however, upgraded the title for the folio to 'Preached before the Kings Majesty at Whitehall'. Chamberlain comes down on the side of the quarto's title when, sending a copy of the quarto to Carleton, he described it as 'preached on Easterday last to the Lords and rest of the houshold at court, which was so much commended that the King wold needs have him sett yt out'. Perhaps here we have the sermon that Neile teased the king for having missed, 'which, though prepared for household fare, yet would have served a royal palate'.[203]

Finally, Chamberlain's account of events in the Whitehall chapel on Christmas Day, 1622, gives us perhaps the clearest indication of the tensions created by Mountaigne's preferment to the Almonership, and perhaps even James's regret for doing so. 'Somwhat' in Mountaigne's sermon *coram rege* 'gave the King so litle content that he grew lowde, and

---

[200] *XCVI Sermons*, 723–34; *Works*, vol. III, 344–60. Chamberlain also makes clear that Andrewes's sermon for Easter, 1 April 1621 (*XCVI Sermons*, 543–52; *Works*, vol. III, 23–38) was not preached before the king (*Letters*, vol. II, 362). Compare also Mountaigne's appointment to preach before the king on Easter Sunday, 21 April 1622 (WAMB 15, fol. 44), and Andrewes's sermon, purportedly preached before the king on the same day (*XCVI Sermons*, 553–65; *Works*, vol. III, 39–59).

[201] *XCVI Sermons*, 923–33; *Works*, vol. IV, 261–76; Chamberlain, *Letters*, vol. I, 388.

[202] Chamberlain, *Letters*, vol. II, 426–8; Andrewes, *XCVI Sermons*, 227; *Works*, vol. I, 398.

[203] Chamberlain, *Letters*, vol. II, 309. For the editions of this sermon see the 'Calendar' disk supplement entry for 16 April 1620. For Neile's remark, see above, note 54.

the bishop was driven to end abruptly'. The letter-writer could not find anyone with a satisfactory explanation for the king's outburst, since the sermon was 'smooth and plausible enough', so he offered his own interpretation of court gossip about Mountaigne's predicament:

Some speach there is that he shold leave the almonership, for beeing to preach so often and to be so much about the King he is not found so able a man as his predecessor . . . Indeed he hath some disadvantage to follow the bishop of Winchester so close both in the place and in the pulpit, who as Deane of the chappell preaches the morning sermon on those high feasts and communion dayes to the Lords and houshold with great applause.[204]

Andrewes, eulogized as 'an *Homer* among Preachers', was clearly a tough act to follow.[205] We are left, then, with the distinct possibility that, although Andrewes's stature as the greatest preacher of the Jacobean court can hardly be challenged, the frequency of his pulpit appearances before the king himself decreased significantly after resigning the Almonership in 1619–20, and that the festival sermons preached after that date have been misattributed to a royal, rather than a merely courtly, auditory.

The sheer weight of Andrewes's surviving bibliography further increases the chances of over-stating his pre-eminence as a preacher at James's court, before as well as after 1619. Although no other preacher – at least from 1604–20 – competed with Andrewes for the pulpit on major feast days, these solemn sermons were only a tiny fraction of those preached throughout the year. Although they were occasions of great solemnity they did not monopolize the sermon-going public's attention, but competed with the Lent series as well as routine Sunday and Tuesday sermons that showcased preachers quite unlike Lancelot Andrewes but not less respected by King James. We would do well to remember also that the bulk of Andrewes's sermons come down to us only because at the time of his death his ecclesiology and theology were in the ascendant under Charles I and Laud. There can be little doubt that the 1629 folio, commissioned by Charles and produced by Laud himself with the assistance of his Oxford tutor, John Buckeridge, was a polemical manifesto of the Carolo-Laudian programme.[206] Significantly, we have no *XCVI Sermons* of George Abbot, John King, or Tobias Matthew, for example, all great Calvinist preaching prelates and contemporaries of Andrewes favoured by James to balance the disproportionate survival of Andrewes's court-sermon *corpus*. It is true that no other preacher had so many court sermons – ten in all – published

[204] Chamberlain, *Letters*, vol. II, 470. Again, a sermon by Andrewes for this day appears in the folio as 'preached before the King's Majesty' (*XCVI Sermons*, 139; *Works*, vol. I, 249).

[205] Hacket, *Scrinia Reserata*, vol. I, 45.

[206] Peter McCullough, 'Making Dead Men Speak: Laudianism, Print, and the Works of Lancelot Andrewes, 1625–1642', *Historical Journal* (1998).

during James's reign, and those all by royal authority.[207] James's reasons for preferring Andrewes to both print and pulpit seem clear. First, there was an obvious political expediency for broadcasting Andrewes's enthusiastic defences of royal objectives for ecclesiological conformity in both England and Scotland. Less tangible, but perhaps even more important, was a sheer delight in Andrewes's learning and rhetorical sophistication, which pleased the king personally and contributed an intellectual dimension to the magnificence of his court. But it was precisely this kind of passionate enthusiasm for a good sermon that sowed the seeds of a reaction – led by Andrewes – against the court cult of the sermon.

THE REACTION: *ORATORIA* OR *AUDITORIA*?

James made one other radical change from Elizabethan court-sermon practice, which had far-reaching effects. As we have seen, eyewitnesses confirm Camden's assertion that 'always on *Sundays* and *Holydays*' Elizabeth attended public service in her chapels royal.[208] If the queen heard a sermon, it was preached in the afternoon as in Lent, or as an adjunct to morning service on Sundays and feast days. James, however, had his own peculiar routine for sermon attendance. In September 1626, Lancelot Andrewes was not dead 'above nine days' when William Laud was nominated to the now-vacant Chapel deanery and instantly set about reforming what he considered to be offensive customs in chapel. Foremost was one 'used in the Court since the first entrance of King *Iames*', namely, 'that at what part soever of the Publick Prayers the King came into his Closet (which looked into the Chappel) to hear the Sermon, the Divine Service was cut off, and the Anthem sung, that the Preacher might go into the Pulpit'. 'This', not surprisingly, 'the new Dean disliked', and he quickly secured Charles's agreement 'that he would be present at the *Liturgy*, as well as the Sermon every Lords day; and that at whatsoever part of the Prayers he came, the Priest who Ministred should proceed to the end of the Service.'[209]

Although a Scottish influence was not long felt at court in terms of chaplains and preachers, it dictated routines of court-chapel attendance until Laud's intervention in 1626. For James's expectation that his entrance was a cue to start the sermon – with an anthem as a bridge during which the preacher made his way into the pulpit – was, as we have seen, precisely the manner of royal attendance of sermons in Scotland: the congregation

---

[207] All Andrewes's imprints were issued from the king's printing house; see also Chamberlain, *Letters*, vol. I, 292, 295; vol. II, 309, 362.

[208] Camden, *History of Queen Elizabeth*, in *A Complete History of England*, vol. II, 371.

[209] Heylyn, *Cyprianus Anglicus*, 158.

sat patiently until his arrival, then sung five psalms, heard the sermon, sung five more psalms, and watched the king depart. However routine this might have been in Scotland, it must have been surprising, if not shocking, to an English court used to a queen who, if anything, gladly dispensed with sermons, but religiously attended the complete sung service in chapel every Sunday and feast day. Camden's potted summary of Elizabeth's churchmanship should, then, be read not only as an accurate account of Elizabeth's piety, but as an incisive commentary on that of her successor. She 'not only paid her private and daily Addresses to God, the first thing after she rose' – referring to daily private prayers, said with a chaplain and attendants in her privy closet – but also 'attended the publick Service at her own Chappel'. Camden then added, not without reference to James's cavalier interruption of chapel services, that she attended the public services 'at the appointed Times, and always on *Sundays* and *Holydays*; where she behaved herself with a Reverence and Devotion suitable to her Greatness'. When the historian gave the queen credit for 'attentively' hearing the Lent sermons, he balanced that endorsement of royal sermon-going with the important caveat that Elizabeth often mentioned her predecessor Henry III's preference for prayer over preaching.[210] Several of James's most important, and most favoured, preachers laboured from the court pulpit throughout his reign to revive sentiments – and practices – to bring James's churchmanship closer to Elizabeth's and Henry's.

James's brusque elevation of sermon over service focused and fuelled a debate over the efficacy of preaching versus prayer that had simmered in England since the Reformation. Understanding James's peremptory interruption of prayerbook service for preaching in his own chapel radically alters the valence of sermons by a number of court preachers, notably those of Lancelot Andrewes, from a generalized critique of sermon-centred piety to direct rebuke of royal practice. The first, and one of the most direct, criticisms of James's chapel attendance came not from Andrewes, but from a contemporary, Richard Meredeth (1559?–1621). Meredeth made his court debut in Lent 1599, when chaplain to Cecil, and was sworn Chaplain in Ordinary to James in 1607.[211] Nicholas Tyacke has called attention to Meredeth's two surviving sermons, preached during his attendance at court in February 1606 and printed together the same year, as important early evidence of English anti-Calvinism in the circle of another Cecil chaplain, Richard Neile, James's Clerk of the Closet. Meredeth's sermons, one of the few books known to have been licensed by Neile, asserted universal grace, and, more pertinent for this discussion, unequivocally gave pride of place

---

[210] Camden, *History of Queen Elizabeth*, in *A Complete History of England*, vol. II, 371.
[211] WAMB 15, fol. 27; *HMC Salisbury*, vol. IX, 400.

to prayer over preaching.[212] Moreover, this latter theme was reinforced
through allusions both typographical and textual to an ecclesiology centred
on the prayerbook liturgies. *Two Sermons* was printed in black-letter
gothic, a typeface that had been largely abandoned for printing sermons in
the 1580s and that looks noticeably, even deliberately, antiquated in a 1606
quarto.[213] But black letter continued to be used throughout the seventeenth
and even into the eighteenth century, either for pamphlets, ballads, and
proclamations aimed at unsophisticated audiences or as the standard typeface for official government and church documents including *The Book of
Common Prayer,* the *Homilies,* Bibles, and Psalters.[214] The typeface of
Two Sermons visually linked Meredeth's book with the printed liturgical
texts of the English Church, a connection made explicit in the text of the
second sermon, where the preacher made unprecedented use of passages
from the prayerbook as exempla and proof texts. To prove his claim that
only four things could be prayed for without qualification, 'to wit, Remis-
sion of sinnes, Grace, Perseuerance, and Glorie', Meredeth cited the *Te
Deum Laudamus,* noting that in that hymn 'which is sung in the Morning
prayer, you haue all these' petitions. Similarly, three other things that could
be asked for in good conscience – mercy for the past, grace for the present
and illumination for the future – were all found 'in the Psalme which is
sayde in the Euening prayer'. Summarizing his point that all Christian
prayers were properly offered only in the name of Christ, Meredeth pointed
out that the church concluded 'euery prayer and Collect as you may see in
the communion booke with this clause, *Per Iesum Christum Dominum
nostrum,* Through our Lord Iesus Christ'.[215] To appreciate fully how
avant-garde Meredeth's references to the prayerbook were, one must
appreciate that, however surprising it may seem, no preacher in any
surviving court sermon after 1559 made so much as a glancing allusion to
the English formularies. Suddenly to have three such elementary lessons on
prayerbook usage in one sermon suggests that this preacher had a grievance
with James that no one had had with Elizabeth. That Meredeth had the

---

[212] Richard Meredeth, *Two Sermons Preached before his Maiestie in his Chappell at Whitehall* (1606); Tyacke, *Anti-Calvinists,* 112–13.

[213] The first court sermon printed in roman type was Peter Wentworth's *A Sermon . . . at the
Courte, at Greenewiche* (1587).

[214] Keith Thomas, 'Literacy in Early Modern England', in Gerd Baumann, ed. *The Written
Word: Literacy in Transition* (Oxford, 1986), 99. I owe this reference to David Armitage.
See also Charles C. Mish, 'Black Letter as a Social Discriminant in the Seventeenth
Century', *PMLA* 68 (3) (June 1953), 627–30.

[215] Meredeth, *Two Sermons,* 32, 37. The Psalm alluded to is Psalm 67, the *Deus misereatur,*
appointed as an alternative second canticle. Tyacke calls Meredeth's endorsement of
prayers for perseverance 'only just within the bounds of the doctrinally permissible at this
date' (*Anti-Calvinists,* 112).

king specifically in mind became unequivocally clear in the closing
moments of the sermon.

In conclusion Meredeth explained pointedly that, 'I haue thus magnified
and extolled this holy exercise of prayer . . . to diminish and abate the
credit, of a certaine newfangled, and ouer-licentious opinion . . . that all
the chiefe parts, and points of the christian religio[n] consisteth in the
reading of scriptures, frequenting of Lectures, and hearing of Sermons'.
After explaining why he found prayer more vital to both Christian
individuals and Christian commonwealths, he loosed a fierce attack on the
present preaching age and invoked the time when his auditors' ancestors
had worshipped with 'knees as hard as Camels hoofes, with continuall
praying' and left as their 'godly exercises' not sermon notes but 'oratories,
churches, Colleges, chappels'. But whom did Meredeth address here? Who
were those who thought it 'the height of religion, if so be they are come to
church, turned ouer their bookes, found the text, looke on the preacher,
marke his diuision, heard the sermon'? Was Meredeth only parodying
godly Cits who gadded to sermons and lectures? He left no one in doubt
when, raising his eyes to the closet, he said,

> I will speake what I intend more plainly. Your sacred presence (most dread and
> mightie Soueraigne,) at the morning and euening Sacrifice, will induce others to
> present themselues, they will come, they will runne, they will prostrate themselues,
> they will worship they will adore in the holy Sanctuarie of God, the sweete odor of
> the oyntments of this your gratious deuotion, hath, and doth, and will drawe on
> others, yea many others for to follow . . . for this cause of set purpose haue I
> compiled this Sermon.[216]

Meredeth's 'set purpose' throws a number of issues into sharper focus. The
publication design of *Two Sermons* seems to echo the second sermon's
indictment of James's sermon-centred piety and the call for the king to give
due regard, and due attendance, to the prayerbook liturgies. The choice of
the black-letter typeface, with its liturgical connotations, might itself
suggest that the sermon should be a component, or even subordinate, part
of a larger liturgical whole.[217] But even more specific to James and his
household, Meredeth had begged for the court chapel to be a royal house
of liturgical prayer, not a royal sermon hall, and for James to set an
example for all the nation's churches to be *oratoria* not *auditoria*.[218] This
plea seems to emanate from the very title page of *Two Sermons* with the

---

[216] Meredeth, *Two Sermons*, 40, 44, 46.

[217] It is, of course, dangerous to ascribe authorial intention to the design of an early printed
book. However, Neile's special interest in this volume suggests a concern for its ideological
content, and therefore perhaps for its presentation in print. The printer, George Eld,
printed no other works in black letter in 1606 (using the handlist in *STC*, vol. III, 58).

[218] Meredeth, *Two Sermons*, 44.

subtitle's unprecedented emphasis on the chapel as the site of preaching: '*Two Sermons Preached before his Maiestie, in his Chappell at Whitehall*'. Like the return to black-letter type, the titular identification of the chapel royal as the place of preaching departs wholly from convention. No Elizabethan or Jacobean court sermon printed before this date designated the place of preaching so exactly, but only gave formulaic notice of the auditory and the manor where the sermon was preached (e.g. 'before the Queen at Whitehall', or 'at the Court at Greenwich'). Meredeth's volume insisted on the distinctly liturgical identification of the king's 'Chappell at Whitehall'. It was in this space that the king and court, like their predecessors, who had knelt in it 'with continuall praying', should not only hear sermons, but hear divine service.

To be sure, the king was not the only person in the realm who gadded to sermons instead of prayerbook services, nor was Meredeth the first to fret over the cult of the sermon; during Elizabeth's reign, excess sermon-hearing had been decried by establishment spokesmen as a singularly dangerous aspect of Puritan nonconformity.[219] Even without Meredeth's direct application of the service-above-sermon argument to James himself, his 1606 sermon would still be significant as the first sustained court-pulpit criticism of sermon-centred piety in the period under consideration here.[220] Until 1603 the cult of the sermon had flourished, and was checked, in municipal lectureships, market-town prophesyings and godly City parishes; after that succession year, the struggle also took place at court.

However, if Richard Meredeth sounded the first alarum against the Jacobean court's privileging of sermon over service, it was Lancelot Andrewes who kept up the offensive for the entire reign.[221] Peter Lake has already called very needed attention to Andrewes and his colleague John Buckeridge as vital links between Hooker and Laud, and to the uniqueness of their churchmanship at the Jacobean court.[222] Both men departed from conventional Elizabethan–Jacobean Calvinism not only in their liberal views on grace, but also in their emphasis on the sacraments and the public liturgy, and anathema to both was what they saw as a hypocritical, word-

---

[219] For this thread of conformist apologetic, see Peter Lake in *Anglicans and Puritans? Presbyterianism and English Conformist Thought from Whitgift to Hooker* (1988), 162–4.

[220] In November 1601, Andrewes had complained at court that England could 'not canonise *Preaching*, but *Prayer* must grow out of request' (*XCVI Sermons*, 2.91; *Works*, vol. V, 131). Richard Eedes glanced briefly at 'that idle and profunctorie hearing of sermons, which too many make the whole both dutie & fruit of their religion, as if they ought nothing but their eares vnto the Lord' at Hampton Court in August 1603: 'Dutie of a King', in *Six Learned and Godly Sermons*, 15ᵛ.

[221] No other sermons by Meredeth survive; he was appointed among the court Lent preachers in 1608 and 1611: WAMB 15, unfoliated leaf (formerly fol. 34ᵛ), fol. 37.

[222] Lake, 'Avant-Garde Conformity'; Fincham, *Prelate as Pastor*, 231–40.

centred piety built around sermon-hearing. Lake has shown that Andrewes and Buckeridge were indeed 'a very central strand in the religious ideology of the court', and his *florilegium* of quotations from their court sermons captures their fear that 'the church was full of "sermon hypocrites"'.[223] But if we place these sermons even more directly in their court context, that is by applying to them what we know of James's chapel attendance, Andrewes's anti-sermon sermons prove to be much more court-specific than has been hitherto acknowledged. That 'central strand in the religious ideology of the court' was, at least in regard to sermons, a directly oppositional one.

Although Andrewes had established himself as a leading critic of Puritan piety as early as 1592 in a parochial sermon against 'the worshipping of imaginations', the majority of his specific criticisms of the sermon cult date from James's reign, and more importantly, from James's court.[224] Andrewes, like Meredeth, preached a sermon at court early in the new reign that leaves little doubt that his criticisms were not only meant for persons outside the court gates. In 1607, Andrewes explained at Greenwich that he preached on James 1:22 – 'And be ye doers of the word, and not hearers only, deceiving your own selves' – because they lived in a time 'when *hearing* of the *word* is growen into such request, as it hath got the start of all the rest of the parts of GOD's service'. For 'proofe' that increasingly 'all *godlinesse* were in *hearing of Sermons*', he challenged the court to 'take this verie place, *the House of* GOD, which now you see meetly well replenished: Come at any other parts of the *Service of* GOD (parts, I say, of *the service of* GOD no lesse then this) you shall find it (in a manner) *desolate*'. Although he added that one could 'goe any whither els' and 'finde even the like', the pertinence of his message for the court is clear, and it confirms Heylyn's description of James as frequently, if not routinely, attending only sermon and not service in chapel.[225]

We must recall that the king could only reach the chapel by processing through the public chambers of the palace with his attendants, and that most courtiers made it a point to advertise their presence to the king on these occasions. Because of this, precious few members of the court could have attended any part of a chapel service that the king did not attend. Significantly, the only account of James (and Queen Anne) publicly attending chapel service at a time other than a major feast is from the highly choreographed display of the English chapel service ('the haill solemnitie of ceremonies in the Kingis Chappel') staged for the Scottish

---

[223] Lake, 'Avant-Garde Conformity', 114, 115–16, 123–6.

[224] Andrewes, *XCVI Sermons*, pt 2, 25–38; *Works*, vol. V, 54–70. Even Andrewes's early lectures on the Lord's Prayer do not systematically oppose prayer to preaching (*Works*, vol. V, 362–476).

[225] Andrewes, *XCVI Sermons*, pt 2, 129–30; *Works*, vol. V, 186–202.

Presbyterians at Hampton Court in September 1606.[226] Since on more routine occasions the king's entrance was a cue to cut off the service and begin the sermon, most of the court as well as the king must have missed common prayer and heard a sermon sandwiched between two anthems. During service time the Jacobean chapel royal was indeed 'in a manner desolate', while during sermon it was 'meetly well replenished'. The emphasis here is on the king's attendance of public service in chapel, distinct from the private devotions he maintained in his privy oratory, which, although regular and said according to the prayerbook, were not in any way as visible as his sermon attendance. In addition, James professed a high regard for the holy communion, and there is no evidence that his attendance on festival communion days was so cavalier.[227] But, with respect to routine practice, Andrewes found James, and not just some of his godly subjects, 'carried away with the common error, that *Sermon-hearing* is the *Consummatum est* of all *Christianitie*'.[228]

Few passages in Andrewes's court sermons crackle with more righteous indignation than those against infatuation with sermons. Knowing that those same passages so directly chastised a royal practice should qualify the portrait of Andrewes as 'a man chronically devoid both of political sense and gumption, unwilling to take the necessary risks to fight for what he believed in'.[229] Like Meredeth, Andrewes believed that an over-emphasis on sermons devalued prayer and the sacraments and thereby placed in inverse order of efficacy the means by which God bestowed grace on believers. For Andrewes, nothing less than the salvation of souls was at stake: as he reminded the court in 1607, to those who heard even Christ himself preach daily but followed none of his commandments, 'for all their *hearing*, He telleth them againe, *Nescio vos*'.[230] It was with this urgency that Andrewes preached to the king and court about the spiritual dangers of sermon-centred piety, using his esteemed pulpit eloquence to wean his auditory from a juvenile reliance upon it. He had no contempt for preaching *per se*, and it would be an error to think that he took his role as preacher at court lightly. According to Buckeridge, Andrewes considered it his chief role there; in his last illness 'he began to goe little to the Court, not so much for weaknesse, as for inabilitie to preach'. He even thought the preparation of a worthy sermon so demanding that it was a contradiction

---

[226] Melvill, *Autobiography and Diary*, 653, 657, 663–4.

[227] James ordered morning and evening prayer to be read daily by a chaplain in Prince Henry's privy closet (BL Add. MS 39853, fol. 16ʳ). Camden, *Annals*, in *A Complete History of England*, vol. II, 645, 652; King James, *A Meditation vpon the Lords Prayer* (1619), sig. A7ʳ.

[228] Andrewes, *XCVI Sermons*, 142; *Works*, vol. V, 202.

[229] Lake, 'Avant-Garde Conformity', 132.

[230] *XCVI Sermons*, 2.141; *Works*, vol. V, 201.

in terms to say one had preached twice in the same day.[231] In this sense, his view of the sermon was more exalted than most Puritans'.

   More importantly, Andrewes always laboured to integrate the sermon into a larger liturgical context. The hallmark of his Christmas, Easter, and Whitsun sermons is their refusal to become metonymic stand-ins for divine service, always leading as they do to invitations to communion. Andrewes revelled in these rare occasions that saw the celebration of the church's full service when 'no *part* is missing, when all our *dueties* of *preaching*, and *praying*, of *Hymnes*, of *offering*, of *Sacrament* and all, meet together'. Sermons were not to be excised, but rather prepared with the greatest possible scholarly precision and verbal skill and then heard in their proper context as preliminary components of a larger service made complete only with communion: 'No *fulnes* there is of our *Liturgie*, or publike solemne service, without the *Sacrament*.'[232] So, in his sermon for 5 November 1617 he complained again about the contrast between service and sermon attendance and chastised the court for using locutions such as 'At Seruice time' and 'the Seruice booke', but then refusing 'to be present at Diuine seruice'. In the same sermon, the royal practice of being absent from service but then present at sermon must have infused an uncomfortable irony into the preacher's lesson that in the primitive church the sermon, an extraneous appendage to the service proper, was the only part of Christian worship open to the heathen who were promptly 'voided' before the liturgy began. The king and court, Andrewes implied, perverted ancient practice when they ennobled by their presence the least noble part of the church's service.[233] Similarly, on Whitsunday 1618 he asked in exasperation, 'For what? is the *powring of the Spirit* to end in *preaching*? and *preaching* to end in it self (as it doth with us) *a circle of preaching* & in effect nothing els?' What might sound to us like a generalized parody of those who 'make Religion nothing but an *auricular profession*, a matter of ease, a meer sedentarie thing' was in fact a daringly accurate description of the court sermon routine: 'sitt still, and hear a *Sermon*, and *two Anthems*, and be *saved*: as if, by the act of the *Queer*, or of the *Preacher*, we should so be'.[234] Dr Fincham is correct to point out that Andrewes's (and Buckeridge's) court sermons 'were calculated attempts to persuade the King . . . to tighten ceremonial discipline

[231] Buckeridge, 'A Sermon Preached at the Funeral,' appended to Andrewes, *XCVI Sermons*, 21; *Works*, vol. V, 295–6.
[232] Lancelot Andrewes, *A Sermon Preached before the Kings Maiestie at White-hall, on Munday the 25. of December* (1610), 38; *Works*, vol. I, 62.
[233] Andrewes, *A Sermon Preached . . . at Whitehall the Fift of Nouember Last*, 34, 35; *Works*, vol. IV, 376, 377.
[234] *XCVI Sermons*, 719–20; *Works*, vol. III, 318–19.

and curb excessive preaching'.[235] But what has been missed is that the king himself was the prime offender.

James's practice obviously galled Andrewes. But did he speak out against it at the risk of losing favour with the king? To be sure, at times, Andrewes gave preaching high praise, and often cast his critiques of sermon-centred piety as satires against crazed Puritans.[236] But perhaps Andrewes and James both knew that the latter was so resolute in his custom that criticism of it was only proffered out of conscience from the pulpit and benignly indulged from the royal closet. Indeed, Andrewes struck precisely such a note of frustration at the outset of the 1607 Greenwich sermon, when he said frankly that preaching 'is not the only thing, and so much we must and do testify unto you, though our witness be not received'. Professor Lake has already suggested that, try as they might, Andrewes and Buckeridge had to wait until the next reign for the full implementation of their avant-garde programme.[237] At least in the case of court-sermon attendance, Andrewes seems to have acknowledged even in the first years of the reign that his criticisms would go unheeded; but he continued to express them with consistency and conviction.

Of even broader significance, though, is the light these court reactions against excessive preaching throws on the ecclesiastical polity of the Jacobean Church. First, James's court practice departed significantly from what he, and at least his first two Archbishops, publicly demanded from his subjects – that is, minimum weekly attendance at the public liturgy. In this respect, James reflected in his own household the tacit distinction that he and most of his bishops made between the parochial clergy's subscription to canonical authority and actual conformity to it. After Hampton Court James and his bishops pursued an ecclesiastical policy that, in exchange for a minister's oath to uphold the rites and ordinances of the church, quite often disregarded 'occasional nonconformity', or 'minor infringements of the liturgy'.[238] To James, conformity in religion was a matter of swearing loyalty to the Crown, not the unflagging observance of rites and ceremonies, hence his strict pursuit of subscription but comparatively soft line on nonconformity. Not until the Caroline regime were observances of the visible church – strict adherence to the liturgy and ceremonies – elevated from things indifferent to professions of faith. So it is perfectly in keeping with James's nationwide ecclesiastical *laissez-faire* to find such a disparity between the letter of the 1604 Canons, with their evident concern to leaven

---

[235] Fincham, *Prelate as Pastor*, 237.
[236] See *XCVI Sermons*, 134, 138–9; *Works*, vol. V, 192, 197.
[237] Lake, 'Avant-garde Conformity', 133.
[238] Fincham and Lake, 'Ecclesiastical Policy', 171–82; Fincham, *Prelate as Pastor*, 228.

the English Church's diet of preaching with more public prayer, and his own privileging of sermon over service at court.

Secondly, the 'reaction' against preaching had been launched decades before the advent of 'Carolinism', or for that matter, the 1622 promulgation of James's directions for preachers. For if, as has been argued, Jacobean England was a kind of evangelical Arcadia, a 'country on the move as the godly gadded between churches and households to hear sermons, to hold repetitions and fasts, and to participate in fellowship', there were not a few who considered this golden preaching age a brazen one for the church.[239] The groundwork had been laid, first in political terms by Whitgift against the perceived levelling impulses of Puritan preaching in the 1580s, and then on more ecclesiological grounds by Richard Hooker and John Howson in the 1590s.[240] Elizabeth herself – out of a combination of public policy and personal taste – had also checked the growth of popular preaching during her reign. The Jacobean father of the restraint of preaching was no Arminian, but the conformist-Calvinist Richard Bancroft, who spoke out at Hampton Court against excessive preaching and then steered the Canons of 1604, with their attempts to subordinate sermon to service, through Convocation.[241] John Burgess objected not only to forced ceremonial conformity, but complained that the new canonical requirement for reading complete service on Sundays wasted time much better spent on a sermon. He singled out as the root of his predicament 'my Lo: of Londons [Bancroft's] motion at the Conference for a praying Ministrie as more needfull in a Church planted then preaching (as his speeches also since have professed)'. And just as Meredeth had argued at court the previous year, royal chaplain Martin Fotherby lamented before Bancroft in a Canterbury visitation sermon that Scripture reading and public prayer had been 'iustled out of the Church' by sermon-goers.[242] By 1603, the case against excessive preaching was a well-rehearsed one.

The accession of a king who not only established what amounted to a weekly combination lecture at court (Tuesday sermons) and disregarded public attendance of liturgical service in favour of sermon-hearing galvanized a small but very prominent group of clergy to focus their attention on the court as a crucial battleground in a long campaign to reorient the ecclesiology of the English church. The increasing stature of the English clergy, in terms of both academic training and social status, from the rather

---

[239] Julian Davies, *Caroline Captivity of the Church*, 126; see also 292. For 'Carolinism', see ibid., ch. 1; for the centrality of the supression of preaching to it, esp. 27 and ch. 4.

[240] Richard Hooker, *The Folger Edition of the Works of Richard Hooker*, 6 vols. (Cambridge, Mass, 1977–93), vol. II, 65–121; John Howson, *A Second Sermon, Preached at Paules Crosse* (1598), 40–6; see Fincham, *Prelate As Pastor*, 232–3.

[241] Fincham, *Prelate as Pastor*, 65, 291–2.

[242] Bodl. MS Rawl. D.353, 219–29; Martin Fotherby, *Fovre Sermons* (1608), 44.

bedraggled lot that set out to preach the Elizabethan Settlement in 1559 to the '*stupor mundi*' hailed by Joseph Hall in 1624 has been admirably charted by Professor Collinson. In his telling, if the story of that clergy between 1559 and 1625 was a success story, it was so most notably in terms of preaching: by the end of James's reign university graduates manned the pulpits, and an elaborate network of lectures supplemented regular parochial preaching.[243] Lancelot Andrewes himself would have been the first to agree that years of labour in the parishes and universities had indeed raised up a mighty preaching clergy in England. Yet, he and others asked, could they do anything but preach, and had the single-minded emphasis on preaching and developing a preaching clergy actually benefited the church?

Sermons at court on Whitsunday, the feast that commemorated the descent of the Holy Ghost and distribution of gifts that included preaching and the calling to ordained ministry, often afforded Andrewes occasion to comment on preaching and the priesthood. His most sustained treatment of these subjects came on Whitsunday 1608, before the king at Greenwich, preaching on Acts 2:4 ('And they were all filled with the holy Ghost, and began to speake with other tongues, as the spirit gaue them vtterance'). At the heart of the sermon was a conviction that preaching had become so popular and frequent that men were preaching (the text's 'speaking in tongues') without having first been filled with the Holy Ghost, by which Andrewes understood not only having been called and ordained, but deeply educated in fundamentals of Christian faith and practice. The '*godly brethren*', he said, had 'all out of order, to have the *tongues* come, before the *wind*'. The nation had clamoured for preachers and sermons, and whether the former were properly called or the latter properly preached had become beside the point. At the same time, patrons sought curates who would meet the demand for sermons at the smallest possible wage – sometimes 'but eight pound a yeare'. The result was an inferior group of men preaching inferior sermons. Andrewes told the ruling élite, you 'send us a sort of *foolish sheepheards*; and send us this senselessnesse withall, that, speak they never so fondly, so they *speake*, all is well; it shall serve our turne as well as the best of them all'.

To Andrewes, decades of effort to establish a preaching clergy in England had actually devalued preaching. Clergy and laity had been taught by precept and example that preaching well and frequently was all that mattered, resulting in an emphasis on the externals of style, elocution, and rhetoric: 'all their religion is in common phrases and terms well got by heart', and their sermons judged on '*volubilitie* of *utterance, earnestnesse*

---

[243] Patrick Collinson, *The Religion of Protestants* (Oxford, 1982), ch. 3, but see esp. 130–40.

of action, streining the *voice* in a *passionate deliverie, phrases* and *figures'*. If a preacher could make his congregation 'a little *sermon-warme* for the while', it was a job well done. Lost in this preaching culture, Andrewes claimed, was attention to fundamentals of the faith preached by the Apostles, who, 'when they spake, they spake *magnalia: Magnalia,* great and *high Points*; not *Trivialia*, base and *vulgar stuff*, not worth the time it wasteth, and taketh from the hearer'.[244] With this, Andrewes essentially inverted the arguments for establishing a preaching clergy that had echoed from the same pulpit early in Elizabeth's reign. Whereas Edward Dering had excoriated the English clergy as 'dumb dogges' precisely because they did not preach, fifty years later Lancelot Andrewes lamented another breed of dumb dogs that had evolved through generations of training to do nothing but preach.

King James, like Queen Elizabeth, died in March; even more fittingly, James died close to sermon-time on mid-Lent Sunday morning, 27 March 1625. An hour before the king's passing, royal chaplain Daniel Price had preached to Prince Charles and those gathered at Theobalds, taking full advantage of the pathos of the moment: 'for it is the *day of our Royall Iacobs wrestling*, and . . . my *heart* trembleth to thinke it, and my *eares* tingle to *heare*, the *heauie* and sad *approach* of *pale Death* entring into this *Kingly Palace'*.[245] Price – the son and brother of godly Shropshire preachers, servant of Lord Chancellor Ellesmere, the godly preachers' patron *par excellence*, Prince Henry's chaplain, and now a chaplain to the dying king – is, on the one hand, the consummate example of the kind of career made possible, probably even intended, by James's remarkable patronage of preaching at court. But, on the other hand, the future belonged to men of another kind of churchmanship, which defined itself in opposition to the preaching model apotheosized at court by King James. As at Elizabeth's death, the court Lent sermon series was in progress at James's death, and word of the king's passing reached London during the delivery of the mid-Lent Sunday sermon. In the pulpit was William Laud. Before he reached the middle of his sermon, the murmurs of the crowd and 'the dolorous complaints made by the Duke of *Buckingham*' confirmed the fact of the king's death and, according to Heylyn, 'occasioned him to leave the Pulpit, and to bestow his pains and comforts where there was more need. He did not think (as I believe few wise men do) that the carrying on of one particular Sermon was such a necessary part of *Gods business*, as is not to be intermitted upon any occasion.' One expects Price would have finished his sermon had the king died during it. James, the king who interrupted

---

[244] *XCVI Sermons*, 609–10, 614–15; *Works*, vol. III, 132–3, 141–3.
[245] Price, *Heartie Prayer*, 24.

chapel services for a sermon, probably would have wanted him to. But the church was now in Laud's and Charles's hands, and Laud soon asked his new king to correct his father's practice and attend the whole of divine service as well as sermon. So too in the dioceses, parishioners would complain that their sermons were made prisoner to the whole 'quier service'. Sermons, like Laud's own on that Midlent Sunday in 1625, were to be 'intermitted'. We may indeed be able to consider the Caroline captivity of the church, or at least the Caroline captivity of preaching, but the trap had been set by the Jacobeans.[246]

[246] Heylyn, *Cyprianus Anglicus*, 126, see Laud, *Works*, vol. III, 157–8; J. Wickham Legg and W. H. St John Hope, eds., *Inventories of Christchurch Canterbury* (1902), 246; Davies, *Caroline Captivity*, ch. 4.

4

Denmark House and St James's: sermons for the Jacobean queen and Princes of Wales

PREACHING TO A COURT PAPIST? SERMONS AT THE COURT OF
QUEEN ANNE

In his sermon on the day of King James's death, royal chaplain Daniel Price lamented the *'fatality* of this *bloody Moneth'* by recalling the 'ancient *Triumph* of *Funerall Solemnities* in *March'*, which included the deaths of both James's royal predecessor and his wife. Elizabeth was eulogized conventionally as that *'Paragon* of *mortall Princes'* and likened to the Virgin Mary. About Queen Anne, however, Price asserted rather strongly that she was 'not *superstitious,* not *factious,* not *tyrannous,* but *religious* to her God'.[1] The defensiveness of Price's allusion suggests that some, perhaps even Price himself, *did* believe that Anne of Denmark was superstitious, factious, tyrannous, and irreligious, or, at the least, that her reputation needed defending against charges of false religion. Anne's confessional allegiance had been a point of some concern in England at least since June 1603, when she very publicly did not receive communion at her and her husband's coronation in Westminster Abbey. Fr A. J. Loomie has documented how Anne was rumoured to have Roman Catholic sympathies as early as 1593, and that Jesuit missionaries reported her formal conversion at 'about the year 1600'. After her arrival in England she repeatedly made overtures to Rome and insinuated to Catholic ambassadors that she was of their religion. Yet, eager to secure a reliable Catholic influence on her husband, these men found Anne's frequent attendance at Protestant preaching and prayers and her unwillingness to become the anchor of a Catholic interest at court dubious confirmation of her Catholicism. Like Loomie, they found her religious beliefs 'elusive' at best.[2] But combining our knowledge of Anne's 'elusive' Catholicism with attention to her attendance at establishment services and

---

[1] Daniel Price, *A Heartie Prayer* (1625), 31–2.
[2] Albert J. Loomie, S.J, 'King James I's Catholic Consort', *Huntington Library Quarterly* 34 (August 1971), 303–16.

her overt patronage of Protestant preachers in her own household lends supportive detail to the recent thesis that there were in early modern England an underestimated number of Catholics for whom routine compliance with the Church of England and committed Catholicism were not mutually exclusive.[3] Anne might not have been such a religious enigma after all, but rather one of Jacobean England's consummate 'church papists'.

As early as 1601, Anne personally petitioned Pope Clement VIII for his 'absolution and a blessing' for her to attend 'the rites of heretics' not out of belief, but political expediency. This practice was in keeping with the official policy of the Scottish Jesuit mission and its superior, Robert Abercrombie (reportedly Anne's quondam confessor) who required his priests to allow Catholics in their charge to attend Protestant sermons when necessary for a show of conformity.[4] As Walsham has shown, the practice of such conformity or 'church papistry' was indeed an option practised by the laity and tacitly allowed by the Catholic mission on a scale much greater than official Roman Catholic propaganda for a strictly separatist recusancy might suggest.[5] What was observed by contemporary ambassadors and cited by modern historians as Anne's puzzling appearances at her husband's Protestant services and sermons was in fact a form of religious dissimulation widely practised in both Scotland and England. If anything, the frequency with which Anne publicly played the Protestant has been underestimated. According to the precedent book of the Chapel Royal, she was churched according to the form of *The Book of Common Prayer* after the births of both English-born princesses, Mary (1605) and Sophia (1606), and on Good Friday 1611 she attended Princess Elizabeth's confirmation and the sermon following in the chapel at Whitehall.[6] The accounts of the Treasurer of the Chamber indicate that she routinely joined the king and Prince of Wales in the Council Chamber window to hear the Lent sermons preached from the outdoor pulpit at Whitehall.[7] The Scottish minister James Melville, during his enforced visit to Hampton Court in September, 1606, noted that the queen was present with the king at the sermons preached in chapel on Sunday and Tuesday, 21 and 23 September, and on St Michael's Day, the 29th, he 'saw the King and Quein offer at the

[3] Alexandra Walsham, *Church Papists: Catholicism, Conformity and Confessional Polemic in Early Modern England* (Woodbridge, 1993), 77.

[4] Bib. Vaticana, MSS Marberini Latini 8618, fols. 15–16, quoted in Loomie, 'Catholic Consort', 305.

[5] Walsham, *Church Papists*, ch. 3.

[6] *The Old Cheque-Book . . . of the Chapel Royal*, eds., Edward F. Rimbault, Camden Society, n.s. 3 (1872), 169–72.

[7] Anne is specifically mentioned in preparations for the outdoor Lent sermons in 1606, 1608, 1609, 1611, and 1612 (PRO E351/543, fols. 153^v, 189^r, 211^r, 247^r, 260^v).

altar' at the service of ante-communion.[8] When James was absent on his 1617 progress to Scotland, Anne, attended by the Lords of the Council, dutifully presided at the court Lent and Easter sermons.[9]

Furthermore, the conventional titles used for printed sermons preached *coram rege* have erased from historical memory some of the queen's participation in conformist court religious life: even if other members of the royal family were present at sermons that were printed, only the king's presence goes noticed on the title page. For example, the printed editions of the two September 1606 Hampton Court sermons that she attended, those preached by William Barlow and John Buckeridge, are titled, respectively, 'ONE OF the foure Sermons PREACHED *BEFORE THE KINGS Maiestie*, at *Hampton Court* in *September* last . . .' and 'A SERMON PREACHED AT Hampton Court before the Kings Maiestie'. Similarly, the titles of Lancelot Andrewes's many holiday court sermons, both those printed in his own lifetime and those gathered into the posthumous folio of 1629, make no mention of the queen. But, as the Treasurer's accounts show, Anne sat in her chapel closet next to the king on all of the principal feast days for which Andrewes preached.[10] The queen not only joined her husband at services and sermons, but made a point to attend them on her own. During her western progress in late summer 1613, she heard service three times in Salisbury Cathedral, five times in Bath Abbey, and a sermon in the cathedral at Wells. In May of the same year, she had also attended a cathedral sermon as part of her public welcome to Bristol.[11]

Moreover, the queen did not limit her attendance at reformed preachings to quasi-public events such as outdoor Lent sermons and progresses, but also sponsored Protestant preaching in her own household. As we shall see, John Donne preached before her at Denmark House in 1617, and shortly before her death one year later John Chamberlain dismissed rumours of her 'desperat' health on the evidence that 'she was able to attend a whole sermon on Christmas day preached by the bishop of London in her inner chamber'.[12] But even more significantly, the list of mourners for her funeral confirms that the queen, like the king and Princes of Wales, was served by a college of sworn chaplains. Of the men among the eighteen listed who can

---

[8] James Melvill, *The Autobiography and Diary of Mr. James Melvill*, ed. Robert Pitcairn (Edinburgh, 1842), 653, 657, 664. For ante-communion as the routine service on Sundays and minor feast days, see above, 72.

[9] Bodl. MS 74, fol. 371.

[10] Payments for preparing the Queen's chapel closets are myriad and routine, e.g. 'for makeing ready the Chappell and Clozett at Whitehall on both the kinge and Queenes side against Allhallowtide', October 1607 (PRO E351/543, fol. 188ᵛ).

[11] PRO E351/544, fols. 8ᵛ–9ʳ; John Nichols, *The Progresses, Processions, and Magnificent Festifivites of King James the First*, 4 vols. (1828), vol. II, 645–6.

[12] Chamberlain, *Letters*, vol. II, 196–7.

be positively identified, the majority had solid conformist credentials.[13] Two were even pillars of a notable evangelical revival in the West Country: Edward Chetwynd, lecturer at Bristol, who, through the patronage of James Montagu, became Dean of Bristol in 1617; and Samuel Crooke, who died a near-legendary Puritan patriarch after forty years of godly preaching at Wrington, Somerset.[14] During Elizabeth's reign Crooke, educated at Merchant Taylor's School and Pembroke Hall, Cambridge, was barred by Pembroke's then-master Lancelot Andrewes from a Pembroke fellowship and instead took one up at the Puritan seminary of Emmanuel College; at Cambridge he was a disciple of William Perkins. After his appointment as Rector of Wrington in 1602, and therefore throughout whatever years he was associated with Anne's court, he preached godly Puritanism 'for the space of forty seven years (wherein he could give an account of above seven thousand elaborate Sermons preached . . .)', and in 1648 he oversaw the introduction of presbyterian church government in the former diocese of Bath and Wells.[15] One of the other ordinary chaplains, Roger Mainwaring, was to become a zealous advocate of Charles's royal prerogative and of Laud's ceremonialism, but never held Arminian views on grace.[16] Among Anne's chaplains only Godfrey Goodman, later bishop of Gloucester, ever made overtures to Rome; his Catholicism was rumoured as early as 1635, and in fact asserted in his will in 1656.[17] Beyond her chaplaincy Anne seems to have cultivated associations with two notable episcopal scourges of popery. Archbishop of York Tobie Matthew, a preaching prelate scandalized by his own son's conversion to Rome, often graced the queen's pulpit during his Parliament-time visits to London – an association that dated from Matthew's escorting the queen and her two eldest children south from Scotland in 1603.[18] And the Christmas sermon Anne heard from her sickbed in 1617 was preached by John King, Bishop of London,

---

[13] Listed as 'Chaplaines to ye Queene' are: 'D^r [Edward] Chettwind deane of Bristow, D^r [George] Goldman, D^r [William] Swadden, D^r [Godfrey] Goodman, William Tunstall, M^r [John?] Shawe, Mr Samuell Prockter, Mr William Ashfield, Edward Tapsall, M^r [John?] Bretton, Mr Smith, Mr Samuell Crooke, [Ro?]ger Mainwaryinge, Mr Hilliard, Mr George Needham, Mr Lamplugh, Mr Serrein dutch chaplaine, M^r [John?] Day'. PRO LC 2/5 fols. 36^v–37^r. I am indebted to Dr John Considine for transcribing this list for me.

[14] Kenneth Fincham, *Prelate as Pastor: the Episcopate of James I* (Oxford, 1990), 193–4.

[15] W[illiam] G[arrett], *Anthologia. The Life & Death of Mr Samuel Crook* (1651), 4, 44. Garrett very carefully disguised evidence of Crooke's court associations: he mentioned Crooke's 1618 funerary sermon for Anne only by the title '*Death subdued*', but tacitly suppressed its occasion and date (16, 60–1).

[16] Mainwaring (1590–1653) was Chaplain in Ordinary to King Charles and Caroline Bishop of St David's. See Nicholas Tyacke, *Anti-Calvinists: the Rise of English Arminianism, circa 1590–1640* (Oxford, 1990), 159, 216.

[17] Geoffrey Soden, *Godfrey Goodman, Bishop of Gloucester, 1583–1656* (London, 1953), 224–35, 246–66. Goodman dedicated his 1616 treatise *The Fall of Man* to Anne.

[18] YML Add MS 18, 70–1, 82, 108.

whom we have already encountered as one of England's leading evangelical Calvinists and a vehement critic of popery. None the less, King's son reminded King Charles I 'how great an interest your Princely Mother, our late Gracious Queene, vouchsafed to challenge in my deceased Father', adding that Anne accounted Bishop King 'as one of Hers . . . by all the tyes a Royall Mistris might engage a Servant'.[19]

The churchmanship of Anne's preachers corresponds with the religious sympathies of her favoured inner circle, described as 'the Essex group'. This group was centred on Lucy Russell, Countess of Bedford, the queen's fast favourite, and Sir Robert Sidney, brother of the late Sir Philip, Anne's Lord High Chamberlain, and later Viscount de Lisle and Earl of Leicester. Around Bedford and Sidney orbited those allied families such as the Haringtons, Devereux, and the Herberts who were closely linked by association or blood to the ill-fated second Earl of Essex. In addition to being generous Jacobean patrons of the literary arts, these families continued the tradition of patronizing a militant, anti-Catholic Protestantism that stretched back to Sir Philip Sidney and Robert Dudley, Earl of Leicester. Anne would not find, indeed probably did not look for, kindred religious spirits in this group; their predominance in Anne's household establishment owed itself to what has been termed the 'lightning strike' of amity between Anne and the Countess Lucy as well as the general revival of Essexian fortunes under King James.[20] But it is apparent that the 'Essex group' played a role in determining the religious temper of Anne's preaching chaplaincy, perhaps most directly through Sidney, who, as Lord Chamberlain, would have overseen personnel above-stairs, including chaplains. Samuel Crooke printed the only surviving text of a sermon for Anne's court by one of her ordinary chaplains and dedicated it to Robert Sidney and his 'MVCH honoured and worthy *friends*' in the queen's 'family'. The Essex thread can be traced through others of the queen's preachers: Donne had accompanied Essex to Cádiz and considered the Countess of Bedford a patroness; the first printed sermon preached before Anne was by John Hopkins, a royal chaplain who had served as one of Essex's chaplains on the Cadiz expedition; and the queen's chaplain, Edward Topsell, credited Essex's successor in Ireland, Charles Blount, Lord Mountjoy with his early preferment.[21]

---

[19] *The Sermons of Henry King (1592–1669), Bishop of Chichester*, ed. Mary Hobbs (1992), 63.
[20] Leeds Barroll, 'The Court of the First Stuart Queen', in *The Mental World of the Jacobean Court*, ed. Linda Levy Peck (Cambridge, 1991), 200–5.
[21] Samuel Crooke, *Death Subdued . . . in a Sermon at Denmarke House on Ascension Day* (1619), sig. A4ʳ.; John Hopkins, *A Sermon Preached Before the Qveenes Maiestie* (1609). R. C. Bald, *John Donne: a Life* (Oxford, 1970), 80–5. Hopkins attended Essex during the first months of his house arrest in August 1599 (*HMC Salisbury* vol. IX, 410).

Does this suggest not so much Anne's church papistry as the likelihood that she was in fact a good Protestant, albeit a Lutheran one with scruples about the Calvinist English communion? To assume so requires discrediting Anne's own professions of a Roman faith. Rather, affinity, kinship, and patronage ties often transcended religious differences between Anne and her preachers, just as they did between herself and her inner circle. More importantly, the queen, like so many conforming Catholics, opted for conformity to the routine non-Eucharistic services of the church instead of the staunch recusancy urged by Catholic missionary propaganda. If avoiding the weekly parochial services 'whose very seating arrangements visibly embodied and reinforced the social hierarchy' was 'a grave dereliction' of a country gentleman's 'duty to bolster parochial discipline and stability', how much more unthinkable would it have been for the queen consort not to show herself reigning from her closet window next to the king's in the chapel royal? And if a Catholic matriarch 'circumspectly recruited conformist tutors after she was required to notify the Privy Council regarding the private education of her son', is it really surprising to see Anne, so much more in the public's eye than Elizabeth Vaux, compensating for rumours of her Catholicism by packing her chaplains' rota with unobjectionable, indeed godly, ministers?[22] She perhaps chose, however, as her one public conscientious objection to the Church of England, to abstain from its communion, a tack popular among conformists as an 'appealing alternative to insolent refusal to attend weekly services'. For the ordinary layman, avoiding a service required only three times a year was not a difficult business.[23] For a prince living in a Tudor palace with the tradition of more or less private services for the prince in a private closet or oratory fitted for the celebration of the Eucharist, Anne's not descending to the body of the chapel royal for communion on Christmas, Whitsun, or Easter was no proof that she had not received a lawful communion in the seclusion of her private closet; and, of course, the privy closet would have provided the perfect place for clandestine celebration of the Mass. Anne's Catholicism, whether devout or dabbling, was a matter of private faith, and she seems to have decided early in her marriage that she would not make it a factional issue. Therefore it is not remarkable that her patronage and involvement in court intrigue, both religious and secular, did not observe neat confessional boundaries.

Anne clearly did not let any confessional loyalties dictate her politicking at her husband's court. In matters of preaching she was apparently glad to offer shelter to an anti-Catholic preacher who taunted from the king's

---

[22] The conformist Catholic exempla are from Walsham, *Church Papists*, 84, 82.
[23] Walsham, *Church Papists*, 85–6.

pulpit one of her inveterate enemies who was himself a crypto-Catholic. In 1616, Thomas Scott dedicated the printing of two sermons preached before King James (one on Easter Tuesday 1613, the other undated) to Anne.[24] In the epistle, he mentioned that the first of these was one

for which I was calld in question, and in defence whereof whilst you stood, a great affront was giuen you by an vnequall opposite; so that I seemed not to suffer for it alone, but your Maiestie with me. I haue now sent it to your Highnes, that you may see wherein it deserued so many great exceptions, or I for it so strict a censure.[25]

Chamberlain's account of Scott's troubles supplies the name of Anne's 'vnequall opposite'. Scott, he said, 'glaunct at matters somwhat suspiciously, wherupon he was called before the counsaile, and the Lord Priviseale insisted much to know yf he had any particuler meaning to him'.[26] Given the wave of public sentiment against the Lord Privy Seal, Henry Howard Earl of Northampton, that was cresting at the time, and Northampton's obvious distaste for Scott's sermon, it seems likely that he was the target of the preacher's criticism.[27]

Scott's sermon in fact belongs to a rash of anti-Northampton libels from 1612–13, in both verse and sermon, that decried the Earl's crypto-Catholicism and his favour and influence at court, and in turn inspired what recent work describes as 'a programme of sustained suppression by the Earl'.[28] Chamberlain's account of Northampton's rough handling of Scott immediately followed his bemused notice of the Lord Privy Seal's severe and illogical Star Chamber sentence – the 'straunge medley' of a 5,000-mark fine and whipping – against two 'seelie men' for allegedly retailing rumours

---

24 Thomas Scott, *Christs Politician, and Salomons Pvritan* (1616). The sermons are undated in the published text; I date the first following Chamberlain, *Letters*, vol. I, 453–4. The biographical tangle of anti-Catholic, anti-Spanish Thomas Scott(s) in Jacobean England is bewildering. This royal chaplain could be any of three Thomas Scotts who graduated from Cambridge and have been conflated by *STC* and *DNB*; see *Alumni Cantab*, vol. IV, 33. It seems unlikely that our author was the anti-Spanish radical of *Vox Populi* (1620) and *The Belgicke Pismire* (1622), for the court sermons do not appear in his posthumous *Workes* (1624), and he did not proceed BD at Cambridge until 1620 (the court sermons' author was, according to the 1616 title page, already BD). The royal chaplain was probably Thomas Scott from Trinity College, Cambridge, BD 1611 and Rector of St Clement's, Ipswich, 1612–38.

25 Scott, *Christs Politician and Salomons Pvritan*, sig. A2ᵛ.

26 Chamberlain, *Letters*, vol. I, 453–4. Chamberlain's account of a sermon on the text 'beware of men' by 'one Scot' on 'Easter Tewsday' 1613, fixes the date of 'Christs Politician' (Chamberlain's editor mistakenly assigns the sermon to 'John Scott').

27 Margot Heinemann has suggested that Scott's sermon alludes to the 1615–16 fall of Somerset; but this is without the benefit of Chamberlain's positive dating of the sermon in 1613. See *Puritanism and Theatre: Thomas Middleton and Opposition Drama under the Early Stuarts* (Cambridge, 1980), 275–6.

28 Alastair Bellany, 'The Poisoning of Legitimacy? Court Scandal, Public Opinion and Politics in England, 1603–1660' (unpublished PhD dissertation, Princeton University, 1995). I am very grateful to Dr Bellany for sharing drafts of his work in progress.

that Northampton was an 'arch-papist' who had petitioned the king for favours to Catholics after the death of Prince Henry.[29] There was plenty in Scott's sermon to anger an already defensive Henry Howard. For not only did Scott rant against conniving flatterers, a commonplace in the court pulpit, but he specifically warned the king to 'aboue all other beware of them, that do acknowledge *England* to be their country, but will haue *Rome* to be the randeuoue and rule of their religion' – a sure glance at Northampton's ambidextrous ability to defend Protestant royal supremacy while practising Roman Catholicism.[30] Scott then went on to caution against traitorous Catholics who sat at the king's own board. In a thinly veiled biblical allegory that made a daring twist on the common alignment of the king with Christ, Scott told James to beware

when *Iudas* sitteth with Christ at his owne table, and in his owne messe, and is one of the next men to him, yea when he embraceth him in his armes and kisseth him with his lippes, he betraieth him into the handes of his enemies, and hath an armie of *Romane* souldiers in a readinesse to rescue him from his Apostles.[31]

Why was Anne willing to be Scott's '*protection against the torrent of violent greatnes*' unleashed by his sermon? Anne and Northampton were hardly allies in the spring of 1613. First, the queen was no doubt still nursing the insult she had received by Northampton's late December 1612 victory in a battle with her over rights to Greenwich Park.[32] Moreover, Anne, out of a combination of her allegiance to the Essex group, her enmity for Northampton, and her bitter resentment of Robert Carr's confidant Sir Thomas Overbury, stood squarely opposed to the Essex–Howard divorce then being engineered by Northampton.[33]

But why did Scott wait until 1616 to print these sermons? Northampton's continued existence and influence is the most obvious answer. As Scott mused in his dedicatory epistle to the queen, there was a time 'for all things', and even if James did rebuke his Lord Privy Seal for harrassing Scott, to have printed the sermons would have been foolishly 'out of season'. Northampton was out of the picture, though, after June 1614; this

---

[29] Chamberlain, *Letters*, vol. I, 453.

[30] Scott, *Christs Politician and Salomons Pvritan*, part 1, 24. A libellous animal fable of 1616 by yet another Thomas Scott cast Northampton as the griffin, a hybrid beast who 'halts to either side' and '*Who hath two faiths, doth true to neither stand*': Thomas Scot, gent, *Philomythie or Philomythologie* (2nd edn, 1616), sigs. C2ʳ, C3ʳ, a reference I owe to Alastair Bellany.

[31] Scott, *Christs Politician and Salomons Pvritan*, part 1, 25–6.

[32] Linda Levy Peck, *Northampton: Patronage and Policy at the Court of James I* (1982), 40, 74.

[33] David Lindley, *The Trials of Frances Howard: Fact and Fiction at the Court of King James* (1993), 84. For Northampton's involvement and Catholicism, see Peck, *Northampton*, 38–40.

still leaves us a full year-and-a-half before Scott printed the sermons. They were made suddenly and sensationally topical, however, in the autumn of 1615, when the revelation of Frances Howard's successful plot to murder Sir Thomas Overbury, and the trials and executions of her alleged accomplices, mesmerized the public. Rumours of foul play circulating in September led in rapid succession to house arrest for the Somersets in early October, the trial of the accomplices Richard Weston and Anne Turner beginning late that same month, and their subsequent executions on 25 October and 14 November.[34] Meanwhile, Somerset's presumed involvement in the Overbury murder was feared to be part of a larger, pro-Spanish, pro-Catholic plot that included not only Somerset, but the deceased Howard patriarch, Northampton, now said by some not to lie mouldering in a tomb at Dover Castle but to walk the streets of Rome orchestrating an international popish plot.[35] So the old charges from 1613 of Northampton's traitorous popish conniving suddenly had a new-found currency in the rather sordid heat of November 1615's scares, trials, and executions. And on 19 November, Thomas Scott's two sermons, with their dedication to the queen, were entered in the Stationer's Register.[36] Scott's – or possibly the queen's – time had finally come to advertise what he no doubt wanted to suggest was his prophetic 1613 indictment of Northampton as a crypto-Catholic traitor. By publishing at the height of the Overbury murder scandal what in 1613 had been an attack on Northampton, Scott could use his early 'glance' at Howard treachery to parrot in his dedicatory epistle providentialist assurances invoked during the murder trials that time, and God would always avenge evil.[37] '*God hath his time neuer limited*', Scott moralized, '*and yet in respect of the execution of his will, he hath his time too, as we see lately by wonderfull example. What this age hath seene were enough to make a heathenish Atheist a Christian, and a licentious Christian, a Saint*'.[38] The 1615 fall of the Somersets and the further posthumous fall of Northampton on their Howard coattails gave Anne a convenient vindication of her past enmity with Northampton. And the conflation of those things in Scott's dedication to her and in his sermons gave the queen an even more convenient means of advertising not

[34] Lindley, *Trials of Frances Howard*, 146–8.

[35] Bodl. MS Eng. Hist.c.477, cited in Bellany, 'Poisoning of Legitimacy?', 304.

[36] The sermons were licensed by Dr William Pierce, then chaplain to Bishop King of London. Pierce was one of four of King James's chaplains chosen to walk in Queen Anne's funeral procession: Edward Arber, *A Transcript of the Register of the Company of Stationers of London 1554–1640*, 5 vols. (1875–94), vol. III, 577; PRO LC 2/5, fol. 37ʳ.

[37] For the topos of *Veritas filia Temporis* ('Truth the daughter of Time') see Lindley, *Trials of Frances Howard*, 188–9. Dr Bellany has examined the providentialism that animated the murder trials themselves in 'Poisoning of Legitimacy?'

[38] Scott, *Christs Politician, and Salomons Pvritan*, sig. A2ʳ.

only her distance from the crumbling Howard axis at her husband's court, but, by implication, her alignment with the ascendant Essexians who stood ready to fill the gap left by Somerset's fall.[39]

Finally, if Anne was a conforming Catholic, would not her reformed preachers have known or at least suspected as much and left some trace of admonition in their sermons? Texts of only three sermons preached before the queen survive. Two – those by John Hopkins, and the post-mortem sermon by Samuel Crooke – contain nothing that is not conventional.[40] But, I argue, the third, preached by John Donne on Sunday, 14 December, 1617, is an extended condemnation of church papistry addressed directly to Anne herself.[41] As we have seen in the cases of John Burgess and Thomas Scott, couching criticism of the monarch or another prominent courtier in a court sermon was a delicate business. Preachers, anxious to avoid Burgess's fate, honed their skills of veiled speech to such a degree that, especially across centuries as many allusions lose their sharp edge, it is difficult to prove who the intended subject of any given 'glance' or 'touch' might have been. The whole valence of a sermon can depend, as it does in the case of Donne's sermon before Anne, on who the 'you' addressed by the preacher actually was. We might begin with the heading given the sermon when it was first printed in the 1661 folio *XXVI Sermons* – 'A *Sermon Preached to Queen Anne, at Denmarke-house. December. 14. 1617*' – which seems direct enough about who the addressee was, especially by virtue of its subtle but significant use of the preposition 'to' instead of the conventional 'before'.[42] In the sermon text itself Anne is never directly addressed by name or title in the way used on some occasions by preachers before her husband. But Donne also shuns the other extreme, which is to preach in a first-person plural voice that includes the preacher as well as the auditory in his admonitions, and thereby gives the sermon a less confrontational tone. In the first part of the sermon there are brief, witty allusions to

[39] Lindley, *Trials of Frances Howard*, 83–4. William Herbert, Earl of Pembroke, a leader of the Essex interest, succeeded Somerset as Lord Chamberlain. Heinemann (*Puritanism and Theatre*, 275–6) presents evidence that this Thomas Scott was his chaplain. For a case study of how this realignment literally played itself out in the 1616 Christmas masque, see Martin Butler, 'Ben Jonson and the Limits of Courtly Panegyric', in Kevin Sharpe and Peter Lake, eds., *Culture and Politics in Early Stuart England* (Basingstoke, 1993), 104–8.

[40] Crooke, *Death Subdued*, Hopkins, *A Sermon Preached before the Qveenes Maiestie*.

[41] John Donne, *The Sermons of John Donne*, 10 vols., ed. G. Potter and E. Simpson (Berkeley, Calif., 1953–62), vol. I, 236–51; subsequent references appear in the text. Donne's sermon text was Proverbs 8:17 ('*I love them that love me, and they that seek me early shall find me*').

[42] The two surviving manuscript copies have no title or heading and mention only the Scriptural text of the sermon. These are the 'Merton' manuscript (Bodl. MS Eng.the.c.17, fols. 116–22), and the 'Ellesmere' manuscript, both of which date from the 1620s–1630s. See Donne, *Sermons*, vol. I, 33–45 and vol. II, 365–7; Peter Beal, *Index of English Literary Manuscripts, Volume I 1450–1625, Part vol. I, Andrewes–Donne* (1980), 555.

things feminine that suggest Donne was playing to the female household, as when he explained somewhat wryly that '*Salomon,* whose disposition was amorous, and excessive in the love of women' naturally 'conveyes all his loving approaches and applications to God . . . into songs, and Epithalamions' (237). But who is the preacher's intended 'thou' in the sermon's passages of sharp exhortation? To picture the preacher literally eye to eye with the queen, we are forced to entertain the possibility that she was the intended 'thou'. If she was, Donne's sermon contains criticisms, both oblique and direct, of institutional and covert Catholicism that provide rare evidence of a contemporary critique of Anne's church papistry.

The puzzle of just how specific Donne's address is to his queen is perhaps solved by a brief but important allusion in the sermon's conclusion to an event in the queen's own life. In his urgent call to turn to Christ from the follies of a sinful youth – based on his text's latter portion, '*they that seek me early shall find me*' – Donne invited those present to 'seek Christ early . . . now as soon as you begin your day of Regeneration, seek him the first minute of this day' (250). Does 'your day of Regeneration' simply refer to the entire auditory's new life of commitment to Christ as inspired by God's word preached by Donne? The date of the sermon, 14 December, suggests otherwise. Anne was born on 12 December, and Donne's description of the day two days thereafter as her 'day of Regeneration' suggests that it was the day of her baptism, the day on which, in the words of *The Book of Common Prayer,* the baptized was made 'regenerate and born anew'.[43] Immediately before his reference to the 'day of Regeneration', Donne dwelt on themes appropriate to the anniversary of the queen's birth, namely the passing of mortal years and the folly of delaying one's return to Christ until the end of one's life. 'For thus,' Donne warned, 'we shall by this habit carry on this early to our late and last houre, and say we will repent early, that is, as soone as the bell begins to toll for us' (250). From this allusion to the passing of mortal years, Donne then recalled the queen to the new life initiated so many years before at her baptism, but now neglected. Hence, Donne's sermon could be read as a commemorative sermon marking the anniversary of the queen's 'day of Regeneration', or her new life sealed by the sacrament of baptism, and therefore as a sermon intended quite specifically and personally for her.

In part one of his sermon, treating the phrase '*I love them that love me*',

---

[43] *The Book of Common Prayer 1559,* ed. John Booty (Washington, D.C, 1976), 270 (from the opening collect for Public Baptism). I have met no success finding documentary evidence for Anne's christening. A contemporary chronicle written for Anne's father, King Frederick of Denmark and Norway, records only Anne's birth: *Kong Frederichs Den Andens Kronicke,* ed. Peder Hanson Resen (1680), 278.

Donne offered meditations on the nature of sacred and profane love. But in part two, on the need to seek Christ and his love early, Donne abandoned abstract definitions and applied his text with some vigour to the wrongs of Roman Catholicism, a profession that discarded rather than sought Christ. He began by turning the Magdalene's cry at the tomb, 'They have taken away my Lord', into a cry against Catholics who 'have taken away Christ, by a dark and corrupt education, which was the state of our Fathers to the Roman captivity'. Immediately after this quibble over papist use and abuse of patristic authors Donne applied his text to the present, and in the presence of the queen Donne's words must have electrified the entire chapel: 'the *abjecerunt Dominum*, which is so often complained of by God in the Prophets, is pronounced against thee, when thou hast had Christ offered to thee, by the motions of his grace, and seal'd to thee by his Sacraments, and yet wilt cast him so far from thee, that thou knowest not where to find him'. The complaint of the 'Prophets' was the complaint 'pronounced against' the queen by Donne himself. Anne, Donne seems to suggest, had been sealed as Christ's own in the sacrament of baptism some forty-two years before, and although Christ had continued to be 'offered' to her in the Church of England's holy communion, she had spurned him by refusing to receive. But Donne went on to chastise Anne for things done as well as things left undone. The tears that should have been 'thy souls rebaptization for thy sins' had instead been poured out in 'prophane and counterfeit tears', and sighs of reconciliation with God were but 'corrupt and ill intended sighs', and 'execrable and blasphemous oathes'. So far had Christ been pushed aside that, Donne summarized, 'thou knowest not when thou didst lose him, no nor dost not remember that ever thou hadst him' (244–5).

Where had Anne 'lost' Christ? Just as Mary and Joseph had lost Christ 'in the holy City, at *Jerusalem*', Donne told the queen, 'we may lose him at *Jerusalem*, even in his own house', and more pointedly, 'even at this present, whilst we pretend to doe him service'. That last remark was a stock criticism of the conforming Catholic, who, in the eyes of faithful Protestants, of course offered no true worship or 'service' by sitting through the established church's liturgies and sermons for mere conformity's sake.[44] And, Donne continued, if Christ could be lost in the practice of a *faux* godliness within the 'Jerusalem' of the Church of England, how much more could he be lost 'if our dwelling be a *Rome* of Superstition and Idolatry'. Donne's subsequent advice on where to find Christ continued his criticism of popery, but palliated it with an indictment of the opposite extreme, Genevan Calvinism, and held up the Church of England as the

---

[44] Walsham, *Church Papists*, 104–6.

desired golden mean. First, against the necessity of saintly and priestly intercession to Christ he said, 'thou must not so think him in heaven, as that thou canst not have immediate accesse to him without intercession of others'. So, too, Christ was not 'so beyond Sea' as to be found only in 'a forrein Church, either where the Church is but an Antiquaries Cabinet, full of rags and fragments of antiquity . . . or where it is so new a built house with bare walls, that it is yet unfurnished of such Ceremonies as should make it comly and reverend'. Anne was to find Christ domestically, as it were, both in her own household and heart, and in her adopted land: 'Christ is at home with thee, he is at home within thee, and there is the neerest way to find him' (245–6). Since Christ 'may easily be found', Donne argued, the practice of his religion was by definition and necessity a public, proclaimed one, not a religion observed covertly or in hiding. Again, Donne glanced first at institutional Catholicism, saying that true religion, unlike that of Rome, 'is not confined to Cloysters and Monasteries, and speculative men only, but is also evidently and eminently to be found in the Courts of religious Princes'. He then proceeded to the case of crypto-Catholicism, the dissimulating practice of religion in 'private Conventicles and clandestine worshipping of God in a forbidden manner, in corners'. Perhaps Donne had heard the report retailed by the Spanish ambassador less than two months before this sermon was preached, that the queen maintained two Roman priests at Oatlands where mass was said secretly every day.[45] No amount of sermon-hearing could redeem such forbidden worship of God 'in corners'. True religion did not hide; it heard the voice of Christ, not the whispers of priests, and inspired the true worshipper to 'confidently doe whatsoever he commands thee, in the eye of all the world' (247).

'To make haste' to his conclusion, and thereby to the end of a sensitive, if not dangerous sermon, Donne recalled the queen again to her membership in Christ's church by virtue of having been sealed by 'his word and sacraments'. Anne, Donne reminded her, had not been born into false religion, but born and baptized into a resolutely Protestant family: God 'hath sought thee amongst the infinite numbers of false and fashionall Christians, that he might bring thee out from the hypocrite, to serve him in earnest, and in holyness, and in righteousness'. To revoke this heritage, to regress to Rome, was indeed to reject Christ, to reject a birthright that had been sealed in baptism. God had picked her out from 'the Herd of the nations and Gentiles, who had no Church' at all, from creatures without souls, indeed from primal nothing at the general Creation. 'Yea', the preacher concluded, 'millions of millions of generations before all this he

[45] Loomie, 'Catholic Consort', 312.

sought thee in his own eternal Decree . . . not only from the beginning of this world, but from the writing of that eternal Decree of thy Salvation' (249). Then Donne gathered up the themes of his sermon's two parts – affirmation of God's love and exhortation to turn from idolatry and seek that love – in a remarkable collect composed for the occasion. Opening with an Augustinian invocation, 'O glorious beauty, infinitely reverend, infinitely fresh and young', he held out the hope of receiving, in spite of past sins, God's regeneration: 'we come late to thy love, if we consider the past daies of our lives'. He alluded once more to the significance of the day as an anniversary of baptismal regeneration by asking God to 'reckon with us from this houre of the shining of thy grace upon us'. Then Donne modulated into an embellished version of the Collect for Grace, the third collect read daily at the close of Morning Prayer (250–1). This not only conflated the Biblical text's theme of seeking Christ 'early' with the actual time of day, but also inscribed upon the sermon – and its royal audience – a participation in the rites of the Church of England.[46]

Donne clearly hoped that his sermon would inspire Anne to move from outward conformity to full communion. As a convert from Roman Catholicism himself, he must have spoken with a special authority on the subject that made him, more than any other preacher, able to deal so frankly with the queen's covert Catholicism. The queen's Chaplains in Ordinary, and visiting preachers, such as Bishop John King, could, and no doubt did, serve up healthy doses of vitriol about the international threat of the papist conspiracy. But Donne approached the topic in a much more personal way, with Catholicism treated as a threat to a soul, not the state. In his sermon, the covert practice of Catholicism estranges a prince from the faith of her birth and baptism. Donne, of course, had travelled the opposite path, born into Catholicism but converted to the Church of England; indeed, there is a hint of knowing sympathy between Donne, the former Catholic, and the royal mistress he perceived as having slipped into the clutches of Rome. In addition to Christ being found 'in the Courts of religious Princes', Donne said he was to be found 'in the Courts of Justice (in the gates of the City)'. 'Both these kinds of Courts', he said, 'may have more diversions from him then other places; but yet in these places hee is also gloriously and conspicuously to be found' (247). So Donne, the Reader of Divinity at Lincoln's Inn, drew himself into society with the queen as both were members of reformed 'courts', and seemed to say, 'I have found and do preach Christ in an Inn of Court, you too can find him in your royal one'.

---

[46] *Book of Common Prayer*, ed. Booty, 60.

PRINCE HENRY AND THE 'COLLEGIATE SOCIETY' OF ST JAMES'S

Prince Henry Frederick governed the household established for him at St James's in 1610 with a strictness that was moral, religious and military. He was famous for the alms boxes in which swearers were required to make expiatory offerings, and for his household's regular attendance at prayers and sermons.[47] When Sir Roger Wilbraham made an obituary entry for the prince in his diary, he noted approvingly that Henry 'attended himself praiers & sermons att sett tymes, & tyed his servants therunto'.[48] But modern scholars, perhaps influenced by the hagiography that followed his sudden death in 1612, have been too inclined to believe that the prince sprung from his mother's womb a militant Protestant, a Jacobean Sir Philip Sidney, ready to counter the irenicism of his father and the high-church-manship of his younger brother. The origins of Henry's advanced Protestantism need to be reconsidered in the context of the clerics who were placed around the impressionable boy prince as his tutors and household chaplains. The best recent work on Henry's court circle has rightly stressed Robert Cecil's oversight in its formation, and his conscious efforts to integrate there the estranged Essex and Cecil factions.[49] But Prince Henry's churchmanship and the preachers planted at his court bear the mark not of Cecil's nascent ceremonialism and anti-Calvinism, but of the progressive and politicized Calvinism of the Leicester–Sidney–Essex tradition.[50] More specifically, many of Henry's chaplains were clerical clients of the families of Henry's two closest childhood companions, both of whom had strong alliances with the Sidney–Essex axis: Robert Devereux, third Earl of Essex, son of the rebel second Earl and Sir Philip Sidney's widow, Frances, *née* Walsingham; and a Sidney cousin, John Harington, younger brother of Lucy, Countess of Bedford, Queen Anne's favourite.[51]

Ministers under the patronage of the executed second Earl of Essex and his disgraced followers stood to gain much from James's restoration of

---

[47] Thomas Birch, *The Life of Henry Prince of Wales* (1760), 85–6.

[48] *The Journal of Sir Roger Wilbraham*, ed. Harold Spencer Scott, *Camden Miscellany*, vol. X (1902), 109.

[49] Timothy V. Wilks, 'The Court Culture of Prince Henry and his Circle, 1603–1613', (unpublished Oxford D.Phil thesis, 1987).

[50] For Cecil, see Pauline Croft, 'The Religion of Robert Cecil', *Historical Journal* 34 (1991), 773–96. One notable anti-Calvinist exception among Henry's early circle was Benjamin Carier, who sensationally converted to Rome in 1613. He styled himself 'one of the Prince his Chaplaines' in his *Sermon Preached before the Prince* (1606), sig. A2ʳ, and a manuscript tract by him for the prince survives (*DNB*, s.n. Carier). He was not among the chaplains appointed at the formal establishment of the prince's household in 1610.

[51] For the Essex circle see Wilks, 'Court Culture', 22–8, and Leeds Barroll, 'The Court of the First Stuart Queen', 201–6. Wilks considers the Haringtons in light of their Cecil connections, but not their quite different ties with the Montagues and Sidneys.

favour to the houses of Essex, Rutland, Southampton, and Bedford. But clerical patronage in the form of coveted royal chaplaincies would have been difficult to obtain, since James had inherited a full complement of chaplains – most of them clients of Whitgift, Cecil, and the Howards – from Queen Elizabeth. The obvious openings for the more progressive Protestants formerly under the patronage of Essex and his circle, but shut out from court influence by the consolidation of patronage under Cecil and Whitgift, would be in the yet-to-be-formed household of the future Prince of Wales; and likely candidates wasted no time presenting themselves to the eight-year-old prince.

One of the first to appear, probably as tutor to the prince's young retainer Rowland Cotton, was Hugh Broughton, a divine noted for his rabbinical learning and Puritanism. Broughton, patronized at Cambridge in the 1580s by the Earls of Essex and Huntington, earned the contempt of both Whitgift and Bancroft and spent the last decade of Elizabeth's reign in scholarly exile in Germany. But on 13 August, 1603, hardly one month after Henry had settled in England, Broughton reappeared and preached before the prince at Oatlands a sermon that, presumably in the hopes of protection by the new royal family, rehearsed all the controversial points for which the Whitgiftian establishment had censured him.[52] Another who turned his attentions to the new prince was Dr Lionel Sharpe, who had served Essex as chaplain both at Tilbury camp in 1588 and on the expeditions to Cádiz (1589) and Portugal (1596). Sharpe was listed among the court Lent preachers in 1595, 1597, and 1599 – precisely the years of Essex's greatest popularity and favour with the queen. But his name conspicuously disappeared in the first Lent after Essex's fall (1600), and after Essex's execution Sharpe was rusticated to his Devonshire benefices.[53] He was not, as his *DNB* biographer suggests, made an ordinary royal chaplain in the last years of Elizabeth's life, but had to wait for that dignity until the Jacobean resurrection of Essexian fortunes.[54] The discovery of the Gunpowder Plot in 1605 gave opportunity for a Latin letter from Sharpe to Prince Henry warning of the dangers of popery and the Jesuits, and shortly thereafter he was made one of the prince's chaplains.[55]

---

[52] Hugh Broughton, *An Exposition vpon The Lords Prayer . . . in a Sermon, at Oatelands: before . . . Henry Prince of Wales* (n.d., 1603?). Broughton also dedicated three printed works of divinity to the Prince (Birch, *Life of Henry*, 44–5). For Broughton and Cotton, see Wilks, 'Court Culture', 231–2.

[53] WAMB 15, fols. 24, 25, 27. In December 1599 Essex chose Sharpe to attend him while under house arrest (*HMC Salisbury*, vol. IX, 410).

[54] In February 1603 Sharpe's name appears as an extraordinary chaplain, and shortly after the accession as one of those suitable to preach *coram rege* but 'that are no Chapleins' (WAMB 15, fols. 2, 6).

[55] Birch, *Life of Henry*, 62–4, 414–16. Sharpe does not appear among the chaplains in the 1610 household establishment lists, having by this time transferred his service to King James.

Efforts by godly Essexians to gain a foothold in the new prince's household also came from within James's court. Patrick Collinson has shown that the operatives at court for the Puritan interest during the first two years of the reign were Lewis Pickering, a Northamptonshire gentleman, and James's Scottish preacher, Patrick Galloway.[56] But recent work adds to this picture of Puritan manouevring at court no less a personage than James's first Dean of the Chapel Royal, James Montagu.[57] Montagu, the first master of the Puritan seminary Sidney Sussex College in Cambridge, was, like Pickering, from godly Northamptonshire. Even more significantly, his maternal uncle was Lord John Harington of Exton, thereby making Montagu first cousin of Lucy, Countess of Bedford, and uncle to Prince Henry's companion, the young Sir John Harington. Both Lord Harington and his son were generous benefactors of Sidney Sussex, which had been founded by Montagu's great-aunt, Lady Frances Sidney, Countess of Suffolk and aunt of Sir Philip.

With these connections along the Sidney–Essex axis, Montagu, if somewhat timidly, used his great influence with the new king to advance the godly cause at court by placing reforming ministers in Prince Henry's household. Dr Bellany has charted how Montagu found himself between Scylla and Charibdys in 1605 when an anti-Puritan backlash came close to discrediting him at court and his subsequent distancing of himself from his Puritan contacts discredited him with the godly. Pickering, in prison for allegedly penning a libel against the deceased Archbishop Whitgift, accused Montagu to the Earl of Salisbury of sympathizing with the nonconformists who were now being deprived of their benefices, and he offered the names of four ministers who would swear to having heard the royal Dean say that they would be sinning if they conformed and that 'his Majesty did ill in urging them'.[58] One of the ministers Pickering claimed had heard such things 'from the Dean himself' was John Burgess, who, as we have seen, preached an infamous, and injudicious, critique of James's policy for ceremonial conformity in June 1604.[59]

There is little doubt that Burgess's primary mission that day at Greenwich was to petition the king on behalf of those Puritans whose early hopes for further reform under James were dispelled at the Hampton Court Conference. But Burgess's sermon was also an audition – a sermon arranged by Montagu with a view toward placing Burgess in Prince

[56] Patrick Collinson, *The Elizabethan Puritan Movement* (1967; Oxford, 1990), 450–1.
[57] Alastair Bellany, 'A Poem on the Archbishop's Hearse: Puritanism, Libel and Sedition after the Hampton Court Conference', *Journal of British Studies* 34 (April 1995), 160. I am very grateful to Dr Bellany for sharing his work with me before publication.
[58] Bellany, 'Archbishop's Hearse', 160–1; *HMC Salisbury* vol. XVII, 28–9, 288, 270.
[59] See above, 141–7.

Henry's household. The godly City lecturer Thomas Gataker, who was himself Montagu's associate as one of the first fellows of Sidney Sussex, wrote late in life that he had been canvassed as a potential chaplain to the prince by the young John Harington, who, with other members of Henry's court, frequented the sermons he preached at Lincoln's Inn. According to Gataker, Harington hoped to use 'the assistance of Bishop Montagu, then in favour with the king his father, to procure for me that place of constant attendance . . . that was sometime designed to Mr. John Burges, had not the design miscarried by a sermon, which he preached before the King, and cost him much trouble'.[60] Trouble indeed it cost Burgess – and no doubt Dean Montagu as well.

Corroboration of Gataker's recollection is found in a very reliable source – Burgess's own letter of supplication to the king. Writing from the Tower, he asserted that he preached the sermon 'without counsell or conference wth other person or persons', probably a disclaimer to shield Montagu. He further maintained that in defending the nonconformist position he did not 'prefer mine own possibilities of attaining the Princes service to this duty'.[61] This episode reveals the Essex group at work trying to mould the religious environment of the young heir apparent: Sir John Harington, confidant of the prince, enlisting not only a godly preacher, but a *bona fide* nonconformist for the prince's service *via* the court connection of his uncle, James Montagu, Dean of the king's Chapel Royal. Burgess's sermon backfired famously, of course, and was no doubt one reason why Montagu tried desperately to distance himself from the likes of Lewis Pickering in 1605. But, as Gataker's recruitment shows, Montagu could still be counted on by his nephew as a valuable agent at James's court for placing evangelical preachers around Prince Henry. In the end, the wider Essex circle did not forget Burgess. On his return from the Continent as an MD in 1612, one of the most fashionable ladies who frequented his fashionable Isleworth practice was Lucy, Countess of Bedford. Chamberlain thought that Burgess 'did her more good with his spirituall counsaile then with naturall phisicke', but John Donne was scandalized by his patroness's association with the Puritan doctor–preacher. Perhaps as a belated apology, it was Montagu, then Bishop of Winchester, acting in concert with the Countess, Francis Bacon, and the new favourite Sir George Villiers, who helped secure Burgess's conformity and restoration to a living in 1616.[62] Burgess's

---

[60] Thomas Gataker, *Discourse Apologetical* (1654), 36, quoted in Birch, *Life of Henry*, 390–1.

[61] John Burgess, *A Sermon Preached before the Late King James . . . with Two Letters in Way of Apology* (1642), 29.

[62] Chamberlain, *Letters*, vol. I, 470; Bald, *John Donne*, 275, 296–7; J. Spedding, ed., *The Letters and the Life of Francis Bacon*, 7 vols. (1862–74), vol. V, 372–3; Fincham, *Prelate as Pastor*, 230.

reinstatement might be seen in part as yet another ramification of the ascent of the Essex circle after the fall of Somerset and the Howards.

However, to emphasize the role of the 'Essex group' in the formation of Prince Henry's zealous Protestantism is not to suggest that the prince was a cipher who had no opinions of his own about his chaplains and preachers. As early as 1607, at the age of thirteen, Henry had been much impressed by Joseph Hall's *Meditations* (1606), and, after hearing a probationary sermon by him, swore him as his chaplain. But even in Hall's case, it was the young Earl of Essex's tutor, Mr Gurry, who made the initial overtures of patronage from the prince.[63] The very early positioning of this group and its clerical clients around the young Henry must certainly have confirmed him in a brand of English Protestantism that was doctrinally Calvinist, vehemently anti-Catholic, and sympathetic to military evangelism. And here we must suspect the helping hand of Henry's governor and Lord Chamberlain, Sir Thomas Chaloner, identified as 'the principal agent' in the formation of Henry's circle. Chaloner had not only served Leicester and Essex, but had himself been tutored by the staunch Calvinist Laurence Humphrey at Oxford.[64] Assuming that officers' duties were the same at the king's and the prince's courts, it would have been Chaloner's duty as Lord Chamberlain officially to admit chaplains to service in the prince's household. Finally, though, it seems impossible that the king himself did not influence the appointment of Henry's chaplaincy. In the same month that the prince's new household chaplains were sworn in, James chartered another society of divines as Provost and Fellows of the new Chelsea College. In Anthony Milton's estimate, Chelsea's *raison d'être* was 'the systematic production of anti-papal polemic'. Zeal for precisely the same mission was to distinguish the chaplaincy assembled at St James's until 1625. James's commitment to anti-Catholic controversy and his patronage of conformist Calvinist divines – both at their height in the years around 1610 – must have informed both royal foundations.[65] It is therefore no surprise that the twenty-four Chaplains in Ordinary appointed to wait on the prince 'by two and two every month' included some of the day's most noted Calvinists and future opponents of Arminianism and of peace with Spain.[66]

---

[63] Joseph Hall, *The Shaking of the Olive Tree* (1660), 23–5.

[64] Wilks, 'Court Culture', 4.

[65] Anthony Milton, *Catholic and Reformed: The Roman and Protestant Churches in English Protestant Thought, 1600–1640* (Cambridge, 1995), 32. For Chelsea College, see D. E. Kennedy, 'King James I's College of Controversial Divinity at Chelsea', in Kennedy, ed., *Grounds of Controversy: Three Studies in Late 16th and early 17th Century English Polemics* (Melbourne, 1989), 97–126.

[66] The 1610 list of Henry's chaplains is printed in Birch, *Life of Henry*, 454–5. This should be supplemented by the list of mourners at Henry's funeral (PRO LC 2/4/6, fol. 42ᵛ). Various

Five of these became bishops: Richard Milbourne, successively of St David's (1615) and Carlisle (1621), Robert Snowden of Carlisle (1616), Lewis Bayley of Bangor (1616), John Prideaux of Worcester (1641), and Joseph Hall, successively of Exeter (1627) and Norwich (1641). Although the first three were unremarkable as bishops, all conformed to the model of the anti-Catholic evangelical 'preaching pastor'.[67] Bayly, from the parish pulpit at St Martin's-in-the-Fields, used the occasion of his royal master's death to decry the foothold that popery had gained at Whitehall – a glance at the crypto-Catholic Northampton. On Sunday, 15 November, only nine days after the prince's death, he even alleged that the prince himself had lamented how 'religion lay a bleeding', and cited as proof that 'divers counsaillors heare masse in the morning, then go to a court sermon and so to the counsaile'.[68] Bayly considered Whitehall a seedbed of hypocritical religion – a place, presumably unlike the godly St James, where sermons were used as a cover for Catholicism rather than for the edification of true religion. John Prideaux (1578–1650), as Vice-Chancellor of Oxford, led the Jacobean offensive against Arminianism at that university, and, in 1624, joined forces with Joseph Hall to denounce in Parliament the Arminian writings of Richard Montagu. The fifth future bishop among Henry's chaplains, Joseph Hall, more notably combined Calvinist orthodoxy with Caroline conformity, but always laboured under Laud's distrust and surveillance.[69] Among the other custodians of religion in the prince's household, Henry Burton, Clerk of the Closet, maintained throughout his life that the Pope was the anti-Christ, and during the reign of Charles I became a vociferous opponent of episcopacy and suffered the pillory, the loss of his ears, and years of imprisonment. Less sensationally, Richard Fowns dedicated an 800-page anatomy of Romish abuses, his *Trisagion*, to Prince Charles in 1619. Several of Henry's original chaplains later spoke out against the Spanish Match and in favour of military intervention in the Palatinate: Andrew Willet was imprisoned in 1618 for anti-Spanish writings, and Christopher Swale, in a sermon preached before James in 1621, lamented that while the English sit 'vnder our owne Vines . . . in peace and rest', no one is '*sorrie for the affliction of* Ioseph, the extreame miseries of our Brethren in neighbour-Countries'.[70] Significantly, of the twenty-four

copies of these and other lists have caused confusion. See the lucid summary appendix in Wilks, 'Court Culture', 274–9.

[67] Fincham, *Prelate as Pastor,* 250–76.

[68] Chamberlain, *Letters,* vol. I, 392.

[69] Tyacke, *Anti-Calvinists,* 72–3, 148; Kenneth Fincham, 'Episcopal Government, 1603–1640', in Fincham, ed., *The Early Stuart Church, 1603–1642* (Basingstoke, 1993), 85.

[70] Christopher Swale, *Iacobs Vow. A Sermon Preached before his Maiestie* (1621), 12. The sermon was printed by the king's printer.

chaplains in the 1610 establishment list that can be identified, only Samuel Brooke later aligned himself with Laudianism.[71]

From this original establishment-list group (excluding Burton, whose responsibilities did not include preaching) only Hall published any of his sermons preached *coram principe*. But to Hall's sermons can be added a significant number preached to Henry's household by two others: Daniel Price, who in print styled himself Chaplain in Ordinary to Henry from 1608 but does not appear on the 1610 list, and Robert Wilkinson, a chaplain to James who was a favourite preacher of Henry's. Together these sermons demonstrate that the prince's chaplains and preachers, as well as the prince's own practice, nurtured a religious culture and a sermon style at St James's noticeably different from that found at Whitehall.[72] First, the prince's preachers spoke much more univocally. At James's court one could hear in the course of the same week the filigreed textual exegesis of Lancelot Andrewes and a doctrine-and-uses jeremiad by George Meriton; one could hear sermon-hearing satirized as the greatest abuse of the age, and then lauded as the only way to salvation. No such variations in churchmanship or sermon style exist in the surviving sermons preached at Henry's St James's.

Wilkinson, Hall, and Price all preached in the prophetic voice of Tudor reformers such as Latimer, Dering, and Sandys. Recent work on Joseph Hall points to his homiletic blend of classical satire and Old Testament prophecy.[73] But this pose struck so consistently by Hall and Henry's other preachers was not only a matter of style, but rather of historical tradition, namely, the brand of 'apocalyptic utterance' and 'prophetic discourse' that Patrick Collinson has pointed to as the ground-base of English national Protestantism.[74] In bold satiric digressions on such subjects as court vices and the natural depravity of man these preachers focused on individual morality and its consequences for the nation-state. Price blamed Henry's death, for example, on the lethal combination of the state's leniency to Catholics, the vanity of 'the quaint Crane-paced Courtiers of this time' and the sins of 'this *Citie* and *Court*' which included 'men like women, women like Diuels . . . cheating, whoring, drinking, swearing', and were 'as

[71] Tyacke, *Anti-Calvinists*, 40, 57.

[72] Daniel Price, *Prælium & Præmium* (Oxford, 1608), title page; in Henry's funeral lists two Prices appear (one as chaplain, another as almoner), presumably Daniel (1581–1631) and his brother Sampson (1585–1630). Robert Wilkinson (*ob.* 1618) was designated by Whitgift in 1603 as a bishop's chaplain 'fitt to preach' before the king (WAMB 15, fol. 6); Daniel Price identified him as the king's chaplain in 1612 in *Prince Henry His First Anniversary* (Oxford, 1613), 8.

[73] Richard A. McCabe, *Joseph Hall: a Study in Satire and Meditation* (Oxford, 1982), 32, 283–7.

[74] Patrick Collinson, *The Birthpangs of Protestant England* (New York, 1988), ch. 1 *passim*, but esp. 17–20.

common as breathing'. He went on to suggest that God had taken Henry in order to spare him from the judgmental fire that would soon rain down upon sinful England. And, in a move that not only linked Henry, but Price himself to the early Tudor reformation tradition, Price compared the present tragedy to that acted under Queen Mary when '*England* was persecuted and fiered, but blessed King *Edward* must first be receiued into *Abrahams* bosome'.[75] If Henry was another Edward, then Price as preacher to the prince assumed the mantle of a Latimer or Ridley. Like their Tudor predecessors, Henry's preachers considered it part of their duty to school princes and nobles, and in harsh terms. Price minced no words in his probationary sermon before Henry when he said that he delivered truth that 'would serue to let you blood in the swelling vaines of pride, to launce the impostumes of greedy desires, to purge your ambitious, malitious, voluptuous thoughts, to cure wantonnes, & to curbe the lest thought of wickednesse', and even threatened to 'exhort and by violence drawe some conuersion, or compunction, or deuotion from you'. In a similar vein, Robert Wilkinson, preaching only days before Henry fell into his fatal illness, told the prince that although when living he was known for 'your matchlesse wisedome, your incomporable valour, your equitie, piety, and Princely Maiestie', once dead 'euery Hare' would 'dare dance vpon his carkase, and dogs dare barke, and Poets then dare raile and rime with pen and tongue'.[76] Henry seems to have valued and rewarded such plain-dealing. Whether by training or temperament, Henry was an auditor from every godly preacher's dream, not only attending sermons regularly, but listening attentively and humbly. He once told his chaplain Richard Milbourne that he had the highest regard for those chaplains who challenged him from the pulpit with a demeanour that suggested, '"Sir, you must hear me diligently: You must have a care to observe what I say"'.[77] In the sermons themselves there is a candour with which Henry's preachers address him directly that is unlike both the elaborate pulpit compliments and the carefully veiled criticism offered to his father.

Indeed, one is consistently struck by evidence in the sermons of a unique intimacy that bound all members of Henry's household. More than euphemism was at play when Hall titled his last sermon to the household '*A Farewell Sermon, Preacht to the Familie of Prince* Henry', or when Daniel Price dedicated his first sermons after the prince's death to 'that

---

[75] Daniel Price, *Lamentations for the Death of the Late Illustrious Prince Henry* (1613), 19–20, 25 (*vere* 21).

[76] Daniel Price, *Recvsants Conversion: a Sermon . . . before the Prince* (Oxford, 1608), 15, 32; Robert Wilkinson, *A Paire of Sermons Svccessively Preached to a Paire of Peereles and Succeeding Princes* (1614), 21.

[77] Birch, *Life of Henry*, 377.

Princely familie'.[78] The intimacy of Henry's court fostered a society that was self-consciously fraternal, or more specifically, collegiate. The sermons for Henry's household provide further evidence of what Dr Wilks describes as an establishment 'pervaded by the fervour to provide collective courtly education' at a princely academy. Just as Sir Thomas Chaloner wrote in 1607 that 'his Highness's household ... was intended by the King for a *courtly college* or *collegiate court*', Price would lament the dissolution 'of this *Collegiate societie*'.[79] As we have already seen, a common churchmanship united the 'Reuerend *Brethren* the Chaplaines' and they spoke frequently of one another in their sermons – an expression of confraternity that is completely absent in the sermons preached by Elizabeth's or James's chaplains. Price, in his first printed dedicatory epistle to Prince Henry, alluded to the prince's chaplains in an explicit bid to join that select group. In fact, he spoke of them and their preaching styles individually, but in the veiled speech of Biblical personæ: '*Your highnesse hath already cunning Aholiab, and Bezaleel, sweet singing David, Parable speaking Ecclesiastes, Sinne smiting Micaiah, Ionas powerfull for Contrition, Peter potent for compunction, Barnabas singuler for Consolation.*' Not only does Price's allegorized list suggest the familiar reputations of Henry's prized preachers, but also marks a closed, if not an almost secret, society whose members had, in Price's own words, '*dedicated and consecrated their labours to the building of Gods temple*' in the prince.[80] The society was a fraternal one in the most literal sense; compared with James's court at Whitehall, Henry's was far less diverse in both age and sex.

The prince's court was '*the* Spring garden *of this land*', where a preacher could instruct the 'springes of Nobilitie' to 'remember now euen now in your tender yeares, to tender your selues to your God'.[81] Even more distinct from the paternal court, St James's had no female residents above stairs, and the auditory in the chapel there would have been predominantly male. Where James's orders for seating in the Whitehall chapel divided the stalls between the sexes, those for Henry's chapel assumed only male worshippers and divided the stalls by rank. The Yeomen of the Vestry were instructed to 'be carefull y^t upon dayes appointed for Sermons ye Chappell be decently ordered, reserving one syde thereof for his Highnes Officers'. Moreover, 'especiall regard' was to be taken 'y^t ye seates be not pestered & taken up by men of meane quality, but y^t there may be convenient roomes for his

[78] Joseph Hall, *The Works of Ioseph Hall* (1625), 459; Price, *Lamentations*, sig. A2^r.
[79] Wilks, 'Court Culture', 59; Birch, *Life of Henry*, 97; Daniel Price, *Teares Shed Over Abner*, part 4 of *Spiritvall Odours to the Memory of Prince Henry* (Oxford, 1613), part 4, 18.
[80] Daniel Price, *Recvsants Conversion*, sig. A2^r.
[81] Daniel Price, *The Spring. A Sermon Preached before the Prince* (1609), sig. A2^r; *Recvsants Conversion*, 35.

Highnes Servants'.[82] This social fact permeates the tone and even the subject matter of the sermons preached in Henry's chapel. Wilkinson, in his sermon for the marriage of James's favourite Lord James Hay to Honora Denny at Whitehall in 1607, satirized female vanities and was judged '*too bitter*' because of it. But his criticisms were conventional – against excess in dress, dominance over the husband – and he ended his sermon with a disclaimer that he preached 'nothing against the sex, but all against the sinnes of women', a caution to the husband to temper authority 'with equalitie', and finally a gracious series of compliments to the bride and her family.[83] But preaching at Henry's exclusively masculine household in 1612 on the text '*Man that is borne of a Woman, Short in continuance, And full of trouble*' (Job 14:1), Wilkinson hardly tempered his anti-feminism. Instead he pursued it with a humour fashioned specifically for men, as in his differentiation between the sorrows felt by men and women in marriage: 'shee to sorrow in her subiection to him, and hee to sorrow, yea a great deale of sorrow, in passing his time with her'.[84]

However, the differences between the churchmanships preached and the courtly lifestyles practised at Whitehall and St James's were no laughing matter, and in fact occasioned pulpit evidence of the oppositional tensions that grew up between James and his heir-apparent. When compared with the balancing act of opposed political and ecclesiological interests at James's court, Henry's offered an unambiguous agenda of anti-Catholic militant Protestantism. As patron of such, Henry, unlike his father, could become the charismatic focal point of hopes for a well-defined vision of the Church of England as well as of pan-European Protestantism. The sincerity of Price's almost histrionic eulogies for the deceased Henry might be suspected of self-interest and the emotionalism of bereavement. But years before his death, Henry had attracted the ideological devotion of Price and others. Upon completing a refutation of an English convert to Rome in 1610, Price asked, 'To whom shoulde I dedicate it? But to your Princelie goodnes, to whose service I haue consecrated my tongue, and pen, and heart, and all the offices of my life.' According to Price, 'the eies, and harts, and hopes of all the Protestant world, be fixed vpon your *Highnesse*, all expecting your *Gracious* faithfulnes, & readines in the extirpation' not just of popery, but the Pope himself, 'that man of sinne'.[85] Henry's example permeated the whole of St James's. To Price in his first sermon before him

---

[82] BL MS Add 39853, fol. 16ʳ.

[83] Robert Wilkinson, *The Merchant Royall. A Sermon Preached at White-Hall . . . at the Nuptials of . . . Lord Hay* (1607), sig. A3ᵛ, 35, 37–8.

[84] Wilkinson, *Paire of Sermons*, 1, 31.

[85] Daniel Price, *The Defence of Trvth* (Oxford, 1610), sig. 2ʳ⁻ᵛ. Price was not without other powerful patrons as likely dedicatees, including Archbishop Abbot who had encouraged him in the enterprise.

he was the *'young Cedar'* that drew 'all that make their nest vnder the shade of his Greatnesse' to it. Although proverbial wisdom held that 'Godlinesse is no good Courtier', Price confidently prayed 'that that position neuer take place here, but that holinesse may Crown this house for euer' not only in the chapel but even in 'the inmost Priuy Chambers . . . that so this Court *may bring forth encrease'*.[86] James could be lauded from his pulpits in benign general terms as a Solomonic prince of peace or patron of learning, but his own political style of compromise and the religious and political heterogeneity of his court and chaplaincy prevented praise – and commitment – like Price's ever being heard in Whitehall.

There were pointed attempts, though, by the collegians from St James's to export this ethos to Whitehall. As we shall see, military evangelism would become a keynote of Henry's and Charles's chaplains preaching at court and City during the mounting crisis in Germany after 1618. However, Price, for one, carried to Whitehall as early as 1608 the banner of revived Protestant chivalry for which Henry's court was famous. Preaching on Revelation 2:26, *'He that overcommeth, & keepeth my works to the ende, to him will I giue power over nations'*, Price's application of his text to his auditory – 'what subiect more fit for Heroicall spirits then an encitement to chiualtrie' – sounds out of place in a Jacobean Whitehall sermon. But Price pressed on. Though the preacher commended a sub-limated spiritual warfare ('The vse of the doctrine is to encite al the serua[n]ts of the Lord to be Martialists to be souldiers in this wicked world'), the vocabulary was painfully inappropriate for the chapel of the self-proclaimed *Rex Pacificus*. Price even acknowledged as much when he begged the king's pardon 'that I haue beeene [*sic*] so bould in a time of such gratious and glorious *peace* to moue this assembly to fight especially, seeing the Gospel, *is a Gospel of peace'*.[87] That such gestures were more than simply miscalculating one's audience, and were actually rather pointed comparisons that obliquely criticized the paternal court became much clearer in the sermons Price preached at St James's between Henry's death and funeral. In one the prince was cast as King David's military ally Abner, 'the *grace* of the *Court*, & the *hope* of the *Campe* . . . the *bearer* of the *sword*, and the *ioy* of the *souldiers'*. Henry *cum* Abner was of course the '*glory* of the king, & the *supporter* of the *kingdome'* – but Price's praise of his late master's military prowess implicitly lamented the absence of the same virtues in the king.

Inverting James's own professed priorities for kingly government, Price asserted in conclusion that 'certainly the *souldier* how ever he paceth, the same *measure* of *miserie* with the *scholar*, yet in all *ages* hath beene euer in

---

[86] Price, *The Spring*, sig. E2ʳ.   [87] Price, *Prælium & Præmium*, 3, 11, 30.

high *esteme*, til these daies'. Without a martial prince the country was vulnerable, for 'the *souldiour* is the *hart*, and *arme* of the *state* . . . and the most laudable *improver* of his Cou[n]try. For *alwaies* the *oliue* garlands of P*eace* bee not so *glorious* as the *Laurell wreathes* of *victory*, seeing P*eace* only *keepeth* and often *rusteth* good spirits'.[88] In another sermon, preached only the week before, Price had described the kind of moral 'rust' he saw spreading under James's irenic rule. To do so, he turned to Ezekiel's catalogue of abominations committed in Israel (Ezekiel 8) – precisely the exemplum appropriated by Edward Dering for his famous schooling of Queen Elizabeth in 1569. Ezekiel's prophecies revealed idolatry by noblemen '*priuatly in their chambers*', by noblewomen openly 'at the *doore* of the *Lords house*', and by priests 'betweene the *porch* & the *altar*', prophecies that implicated '*people*, and *Prince, women, Priests*, all are found *faulty*, all are *abominable*'. Moreover, Price continued, 'in this *dysastrous* time of my distracted *meditations* I haue beene at *a maze* to co[n]sider whether these *prophecies* . . . be *Oracles* for Ierusale[m] only, or the *Chronicles* of our owne *lands*'. For popery was practised by the great, 'we haue some *Idolatrous* Ancients, noble *Idolaters*, Idolatrously *luxurious women*', and the Church of England was infected by 'Priests . . . of our owne *Temple*, who wish more *Rome* in the *Land*, who often offer strange *fire* vpon the altar even in *Bethel*'. Not far from the minds of anyone listening could have been prominent court Catholics such as Northampton and the court presence of ceremonialist bishops and chaplains such as Andrewes or Roman sympathizers such as Benjamin Carier, the former royal chaplain who converted only months before Henry's death. The likes of these were '*spurious, Heterogeneous* monsters', who, indulged by a moral as well as a political pacifism, bred a heterogeneous religion, for which England was now being punished by the death of her prince. To Price's ears, Jeremiah 'as if hee cried to the *English Court*, vseth these words, *Say vnto the King & Queene, humble your selues for your Principality is come down, even to the Crown of your heads*'.[89]

EPILOGUE: 'OUR SUCCEEDING *CHARLEMAINE*'

We know precious little about the future King Charles as Prince of Wales before his infamous voyage to Spain in 1623. Particularly obscure are the early religious convictions of the man who would preside over the Laudian revolution and disintegration of the Church of England. In connection with discussion of Tobias Matthew's churchmanship – 'his

[88] Price, 'Teares Shed Ouer Abner', part 4 of *Spirituall Odours*, 3, 24–5.
[89] Daniel Price, 'Sorrow for the Sinnes of the Time', part 3 of *Spirituall Odours*, 19–20, 22, 24–5.

evangelical leanings, connivance at nonconformity, staunch anti-Popery and courtesy towards lay society' – and mention of a 1606 suggestion that Matthew be appointed tutor to Prince Charles, a recent historian muses, 'if this had happened, would English history have been rather different?'[90] I would suggest not; for the chaplains and tutors appointed to attend Charles in his youth were just as godly as Matthew, if not more so. More to the point, they mark not a break but a continuity with the progressive Protestant character of Prince Henry's chaplaincy. Upon coming to England in 1604, Charles was entrusted to the guardianship of Sir Robert Carey, whose wife, Lady Elizabeth, took primary responsibility for rearing the prince.[91] Prince Henry's chaplain, Daniel Price, lauded Lady Carey as a 'holy *example*' of the godly woman who would rise to glory while 'Painted *sepulchers* shall rot, and Popish *Hypocrites* shall rise to sorrow.'[92] The Careys' entrusted their own sons' education to the Puritan Henry Burton, who, as we shall see, owed his service to both Jacobean Princes of Wales to the Carey's patronage. In 1611, the Duke of York's household was enlarged, with Carey at its head as Chief Gentleman of the Bed-Chamber. No ordinary chaplains seem to have been appointed to attend the young duke in this minimal establishment. His religious instruction was presumably entrusted to members of the Careys' household, a model of provision that can be documented for his sister, Princess Elizabeth, who had for her chaplain Daniel Dyke, chaplain to her guardians, Lord and Lady Harington.[93] Charles did, however, frequent Henry's court, and we know that he accompanied his brother to sermons there.[94] Most significantly, when Charles succeeded Henry as the apparent Prince of Wales (he was not so created until November 1616), he, as James did at his succession, seems to have inherited some of his predecessor's chaplains. The reforming vigour of Henry's household lived on at St James's under Charles – so robustly that it haunted King James when the furore over the Spanish Match polarized England and played havoc with the king's broad-based ecclesiastical polity.

In the months immediately following Henry's death in November 1612, grief mixed with fear and anxiety as the prince's household servants faced promises from Whitehall that Charles would not have a full-scale household for at least three years. As Dr Wilks has shown, many turned their

[90] Fincham, *Prelate as Pastor*, 299 *n*.12.
[91] Peter Heylyn, *A Short View of the Life and Reign of King Charles* (1658), 4.
[92] Price, *Spiritvall Odovrs*, sig. G4^{r-v}.
[93] See Daniel Dyke, *Certaine Comfortable Sermons . . . Preached before the Lady Elizabeth her Grace* (1616); Prince Henry's funeral list includes 'Mr Daniell Dike Chaplaine to the Ladie Eliz:' (PRO LC/2/4/6, fol. 42^v); see Thomas Fuller, *History of the Worthies of England*, 3 vols., ed. P. Austin Nuttal (1840), vol. II, 54–5.
[94] Wilkinson, *Paire of Sermons*, sigs. A1^r, A2^r.

eyes to the alternative patronage of the Palatine court after the Princess
Elizabeth's 1613 marriage. Among them, one of Henry's former chaplains,
Alexander Chapman, travelled to Germany as chaplain and almoner to the
princess. But for most, all hopes were pinned on Charles, the twelve-year-
old boy who Daniel Price styled 'THE IOY OF OVR SORROW AND THE HOPE
OF SVCCESSION, ENGLANDS *CHARLEMAINE*'.[95] Price's 'hope of succession'
was not only for the regal succession, but successive employment in the
new prince's household. In his sermons to the household post-mortem,
Price tried to temper worldly anxieties over court employment with some
practical comforts, such as, 'to *you this* is a *dissolution*, not a *dispersion*
. . . *you* onely returne to your owne *Families*', or by decrying court
preferment as 'but *splendida miseria*', and warning against putting trust in
earthly princes.[96] But these moralisms ring rather hollow, for clearly Price
was just as desperate as his fellows to reassemble Henry's circle around his
younger brother. Certainly one of the most disingenuous utterances from a
court pulpit has to have been Price's teasing exhortation to the household,
'You are all of *you*, I *hope* to serue another *Prince*, I doubt not but you are
in *Check-roll* already: *mistake* mee not, I meane no other *Prince* then the
Prince of Peace'. Few in Price's auditory would have disagreed that
ultimately they were Christ's servants, but most were at the moment
interested in being Charles's. As Price himself put it only a few days later,
'Wee haue yet the *sunne* and *moone*, and *starres* of a *Royal* firmament; and
though we haue lost the *morning* starre, yet we haue *Charls-waine* in our
Horizon'.[97] Most secular servants of the former household were cruelly
disappointed in their hopes. Only half of the small household created for
Charles in 1613 were formerly servants to Henry, and among those missing
or demoted were some senior office-holders. Significantly, in the case of Sir
David Murray, Henry's Groom of the Stool and Keeper of the Privy Purse,
charges of Puritanism by king and Council were vaunted as reasons for his
exclusion from the new prince's household. But if, as Dr Wilks sees the
case, James's fears of a progressive, militant Protestantism and its implications for his foreign policy lay behind the exclusion of so many of Henry's
servants, it is certainly ironic that, unlike the secular servants, the chaplains
of the former household continued to receive court appointments.[98] Several

[95] Price, *Lamentations*, sig. A1ʳ. The best account of the circle's demise is Wilks, 'Court
     Culture', chs. 9 and 10, esp. 218–20. For Chapman see 'An Account of . . . the Expenses of
     Lady Elizabeth', *Archaeologia* 35 (1853), 9, 12 (cited in Wilks); Alexander Chapman,
     Jesvitisme Described (1610), sig. A3ʳ–4ᵛ.
[96] Price, *Lamentations*, 37 (*vere* 39); 'Sorrow for the Sinnes of the Time', part 3 of *Spiritvall
     Odovrs*, 14.
[97] Price, *Lamentations*, 40; *Spiritvall Odovrs*, part 1, 25.
[98] Wilks, 'Court Circle', 218, 221.

became the king's own Ordinary Chaplains: Joseph Hall, Lewis Bayly, Samuel Brooke, John Prideaux, and Christopher Sutton.[99]

There were distinct continuities between Henry's and Charles's religious establishments. Within one month of Henry's death, news circulated that, in order to protect the prince-apparent from the wiles of popery, 'two sober divines, Dr Hackwell and another, are placed with him, and ordered never to leave him'. The earliest establishment list for Charles, from the spring of 1613, shows two chaplains, Dr George Hakewill and Richard Milbourne, Dean of Rochester, as well as Henry Burton as Clerk of the Closet. Milbourne and Burton were old members of Henry's 'collegiate society'. Burton probably owed the reversion of his post to his patron Sir Robert Carey, and Milbourne, who had headed the 1610 list of Henry's chaplains, might have had his by seniority.[100] Hakewill, the new member of the '*first-sworne*' chaplains, was a logical addition to the group. Like Henry's chaplains Daniel and Sampson Price, John Prideaux and Lewis Bayly, Hakewill hailed from the stoutly Calvinist Exeter College, Oxford, and had augmented his reformed credentials with study in Heidelberg.

With this training and his fame as an orator and a preacher, Hakewill was a likely candidate not only to ward off popery, but to continue the tradition of evangelical Protestantism associated with the household of the Prince of Wales. He discharged his duties with zeal. Perhaps his first responsibility was to tutor Charles for his confirmation in the chapel royal at Whitehall on Easter Monday 1613. There, Hakewill watched with pride as his young charge, '*vpon strict and long Examination*' by Bishop Montagu and Archbishop Abbot, proved his knowledge of '*the Grounds and Principles of Christian Religion*'. According to Hakewill, the prince's exemplary responses inspired him to write a tract on the validity of episcopal confirmation, a prototypical conformist Calvinist treatise defending the English rite out of primitive and Reformation sources.[101] Appropriately, it was also Hakewill who published with royal approbation a refutation of Henry's and James's former chaplain turned Roman Catholic, Benjamin Carier. Hakewill produced a 300-page response to Carier's short, printed epistle that had explained his conversion and called for James to reject the Calvinism that hindered the Church of England's communion with Rome. Although Hakewill wrote in large part to vindicate the king against a religious traitor, his duties to the prince in the under-

---

[99] Corpus Christi College Oxford, MS E 297 fol. 188, transcribed in Nicholas Cranfield, 'Early Seventeenth Century Developments and Change in the Doctrine of [Episcopacy] and Understanding of the Office of [Bishop] in the Church of England, 1603–1645' (unpublished Oxford DPhil 1988), 232–3.

[100] *CSPD 1611–1618*, 160; PRO SP 14/72/111.

[101] George Hakewill, *The Avncient Ecclesiasticall Practise of Confirmation* (1613), sig. A2ʳ.

taking were clear from the very title page, which carried the epigram, 'Giue thy iudgements to the King (O God,) and thy righteousnesse to the Kings sonne'. In the dedication, he went on to claim that the *Response* was to be a reference manual for the prince in questions of controversy with papists that was based on the king's own disputative works. '*My selfe sworne to your* Maiestie, *for the seruice of your most Noble Sonne the Prince, my most sweete and gracious Master*', Hakewill explained, '*I thought I might herein doe him some seruice for his better information, to marke out vnto him such passages in your* Maiesties *writings, as serue for a satisfaction to such passages of the letter as may concerne him*'.[102]

Hakewill's writings also contain evidence that the fraternal ethos of Henry's St James's was kept alive under Charles. He dedicated a 1621 collection of St James's sermons not only to 'my Gra*cious Lord and Master*', but also to 'the PRINCE his Family'. This double dedication not only recalls Daniel Price's similar dedication of *Lamentations for the Death of the Late Illustrious Prince Henry* (1613) to both the young Charles and the members of his brother's former household, but captures again the strong sense of group identity fostered at St James's. Price had looked upon Henry's chaplaincy as a select fraternal order, set apart from the world by its dedication to the prince and to shared ideals of reforming godliness. Similarly, Hakewill addressed his fellows as the most '*sufficient Masterworkmen in their kindes as the Land affords*'. They were not courtly sycophants '*thrusting themselves into the Place, but all of them culled out and called thither*', and rewarded by their prince not for vain flattery but for lighting his way with truth. Allegiance to this élite order was fierce, and identification with it all-consuming. Even allowing for the warmer rhetoric of a dedicatory epistle, Hakewill describes membership in a remarkably self-consciously defined fellowship: '*whatsoever I am, I am for your service*', he told the other members of the household, '*ready to bee imployed by the meanest of that Family, for which I daily pray as for myself*'. Finally, Hakewill seems to have himself appealed consciously to Prince Henry's legacy at St James's. If Charles heeded his preachers' lessons, he said, 'we may by Gods helpe one day promise to our selves another *Charlemaine*, or rather the perfections of all the *Edwards & Henries, & Iameses* your renowned progenitors united in one *Charles*'. There can be little doubt that the '*Edwards & Henries*' were the reforming princes Edward Tudor and Henry Stuart. The '*Iameses*' were a necessary compliment to the royal father who in Hakewill's view, as we shall see, threatened the ideals of those Edwards and Henrys.[103]

---

[102] George Hakewill, *An Answere to a Treatise Written by Dr Carier* (1616), sig. A1ʳ, 7.

[103] George Hakewill, *King Davids Vow for Reformation . . . Delivered in Twelue Sermons before the Prince* (1621), sig. A2ʳ–A6ᵛ.

Charles's princely household also resembled his late brother's in the strong presence there of Scotsmen. James had entrusted Henry's education in both Scotland and England to the Scottish tutor Adam Newton, and the domestic posts closest to the prince were held by the Scot Sir David Murray.[104] Perhaps not surprisingly, then, of the chaplains who attended James to Scotland in 1617, the one who found 'great love, and respect . . . both from the Ministers, and People' in the northern kingdom was Henry's former chaplain, Joseph Hall.[105] Although Sir Robert Carey, later Lord Carey, always maintained a dominating presence in Charles's establishment, as the young Duke of York attained a more independent household Scots manoeuvred for influential positions about him. When, at the age of six, Charles was 'taken from the charge of his Women (though not from the Motherly super-inspection of the Lady *Cary*)', he was given to the tutelage of Sir Thomas Murray. According to Heylyn, Murray was 'sufficiently qualified for that service, but otherwise ill Principled in the Rites and Ceremonies of the *Church* of England'.[106] Indeed, Murray was known as the special friend and advocate of King James's Presbyterian nemesis, Andrew Melville, and in 1615 the Archbishop of St Andrews recommended that he be removed from Charles's household; when Murray missed the Provostship of Eton in 1617, owing to fears of his Puritanism, he was instead made Secretary to the prince. In 1611, a scheme was set afoot to supplant Carey in his chief household offices with another Scot, Sir James Fullerton. In council, the king's own Lord Chamberlain, the Earl of Suffolk, successfully argued for the retention of Carey. But then Prince Henry intervened in favour of placing his brother in Fullerton's charge, telling Suffolk that he would see if he could '"get Sir Robert Carey himself to accept of the second place."' After an interview with Henry, a compromise was struck in which Carey and Fullerton divided the spoils of the principal offices.[107] Although it was Prince Henry who was the subject of the proverb, '*Henry the 8.* pulld down Abbeys and Cells / But *Henry the 9.* shall pull down Bishops and bells', Charles presided over household establishments with similar sympathies.[108] By the time of his creation as Prince of Wales in 1616, his St James's combined a potent mix of evangelical English Calvinism in chaplains such as George Hakewill and Scots Presbyterianism in tutors such as Murray, laced with more radical Puritanism (at least *in potentio*) in Clerk of the Closet Henry Burton.

In both churchmanship and theology the sermons preached before

104 Birch, *Life of Henry*, 13–14, 372–5 (for Newton); 16, 218 (for Murray).
105 Hall, *Shaking of the Olive Tree*, 33.   106 Heylyn, *A Short View*, 6.
107 Birch, *Life of Henry*, 231–5.
108 Sir John Harington, *A Supplie or Addicion to the Catalogue of Bishops to the Yeare 1608*, ed. R. H. Miller (Potomac, Md., 1979), 5.

Charles echoed those preached before Henry. In 1614, George Meriton, Dean of Peterborough, printed a sermon preached before Charles and so well liked by him that the young prince commanded a copy and inspired the wonder that *'your Grace at these yeares is so religiously disposed'*. If *'religiously disposed'* meant Charles's endorsement of the sermon's contents, then he endorsed first of all a sermon-centred piety. According to Meriton, of the three focal points in churches – 'The *Fonte* for dipping or baptizing; the *Altar* for offering: the *Pulpit* for teaching' – the pulpit had 'the first place'. Salvation was only to be secured 'by application of the promise of the Gospell . . . by the Ministers of the Gospell, set apart for that purpose', not with 'a mumbling ouer of mattins for fashions sake'.[109] The theology of grace Charles seems to have endorsed in this sermon was a strictly Calvinist one. Meriton had told Charles and his household that 'some are actually saued, others reiected . . . because God before all worlds did purpose and ordaine the same', and that God did not determine election by 'foresight of faith and good works' but on His will alone. The assurance of salvation, he maintained, was 'no vniuersall respect, vnlesse we make the streame more large than the fountaine'.[110] Although we might be cautious about holding a boy of fourteen to the theological fine points of predestination, Meriton's views were certainly those of the prince's principal chaplains, Milbourne and Hakewill, and their young prince in the 1610s could hardly have been farther from Laud's king in the 1630s.

New chaplains appointed to serve the prince were logical additions to the late Prince Henry's 'collegiate society of St James's'. Robert Wilkinson, one of Henry's favourite preachers, was officially the king's chaplain, but continued his favoured status under Charles.[111] Thomas Winniffe (1576–1654) became chaplain at an uncertain date and further cemented the Exeter College, Oxford, connection with St James's.[112] Richard Senhouse hailed from godly St John's College, Cambridge and, as a client of the Earl of Bedford, kept up the long-standing Essexian connection with the Prince of Wales's household. Well into the 1620s the Scots about the prince kept alive at St James's the Kirk – Puritan axis that had been effectively dispersed at James's court by 1607. George Carleton, who would maintain the tenets of classical English Calvinism as a delegate to the Synod of Dort in 1619, entered Prince Charles's service in 1615 through the motions of Sir James Fullerton, who had secretly vetted his nomination

---

109 George Meriton, *The Christian Mans Assvring House. And a Sinners Conuersion. Two Sermons* (1614), A2^{r-v}, 1, 17, 18.
110 Meriton, *Christian Mans Assvring House*, 1, 10–11.
111 Wilkinson, *Paire of Sermons*, sig. A3^v.
112 Anthony Wood claimed that Winniffe was also chaplain to Prince Henry, although he does not appear on the establishment list: *Athenæ Oxoniensis*, ed. James Bliss, 4 vols. (1820), vol. IV, 813.

with Archbishop Abbot and the king.[113] John Hacket, though not above some partisan resentment, probably recorded truth when he wrote that the Cambridge Puritan John Preston 'preferr'd himself to be Chaplain to the Prince . . . through the Scotch' in Charles's bedchamber who favoured him because 'he prosecuted the Endeavours of their countryman Knox'. With men such as Henry Burton and the chaplains already established at St James's, Preston, appointed in 1621, was not an anomaly at Charles's court and not the first to merit the sobriquet, 'Prince Charles's Puritan chaplain'.[114]

However, with the crisis of the early 1620s over the Spanish Match and Habsburg aggression on the Continent, the progressive Protestant chaplains from the 'collegiate society' of St James's found themselves at odds with King James's foreign policy. The Prince of Wales's chaplains were part of the zealous anti-Catholic cornerstone of James's broad-based ecclesiastical polity, which was now forced into open opposition by the king's leniency to Spain and Roman Catholics. Was Charles willing himself to marry a Catholic princess in the early 1620s? Recent work suggests that his disposition to his father's wider foreign policy was closer to that of his godly chaplains and preachers than we have come to expect. Thomas Cogswell has reminded us that the Prince Charles of the 1610s and early 1620s was not the king Charles of the 1930s. Most important for our purposes here is his recovery of Charles's and Buckingham's impatience – long before their trip to Madrid – with James's protracted peace negotiations and their eagerness for English military action on behalf of the prince's sister, Elizabeth of Palatine.[115] At his court, Charles had a chaplaincy created in the image of his late brother's that was ready and willing to trumpet precisely such a cause, for hand in hand with their evangelical Calvinism went a dedication to stopping the advance of Catholic, which was to say Spanish, expansionism in Europe. And trumpet they did. As Cogswell has noted, clerical opposition to the Spanish Match came 'from preachers at Court who had powerful patrons to save them from serious harm when they stepped into the arcana imperii'.

To take this point a step further, clerical opposition to the Spanish Match came from court preachers who were alumni of Prince Henry's chaplaincy, whose 'powerful patron' was Henry's successor, Prince Charles. The two celebrated cases cited by Cogswell, the autumn 1623 sermons by Joseph

[113] PRO SP14/80/27. Carleton was successively Bishop of Llandaff (1618) and Chichester (1619); see Fincham, *Prelate as Pastor*, 289–91; and Tyacke, *Anti-Calvinists*, 91–2, 75–6.
[114] John Hacket, *Scrinia Reserata* (1693), 204, quoted in Irvonwy Morgan, *Prince Charles's Puritan Chaplain* (1957), 74.
[115] Thomas Cogswell, *The Blessed Revolution: English Politics and the Coming of War, 1621–1624* (Cambridge, 1989), 58–69.

Hall and Dr Whiting, were performances by two of Prince Henry's original chaplains.[116] One must wonder if these two preachers would have suffered the royal opprobrium they did for their anti-Catholic sermons had Prince Charles not been abroad at the time. For it was the prince himself who had shielded several anti-Spanish court preachers from his father's wrath in the preceding years. King James fumed that he would 'hang' Sampson Price for being 'too busy with Rochelle, the Palatinate, and the Spaniard' in a sermon before him in July 1621. But when Joseph Mead reported the end to Price's very brief arrest, he said knowingly, 'He is the prince's chaplain'.[117] And at court on Passion Sunday (7 April) 1622, Charles's chaplain Thomas Winniffe likened the Palatinate to an innocent sheep savaged by a Spanish wolf. He was promptly whisked from the pulpit to the Tower, but, through Charles's supplications to the Spanish ambassador, was released the next day.[118] Similarly, Charles summarily dismissed two of his own chapel musicians when he learned that they had sung mass in Gondomar's embassy chapel at Christmas 1622, and he was 'exasperated' by his father's reinstatement of them over his own wishes.[119] Charles did not wait for his disgruntled return from Spain to turn a cold shoulder to Spanish Catholicism.

Perhaps the most sustained attack on Whitehall policy from the chapel in St James's came from George Hakewill, no doubt doing his job, he thought, as Charles's anti-Catholic bodyguard. Early in August, Hakewill presented to the prince a treatise against the Spanish Match, 'whereat the King being offended, sent . . . all those who were privy to the Business, to Prison', among them Hakewill and the prince's secretary, Sir Thomas Murray.[120] At precisely the same time, or perhaps shortly before, there appeared Hakewill's collection of twelve sermons preached before Prince Charles and dedicated to him and his household. All twelve sermons were preached on Psalm 101, which Hakewill described as King David's charter 'for the reformation and government of himselfe, his housholde and State'.[121] Hakewill's explication of the Psalm text followed the polemical agenda of his own treatise against the Spanish Match, and left little doubt that the household and state he thought in need of reformation were James's. First,

---

[116] Cogswell, *Blessed Revolution*, 44–5; Joseph Hall, *A Sermon Preached to the Court at Theobalds* (1623); *CSPV 1623–25*, 131; Chamberlain, *Letters*, vol. II, 517.

[117] Thomas Birch, *The Court and Times of James the First*, 2 vols. (1848), vol. II, 265–7.

[118] Chamberlain, *Letters*, vol. II, 432; Birch, *Court and Times*, vol. II, 304.

[119] *CSPV 1621–23*, 555, 558. John Chamberlain thought that by his action Charles 'gave good testimonie' for the true religion (*Letters*, vol. II, 473).

[120] William Camden, *Annals of . . . the Reign of King James I*, in *A Complete History of England*, 3 vols. (1706), vol. II, 658; *CSPD 1619–23*, 284.

[121] Hakewill, *King Davids Vow*, sig. A2ᵛ. Hakewill's sermons were entered in the Stationers' Register on 1 June (*STC* 12616).

the king's Solomonic pacifism came under attack as Hakewill expounded the Psalm's second verse, '*I will behave my self wisely in a perfect way*'. Turning the well-known theatrical metaphor for kingship that James had employed in *Basilikon Doron* back on its royal author, Hakewill reminded the court that 'Princes as they act their parts upon an high stage, so is the least errour in their action presently discerned'.[122] Since the 'vulgar' were better led 'by example then by reason', he explained, wisdom had to be set forth in actions, not merely projected as a royal image or title: 'It is not wise thought, or wise speaking, or wise writing, or wise gesture & countenance, will serve the turn; but wise behaviour.' James had to give substance through action to his image as Britain's Solomon, and for Hakewill the most tangible evidence of a king's wisdom was edification of true religion. As we have seen, 1621 saw the complete redecoration of the Whitehall chapel royal along vividly Catholic lines, including images and a silver crucifix, all in preparation for the hoped-for signing of a Spanish marriage treaty and 'the spannish Ladys coming'.[123] This was not the kind of edification Hakewill had in mind, however, and he said so in explicit terms in the sermon that treated the Psalm's third verse, '*I will set no wicked thing before mine eyes*'. Nothing, he insisted, 'be it never so curiously wrought, never so artificially graven or carved, never so lively coloured, or richly attired: nay, be it of massie silver & gold, garnished with jewels and precious stones; yet beeing put to religious use, it is still a thing of Belial'. More to the point, 'The Ark and Dagon will not stand together: neither can a Crucifix, ordained to such an use, and Christ himselfe well dwell together under the same roof'.[124] Concessions to Catholics had now compromised the very integrity of the king's place of worship. Finally, since the king, in the words of the Psalmist, should '*hate the worke of them that fall away, or turne aside*', Hakewill considered it self-evident that 'he should proclame them his enemies, who had proclaimed themselves enemies to God and religion': declaration of war, not peace with Spain was the godly king's duty.[125] But not only did James pursue peace with Spain, he pursued it through matrimony, something that appalled Hakewill even more. 'The practice of the Church of Rome, that *Faith plighted to Hereticks is not to bee held*', he argued, should make it clear that there was no possible way to 'rely upon the contracts made with her or her adherents'. Peace was an admirable goal as long as it was not achieved by dallying with the Roman harlot – Catholicism in the person of

---

[122] Hakewill, *King Davids Vow*, 41. For James's use of the metaphor in *Basilikon Doron*, see *The Political Works of James I*, ed. Charles Howard McIlwain (Cambridge, Mass., 1918), 5.

[123] See above, 33–4.

[124] Hakewill, *King Davids Vow*, 109–10.   [125] Ibid., 120, 132.

the Spanish princess – 'for what peace can there bee as long as the whoredomes and witchcrafts of that *Iezebel* remaine yet in such abundance?'[126] Hakewill's pulpit attacks on the idolatry of images and the folly of pursuing a Catholic peace through marriage fit squarely with Chamberlain's summary of the same chaplain's offending treatise against 'marieng with one of a contrarie religion and an ydolater'.[127] The fact that the preacher was jailed for a prose treatise against the Spanish Match, but apparently left unmolested for setting out a collection of sermons treating the same matters speaks for the importance of the sermon as a means for viable political commentary upon the *arcana imperii*, both orally and in print. Sermons functioned well not only as veiled speech, but also as veiled print.

Did James sit idly by while his son's preachers carped at his dreams for dynastic union and confessional *rapprochement*? As we have seen, house arrest and confinement in the Tower, however brief, were used. But since the problem had been created, at least in part by institutional means – the flourishing of a household staff and chaplaincy at St James's with strong confessional and political biases – institutional means were taken to address it. Lancelot Andrewes, for one, was alarmed by the potentially nonconformist religious culture bred in the Prince of Wales's household, and when James lay in what was feared to be the grip of a mortal illness at Easter 1619, Andrewes seized the opportunity to influence matters. At the king's bedside the bishop 'bewailed with great Affliction the sad condition which the Church was like to fall into, if God should take away his life; the Prince being in the hands of the *Scots*, which made up the greatest part of his Houshold, and not well principled by those which had the tutelage of him, either as to the Government or *Liturgie* of the Church of *England*'. James was moved by Andrewes's argument, confessed his 'negligence', and vowed to take Charles under his own wing for education in matters ecclesiastical.[128]

The king seems to have moved decisively on Andrewes's advice. Even though Sir Thomas Murray was still out of favour at court for his opposition to the Spanish Match when the provostship of Eton fell vacant in January 1622, he was granted the post by the express direction of the king.[129] Here was an excellent opportunity for James to free the prince from 'the hands of the *Scots*', as Andrewes had put it, or, more pertinent for the king, to free the prince from the influence of one opposed to the Spanish Match. Significantly, James had already recalled one of his English agents in Spain and a proponent of the Match, Sir Francis Cottington, to replace

---

[126] Ibid., 259, 298.   [127] Chamberlain, *Letters*, vol. II, 393.
[128] Heylyn, *A Short View*, 11.
[129] *CSPD 1619–23*, 339, 349–50; Chamberlain, *Letters*, vol. II, 425.

Murray as Secretary to Charles.[130] Another part of James's strategy was a leavening of Charles's godly chaplaincy with ministers more akin to those who, since 1618, had been in the ascendant at his own court, that is, men amenable to the Spanish Match and committed to a strict observance of the ceremonies and hierarchy of the English church as a defence against the perceived threat of popular Puritanism. Significantly, it was Lancelot Andrewes who James commanded to Whitehall to refute Hakewill and his anti-Match treatise. The bishop, newly appointed Dean of the Chapel Royal, countered Hakewill by citing Biblical precedents for marriages to one of another faith, and maintained that 'every papist was not an idolater'.[131] So too it was Andrewes's own creature and domestic chaplain, Matthew Wren, whom James appointed to serve as Charles's chaplain in January, 1622, an appointment, with that of Leonard Maw, that Heylyn attributed to Andrewes's sickbed counsel to James in 1619.[132] Only with an understanding of the godly cast of Charles's chaplaincy before 1621 can we appreciate what a cuckoo Wren really was in the St James's nest. Small wonder that it was considered something of a coup that Wren's insinuation into Charles's college of chaplains 'was carried on so privately, as to render it doubtful, whether he was assign'd by the *King* himself, or petitioned for by the *Prince*; which Ambiguity was still happily improv'd, in that he was equally acceptable to *them both*'. Only with the same understanding can we appreciate the irony in Wren's biographer's account of his appointment:

Wherefore, in that Point of Time, when the Family of his Royal Highness *Charles*, Prince of *Wales*, needed a true Son of the Church of *England*, and one of the most approv'd Fidelity, this was the Man, whom above all others, his *Majesty* out of his own Inclination, and guided by his own exquisite Judgment, was pleas'd . . . to appoint *Chaplain* to *his Son*.[133]

The household 'Family' of both princes Henry and Charles had very self-consciously defined itself as made up of 'true sons of the Church of England' – indeed, James had chartered both chaplaincies as unique defenders of the English faith against Rome. They no doubt would have scowled at the idea that their number needed to be supplemented by 'a true Son of the Church of England'. But by 1621 the definition of 'true sons' had changed. 'True sons' would not, like Charles's present chaplains, carp at the Spanish Match and they would defend worship that revived Catholic

---

130 *CSPD 1619–23*, 296; Chamberlain, *Letters*, vol. II, 455.
131 Chamberlain, *Letters*, vol. II, 393–4. Chamberlain was reporting his own dinner conversation with Andrewes; he was not impressed with the bishop's arguments, which he summarized as 'a great deale more of that kind'.
132 Heylyn, *A Short View*, 11. For Maw see Tyacke, *Anti-Calvinists*, 46. For Wren and Andrewes, see Christopher Wren, *Parentilia, or the Family of the Wrens* (1750), 2.
133 Wren, *Parentilia*, 2.

ritual and furnishings; which is not to say that anti-Catholicism was no longer on the agenda. On the contrary, Wren's biographer would go to great lengths to point out that while in Spain with Charles, it was due to Wren's religious counsel that 'the *Prince* stood like a Rock, firm, and immoveable in the *true Religion*; and in the end, triumph'd over all the Efforts, Policy, and Machinations of the *Romish* Churchmen'. But if refuting Roman prelates was what was needed in Spain, Charles had other chaplains on his rota far better fitted for the task, not least of whom were those original anti-papal chaplains, George Hakewill and Richard Milbourne. But James knew that the marriage negotiations could not go forward with repeated embarrassments from the proposed bridegroom's own chaplains; just as the chapel royal at Whitehall needed embellishment, Charles's chaplaincy needed some high-church decor. In this context it is easier to understand James's insistence that Wren and Maw follow the prince and Buckingham to Spain in 1624, where they were needed to assure Spanish observers that their princely master was no Puritan.

Did the 'collegiate society' of St James's finally begin to dissolve with the trip to Madrid? Henry Burton thought it his prerogative as Clerk of the Closet to Charles and his brother Henry to join the entourage sent to Spain, and he was right. None the less, he was rudely excluded. Lord Robert Carey, the prince's Chamberlain and Burton's long-time patron, wrote in exasperation to Secretary Conway against the king's command to keep Burton at home. He cited Burton's seven years' service to Henry and continuous service to Charles, as well as pointing out how the Clerk's rather menial duties – 'to keepe the Bookes together to looke to the Candlestyckes and other plate . . . to looke to the surplesses lynnen and all other ornamentes belonginge to the Chappell' – were not for chaplains to attend to. And, he hinted, 'yt may be the Prince wilbe displeased if a straunger should supply his owne servants place'. But the king's position was immovable; he had, as Carey put it, been 'informed against Mr Burton' and no room could be found on board.[134] Scarcity of berths notwithstanding, James wanted a churchmanship radically different from Burton's to be on display in Spain. Although Burton would ride through the streets of London in triumph in 1640, his clipped ears a reproach to Laud and King Charles but a badge of martyrdom to City Puritans, the likes of Wren and Maw were in the ascendant in 1623.[135]

---

[134] PRO SP14/139/106. See also *CSPD 1619–23*, 523, 525, 531, 533, 535.

[135] Burton retained his Clerkship until one month after King James's death, when he wrote a letter to Charles decrying Laud's and Neile's high churchmanship. He was told not to present himself at court until summoned, a call that never came. See Samuel R. Gardiner, *History of England . . . 1603–1642*, 10 vols. (New York, 1965), vol. VII, 12; also the partisan accounts in Peter Heylyn, *A Briefe and Moderate Answer to . . . Henry Burton*

However, this was an ascent engineered from without, not fostered from within Charles's household. Just as James had imposed his chapel royal staff and practice on Holyrood in 1617, he now imposed it at St James's. And just as his obsession with achieving peace in Europe through concessions to Spain alienated him from a significant portion of his subjects' affections, it constituted what must have seemed a shocking volte-face to the servants of Prince Charles. In Hakewill's case, his express commission to guard the prince from popery was traduced by the very king who had charged him with his duty. So, too, Henry Burton who, after eighteen years of service to both Jacobean Princes of Wales, suddenly found himself *persona non grata* in his own post. The prince's servants considered Charles a hostage to his father's policies. Hakewill, ever the prince's catechist, had been prompted to set out his 1621 admonitory sermons 'specially now that your frequent presence with his Majesty enforceth your often absence from your Familie', he told Charles. But the subsequent journey to Spain was the king's ultimate act of estranging his son from that family.[136] So Charles's jubilant return from Spain was a homecoming of a very special sort. Prince Henry's former chaplain, John Prideaux, rhapsodized to Hakewill that his dedication of the new chapel at Exeter College, Oxford on 5 October 'will proue . . . more *auspicious*, in that it was contriued by you to bee *consecrated* vpon the *Day*, which made *England* most happy and triumphant, by your Noble Master *Prince Charles* his *Return* from beyond the Seas'.[137] Not insignificantly, Charles's and Buckingham's landfall on 5 October was made not at Whitehall but at Lambeth Palace, from which Archbishop Abbot, the patriarch of anti-Spanish conformist Calvinism, orchestrated their triumphal entry into London.[138] Charles and Buckingham were hailed as sound Protestants, and in 1624 they underwrote a 'mild persecution' of Catholics while they lavished favour on conformists.[139] This is to say that, with the Spanish Match discredited, Charles and Buckingham could now claim the legacy of militant anti-Catholicism and native conformist Calvinism that had been nurtured at St James's since Prince Henry's time. Prince Charles was back where he belonged, inspiring hope among godly court preachers such as William Loe, chaplain to James, who suddenly had a new use for an old court sermon. In January 1623,

(1637), sig. a3ᵛ–b1ʳ; and Christopher Dow, *Innovation Unjustly Charged upon the Present Church and State* (1637), 8–10.

136 Hakewill, *King Davids Vow*, sig. A2ᵛ.
137 John Prideaux, *A Sermon Preached on the Fifth of October 1624* (Oxford, 1625), sig. &4ᵛ.
138 Elisabeth Bourcier, ed., *The Diary of Sir Simonds D'Ewes, 1622–1624* (Paris, 1974), 161–3, quoted in David Cressy, *Bonfires and Bells: National Memory and the Protestant Calendar in Elizabethan and Stuart England* (1989), 94.
139 Cogswell, *Blessed Revolution*, 91–3.

Loe, preaching before both James and Charles, had urged the defence of true religion with the sword, a sermon he elegantly copied and dedicated to Prince Charles. But he had not presented it immediately after its preaching, when its contents were no doubt too sensitive to commit to paper, but ten months later, after the Spanish journey, as a thanksgiving 'for your prosperous voyage, & safe returne', that is, as a thanksgiving for Charles's return from the ploys of his father's Hispanophile pacifism to an English defence of European Protestantism.[140]

Where, though, was the Charles who would preside over the Laudian reforms of the 1630s? Where was the royal patron of the so-called 'Arminianization' of the Church of England? On witness of their patronage of preachers and preaching at their respective courts, Charles's policies in the 1630s were much less a departure from James's in the 1620s than from Charles's own at that time. Historians have despaired at ever finding the roots of Charles I's religious convictions;[141] but one famous piece of evidence takes on new significance in light of Charles's chaplain-preachers as Prince of Wales. After returning from Spain with the prince, Wren was urgently summoned to his patron Andrewes's episcopal palace in Southwark, where behind locked doors he was interrogated by the anti-Calvinist triumvirate of Andrewes, Neile, and Laud about 'how the Prince's Heart stands to the Church of *England*, that when God brings him to the Crown, we may know what to hope for'. Wren confidently maintained under cross-examination that 'for upholding the Doctrine and Discipline, and the right Estate of the Church, I have more Confidence of him, than of his Father'.[142] Historians have rightly interpreted this episode in light of Charles's later public commitment to Arminian theology and ceremonial worship.[143] But the timing of Wren's interview and the backdrop of James's manipulation of Charles's chaplaincy puts a sharper point on the matter. Charles had just returned to the great rejoicing both of godly citizens and of his godly chaplains, and, with Buckingham, was leading a war party that breathed new life into the hopes of conformist Calvinists, who had begun to despair of betrayal by their own sovereign. Andrewes had been manoeuvring since at least 1619 to weaken precisely this confessional–political alliance in Charles's household, and Wren had been his operative. The

---

[140] William Loe, 'The Kings Sworde . . . Deliuered in a Sermon at Whitehall . . . the 14.th day of Ianuary . . . 1622', BL MS Royal 17.A.XL, fol. 6r.

[141] Conrad Russell, *The Causes of the English Civil War* (Oxford, 1990), 196–7, and n. 41.

[142] Wren, *Parentilia*, 45–6.

[143] Tyacke, *Anti-Calvinists*, 113–14, stresses the theological implications; Kevin Sharpe, *The Personal Rule of Charles the First* (New Haven, Conn., 1992), 275, insists that the 'great stress on ordered ritual and uniformity in worship' was not grounded on theological positions. In the minds of men such as Andrewes and Wren, however, it was impossible to separate the two.

prelates gathered at Winchester House wanted to know from their source at St James's whether they were going to lose the heir-apparent to a revival of his deceased brother's threat to 'bishops and bells'. Their fears, as we know, were unnecessary. But not only does the Spanish journey mark the probable beginnings of Charles's own commitment to what became Laudianism, it also marks the beginnings of his rejection of an entrenched household tradition of conformist Calvinism – and is an emblematic example of the power of preachers and preaching at the early modern English courts.

Appendix

COURT SERMONS PRINTED BY COMMAND, 1558–1625

Sermons are listed chronologically by date of printing, showing author, short title, and source for identification as printed by command. Unless otherwise noted, the command for printing is the sovereign's.

John Jewel	*Certaine Sermons Preached before the Queenes Maiestie and at Paules Crosse* (1583)	Christopher Barker, Queen's Printer
Lancelot Andrewes	*The Copie of the Sermon preached on good Friday* (1604)	Robert Barker, King's Printer
William Smith	*The Black-Smith. A Sermon at White-Hall* (1606)	Commanded by Richard Bancroft, Abp of Canterbury (sig. aaᵛ)
William Barlow	*One of the Foure Sermons Preached Before the Kings Maiestie at Hampton Court* (1606)	Dedicatory epistle (sig. A1ʳ)
John Buckeridge	*A Sermon Preached at Hampton Court before the Kings Maiestie* (1606)	Robert Barker, King's Printer
Lancelot Andrewes	*A Sermon Preached before the Kings Maiestie at Hampton Court* (1606)	Robert Barker, King's Printer
John King	*The Fovrth Sermon Preached at Hampton Covrt* (1606)	Chamberlain, *Letters*, vol. I, 232.
Martin Fotherby	*Fovre Sermons, . . . the Fourth at the Court* (1608)	Commanded by Richard Bancroft, Abp of Canterbury (sigs. A1ʳ A2ʳ)

210

John King	*A Sermon Preached At White-Hall the 5. Day of November.ann.1608* (1608)	Title page; Chamberlain, *Letters*, vol. I, 269
Lancelot Andrewes	*A Sermon Preached Before the Kings Maiestie at White-hall, On Munday the 25. of December* (1610)	Robert Barker, King's Printer; Chamberlain, *Letters*, vol. I, 292, 295
Lancelot Andrewes	*A Sermon Preached before His Maiestie, On Sunday the Fifth of August last* (1610)	Robert Barker, King's Printer
Lancelot Andrewes	*Concio Latiné habita Coram Regia Maiestate, quinto Augusti 1606* (1610)	Robert Barker, King's Printer
Lancelot Andrewes	*A Sermon Preached Before His Maiestie at White-Hall, On . . . Christmas Day* 1610	Robert Barker, King's Printer
Lancelot Andrewes	*A Sermon Preached Before His Maiestie . . . On the 24 of March Last* (1611)	Robert Barker, King's Printer
William Goodwin	*A Sermon Preached before the Kings . . . Maiestie* (1614)	Title page
Robert Wilkinson	*Barwick Bridge: Or England and Scotland Covpled. In a Sermon . . . Preached before the King* (1617)	Dedicatory epistle (sig. A2^{r})
Lancelot Andrewes	*A Sermon Preached before His Maiestie . . . the fift of Nouember last* (1618)	John Bill, King's Printer
John Buckeridge	*A Sermon Preached before His Maiestie At Whitehall* (1618)	John Bill, King's Printer
Lancelot Andrewes	*A Sermon Preached before His Maiestie at Whitehall, on Easter Day last. 1618* (1618)	John Bill, King's Printer
John Williams	*A Sermon of Apparell, Preached before the Kings Maiestie* (1620)	Title page; John Bill, King's Printer
Lancelot Andrewes	*A Sermon Preached at White-hall, on Easter day* (1620)	John Bill, King's Printer; Chamberlain, *Letters*, vol. II, 309
William Laud	*A Sermon Preached before His Maiesty* (1621)	Title page

William Laud	*A Sermon Preached at White-hall* (1621)	Bonham Norton and John Bill, King's Printers; Laud, *Works*, vol. III, 138
Christopher Swale	*Iacobs Vow. A Sermon Preached before His Maiestie* (1621)	John Bill, King's Printer
Walter Curll	*A Sermon Preached at White-hall* (1622)	Title page; John Bill, King's Printer
Edmund Mason	*A Sermon Preached . . . at Oatelands* (1622)	John Bill, King's Printer
John Williams	*Great Britains Salomon. a Sermon Preached at the Magnificent Funerall, of . . . King, Iames* (1625)	John Bill, King's Printer

BIBLIOGRAPHY

MANUSCRIPT ELIZABETHAN-JACOBEAN COURT SERMONS

Abbot, George, 24 Mar. 1624 (private collection)
anon, *temp. Eliz.* (BL MS Add. 41,499a)
    Accession Day 1588 (University of London Library MS 187, fols. 34^r–38^r)
Balcanquall, Walter, 14 March 1623 (Huntington Library MS EL 6867)
Fletcher, Richard, 1587 (SJCC MS I.30)
Godwin, Thomas, 27 March 1566 (CCCC MS 340)
Guest, Edmund, n.d. (CCCC MS 104)
King, Geoffrey(?), July 1604 (Huntington Library Egerton MS D.3.6.)
King, John, *ante* 1611? (Bodl. MS Eng.the.c.71, fols. 1^r–5^r)
Loe, William, January 1623 (BL MS Royal 17.A.xl)
Matthew, Tobias, c. 1572? (Bodl. MS Top.Oxon.e.5, pp. 48–65)
    Good Friday 1581 (Bodl. MS Top.Oxon.e.5, pp. 149–78)
Montagu, James, Ash Wednesday 1615 (Bodl. MS North e.41, fols. 141^r–151^r)
Rawlinson, Francis, December 1619 (Huntington Library Egerton MS 6866)
Simpson, Edward, October 1617 (CUL MS Ff.5.25; BL Add. MS 5960)
Winniffe, Thomas, 12 March 1624 (private collection)

PRINTED ELIZABETHAN-JACOBEAN COURT SERMONS

Adams, Thomas, from *Three Sermons* (1625): 'The Sinners Mourning Habite' (1–27).
Andrewes, Lancelot, *Concio Latinè habita Coram Regia Maiestate, quinto Augusti 1606* (1610).
The Copie of the Sermon Preached on Good Friday (1604).
A Sermon Preached at White-hall, on Easter Day (1620).
A Sermon Preached before His Maiestie at White-Hall, On . . . Christmas Day (1610[–11?]).
A Sermon Preached before His Maiestie, at Whitehall, on Easter Day Last (1614).
A Sermon Preached before His Maiestie, at Whitehall, on Easter Day Last (1618).
A Sermon Preached before His Maiestie, on Sunday the Fifth of August Last (1610).
A Sermon Preached before His Maiestie, . . . on the 24 of March Last (1611).

213

A Sermon Preached before His Maiestie, . . . the Fifth of Nouember Last (1618).
A Sermon Preached before the Kings Maiestie, at Hampton Court (1606).
A Sermon Preached before the Kings Maiestie at White-hall, on Munday the 25. of December (1610).
Opvscula Posthuma (1629). Includes 'Concio Latine habita, in discessu Palatini' (separately paginated).
XCVI Sermons, ed. William Laud and John Buckeridge (1629). Includes 13 Elizabethan and 80 Jacobean court sermons, including the 11 Jacobean sermons printed before 1625 (see above).
anon., *A Godlye Sermon: Preached before the Queenes most Excellent Maiestie* (1585).
Peters Fall (1585).
Archbold, John, *The Beauty of Holines. A Sermon, Preached at the Court* (1621).
B. H. [Hugh Broughton?], *Moriemini: a Verie Profitable Sermon Preached before Her Maiestie at the Court* (1593).
Babington, Gervase, *A Sermon Preached at the Court at Greenwich* (1591).
Bargrave, Isaac, *A Sermon against Self Policy* (1624).
Barlow, William, *The Eagle and the Body* (1609).
One of the Foure Sermons Preached before the Kings Maiestie, at Hampton Court (1606).
Bilson, Thomas, *A Sermon Preached at Westminster before the Kings and Queenes Maiesties, at their Coronations* (1603).
Blague, Thomas, *A Sermon Preached at the Charterhouse before the Kings Maiestie* (1603).
Broughton, Hugh, *An Exposition vpon the Lords Prayer . . . in a Sermon, at Oatelands: before . . . Henry Prince of Wales* (n.d, 1603?).
Buckeridge, John, *A Sermon Preached at Hampton Court before the Kings Maiestie* (1606).
A Sermon Preached before his Maiestie at Whitehall (1618).
Burgess, John, *A Sermon Preached before the Late King James . . . with Two Letters in Way of Apology* (1642).
Carier, Benjamin, *A Sermon Preached before the Prince* (1606).
Chaloner, Edward, *Vnde Zizania?* (Oxford, 1624).
Cole, Thomas, *A Godly and Learned Sermon . . . before the Queenes Maiestie* (1564).
Cowper, William, *Two Sermons Preached in Scotland before the Kings Maiesty* (1619).
Crooke, Samuel, *Death Subdued . . . in a Sermon at Denmarke House on Ascension Day* (1619).
Curll, Walter, *A Sermon Preached at White-hall* (1622).
Curteys, Richard, *A Sermon Preached before the Queenes Maiestie . . . at Grene-wiche* (1574).
A Sermon Preached before the Queenes Maiesty at Richmond (1575).
Two Sermons . . . the first at Paules Croße . . . and the Second at Westminster before ye Queenes maiestie (1576).
Denison, John, *Beati Pacifici . . . Two Sermons Preached before the King* (1620).
Heauens Ioy . . . a Sermon Preached at White-Hall (1623).
The Sinners Acquittance. A checke to Curiositie. The Safest Seruice. Deliuered in Three Sermons at the Court (1624).
Dering, Edward, *A Sermon Preached before the Quenes Maiestie* (1569?).

Donne, John, from *The Sermons of John Donne* (ed. G. Potter and E. Simpson, 1953–62), 20 Jacobean court sermons. Of that number only one was printed before May 1625 (*The First Sermon Preached to King Charles* [1625]); the others appeared in sections devoted to court sermons in the three seventeenth-century folios: *LXXX Sermons* (1640), *Fifty Sermons* (1649), and *XXVI Sermons* (1660/1).

Drant, Thomas, *Two Sermons Preached. the One at S. Maries Spittle . . . the Other at the Court at Windsor* (1570).

Du Moulin, Pierre, *A Sermon Preached before the Kings Maiesty* (Oxford, 1620).

Dyke, Daniel, *Certain Comfortable Sermons . . . Preached before the Lady Elizabeth Her Grace* (1616).

Eedes, Richard, *Six Learned and Godly Sermons: Preached Some of Them before the Kings Maiestie, some before Queene Elizabeth* (1604). These are:

'The Dutie of a King . . . in Two Sermons' (1^r–35^v).

'A Fruitfull Meditation vpon the Sickenesse . . . Preached before the King' (36^r–61^r).

'The Principall Care of Princes to Bee Nurces of the Church. Preached before Queene *Elizabeth*' (61^v–83^v).

'A Sermon of an Heauenly Conuersation' (103^r–122^r).

'A Sermon of the Difference of Good and Evill. Preached before Queene *Elizabeth*' (84^r–102^v).

Roger Fenton, *A Treatise Against . . . the Church of Rome*, ed. Emmanuel Utie (1617). Appended are three Jacobean court sermons (61–88).

Field, Richard, *A Learned Sermon Preached before the King* (1604).

Fotherby, Martin, *Fovre Sermons . . . the Fourth at the Court* (1608), 87–105.

Fulke, William, *A Sermon Preached at Hampton Court* (1570).

Goodwin, William, *A Sermon Preached before the Kings . . . .Maiestie* (Oxford, 1614).

Gordon, John, *ENOTIKON or a Sermon of the Vnion of Great Britannie* (1604).

Hacket, John, *A Century of Sermons*, ed. T. Plume (1675), 731–61. Three Jacobean court sermons.

Hakewill, George, *King Davids Vow for Reformation . . . in Twelue Sermons before the Prince* (1621).

Hall, Joseph, *The Works* (1625): 'The Imprese of God' in two sermons (439–457), 'A Farewell Sermon' (459–68).

The Best Bargaine. A Sermon preached to the Court (1623).

A Sermon Preached before his Maiestie at his Court of Thebalds (1622).

A Sermon Preached to the Court at Theobalds (1623).

The Shaking of the Olive Tree (1660). Includes: 'A Sermon Preacht at Hampton-Court to King James' (separately paginated).

The True Peace-Maker . . . a Sermon before His Maiesty (1624).

Hampton, Christopher, *Two Sermons Preached before the Kings . . . Maiesty* (1609).

A Sermon Preached before the Kings Maiestie (Dublin, 1620).

The Three Severall States of Man . . . in Three Severall Sermons at the Court (Dublin, 1620).

Hodson, Phineas, *The Last Sermon Preached before His Maiesties Funerals* (1625).

Hooke, Henry, *A Sermon Preached before the King* (1604).

Hopkins, John, *A Sermon Preached before the Kings Maiestie* (1604).

A Sermon Preached before the Queenes Maiestie (1609).

James, William, *A Sermon Preached before the Queenes Maiestie* (1578).

Jewel, John, *Certaine Sermons Preached before the Queenes Maiestie and at Paules Crosse* (1583), sigs. H2^r–M1^r. Two sermons preached before the queen.

The *Trve Copies of the Letters betwene . . . Iohn Bisshop of Sarum and D. Cole vpon Occasion of a Sermon that the Said Bishop Preached before the Quenes Maiestie* (1560).

The *Works of John Jewel*, 4 vols., ed. John Ayre (Cambridge, 1845–50), vol. I, 1–80 and vol. II, 1004–24 reprint the court sermon texts from *The True Copies* and *Certain Sermons*.

King, John, *The Fovrth Sermon Preached at Hampton Covrt* (Oxford, 1606).

A *Sermon Preached at Whitehall the 5. Day of November.ann.1608* (Oxford, 1608).

Uitis Palatina (1614).

Lake, Arthur, *Sermons* (1609): Grouped with a separate title page, *Svndrie Sermon Preached at Covrt*, are six sermons of uncertain date, all but the last probably Jacobean.

Laud, William, *A Sermon Preached before His Maiestie* (1621).

A *Sermon Preached at White-hall* (1622).

Loe, William, *The Kings Shoe* (1623).

Mason, Edward, *A Sermon Preached . . . at Oatelands* (1622).

Mason, Francis, *Two Sermons Preached at the Kings Court* (1621).

Maxey, Anthony, *The Sermon Preached before the King* (1605).

Another Sermon Preached before the King (1605).

The Churches Sleepe (1606).

The Copie of a Sermon Preached on the First Friday in Lent (1610).

Five Sermons Preached Before the King (1614), reprints all above, and adds 'The Copie of a Sermon Preached in Lent' (separately paginated).

Certain Sermons (1619) reprints all above, and adds 'A Sermon Preached before his Maiestie at Bagshot' (separately paginated).

Meredeth, Richard, *Two Sermons Preached before His Maiestie in his Chappell at Whitehall* (1606).

Meriton, George, *A Sermon of Nobilitie* (1607).

The Christian Mans Assvring House. And a Sinners Conuersion. Two Sermons (1614).

Playfere, Thomas, *Cæsaris Svperscriptio* (1606).

Ten Sermons Preached by . . . Th. Playfere (Cambridge, 1610). Includes:

'A Sermon Preached at *Hampton* Court . . . the 23. day of *September*. 1604' (29–54).

'A Sermon Preached at the Court at Whitehall. *March* 10. 1598' (75–116).

'A Sermon Preached at White-hall before the King on Tewsday after Lo Sunday. 1604' (236–70).

'A Sermon Preached At *Winsor*. . . the 11. *Day of September*. 1604' (1–28).

'A Sermon Preached before the Kings Maiestie . . . the 2.day of September. 1604' (55–74).

A *Sermon Preached before the Kings Maiestie at Drayton* (Cambridge, 1609).

A *Sermon Preached before the Kings Maiesty . . . at Woodstock*. Printed with separate pagination as part two of *A Sermon . . .at Drayton* (sigs. D2^r–13^v).

The Sick-Mans Couch (1605).

Preston, John, *A Heartie Prayer* (1639).

Lamentations for the Death of the late Illustrious Prince Henry (Oxford, 1613).

Prælium & Præmium (Oxford, 1608).

Prince Henry His First Anniversary (Oxford, 1613).
Recvsants Conversion: A Sermon . . . before the Prince (Oxford, 1608).
Spiritual Odovrs to the Memory of Prince Henry (Oxford, 1613). Four court
    sermons, the final two with separate titles and pagination:
    Sorrow for the Sinnes of the Time.
    Teares Shed Over Abner.
The Spring. A Sermon Preached before the Prince (1609).
Two Sermons Preached in His Highnesse Chappell at Saint IAMES (1613).
Prideaux, John, *Hezekiahs Sicknesse* (Oxford, 1637).
    Perez-Vzzah (Oxford, 1625).
Rawlinson, John, *Fovre Qvadragesimal or Lent Sermons Preached at Whitehall*
    (Oxford, 1625).
Rollenson, Francis, *Sermons Preached before his Maiestie* (1611). Three sermons.
Rudd, Anthony, *A Sermon Preached at Richmond before Queene Elizabeth* (1603).
    A Sermon Preached at Greenwich before the Kings Maiestie (1603).
    A Sermon Preached at the Covrt at White Hall (1604).
    A Sermon Preached before the Kings Maiestie (1606).
S. L. *Resvrgendum* (1593).
Sandys, Edwin, *Sermons Made by . . . Edwin, Archbishop of Yorke* (1585). Four
    court sermons.
    The Sermons of Edwin Sandys, ed. John Ayre (Cambridge, 1841), 78–160.
    Reprints the 1585 texts.
Scott, Thomas, *Christs Politician, and Salomons Pvritan* (1616).
Smith, William, *The Black-Smith. A Sermon at White-Hall* (1606).
Spackman, Norwich, *A Sermon Preached before His Maiestie* (1614).
Stoughton, John, *Choice Sermons* (1640) includes:
    'The Happinesse of Peace: Before K. James at Trinitie College in Cambridge'
    (1–41).
Swale, Christopher, *Iacobs Vow. A Sermon Preached before His Maiestie* (1621).
Ussher, James, *A Briefe Declaration of the Vniversalitie of the Chvrch* (1624).
Wakeman, Robert, *Salomons Exaltation* (Oxford, 1605).
Walsall, Samuel, *The Life and Death of Iesvs Christ* (1607).
Warburton, George, *King Melcizedech* (1623).
Wentworth, Peter, *A Sermon . . . at the Courte, at Greenewiche* (1587).
Westerman, William, *Jacobs Well: Or, a Sermon Preached before the Kings most*
    Excellent Maiestie (1613).
Whitgift, John, *A Godlie Sermon* (1574).
    The Works of John Whitegift, 3 vols., ed. John Ayre (Cambridge, 1851–53), vol.
    III, 566– 85, reprints *A Godlie Sermon.*
Wilkinson, Robert, *The Merchant Royal. A Sermon Preached at White-Hall . . . at*
    the Nuptials of . . . Lord Hay (1607).
    A Paire of Sermons Svccessively Preached to a Paire of Peereles and Succeeding
    Princes (1614).
    Barwick Bridge. Or England and Scotland Covpled. In a Sermon . . . Preached
    before the King (1617).
    The Stripping of Joseph (1625).
Williams, John, *A Sermon of Apparell, Preached before the Kings Maiestie* (1620).
    Great Britains Salomon. A Sermon Preached at The Magnificent Funerall, of . . .
    King, Iames (1625).
Young, John, *A Sermon Preached before the Queens Maiestie* (1576).

OTHER MANUSCRIPT SOURCES

BODLEIAN LIBRARY, UNIVERSITY OF OXFORD

MS Carte 74	Misc. Jacobean correspondence

BRITISH LIBRARY, LONDON

Additional 5750	Royal warrants, C16–17
Additional 34324	Papers of Sir Julius Caesar, including James I's orders for chapel attendance, 1623
Additional 39853	Papers of Sir Charles Cornwallis, including orders for Prince Henry's household
Additional 41499a	Elizabethan royal entertainments, including anonymous court sermon
Harleian 6991	Letters and state papers, 1571–4
Harleian 6992	Letters and state papers, 1575–80
Royal 7.C.xvi	State papers of Thomas Cromwell, including household lists of Edward VI
Sloane 1494	Gentleman usher's handbook, temp. Charles I

CORPUS CHRISTI COLLEGE, CAMBRIDGE

MS 114 (2 vols.)	Papers of Matthew Parker

FOLGER SHAKESPEARE LIBRARY, WASHINGTON, D.C.

MS X.d.428	Miscellanea, including correspondence of James Montagu

HAMPSHIRE RECORD OFFICE, WINCHESTER

44MGA/F5 (Jervoise MSS)	Parliamentary diary of Sir Robert Paulet, 1610–11

ST JOHN'S COLLEGE, CAMBRIDGE

MS D105.337	Letter of Richard Neile

PUBLIC RECORD OFFICE, LONDON

E351/541–544	Treasurer of the Chamber, accounts, 1557–1627
E351/3206	Paymaster of the King's Works, accounts
LC2/4/4	Funeral of Elizabeth I, declared accounts
LC2/4/6	Funeral of Prince Henry, declared accounts
LC2/5	Funeral of Queen Anne, declared accounts
LC2/6	Funeral of James I, declared accounts
LC5/35–38	Wardrobe warrants, Elizabeth I, James I , Charles I
LC5/180	Household Regulations, Charles I, 1630
LS 13/168	Lord Steward's Department, Entry Book of Records
SP 12	Domestic state papers, Elizabeth I
SP 14	Domestic state papers, James I

WESTMINSTER ABBEY, LONDON

Muniment Book 15   Papers of John Whitgift and later, including court Lent lists

YORK MINSTER LIBRARY, YORK

Additional 18   Transcript of Tobie Matthew's sermon diary

OTHER PRINTED PRIMARY SOURCES
(Note: The place of publication is London unless otherwise stated.)

Accounts of the Masters of Works for Building and Repairing Royal Palaces and Castles, 2 vols., ed. Henry M. Paton, John Imrie and John G. Dunbar (Edinburgh, 1957, 1982).

Alumni Cantabrigienses . . . to 1751, 4 vols., ed. John Venn and J. A. Venn (Cambridge, 1922–1927).

Alumni Oxoniensis . . . 1500–1714, 4 vols., ed. Joseph Foster (Oxford, 1891–1892).

Andrewes, Lancelot, *Works*, 11 vols., ed. J. P. Wilson and James Bliss (Oxford, 1841–54).

'Lancelot Andrewes' "Prayer Before Sermon": a Parallel Text Edition', ed. Paul J. Klemp, *Bodleian Library Record* vol. XI, no. 5 (1984), 300–19.

'Notes on the Book of Common Prayer', in *Works*, ed. Wilson and Bliss, vol. XI, 150–1.

anon., *A Deep Sigh Breath'd Through the Lodgings at White-hall* (1642).

Arber, Edward, *A Transcript of the Register of the Company of Stationers of London 1554–1640*, 5 vols. (1875–94).

Athenæ Oxoniesis, ed. James Bliss, 4 vols. (1820).

Bacon, Sir Francis, *The Letters and Life of Francis Bacon*, 7 vols., ed. James Spedding (1862–74).

Bacon, Nathaniel, *The Papers of Nathaniel Bacon of Stiffkey*, 3 vols., ed. A. Hasell Smith and Gillian M. Baker (Norwich, 1979–88).

Ball, Thomas, *The Life of the Renowned Doctor Preston*, ed. E. W. Harcourt (Oxford, 1885).

Birch, Thomas, ed. *The Court and Times of James the First*, 2 vols. (1848).

Calderwood, David, *History of the Kirk of Scotland*, 8 vols., ed. T. Thomson (Edinburgh, 1842–59).

Calendar of Patent Rolls.

Calendar of State Papers, Domestic, 1547–1625, 12 vols., ed. M. A. E. Green (1856–72).

Calendar of State Papers, Ireland, 24 vols., ed. H. C. Hamilton et al. (1860–1912).

Calendar of State Papers, Rome, 2 vols., ed. J. M. Rigg (1916, 1926).

Calendar of State Papers, Spanish, Elizabeth, 4 vols., ed. Martin A. S. Hume et al. (1892–1899).

Calendar of State Papers, Venetian, 38 vols., ed. Rawdon Brown et al. (1864–1947).

Camden, William, *Annals of . . . the Reign of King James I*, in *A Complete History of England*, vol. II.

The History of Queen Elizabeth, in *A Complete History of England*, vol. II.

Cardwell, Edward, ed., *Documentary Annals of the Reformed Church of England*, 2nd. edn, 2 vols. (Oxford, 1844).

Carleton, Sir Dudley, *Dudley Carleton to John Chamberlain 1603–1624: Jacobean Letters*, ed. Maurice Lee, Jr (New Brunswick, 1972).

Chamberlain, John, *The Letters of John Chamberlain*, 2 vols., ed. N. E. McClure (Philadelphia, Pa., 1939).

Chamberlayne, Edward, *Angliæ Notitia . . . the Third Edition* (1669).

Church of England (liturgies), *A Fourme of Prayer with Thankesgiuing, to be Vsed . . . Euery Yeere the Fifth of August* (1603).

    The Book of Common Prayer, 1559: the Elizabethan Prayer Book, ed. John Booty (Washington, D.C., 1976).

    The First Prayer-Book as Issued by . . . King Edward VI, ed. James Parker (Oxford, 1883).

Clark, Andrew, ed., 'Dr. Plume's Notebook', *Essex Review* 15 (1906), 8–24.

Clifford, Lady Anne, *The Diary of Lady Anne Clifford*, intro. Vita Sackville-West (1924).

A Collection of Ordinances and Regulations for the Government of the Royal Household (1790).

A Complete History of England, 3 vols. (1706).

Cranmer, Thomas, *Miscellaneous Writings and Letters*, ed. John Edmund Cox (Cambridge, 1846).

D'Ewes, Sir Simonds, *The Diary of Sir Simonds D'Ewes, 1622–1624*, ed. Elisabeth Bourcier (Paris, 1974).

Dow, Christopher, *Innovation Unjustly Charged upon the Present Church and State* (1637).

Edward VI, King, *The Chronicle and Political Papers of King Edward VI*, ed. William K. Jordan (Ithaca, N.Y., 1966).

England as Seen by Foreigners in the Days of Elizabeth and James the First, ed. William Brenchley Rye (1865).

Field, Nathaniel, *Some Short Memorials Concerning the Life of that Reverend Divine Doctor Richard Field* (1716–17).

Finett, Sir John, *Finetti Philoxenis: Som Choice Observations of Sᵣ John Finett . . . Master of the Ceremonies* (1656).

Fitzneale, Richard, *Dialogus de Scaccario . . . and Constitutio Domus Regis: the Estimate of the Royal Household*, ed. and trans. Charles Johnson (Oxford, 1983).

Foxe, John, *Actes and Monumentes* (1563).

Gardiner, Stephen, *The Letters of Stephen Gardiner*, ed. James Arthur Muller (Cambridge, 1933).

G[arrett] W[illiam], *Anthologia. The Life & Death of Mᵣ Samuel Crook* (1651).

Goodman, Godfrey, *The Court of King James the First*, 2 vols., ed. John S. Brewer (1839).

Grindal, Edmund, *The Remains of Archbishop Grindal*, ed. William Nicholson (Cambridge, 1843).

Hacket, John, *Scrinia Reserata*, 2 vols. in one (1693).

Hakewill, George, *The Avncient Ecclesiasticall Practise of Confirmation* (1613).

    An Answere to a Treatise Written by Dr. Carier (1616).

Hall, Joseph, *The Shaking of the Olive Tree* (1660).

    Works, 10 vols., ed. P. Wynter (Oxford, 1863).

Harington, Sir John, *A Supplie or Addicion to the Catalogue of Bishops to the Yeare 1608*, ed. R. H. Miller (Potomac, Md., 1979).

The Letters and Epigrams of Sir John Harington, ed. Norman E. McClure (Philadelphia, Pa., 1930).

Heylyn, Peter, *A Briefe and Moderate Answer to . . . Henry Burton* (1637).

Cyprianus Anglicus (1671).

Ecclesia Restavrata (1661).

A Short View of the Life and Reign of King Charles (1658).

HMC Bath vol. IV.

HMC Downshire vol. VI.

HMC Rutland vol. I.

HMC Salisbury vols. IX, XI, XII, XIII, XV, XVII, XXI.

Hooker, Richard, *The Folger Edition of the Works of Richard Hooker*, 6 vols., ed. W. Speed Hill (Cambridge, Mass., 1977–93).

Hooper, John, *Early Writings of Bishop Hooper*, ed. Samuel Carr (Cambridge, 1843).

Howson, John, *A Second Sermon, Preached at Paules Crosse* (1598).

Hutchinson, Roger, *The Works of Roger Hutchinson*, ed. John Bruce (Cambridge, 1842).

James VI and I, King, *A Meditation Vpon the Lords Prayer* (1619).

The Political Works of James I, ed. Charles Howard McIlwain (Cambridge, Mass, 1918).

Keynes, Geoffrey, ed., *The Complete Walton* (1929).

King, Henry, *The Sermons of Henry King (1592–1669), Bishop of Chichester*, ed. Mary Hobbs (1992).

The Knyvett Letters, ed. Bertram Schofield (1949).

Laud, William, *Works*, 7 vols. in 9 parts, ed. J. Bliss and J. W. Scott (Oxford, 1847–60).

Le Neve, John, *Fasti Ecclesiæ Anglicanæ*, 3 vols., ed. T. Duffus Hardy (Oxford, 1854).

Letters and Papers . . . of the Reign of Henry VIII, 21 vols., ed. J. S. Brewer, James Gairdner et al. (1864–1920).

Loades, David, *The Tudor Court* (1992).

Machyn, Henry, *The Diary of Henry Machyn*, ed. John Gough Nichols, Camden Society 42 (1848).

Manningham, John, *The Diary of John Manningham of the Middle Temple, 1602–1603*, ed. Robert Parker Sorlein (Hanover, N.H., 1976).

Melvill, James, *The Autobiography and Diary of Mr James Melvill*, ed. Robert Pitcairn (Edinburgh, 1842).

Memoirs of the the Reign of Queen Elizabeth, 2 vols., ed. Thomas Birch (1754).

Nichols, John, *The Progresses and Public Processions of Queen Elizabeth*, 3 vols. (1823).

The Progresses, Processions, and Magnificent Festivities of King James the First, 4 vols. (1828).

The Old Cheque-Book or Book of Remembrance of the Chapel Royal, from 1561–1744, ed. Edward F. Rimbault, Camden Society, n.s. 3 (1872).

Original Letters Relative to the English Reformation, 2 vols., ed. Hastings Robinson (Cambridge, 1846, 1847).

Parker, Matthew, *The Correspondence of Matthew Parker*, ed. John Bruce and Thomas Perowne (Cambridge, 1853).

Price, Daniel, *The Defence of Trvth* (Oxford, 1610).

Prince Henry His First Anniversary (Oxford, 1613).

Prideaux, John, *A Sermon Preached on the Fifth of October 1624* (Oxford, 1625).

The Receyt of the Ladie Kateryne, ed. Gordon Kipling, Early English Text Society 296 (Oxford, 1990).

Royal Commission on the Ancient and Historical Monuments of Scotland, *Fife, Kinross, and Clackmannan* (Edinburgh, 1933).

Stirlingshire, 2 vols. (Edinburgh, 1963).

Rymer, Thomas, *Foedera*, 17 vols. (1704–17).

Say, William, *Liber Regie Capelle*, ed. Walter Ullman and D. H. Turner (1961).

Scott, Hew, *Fasti Ecclesiæ Scoticanæ*, new edn, 10 vols. (1915–).

Scudamore, Richard, 'The Letters of Richard Scudamore to Sir Philip Hoby, September 1549–March 1555', ed. Susan Brigden, *Camden Miscellany* vol. XXX (1990). 66–148.

The Second Part of a Register . . . Intended for Publication by the Puritans about 1593, 2 vols. ed. Albert Peel (Cambridge, 1915).

Spain and the Jacobean Catholics, 2 vols., ed. A. J. Loomie, S. J., Catholic Record Society 64 and 68 (1973, 1978).

Spottiswood, John, *History of the Church of Scotland*, 3 vols., ed. M. Russell (Edinburgh, 1847–51).

Stowe, John, cont. Edmund Howes, *Annales of England . . . Continued unto 1631* (1631).

Strype, John, *Annals of the Reformation*, 2nd edn, 3 vols. (1725–28).

Ecclesiastical Memorials, 3 vols. (Oxford, 1822).

Historical Collections of the Life and Acts of . . . John Aylmer (1701).

Life and Acts of Matthew Parker (1711).

Life and Acts of John Whitgift (1718).

Thomas Platter's Travels in England 1599, ed. and trans. Clare Williams (1937).

Walton, Izaak, *Life of John Donne*, in Keynes, ed., *Complete Walton*, 213–74.

Watson, Thomas, *Twoo Notable Sermons, Made . . . before the Quenes Highnes, Concernynge the Reall Presence of Christes Body and Bloude in the Blessed Sacrament* (1554).

Von Wedel, Lupold, 'Journey Through England and Scotland . . . in the Years 1584 and 1585', ed. and trans. Gottfried von Bulow, *Transactions of the Royal Historical Society*, n.s. vol. IX (1895), 223–70.

Welch, Joseph, *The List of the Queen's Scholars of St Peters College, Westminster* (1852).

Wilbraham, Roger, *The Journal of Roger Wilbraham*, ed. Harold Spencer Scott, *Camden Miscellany* vol. X (1902), 1–139.

Wilson, Arthur, *The History of Great Britain, Being the Life and Reign of King Iames the First* (1653).

Wood, Anthony, *Athenæ Oxoniensis*, ed. James Bliss, 4 vols. (1820).

Wotton, Sir Henry, *The Life and Letters of Sir Henry Wotton*, 2 vols., ed. Logan Pearsall Smith (Oxford, 1907).

Wren, Christopher, *Parentalia, or the Family of the Wrens* (1750).

Wriothsley, Charles, *A Chronicle of England during the Reigns of the Tudors from 1485–1559*, 2 vols., ed. William Douglas Hamilton, Camden Society, n.s. 18 and 20 (1875, 1877).

The Zurich Letters, 2 vols., ed. Hastings Robinson (Cambridge, 1842, 1845).

SECONDARY SOURCES

Adams, Simon, 'Eliza Enthroned? The Court and its Politics', in Haigh, ed., *Reign of Elizabeth*, 55–77.

'A Godly Peer? Leicester and the Puritans', *History Today* 40 (1990), 14–19.

Akrigg, G. P. V, *Jacobean Pageant* (Cambridge, Mass., 1962).

Amussen, Susan D., and Mark Kishlansky, eds., *Political Culture and Cultural Politics in Early Modern England* (Manchester, 1995).

Aston, Margaret, *England's Iconoclasts* (Oxford, 1988).

Bald, R. C, *John Donne: a Life* (Oxford, 1970).

Baldwin, David, *The Chapel Royal: Ancient and Modern* (1990).

Barroll, Leeds, 'The Court of the First Stuart Queen', in Peck, ed., *Mental World of the Jacobean Court*, 191–208.

'A New History for Shakespeare and His Time', *Shakespeare Quarterly* 39 (1988), 441–64.

Beier, A. L., David Cannadine and James M. Rosenheim, eds., *The First Modern Society: Essays in English History in Honour of Lawrence Stone* (Cambridge, 1989).

Bellany, Alastair, 'A Poem on the Archbishop's Hearse: Puritanism, Libel and Sedition after the Hampton Court Conference', *Journal of British Studies* 34 (1995), 137–64.

'"Raylinge Rymes and Vaunting Verse": Libellous Politics in Early Stuart England, 1603–1628', in Sharpe and Lake, eds., *Culture and Politics*, 285–310.

Bickersteth, John and Robert Dunning, *Clerks of the Closet in the Royal Household* (Stroud, 1991).

Birch, Thomas, *Life of Henry Prince of Wales* (1760).

Blench, J. W., *Preaching in England in the Late Fifteenth and Early Sixteenth Centuries* (Oxford, 1964).

Block, Joseph, 'Thomas Cromwell's Patronage of Preaching', *Sixteenth Century Journal* 8 (1977), 37–50.

Butler, Martin, 'Ben Jonson and the Limits of Courtly Panegyric', in Sharpe and Lake, eds., *Culture and Politics*, 91–116.

Campbell, W. C., 'Sermons and Religious Treatises', in Nugent, ed., *Thought and Culture of the English Renaissance*, 305–325.

Chester, Allan G, *Hugh Latimer, Apostle to the English* (Philadelphia, Pa., 1954).

Christian, Margaret, 'Elizabeth's Preachers and the Government of Women: Defining and Correcting a Queen', *Sixteenth Century Journal* 24 (1993), 561–76.

Churton, Ralph, *The Life of Alexander Nowell* (Oxford, 1809).

Cogswell, Thomas, 'England and the Spanish Match', in Cust and Hughes, eds., *Conflict in Early Stuart England*, 107–33.

The Blessed Revolution: English Politics and the Coming of War, 1621–1624 (Cambridge, 1989).

Collinson, Patrick, *Archbishop Grindal, 1519–1583: the Struggle for a Reformed Church* (Berkeley, Calif., 1979).

The Birthpangs of Protestant England (New York, 1988).

'Cranbrook and the Fletchers', in Patrick Collinson, *Godly People*, 399–428.

'The Elizabethan Church and the New Religion', in Haigh, ed., *Reign of Elizabeth I*, 169–94.

The Elizabethan Puritan Movement (1967; Oxford, 1990).

Godly People: Essays on English Protestantism and Puritanism (1983).

'A Mirror of Elizabethan Puritanism: the Life and Letters of "Godly Master Dering"', in Patrick Collinson, *Godly People*, 289–324.

The Religion of Protestants: the Church in English Society 1559–1625 (Oxford, 1982).

'Windows into a Woman's Soul: Questions about the Religion of Queen Elizabeth I', in Patrick Collinson, *Elizabethan Essays*, 87–118.

Colvin, Howard, gen. ed., *The History of the King's Works*, 6 vols. (1963–82).

Cressy, David, *Bonfires and Bells: National Memory and the Protestant Calendar in Elizabethan and Jacobean England* (1989).

Croft, Pauline, 'The Religion of Robert Cecil,' *Historical Journal* 34 (1991), 773–96.

Cuddy, Neil, 'The Revival of Entourage: the Bedchamber of James I, 1603–1625', in Starkey, ed., *English Court*, 173–225.

Cust, Richard and Anne Hughes, *Conflict in Early Stuart England: Studies in Religion and Politics 1603–1642* (1989).

Davies, Julian, *The Caroline Captivity of the Church: Charles I and the Remoulding of Anglicanism* (Oxford, 1992).

Dugdale, Henry Geast, *The Life and Character of Edmund Geste* (1840).

Elton, G. R, 'Tudor Government: the Points of Contact, III: the Court', *Transactions of the Royal Historical Society* 5th ser., 26 (1976), 211–28.

Falkenstein, Ludwig, 'Charlemagne et Aix-La-Chapelle', *Byzantion* 61 (1991), 231–89.

Fincham, Kenneth, 'Episcopal Government, 1603–1642', in Kenneth Fincham, ed., *Early Stuart Church*, 71–91.

'Prelacy and Politics: Archbishop Abbot's Defense of Protestant Orthodoxy', *Historical Research* 61 (1988), 36–64.

Prelate as Pastor: the Episcopate of James I (Oxford, 1990).

ed., *The Early Stuart Church, 1603–1642* (Basingstoke, 1993).

Fincham, Kenneth, and Peter Lake, 'The Ecclesiastical Policy of King James I', *Journal of British Studies* 24 (1985), 169–207.

Fogle, French R. and Louis A. Knafla, *Patronage in Late Renaissance England* (Los Angeles, Calif., 1983).

Gardiner, Samuel R., *History of England . . . 1603–1642*, 10 vols. (New York, 1965).

Girouard, Mark, 'Elizabethan Holdenby', *Country Life* 166 (October 1979).

Gleason, John B., *John Colet* (Berkeley, Calif., 1989).

Goldberg, Jonathan, *James I and the Politics of Literature* (Baltimore, Md., 1983).

Guy, John, ed., *The Reign of Elizabeth I: Court and Culture in the Last Decade* (Cambridge, 1995).

Haigh, Christopher, *Elizabeth I* (1988).

'Puritan Evangelism in the Reign of Elizabeth I', *English Historical Review* 92 (1977), 30–58.

ed., *The Reign of Elizabeth I* (Athens, Ga., 1987).

Harper, John, *The Forms and Orders of Western Liturgy from the Tenth to the Eighteenth Century* (Oxford, 1991).

Haugaard, William P, 'The Coronation of Elizabeth I', *Journal of Ecclesiastical History* 19 (1968), 161–70.

Elizabeth and the English Reformation (Cambridge, 1968).

'Elizabeth Tudor's Book of Devotions: a Neglected Clue to the Queen's Life and Character', *Sixteenth Century Studies Journal* 12 (1981), 79–105.

Heal, Felicity, *Of Prelates and Princes: a Study of the Economic and Social Position of the Tudor Episcopate* (Cambridge, 1980).

Heath, G. D, *The Chapel Royal at Hampton Court*, Borough of Twickenham Local History Society Paper Number 42 (1983).

Heinemann, Margot, *Puritanism and Theatre: Thomas Middleton and Opposition Drama under the Stuarts* (Cambridge, 1980).

Herr, Alan Fager, 'The Elizabethan Sermon: a Survey and a Bibliography' (published PhD thesis, University of Pennsylvania, 1940).

Hope, William St John, *Windsor Castle, an Architectural History*, 2 vols. (1913).

Jones, Norman, *Faith by Statute: Parliament and the Settlement of Religion, 1559* (1982).

Kawachi, Yoshiko, *A Calendar of English Renaissance Drama, 1558–1642* (New York, 1986).

Kennedy, D. E., 'King James I's College of Controversial Divinity at Chelsea', in Kennedy, ed., *Grounds of Controversy*, 97–126.

Kennedy, D. E., ed., *Grounds of Controversy: Three Studies in Late 16th and Early 17th Century English Polemics* (Melbourne, 1989).

King, John N, *Tudor Royal Iconography: Literature and Art in an Age of Religious Crisis* (Princeton, N.J., 1989).

Kipling, Gordon, *The Triumph of Honour: the Burgundian Origins of the Elizabethan Renaissance* (The Hague, 1977).

Kirk, James, ed., *Humanism and Reform: the Church in Europe, England and Scotland 1400–1643* (Oxford, 1991).

Knafla, Louis B., 'The "Country" Chancellor: The Patronage of Sir Thomas Egerton, Baron Ellesmere', in Fogle and Knafla, *Patronage in Late Renaissance England*, 33–115.

Knowles, David, *The Religious Orders in England*, 3 vols. (Cambridge, 1955–71).

Lake, Peter, *Anglicans and Puritans? Presbyterianism and English Conformist Thought from Whitgift to Hooker* (1988).

'Lancelot Andrewes, John Buckeridge, and Avant-Garde Conformity at the Court of James I', in Peck, ed., *Mental World of the Jacobean Court*, 113–33.

'The Moderate and Irenic Case for Religious War: Joseph Hall's *Via Media* in Context', in Amussen and Kishlansky, eds., *Political Culture*, 55–83.

Lee, Maurice, Jr, *Great Britain's Solomon* (Urbana, Ill., 1990).

Lindley, David, *The Trials of Frances Howard: Fact and Fiction at the Court of King James* (1993).

Loades, David, 'The Piety of the Catholic Restoration in England, 1553–1558', in Kirk, ed., *Humanism and Reform*, 289–304.

The Tudor Court (1986).

Lossky, Nicholas, *Lancelot Andrewes the Preacher, 1555–1626* (Oxford, 1991).

Jones, Michael K., and Malcolm G. Underwood, *The King's Mother: Lady Margaret Beaufort, Countess of Richmond and Derby* (Cambridge, 1992).

London County Council, *Survey of London*, 41 vols. (1900–).

Loomie, Albert J., S.J., 'King James I's Catholic Consort', *Huntington Library Quarterly* 34 (1971), 303–16.

MacCaffrey, Wallace, *Elizabeth I* (1993).

MacLure, Millar, *The Paul's Cross Sermons 1534–1642* (Toronto, 1958).

Register of Sermons Preached at Paul's Cross 1534–1642, revised by Peter Pauls and Jackson Campbell Boswell (Ottawa, 1989).

Manning, Roger B, *Religion and Society in Elizabethan Sussex* (Leicester, 1969).

McCabe, Richard A, *Joseph Hall: a Study in Satire and Meditation* (Oxford, 1982).

McCullough, Peter E, 'Making Dead Men Speak: Laudianism, Print, and the Works of Lancelot Andrewes, 1625–1642', *Historical Journal* (1998).

'Out of Egypt: Richard Fletcher's Sermon to Elizabeth I after the Execution of Mary Queen of Scots', in Julia Walker, ed., *Dissing Elizabeth: Negative Representations of Gloriana* (Durham, N.C., 1998).

'Preaching to a Court Papist? Donne's Sermon before Queen Anne, December 1617', *John Donne Journal* 14 (1977), 59–82.

Milton, Anthony, *Catholic and Reformed: the Roman and Protestant Churches in English Protestant Thought, 1600–1640* (Cambridge, 1995).

Mish, Charles C., 'Black Letter as a Social Discriminant in the Seventeenth Century', *PMLA* 68, 3 (June, 1953), 627–30.

Morgan, Irvonwy, *Prince Charles's Puritan Chaplain* (1957).

Neale, J. E, *Elizabeth and her Parliaments*, 2 vols. (1953, 1957).

Newman, J, 'Inigo Jones and the Politics of Architecture', in Sharpe and Lake, *Culture and Politics*, 229–56.

Nugent, Elizabeth M., ed., *The Thought and Culture of the English Renaissance, an Anthology of Tudor Prose, 1481–1555* (Cambridge, 1956).

O'Malley, John, *Praise and Blame in Renaissance Rome: Rhetoric, Doctrine and Reform in the Sacred Orators of the Papal Court, c. 1450–1521* (Durham, N.C., 1979).

Orgel, Stephen, *The Illusion of Power: Political Theater in the English Renaissance* (Berkeley, Calif., 1975).

Owst, G. R, *Preaching in Medieval England* (Cambridge, 1926).

Pantin, W. A., *The English Church in the Fourteenth Century* (Cambridge, 1955; Toronto, 1980).

Parry, Graham, *The Golden Age Restor'd: the Culture of the Stuart Court, 1603–42* (New York, 1981).

Patterson, Annabel, *Censorship and Interpretation: the Conditions of Writing and Reading in Early Modern England* (Madison, Wis., 1984).

Peck, Linda Levy, *Court Patronage and Corruption in Early Stuart England* (Boston, Mass., 1990).

The Mental World of the Jacobean Court (Cambridge, 1991).

Northampton: Patronage and Policy at the Court of James I (1982).

Perry, Curtis, 'The Citizen Politics of Nostalgia: Elizabeth in Early Jacobean London', *Journal of Medieval and Renaissance Studies* 23 (1993), 89–111.

Pollard, A. W. and G. R. Redgrave, *A Short-Title Catalogue of Books Printed in England, Scotland, and Ireland . . . 1475–1640*, 2nd edn, 3 vols., rev. W. A. Jackson, F. S. Ferguson and Katharine F. Pantzer (1986–91).

Quintrell, B. W., 'The Royal Hunt and the Puritans, 1604–1605', *Journal of Ecclesiastical History*, 31 (1980), 41–58.

Reidy, Maurice, *Bishop Lancelot Andrewes, Jacobean Court Preacher* (Chicago, Ill., 1955).

Reinl, Adolf, *Zeichensprache der Architektur: Symbol, Darstellung und Brauch in der Baukunst des Mittlealters und der Neuzeit* (Zurich, 1976).

Rogers, Charles, *History of the Chapel Royal of Scotland* (Edinburgh, 1882).

Russell, Conrad, *The Causes of the English Civil War* (Oxford, 1990).

Sharpe, Kevin, *Criticism and Compliment: the Politics of Literature in the England of Charles I* (Cambridge, 1987).
  The Personal Rule of Charles the First (New Haven, Conn., 1992).
Sharpe, Kevin, and Peter Lake, eds., *Culture and Politics in Early Stuart England* (Basingstoke, 1993).
Shuger, Deborah, *Habits of Thought in the English Renaissance: Religion, Politics & the Dominant Culture* (Berkeley, Calif., 1990).
Smith, D. I. B., *Editing Seventeenth Century Prose* (Toronto, 1972).
Smith, E. Baldwin, *Architectural Symbolism of Imperial Rome and the Middle Ages* (Princeton, N.J., 1956).
Smuts, Malcolm, *Court Culture and the Origins of a Royalist Tradition in Early Stuart England* (Philadelphia, Pa., 1987).
  'Cultural Diversity and Cultural Change at the Court of James I', in Peck, ed., *Mental World of the Jacobean Court*, 298–303.
  'Public Ceremony and Royal Charisma: the English Royal Entry in London, 1485–1642', in Beier et al., eds., *First Modern Society*, 65–93.
Soden, Geoffrey, *Godfrey Goodman, Bishop of Gloucester, 1583–1656* (1953).
Somerville, J. P, *Politics and Ideology in England, 1603–1640* (1986).
Spencer, H. Leith, *English Preaching in the Late Middle Ages* (Oxford, 1993).
Starkey, David, ed., *The English Court from the War of the Roses to the Civil War* (1987).
  'Introduction: Court History in Perspective', in Starkey, ed., *English Court*, 1–24.
Stone, Lawrence, 'The Building of Hatfield House', *Archaeological Journal* 112 (1955), 100–28.
Story, G. M., 'The Text of Lancelot Andrewes's Sermons', in Smith, ed., *Editing Seventeenth Century Prose*, 11–23.
Summerson, John, 'The Building of Theobalds, 1564–1585', *Archæologia* 97 (1959), 107–26.
Surtz, Edward, *The Works and Days of John Fisher* (Cambridge, Mass., 1967).
Thurley, Simon, *The Royal Palaces of Tudor England* (New Haven, Conn., 1993).
Trevor-Roper, Hugh, *Archbishop Laud* (1940).
  'James I and his Bishops', *History Today* 5 (1955), 571–81.
Tyacke, Nicholas, *Anti-Calvinists: the Rise of English Arminianism c. 1590–1640* (Oxford, 1987).
Verbeek, A, 'Die architektonische Nachfolge der Aachener Pfalzkapelle', in W. Braunfels and P. E. Schramm, eds., *Karl der Grosse. Lebenswerk und Nachleben*, vol. IV, *Das Nachleben* (Dusseldorf, 1967).
Walsham, Alexandra, *Church Papists: Catholicism, Conformity and Confessional Polemic in Early Modern England* (Woodbridge, 1993).
Walton, Guy, *Louis XIV's Versailles* (Harmondsworth, 1986).
Welsby, Paul, *Lancelot Andrewes 1555–1626* (1958).
Willson, David H, *King James VI and I* (New York, 1956).
Wilson, Elkin C., *England's Eliza* (Cambridge, Mass., 1939).
Wing, Donald, *Short-Title Catalogue of Books Printed in England . . . 1641–1700*, 2nd edn, 3 vols. (New York, 1972).
Wormald, Jenny, 'Ecclesiastical Vitriol: the Kirk, the Puritans and the Future King of England', in Guy, ed., *Reign of Elizabeth I*, 171–91.
  'James VI and I: Two Kings or One?', *History* 68 (1983), 187–209.
  'James VI and I, *Basilikon Doron* and *The Trew Law of Free Monarchies*: the

Scottish Context and the English Translation', in Peck, ed., *Mental World*, 36–54.

Wright, Pam, 'A Change in Direction: the ramifications of a female household, 1558–1603', in Starkey, ed., *English Court*, 147–72.

UNPUBLISHED THESES

Bellany, Alastair, 'The Poisoning of Legitimacy? Court Scandal, Public Opinion and Politics in England, 1603–1660' (PhD thesis, Princeton University, 1995).

Cranfield, Nicholas, 'Early Seventeenth Century Developments and Change in the Doctrine of [Episcopacy] and Understanding of the Office of [Bishop] in the Church of England, 1603–1645' (DPhil thesis, Oxford University, 1988).

Foster, Andrew, 'A Biography of Archbishop Richard Neile' (DPhil thesis, Oxford University, 1978).

Kisby, Fiona, 'The Early Tudor Royal Household Chapel, 1485–1547' (PhD thesis, University of London, 1996).

Wilks, Timothy Victor, 'The Court Culture of Prince Henry and His Circle' (DPhil thesis, Oxford University, 1987).

INDEX

Titles in the series